Ian Fleming
&
James Bond

Ian Fleming

& *The Cultural Politics of 007*

James Bond

EDITED BY

Edward P. Comentale,
Stephen Watt, and
Skip Willman

Indiana University Press

BLOOMINGTON AND INDIANAPOLIS

This book is a publication of
Indiana University Press
601 North Morton Street
Bloomington, IN 47404-3797 USA

http://iupress.indiana.edu

Telephone orders   800-842-6796
Fax orders   812-855-7931
Orders by e-mail   iuporder@indiana.edu

© 2005 by Indiana University Press

*The paper used in this publication meets the minimum requirements of
American National Standard for Information Sciences—Permanence of
Paper for Printed Library Materials, ANSI Z39.48-1984.*

MANUFACTURED IN THE UNITED STATES OF AMERICA

Library of Congress Cataloging-in-Publication Data
Ian Fleming and James Bond : the cultural politics of 007 /
edited by Edward P. Comentale, Stephen Watt, and Skip Willman.
      p. cm.
Includes bibliographical references and index.
ISBN 0-253-34523-5 (cloth : alk. paper)
ISBN 0-253-21743-1 (pbk. : alk. paper)
1. Fleming, Ian, 1908–1964—Characters—James Bond. 2. Culture—Political
aspects—England—History—20th century. 3. Fleming, Ian, 1908–1964—
Political and social views. 4. Spy stories, English—History and criticism.
5. Bond, James (Fictitious character) 6. Espionage in literature. 7. Cold War in
literature. 8. Spies in literature. I. Comentale, Edward P. II. Watt, Stephen,
1951– III. Willman, Skip, 1967–
PR6056.L4Z725   2005
823'.914—dc22
2004016392

1 2 3 4 5   10 09 08 07 06 05

CONTENTS

Foreword by Andrew Lycett   vii
Introduction   xi
Abbreviations   xxv

I. The Subject Is Bond

1 Fleming's Company Man: James Bond and the
Management of Modernism   EDWARD P. COMENTALE   3

2 "Alimentary, Dr. Leiter": Anal Anxiety in *Diamonds Are Forever*
DENNIS W. ALLEN   24

3 Lesbian Bondage, or Why Dykes Like 007   JAIME HOVEY   42

4 James Bond, Cyborg-Aristocrat   PATRICK O'DONNELL   55

II. Ian Fleming and Style

5 Living the James Bond Lifestyle   JUDITH ROOF   71

6 James Bond, Meta-Brand   AARON JAFFE   87

7 The Bond Market   CRAIG N. OWENS   107

III. Ian Fleming and the Global Imaginary

8 Bond and Britishness   JAMES CHAPMAN   129

9 Shoot Back in Anger: Bond and the "Angry Young Man"
BRIAN PATTON   144

10 Tropical Bond   VIVIAN HALLORAN   158

11 The Kennedys, Fleming, and Cuba: Bond's Foreign Policy
SKIP WILLMAN   178

12 Wanting to Be James Bond   ALEXIS ALBION   202

IV. Structures of Feeling

13 Why Size Matters   CHRISTOPH LINDNER   223

14 007 and 9/11, Specters and Structures of Feeling
STEPHEN WATT   238

Acknowledgments   261
Works Cited   263
Contributors   271
Index   275

FOREWORD

The nearest James Bond came to Bloomington, Indiana, was Fort Knox, Kentucky (in *Goldfinger*). His creator, Ian Fleming, would have been amused to discover that within forty years of his untimely demise in 1964, this relaxed midwestern university town had become an essential destination for anyone with a serious interest in 007.

The main reason is that the world's leading collection of Fleming's books and papers is housed in the Lilly Library, part of Indiana University at Bloomington. Proof copies of the Bond novels can be read there, embellished with their author's autograph notes and corrections. Additional holdings include the manuscript of *State of Excitement*, Fleming's account of his visit to Kuwait in 1960, which, uniquely among his work, remains unpublished because the Kuwait Oil Company, which commissioned it, disliked his comments on the Gulf emirate. Also available are letters and further biographical material, as well as Fleming's remarkable accumulation of "books that made things happen"—essentially, first editions of treatises on ideas and scientific discoveries which changed the world. If nothing else, deposits such as a first issue of Karl Marx's *Communist Manifesto* attest to Fleming's wide interests.

Fittingly, his spirit of curiosity and eclecticism permeated the conference on "The Cultural Politics of Ian Fleming and 007" held in Bloomington under the auspices of Indiana University College of Arts and Sciences from May 29 to June 1, 2003.

This posthumous festschrift showed Bondian cheek since Fleming had only a fleeting experience of higher education. He did spend some time at the Universities of Munich and Geneva as part of an expensive European "finishing" process. Earlier at school his mother had deemed him not bright enough to follow his older brother Peter to Oxford University. Instead, he went into the army class division, where the more intellectually challenged boys were prepared for military careers.

But Ian was blessed with the sort of darting, magpie mind that makes his stories a joy. No doubt he was trying to impress the literary clique around his wife Ann when he declared that his favorite reading matter, particularly for travel, was the *Times Literary Supplement*. His extensive interests certainly provided a stimulating perspective on the life and times of the Cold War era, as he sought to update the traditional

British secret service thriller from the formulaic confections of authors such as Bulldog Drummond and John Buchan.

On one level, Fleming achieved this with his devoted chronicling of the emerging consumer culture, where the brand names of food, drinks, clothing, and even trains are savored. On another, he indulged in erudite mini-essays on topics that interested him, ranging from the life of the buccaneer Sir Henry Morgan or the nature of *accidie* in *Live and Let Die,* through an overview of London clubs and the rules of bridge in *Moonraker,* to a glossary of poisonous plants and an insight into the haiku verse form in *You Only Live Twice.* Such gems from the Fleming knowledge bank enliven any time spent with the literary Bond.

Moviemakers have happily maintained this sort of engaging feature. Even their obsession with 007's tailoring can, if interpreted astutely, inform about the culture of the times. And what would a Bond film be without its up-market in-jokes? This tradition dates back to *Dr. No,* in 1962, when director Terence Young arranged for a reproduction of Goya's recently stolen painting of the Duke of Wellington to appear on a wall in the eponymous villain's island hideaway.

The Bloomington conference latched on to such details and attempted to make sense of them. Bond has now been in the public domain for fifty years, and it is worth trying to understand what he (and his enduring popularity) means and what it tells us about our age.

As Fleming's biographer, I found incontrovertible evidence, as if I did not already know, that Bond is now a film-led phenomenon. Several participants admitted to scant knowledge of the original "anonymous blunt instrument wielded by dolts in high places" found in the novels.

This slightly distanced proceedings from their original begetter. But it also underlined the enormity of Fleming's achievement. For the child of his imagination has outgrown its bookishness and become a mature cross-media brat. John Betjeman saw that this was likely to happen: as he told a morose Fleming toward the end of the latter's life, "The Bond world is as real and full of fear and mystery as Conan Doyle's Norwood and Surrey and Baker Street. I think the only other person to have invented a world in our time is (P.G.) Wodehouse. This is real art."

That colossal invention repaid the attention accorded it at Bloomington. It was clear that Fleming had created a character, a lifestyle, and even an ideology robust enough to bear examination from different scholarly perspectives including history, geography, sociology, philosophy, and gay and cultural studies.

American intellectual life showed no signs of conformity or torpor after the devastation of 9/11. It seemed to have drawn strength from them, encouraging Stephen Watt, for example, to point out, in the Bond context, the correspondences between 007's Cold War mission and the present-day struggle against Islamic fundamentalism and, in particular, between 007 villains and Osama bin Laden.

Picking highlights is invidious, but I enjoyed Patrick O'Donnell's deft placing of Bond in a continuum of movie heroes between the old-fashioned humanist leading man and the programmed cyborg. I was impressed by Ed Comentale's positioning of Fleming's hero firmly in postwar corporatist culture. Alexis K. Albion was illuminating about Bond's "moment in history": how his qualities epitomized what was happening inside and outside the intelligence community in the 1960s.

Vivian Halloran skillfully interpreted the Caribbean as a metaphor for doubleness in Fleming's work, showing the region seesawing between a place of exotic excitement and a boring backwater for secret agents with nothing better to do. Judith Roof was amusingly incisive about the emphasis on style in the Bond oeuvre masking a nostalgia for an old-fashioned sense of order, while Jaime Hovey noted how the progressive feminization of the cinematic Bond (in accordance with the dictates of market research and political correctness) was disliked in the lesbian community, which preferred the deviant "butch" qualities of the original Sean Connery character. When Jeremy Black suggested such readings had moved the subject matter a long way from Fleming, he was only reflecting a modern academic manifestation of the nagging but fruitful trans-Atlantic "special relationship" that Fleming portrayed between MI6 and the CIA. Long may it thrive in this new context.

Andrew Lycett
London, January 2004

INTRODUCTION

Ian Fleming and James Bond: The Cultural Politics of 007 collects essays delivered at a symposium convened in June 2003 at Indiana University in Bloomington. This international meeting, organized to celebrate the fiftieth anniversary of the publication of Fleming's *Casino Royale*, attracted scholars from Britain, Canada, and across the United States, all of whom gathered to participate in what is believed to be the first academic symposium dedicated solely to Fleming's work, particularly the series of novels and short story collections featuring the world's best-known secret agent, James Bond. Indiana may not seem so unlikely a venue for such a conference when one considers the significance of the Ian Fleming Collection housed at the Lilly Library on campus, an important archive purchased by the university after Fleming's death in 1964. Not surprisingly given the general public's fascination with Fleming and Bond, this symposium attracted significant attention from the media—from the London *Times,* the *New York Times,* and National Public Radio, among others—and this anthology reproduces the most exciting and, in some cases, controversial essays presented at the meeting (revised appropriately for publication).

This volume is based on several premises in addition to its editors' intentions to address both a more general academic audience *and* to recreate the terms of an animated intellectual debate that often emerges around such popular figures as James Bond. The first is that before Bond became a cinematic icon, he was the protagonist of a series of successful novels written at the historical moment of a widely perceived decline in Britain's status as an international power, an acceleration of Cold War tensions with the Soviet Union, and an explosion of cultural debates over gender, sexuality, and morality. Importantly, as an emblem of Western superiority in a rapidly changing global history, the figure of Bond gave expression to biases and anxieties that continue to shape our understandings of identity and belonging. Fleming's writing contributed substantially—and provocatively—to debates over such matters, often appearing to be both liberal and conservative at the same time, and thus seriously challenging the traditional ways in which we continue to delineate political boundaries. Here we are speaking specifically about the novels Fleming wrote, not the screenplays based (or not, as the case may be) on them. As Tony Bennett and Janet Woollacott emphasize in their much-quoted study *Bond and Beyond,* with the serial publication of *From Russia with Love* in 1957, Fleming and Bond became "household names" in Britain. By 1961, with the publication of John F. Kennedy's "Ten Favorite Books" in *Life* magazine that listed *From Russia with Love,* and the release of the film *Dr. No* the following year, both Fleming and Bond rose to similar prominence in America as well. As we shall outline below, several contributors to *Ian Fleming and James Bond: The Cultural Politics of 007* investigate Fleming's novels in their original cultural context, tracing not only their influence in Britain, but their global reach as well, from the 1960s to the present.

The process of Fleming's becoming a "household name" in the 1950s and 1960s, needless to say, was facilitated by the appearance of 007 in a series of successful films, inaugurated in 1962. As we have suggested, while several contributors to this anthology are more interested in his novels and the specific readership for whom Fleming wrote, others regard the films as achieving more significant cultural influence during the Cold War era. This latter group explores, for example, the representation of alternative subjectivities in the films, such as gays and lesbians in *From Russia with Love, Goldfinger,* and *Diamonds Are Forever.* Other essays explore the so-called "Bond lifestyle" as it was promoted and cultivated in the films over several decades of cultural change. Crucial to this promotion were—and still *are*—conspicuous product placement and the deployment of accessories that often function either as emblems of a hetero-normative masculinity or as fetishes. In other words, Fleming and 007 contributed to and substantially revised both masculine subject-formation and extant discourses on sexuality during the Cold War, and they still do. All the while, such processes occur within the excesses of capitalism. How many villains routinely take their antagonists on factory tours before pronouncing their executions, as Slavoj Žižek asked recently? *Ian Fleming and James Bond: The Cultural Politics of 007* has much to say about these and many other issues.

Yet another topic central to this volume and to our understanding of James Bond—as written by Fleming and, after his death, by John Gardner and Raymond Benson—is the public's continuing fascination with a secret agent born fifty years ago. How might we account for this unprecedented success? Several contributors to *Ian Fleming and James Bond: The Cultural Politics of 007* address this question, tracing his evolution in the films to our revised understandings of gender, sexuality, and fashion. Other contributors attempt to explicate the relevance of Fleming's fiction to our own times. For, if Bond remains a figure of allure and identification for film viewers, Fleming himself may stand as something of a prophet in predicting a post–Cold War terrorism, complete with radical cells of "sleepers," biochemical weapons, and a kind of invisibility that the old and monolithic Soviet Union could never have achieved. In such novels as *On Her Majesty's Secret Service*, Fleming seems prescient in depicting the devastating possibilities of the deployment of bacterial and chemical agents—anthrax, botulism, smallpox, and others—by terrorists against the West. In his exposition of SPECTRE in *Thunderball*, Fleming anticipates the implosion of the Soviet machine and its replacement by a nearly invisible, wraith-like terrorist organization not dissimilar from today's al-Qaeda network. Such uncanny parallels suggest the renewed importance of representation—how we metaphorize ourselves and our enemies—in contemporary debates over anti-terrorist tactics in a post 9/11 world, thus making Fleming relevant again, albeit in very different ways. In what follows, all of us hope to make Fleming and Bond again relevant for you as well.

Who Owns Bond?

Importantly, *Ian Fleming and James Bond: The Cultural Politics of 007* addresses not only what academics can do for Bond, but also what Bond does for academics. This may seem like a strange formulation, but, when all was said and done that spirited weekend in June, the figure of Bond turned out to be something of a lightning rod for the humanities, at once confounding the lines of critical inquiry, exposing scholarly biases and blind spots, and, in general, forcing us to rethink the ways in which we work and relate to each other. As conference organizers, we knew from the start that this particular topic could generate some critical heat, but we didn't know exactly where tensions might arise. The Bond phenomenon—because of its thematic and cultural range—seems to generate many different responses (both historically and socially) and thus raises many essential academic questions. Is it more productive to focus on the historical figure of Fleming or on his fictional creation Bond? Where does Bond begin and end—in Fleming's mind, in the British spy novel tradition, in the many fan pages and websites devoted to his cult status? Does the cultural franchise of Bond rest on the novels or the films? Do we grant priority to British or American versions of the superspy? Does Bond's excessive masculinity challenge or sustain traditional forms of gender and sexuality? Does it matter anymore that Bond works in the service of empire? These are the kinds of questions that academics today build their careers on, and the dual phenomenon of Fleming-Bond is the best kind of grist for their mill. Historicists and theorists, textualists and culturalists, globalists and nationalists, film buffs and readers—we imagined them masterminding some intricate deconstructive laser to inflict Bond's death-by-academia. Our premeditated solution was twofold: welcome the multiple valences of the Bond phenomenon and invite representative scholars from a variety of approaches. We thought we could accept only what appeared undeniable and then drown out the problems by multiplying them. But the very fact that we recognized these fault lines, and still imagined that we could avoid them, already says much about the present state of intellection.

The oppositional nature of contemporary intellectual inquiry, particularly as it is usually conjoined with the hope of intellectual reconciliation, already suggests that we are working within an exacting ideological system. Long before our first call for papers, long before we designed the conference program, the fix was in. The "fix" or terms of disagreement were, curiously enough, evident at the earliest stages of conference planning in the disparate goals of the Ian Fleming Foundation and Ian Fleming Publications Ltd. The promotional literature of the Foundation, a non-profit, American-based organization, emphasizes that it is not a "fan club or a collector's club," but is rather a group singularly focused on the "goals of procuring, restoring, and archiving Ian Fleming's legacy for the general public," which it achieves in part by generously providing vehicles and other artifacts from Bond films for events like ours. By contrast, Ian Fleming Publications, a British-based organization operated by the Fleming family intent on elevating his reputation as a "serious author," urged us to use only Fleming's name—not Bond's—on our promotional material and to avoid any kitschy display of fan-based adoration. After our befuddlement subsided, we realized that these conflicting imperatives were emblematic of a larger conflict we often paper over in discussions of such disparate topics as "academic" publishing and the intellectual projects of contemporary humanists: namely, the academy's fraught relationship with the domain of popular consumption.

These difficulties, though, hardly prepared us for what we encountered once scholars arrived on campus and began to engage each another. In the very first conference event, James Chapman insisted on the need for historical specificity, which he opposed to overly or overtly politicized theory. He expressed particular dissatisfaction with the general concept of postmodernism and, more precisely, postfeminism, both of which he depicted as confused, willful constructions with little theoretical validity. This, mind you, was hardly representative of a conference roster that also featured Dennis Allen's " 'Alimentary, Dr. Leiter': Anal Anxiety in *Diamonds Are Forever*" and Jaime Hovey's "Lesbian Bondage, or Why Dykes Like 007." The statement proved to be in direct opposition to papers such as Judith Roof's "Living the James Bond Lifestyle," in which Bond is depicted as a mutable construct, a stylish nostalgia for a past that never really existed. In fact, Roof's paper implied that any kind of historicism, and particularly the kind Chapman proposed, only aids in the maintenance of a fictional but "efficacious law"; Roof drew specifically on postmodern deconstruction and postfeminist theory to oppose Bond's tendency to become a "repository of brute patriarchy." These tensions, among others, were apparent to all involved, and attendees all too quickly drew up on opposing sides. It seemed like the Cold War all over again in its silent anxiousness and threat of annihilation, but without any of the real bombs or public interest. Perhaps the most surreal moment was provided by Jeremy Black's concluding keynote address. After two days of conferencegoing, Black apparently ditched his planned address and decided to respond specifically to what he felt were the conference's weakest papers. In what can best be described as a scolding, he outlined the personal (by which he meant gendered and nationalistic) biases that shaped certain presenters' theoretical approaches. This presentation immediately prompted several attendees, Judith Roof among them, to draw up a manifesto and boycott a final roundtable discussion at which Black was scheduled to appear. As the manifesto explained, "As firm believers in unfettered academic exchange and as unflagging advocates of the multivalent richness of the figure of James Bond, we deplore the creation here at this conference of a narrow-minded atmosphere, one where certain approaches and certain philosophies about how texts should be fashioned are used to bully and intimidate scholars who advocate difficult, solid, and creative interpretive practices. . . . We respectfully further decline to participate in an exchange that is *no* exchange, but merely the rehearsal of stereotypes, unexamined prejudices, and anti-intellectual posturing."

As conference organizers, we appreciated many of the sentiments expressed in the manifesto, if not its tone or manner of delivery. As readers may notice, this collection contains essays by both Chapman and Roof, and, we think, this kind of juxtaposition made the occasion a productive one. That said, we feel pressed to account for these tensions, to make some sense of their causes and possible solutions. Obviously, the issue here is largely one of intellectual ownership and property. Who owns Bond? How can we put him to work for *us*? Who has the right to capitalize on his image and popular status? This is serious business. Academics are fighting over who gets to do the work with which they feel most comfortable, identifying at the same time the political stakes of their interests, and the phenomenon of Bond provides the perfect material for such projects. As mentioned earlier, the ideological axes of Bondiana are multivalent and professionally charged: England versus America, History versus Theory, Author versus Text, Straight versus Queer, Word versus filmic Image. More and more, though, it has become clear that this was not a special moment in academic history, but an emblematic one. The Bond conference was a crisis insofar as our work is always confronting this crisis; it was just a more extreme form of what we face all the time. The most telling aspect of the whole experience is that while much of the talk about Fleming and Bond was heated, oppositional, and divisive, the papers themselves were levelheaded and balanced. Scholars were startlingly bold in their spoken claims, but respectful and subtle in their written ones. In this collection, for example, Chapman's paper is interesting precisely because it teeters between a sincere commitment to historical specificity and an edgy awareness of postmodern phenomenology. Roof's paper, too, is valuable precisely because it plays hide-and-seek with the promise of a stable historicism and the persistence of historical subjectivism. This suggests to us that perhaps academics insist on highly binarized categories so that they can then be free to mix them up in their best work. Their starkly contrasting terms sustain the purity of each other, so that they are then readily mobilized to produce ever more complex and productive claims. According to Bruno Latour, this is nothing other than the ideological dynamic of modernity itself. Moderns insist on absolute distinctions in order to mobilize more subtle and productive hybrids, cultural formations that exist somewhere between nature and history, or, say, between the popular and the elite:

> Because it believes in the total separation of humans and nonhumans, and because it simultaneously cancels out this separation, the [Modern] Constitution has made the moderns invincible. If you criticize them that Nature is a world constructed by human hands, they will show you that it is transcendent, that science is a mere intermediary allowing access to Nature, and that they keep their hands off. If you tell

them that we are free and that our destiny is in our own hands, they will tell you that society is transcendent and its laws infinitely surpass us. . . . If you believe them and direct your attention elsewhere, they will take advantage of this to transfer thousands of objects from nature into the social body while procuring for this body the solidity of natural things. . . . Everything happens in the middle, everything passes between the two, everything happens by way of mediation, translation, and networks, but this space does not exist, it has no place. (Latour 37)

Again, the phenomenon of Bond is ideal for this kind of intellectual work and for sustaining its production. His confounding hybridity is everywhere matched by an astounding (and often offensive) swagger. His most essential talent is his ability to rework the codes by playing them all straight. In fact, the secret service and academia are linked by this mode: the success of both depends on an ability to cross and confound rigid oppositions, but they do this work best when playing it straight. In the end, all that happened at the conference was accurate and true to its subject. We captured the spirit of Bond and pushed its critical potential further than we ever thought possible. This collection is a testament to that process. We hope you enjoy its subtlety as well as its bombast.

Contents

The at times volatile debate at the conference, in some respects, was surprising given the rather obvious fact that the interdisciplinary study of popular culture seems so fully incorporated into the university. Were the skirmishes described above merely symptoms of a turf war between disciplines waged passive-aggressively before martinis at the Lilly Library and watching the Bond films that ran continuously in downtown Bloomington? Or is there something in particular about Bond that makes the study of this subject so contentious? One response to this situation may lie in the issue of enjoyment. In an era of political correctness, James Bond is a guilty pleasure of many academics, at least many of those in attendance at this conference. The resurgent Bond films of the nineties even acknowledge this guilty appeal, most notoriously in *GoldenEye* (1995), in which the brand-new female M (Judi Dench) dresses down Bond (Pierce Brosnan) as "a sexist, misogynist dinosaur, a relic of the Cold War." The Bond scholar is engaged in what Slavoj Žižek describes as "fetishistic disavowal": "I know very well that Bond is a sexist, misogynist hero of British imperialism, but nevertheless I find his adventures thrilling and worthy of serious academic attention."

Writing cultural critiques of Bond is a way for the academic to gain a certain cynical distance from it so as to be able to enjoy its forbidden pleasures. Popular culture clearly offers more subversive figures than Bond for analysis, requiring the academic to be less apologetic or circumspect about his or her own private enjoyment. Witness the academic cult of *Buffy the Vampire Slayer*, a television show that flaunted its "transgression" with an ass-kicking female hero whose sidekick was a lesbian Wiccan. However, the obstacle to the direct and immediate enjoyment of Bond contributes to the enjoyment itself. Perhaps debates about the proper way to study Bond are embroiled in the differences in the ways in which we enjoy him.

If enjoyment is such an issue in the study of Bond, does this somehow taint the scholarship, making cultural studies a glorified form of fandom? Is scholarship on James Bond merely an act of bad faith, yet another symptom of what Marxist literary theorist Terry Eagleton derides in *After Theory* (2003) as the "politics of amnesia" in cultural studies today? The essays in this collection demonstrate that the answer to these questions is a definitive no. Attuned to both history and theory, these essays do not, as Eagleton laments, turn aside from political struggles in pursuit of purely intellectual pleasures. Nor do they shoot fish in the barrel, so to speak, by offering easy denunciations of the James Bond novels and films. Quite deliberately, this volume does not rehash warmed-over versions of the "sex, sadism, and snobbery" arguments against Fleming that have been around since the fifties. Rather, it attempts to address the social, political, and cultural matrix within which the Bond novels and films have been produced, received, and recirculated.

Ian Fleming and James Bond: The Cultural Politics of 007 consists of fourteen essays organized according to two areas of interest that emerged at the conference and thus speak directly to current debates within the field of cultural studies: Subjectivities and Histories. The categories are somewhat deceptive insofar as the formation of the subject considered in the opening section is deeply historical, bound to transformations in late capitalism, technology, and the symbolic order, while the histories of the second section inevitably raise questions about subjectivity, specifically the politics of identification. In general, the book considers Fleming's work as it is situated in certain temporal and spatial contexts, as well as how the Bond novels and films give voice to more subtle issues and anxieties that define thought and politics today. We have been careful throughout to avoid easy distinctions between, say, history and theory, film and fiction, reaction and progress. Our goal, here and at the conference, has been to preserve a critical suppleness that allows us to evaluate Fleming's work in its telling contradictoriness.

Subjectivities

The Subject Is Bond

This grouping of essays explores Fleming's work as it responds to post–World War II transformations—theoretical or otherwise—of subjectivity and intersubjective relations. Taking mostly a psychoanalytic approach, these contributors read Bond as revelatory of a variety of new subjective formations and chart a complex historical transformation that extends from economics to aesthetics to sexuality. Edward P. Comentale, in "Fleming's Company Man: James Bond and the Management of Modernism," argues that Fleming's work, despite its racy content, gives expression to the demands and contradictions of a specifically professional society; hence, James Bond is less a champion of consumer culture than a hero of the corporation. More precisely, Comentale regards Bond's professionalism as bound to a specifically anal order that serves to reconfigure the libidinal investments between subjects and thus release a previously untapped desire into larger productive mechanisms. Dennis W. Allen, in " 'Alimentary, Dr. Leiter': Anal Anxiety in *Diamonds Are Forever*," further explores Bond's sexuality, but as it is represented in the films of the seventies and gives voice to a certain anxiety about the wholeness of both the individual male (in the fear of anal penetration but also of the unconscious) and of masculinity itself (because it suggests that not all men are "really" men). Allen shows how this anxiety results in a certain anal-retentive structuring of Bond's imaginary world, particularly as it manifests itself in narrative formula, high-tech gadgetry, and motivated names. Jaime Hovey's essay, "Lesbian Bondage, or Why Dykes Like 007," provocatively explores the Bond films as they map shifting gender roles in the wake of the women's movement. Hovey traces Bond's transformation from excessively masculine hero to stylishly accessorized dandy, arguing that his later incarnation, albeit more politically correct, is less appealing to feminists and lesbians. In "James Bond, Cyborg-Aristocrat," Patrick O'Donnell argues that the space race of the early sixties triggered a new subject-formation in the national security state idealized in the figure of the astronaut. Bond represents one variation of this new subject that O'Donnell calls the "cyborg-aristocrat," a figure caught between an emerging cybernetic posthumanism and what might be termed humanism's last gasp. Bond, he argues, is both a prosthesis and a playboy, a Deleuzian war machine mutating from the animal to the cybernetic, and at the same time a sex machine whose "individuality" is both bolstered and sundered by gadgetry and sexual conquests.

Ian Fleming and Style

These three essays explore what is perhaps the most obvious yet least theorized aspect of the Bond phenomenon: its fashionable appeal. All three scholars explore the ways in which Bond's style—as it is manifested in everything from his gadgetry to his masculine grace—is embedded in a larger cultural logic of consumption and thus serves to enforce the demands of a social order that is at once gendered, economic, and political. Judith Roof, in "Living the James Bond Lifestyle," argues that the stylish figure of James Bond, precisely because he is stylish, represents a nostalgia for an efficacious law. Bond's style, she argues, substitutes for what law can no longer do; it has become a vector for selling the illusion of a nostalgic mastery, the promises of continued individual fortitude in a culture of increasingly dissipated and concealed power. Aaron Jaffe's essay, "James Bond, Meta-Brand," examines the roles of brand names and product placement in Ian Fleming's fiction and the film franchise. Jaffe regards Bond as a kind of meta-branding machine and reads the novels as expressive of a larger cultural shift from the subjective hard sell of earlier advertising techniques to the objective soft sell of modern public relations and thus of the transition from the chaotic public marketplace of the past to today's vast promotional matrix based on the concept of "lifestyle." The soft-sell tactics of the Meta-Brand James Bond presume that the public subscribes to a distinctly Marxist form of commodity fetishism. However, Craig N. Owens, in "The Bond Market," argues that the psychoanalytic account of fetishism works better than the Marxist one at explaining the nuances of Bond's style, particularly as it relates to the accessory. Owens contends that Bond's selection of accessory fetishes is a means to disavow lack, an issue that manifests itself in the frequent scenes of literal or figurative castration in the novels. The figure of James Bond, moreover, marks the emergence of the consuming male, the anonymous postbourgeois man of moderate means who conceives of himself no longer as a particularity, but as an empty site of potential subjectivity realized only in the act of accruing and consuming things.

Histories

Ian Fleming and the Global Imaginary

This grouping of essays explores Fleming's influence as it first emerged in postwar England and then traveled around the globe to America and eventually to the rest of the world. The first three contributors pay careful attention to the ways in which Fleming's writing emerges from a specific historical juncture, replete with its own social contradictions and anxieties. The Bond novels represent a response to the dilemmas and give voice to the hopes and fears of Cold War England. More specifically, they explore the ways in which Fleming's work is enmeshed in a rapidly changing colonial history, particularly as it expresses the contradictions inherent in England's increasingly tenuous position of imperial power and gives voice to a singular fascination with its colonial others. In "Bond and Britishness," James Chapman peruses the ur-scene of Fleming's creation, the British cultural material out of which Bond and his exploits emerged in the fifties, specifically the decline of England as an imperial power, the rise of the welfare state, and the advent of a more permissive attitude toward sex. Chapman contends that while the cinematic Bond has frequently been seen as the quintessential Brit, the literary Bond entertains a far more ambivalent relationship toward his nation. The postwar decline of Britain as a superpower and the emergence of the welfare state also form the historical context explored by Brian Patton in "Shoot Back in Anger: Bond and the 'Angry Young Man.'" Patton shows that while Fleming cursorily dismissed the "Angry Young Men" who rose to prominence at this transitional moment in British history, he nevertheless responded to the same social and economic conditions framing their work, albeit from the distinctly non-working class perspective of imperial and aristocratic nostalgia. This imperial nostalgia is also registered in Fleming's fiction through the representation of the colonies, particularly those in the Caribbean, with which he was intimately acquainted because his winter home was located in Jamaica. Vivian Halloran, in "Tropical Bond," examines Fleming's work as it negotiates ambivalent feelings toward the increasingly unstable colonies and rebellious colonial subjects. She explores Fleming's use of racial hybridity within the ideologically charged geographical space of the Caribbean "ethnoscape" or "contact zone," in which various races and cultures intersect.

The next two essays move into the sixties to explore the global

reception of James Bond. The popularity of Bond was given a tremendous boost stateside when President John F. Kennedy listed *From Russia
with Love* as one of his ten favorite books in a 1961 *Life* magazine article.
In "The Kennedys, Fleming, and Cuba: Bond's Foreign Policy," Skip
Willman explores the ramifications of Kennedy's obsession with Bond,
beginning with an anecdote about an auspicious dinner party in 1960
during which Kennedy asked Fleming about how to topple Castro. Willman shows how the fantasy figure of James Bond shaped the Kennedys'
expectations regarding the CIA's covert activities in Cuba, even after the
fiasco of the CIA-led Bay of Pigs invasion on April 17, 1961. Alexis
Albion, in "Wanting to Be James Bond," takes us into the world at large,
exploring the transformation of Bond from a popular British fiction
hero into a global icon widely acknowledged in the East and West. Analyzing reviews, articles, and essays about James Bond and his widespread
popularity written in North America, Europe, the Soviet Union, and
Asia, she explains how critics around the globe responded to the figure of
Bond on three levels: as a national figure, as a political and economic
symbol of the West, and as a global figure reflective of universal values
and appeal. Furthermore, Albion makes the case that the reception of
James Bond in the sixties was a harbinger of globalism, not merely in the
sense of an international culture, but also in its depiction of a social
reality eerily similar to our post-9/11 world of terror networks bent on
undermining global stability.

Structures of Feeling

The final two essays consider the mutating social feelings
of the post–World War II world as they find expression in the ever-
changing and ceaselessly renewable world of James Bond. These essays
reveal not only Fleming's remarkable prescience in relation to the course
of twentieth-century history, but also the equally remarkable flexibility
by which his creation continues to register and negotiate our greatest
cultural hopes and fears. Christoph Lindner, in "Why Size Matters,"
explores the Bond phenomenon of the sixties and seventies to propose
that the 007 series marks a shift in cultural understanding of crime and
criminality which, following the traumatic experience of two world
wars, the Holocaust, and the dawn of the atomic age, came to include
crimes against humanity. The discussion examines how this shift not
only registers in the magnified scope of Fleming's "criminal vision," but
also gives rise to new ideological imperatives for the detective—a figure
now reconfigured as secret agent, licensed to kill. The issue of size,

Lindner further claims, makes Fleming a particularly relevant voice in the wake of 9/11. Like Lindner, Stephen Watt, in "007 and 9/11, Specters and Structures of Feeling," explores the uncanny resemblance between the international terrorist organizations of Fleming's fiction and the social reality of today. Watt describes a contemporary structure of feeling that is composed of both present fears and the residues of the Cold War. His analysis focuses on Fleming's characterization of SPECTRE and its founder Ernst Stavro Blofeld as it helps us understand the structure and psychical affect of the contemporary terrorist network.

In the opening salvo of the conference, which is reiterated briefly here in his essay, James Chapman described Bond scholarship as oscillating between two poles, the historical and the theoretical, a claim supported by calls for historical specificity that inevitably rankled some audience members. What precisely does historical specificity mean? For some, it presumably means an awareness of the particular British Cold War political context in which the novels were written, the importance of which no one in attendance at the conference would dispute. However, to say that such a perspective focusing on the influential events of the fifties and early sixties in Britain exhausts the legitimate interpretive possibilities regarding Fleming's fiction is another matter indeed. Historical specificity can certainly take on other forms. In this collection, history likewise takes on many guises, from describing changes in subject formation across the twentieth century to more traditional scholarship. We would argue that the dichotomy between history and theory is false, but that it nevertheless describes something like the reality of the appearance. *Ian Fleming and James Bond: The Cultural Politics of 007* aims to provide a stereoscopic view, providing both historical and theoretical perspectives that, taken as a whole, illuminate the work of Ian Fleming and the Bond phenomenon.

ABBREVIATIONS

All quotations and pagination from Ian Fleming's novels and short stories featuring James Bond come from the recently published Penguin editions. Please note that minor differences of pagination emerge in this series between texts published in Britain and those published in the United States. For this reason, essayists were asked to use the American editions, which are abbreviated as follows when necessary. Also note the lack of an abbreviation in the title of Fleming's 1958 novel *Doctor No*, while the title of the 1962 film is generally rendered as *Dr. No*.

Casino	*Casino Royale*, 1953. New York, 2002.
Diamonds	*Diamonds Are Forever*, 1956. New York, 2003.
Doctor	*Doctor No*, 1958. New York, 2002.
Goldfinger	*Goldfinger*, 1959. New York, 2002
Her Majesty's	*On Her Majesty's Secret Service*, 1963. New York, 2003
Live	*Live and Let Die*, 1954. New York, 2003.
Live Twice	*You Only Live Twice*, 1964. New York, 2003.
Man	*The Man with the Golden Gun*, 1965. New York, 2004.
Moonraker	*Moonraker*, 1955. New York, 2003.
Octopussy	*Octopussy and the Living Daylights* [1966]. New York, 2004
Russia	*From Russia with Love*, 1957. New York, 2003.
Spy	*The Spy Who Loved Me*, 1962. New York, 2003.
Thunderball	*Thunderball*, 1961. New York, 2003.
Your Eyes	*For Your Eyes Only*, 1960. New York, 2003.

The Subject
Is Bond

1 Fleming's Company Man

JAMES BOND AND THE MANAGEMENT OF MODERNISM

Edward P. Comentale

I must apologize in advance for what promises to be a dull affair. This essay contains no violence or danger, little vice and crime, and only a whiff of Cold War sex. I have nothing to say about sharks or dry martinis or even firm Russian breasts; in fact, I have little to say about the charismatic figure of James Bond himself. This is not because I have no interest in these issues or because I find them insignificant in Fleming's work. Rather, I believe that even the most titillating aspects of this fiction exist to be processed by an austere managerial consciousness. It is my contention that the novels, insofar as they work to counter painfully obvious signs of England's postwar decline, also work to justify the increasingly corporate structure of the nation. In other words, Fleming's work cannot be read apart from what Harold Perkin calls "the rise of professional society." Despite its racy content, his fiction gives expression to the demands and contradictions of a specifically professional society, and its hero, James Bond, is less a hero of consumer culture than he is a hero of the corporation.[1] More precisely, I want to argue that this fiction—in its plotting, characterizations, and economical, realist style—depicts corporatism as a flexibly resistant medium, capable of avoiding the extremes of anarchy and efficiency, democracy and fascism, and, perhaps most importantly, unrestrained free trade and socialist revolution. In other words, if it adopts a specifically corporatist stance in its attempt to negotiate the pressures of a postwar world, it finds itself both expressive of and responsive to the conflicted energies of modernity at large. At its best, Fleming's work also explores corporate society in its more subtle manifestations, as it slowly revises notions of nationhood, subjectivity, property, and literary form. Most importantly, it investigates the beliefs and values of this society as it remains caught between the humanistic ideals of the modernist project and a certain posthumanistic outlook that seems an inevitable corollary to life under late capitalism. As I hope to show here, Fleming's work proves that this ambivalence is central to the experience of corporate life and helps to explain its psychic constitution and material persistence. Ultimately, the corporate network appears as neither modern nor post-modern, but totemic in a Freudian sense, forcing us to reconceive the comfortable narratives by which we have come to understand the subject and subjective pleasure as well as the theories by which we have come to value certain types of community and communal belonging.

Not surprisingly, Harold Perkin's landmark study begins in the nineteenth century with the division of labor and the growth of industry as these transformations produced an overwhelming need for vast networks of managerial control.[2] Perkin, however, subtly revises Marx's model of revolutionary change by presenting the professionals as a valid emerging fourth class and thus as a decisive influence on the structural relations of twentieth-century life. This group guaranteed its growth and survival by establishing a series of informational networks and by reinforcing these structures with humanitarian ideals of social justice and public service (4–7). The significance of Perkin's study, then, is that it links economic causes with ideological ones. Indeed, the growth of professional society is a direct result of England's failure to maintain its status as an imperial producer and its consequent turn toward banking and stocks. It also emerges out of the need to develop sufficient reform measures and representative channels for the competing class interests of early twentieth-century society. But, most importantly, the triumph of the professional class depended upon its promotion of a social ideal that mediates between competing class ideologies. In their self-presentation, the professionals borrowed from all three classes: they saw themselves as gentlemanly and industrious, as paternalistic, entrepreneurial, and socially responsible. They were, in Perkin's words, "honest, truthful, upright, polite, temperate, courageous, self-respecting, and self-helping," and with this self-promotional mixture, they were able to adopt, adapt, and assimilate the needs of an increasingly dissociated public sphere (120–21, 304–305).[3] To put it bluntly, the professional class emerged to solve the contradictions of modernity at large. They proffered their wares at precisely that moment when the tensions within capitalism could no longer be sustained, when entrepreneurialism collided with corporate growth, market expansion with national boundaries. In this, and in all that follows from it, the professionals did not simply destroy the economic system, but reaffirmed its basic dynamic in ways that seemed to avoid violence and war. As I hope to show, their key redefinitions—of, say, individualism, property, the nation, and even the novel—simply retooled and rewired the dynamic energies of modernity and capital, allowing the entire system to grow ever more efficiently.[4]

With an almost textbook simplicity, the evolution of the Fleming family line exemplifies this larger socio-political transformation. Ian's grandfather rose from the position of bookkeeper at a small jute shop to become one of the first managers of an international investment trust. Ian's father was described as "a young professional in a hurry" who made his way to Parliament to defend the professional ideals of national service, labor reform, and efficient management. At the end of this line, Ian himself appears less like the dashing composer of salacious thrillers and more like a passionate civil servant with little aristocratic clout to his name. His professional specialties were public relations and info-management, whether serving with the League of Nations' International Bureau of Intellectual Cooperation or the Coordinating Section of the Special Branch of the Navy during World War II or as "Foreign Manager" of a worldwide information-gathering network for the *Sunday Times* (Lycett, *Ian Fleming* 1–9, 99–100, 159–60). Not surprisingly, Fleming's political statements, though few and brief, favor the paradoxes of a specifically professional order. In his somewhat facetious essay "If I Were Prime Minister," he expresses a typically professional disinterest in politics, but then proceeds to list a contradictory mélange of reform measures. He argues for collective social responsibility, but he maintains the need for a competitive arena by which skill and talent can be rewarded. He bemoans the rise of the welfare state and the increasingly consumer-based relations of the mid-century socius, yet he calls for a vast pleasure dome to be built on the Isle of Wight where good British citizens may indulge in gambling and sex.[5] Fleming's novels are similarly ambivalent, if not conflicted, in their political allegiances. For every violently ideological socialist on M's hit list, there is an equally reprehensible capitalist. Bond's enemies err on both sides of the political-economic spectrum, and Bond himself, despite his reputation as an unrepentant free marketer, is first and foremost the guarantor of a flexible corporate order. As I hope to show, what is most troubling about this corporate solution is that it advances modern paradoxes in order to combat the paradoxes of modernity. That is to say, England's corporatism is as conflicted as the society it hopes to redeem, and the terms of its triumph mediate and mimic the terms of similar, more abusive regimes in other places on the globe, whether fascist, socialist, or capitalist.

Take, to begin, Fleming's anxious yet sustained critique of postwar England. The novels repeatedly suggest that the nation's practical traditionalism has been eroded by rampant consumerism and a general moral laxity. Yet they also lament the ways in which the country's proud individualism has been hemmed in by creaky political commitments to social equality and reform. As Bond's enemies are quick to point out, a corrupt modernism has unleashed a certain manic yet ultimately dissipating energy; progressive humanist ideals have left the country at once anarchic and brittle. Hugo Drax, for example, lambastes the British as "Useless, idle, decadent fools, hiding behind your bloody white cliffs while other people fight your battles. Too weak to defend your colonies, toadying to America with your hats in your hands" (*Moonraker* 210). Tiger Tanaka argues, "You have not only lost a great Empire, you have seemed almost anxious to throw it away with both hands. . . . Further, your governments have shown themselves successfully incapable of ruling and have handed over effective control of the country to the trade unions, who appear to be dedicated to the principle of doing less and less work for more money. This feather-bedding, this shirking of an honest day's work, is sapping at ever-increasing speed the moral fibre of the British" (*Live Twice* 77). However, to counteract this seeming decline, Fleming peppers his plot with an array of decisively modern professionals who serve to uphold the corporate ideal, working to transform a society that is at once anarchic and static into something more fluid and efficient. These men and women often turn out to be the true heroes of the books as they uphold a solid yet flexible network of power without which Bond would often fail at his missions. Working for the College of Arms, for example, Sable Basilisk shows superior professional foresight when he perceives a link between the Monsieur le Comte Balthazar de Bleuville, who appealed to his office for a royal title, and the criminal mastermind Ernst Stavro Blofeld, who is wanted by the Ministry of Defence. Here, sifting through birth notices, church registrars, and legal documents, Basilisk's sense of personal responsibility and professional pride works to soften, if not enliven, the apparently inhuman relations and static networks of the corporate bureaucracy (*Her Majesty's* 64–65). Later in the novel, Bond and M hold a tense meeting with Leathers, the Head of the Scientific Research Centre, and Franklin, from the Ministry of Agriculture. The group's effort to crack Blofeld's latest plan is at first stymied by professional guardedness and suspicion; the conversation is almost derailed by an aggressively professional "politeness" and a skeptical "reserve" toward competing claims. Somewhat comically, though, the men eventually recognize that there are limits to their professional knowledge, and that they must put aside their inter-ministry testiness in order to solve the mystery. The scene ends in a collective expression of professional reverence, one that embraces even the efficiency of Blofeld's plan for biological warfare: "Marvelous," Leathers claims, "I really must hand it to the man." Bond, in a fit of professional pride, decides not to hand in his resignation, claiming, "When they were pushed, the British could do this sort of thing supremely well. How much coordination had this brief report required? . . . All had contributed, and with tremendous speed and efficiency" (*Her Majesty's* 228).

Relatedly, the novels perform the important ideological work of distancing the increasingly corporate structure of modern England from the similarly corporatized entities duking it out in an international arena. Whether pitted against the nationalistic entities of Germany and Russia or the less formal organizations of SPECTRE, the Union Corse, and the Black Dragon Society of Fukuoko, the work of the Secret Service involves battling vague corporate structures whose strength lies in their ability to mimic and adapt the formal structures of finance capital. At stake here is the recognition that the socio-economic history that created contemporary England has led to more sinister formations elsewhere, and thus the exploits that follow take shape as a race between two equally efficient bureaucratic machines, with England granted only a slight edge because of its ability to loosen up efficiency with humanity, to limit arrogance by protocol. At his best, Fleming anxiously exposes the similarities between corporate England and its equally corporate nemeses; the most exciting missions are those that are threatened by an inevitable formal identification between Bond and his enemy, between the Secret Service and the sinister organizations that overrun the international scene. Take, for example, Bond's earliest battle with Le Chiffre, a nemesis in charge of a communist-controlled trade union. Le Chiffre is a cipher in a professional sense, without personal memory or even personal time, placed in charge of managing the funds of a large government organization. Indeed, his efficient methods are enviable; Bond is "full of admiration" for the ingenious double-crossings that occur in Le Chiffre's camp, and he marvels at the apparently heartless automatism of Le Chiffre's card playing (*Casino* 57, 74). Le Chiffre, of course, fails because of his indulgent tastes, but the threat of identification remains. Bond ultimately loses the ability to distinguish between his own organization and that of his enemy. He recovers from a brutal torture, but his consequent loss of manhood figures as a metaphor for the much larger identity crisis he faces in the recognition that his world mirrors that of his enemy. At the end of the novel, he is psychologically confined to a relativistic limbo state, tortured by the knowledge that "in order to tell the difference between good and evil, we have manufactured two images representing the extremes" (*Casino* 136). Mathis, his confidante in this scene, blames this lack of confidence on Bond's increasing dehumanization and loss of personal relations. But Bond provides a further, more subtle critique of the mechanical efficiency that blurs national boundaries and confounds political characterization in the modern age: "Today we are fighting Communism," he claims, but "If I'd been alive fifty years ago, the brand of Conservatism we have today would have been damn near called Communism and we should have been told to go and fight that" (*Casino* 135).

In *Moonraker,* Fleming handles this crisis to somewhat more efficient effect, but thereby loses the critical edge of the earlier narrative. Perhaps more than any other book of its time, *Moonraker* frames an intriguing analysis of the psycho-social dimensions of professional life. The narrative is organized according to the workweek and contains several intriguing passages about life in a bureaucracy. In fact, despite its sensational plot, it is essentially a book about interiors, contrasting the impact of competing professional structures on the lives that inhabit them. It begins with a description of the architecture and décor of the Secret Service's main offices. The British system is presented as a well-oiled machine that apparently runs on its own: unnumbered doors open and shut by themselves, files appear almost magically, and Bond himself must empty his mind of all personal thoughts in order to "prepare himself for the normal business of a routine day" (5). Yet, despite this formalism, the British system is decisively human, and its activities are infused with an intuitive aura of familial understanding. Bond doesn't need numbers on the doors because he has a deeper, more passional sense of his seemingly anonymous surroundings. Indeed, each nook and corridor contains a second order of pleasure in the teasing possibility of inter-office sex. The professional network is infused with a sensualism that is both traditional and liberating, caught between a creaky paternalism and a kinky fifties swingerism. The presence of Loelia Ponsonby, for example, makes this bureaucratic space a "little more human." She has "married" her career and provides the men with a "cool motherliness"

(5–7). Later in the novel, this living, breathing bureaucracy is contrasted with the "ugly concrete world" of the Moonraker base (144). Drax's place of business is equally efficient, and the order he maintains is strictly professional, but it clearly suffers from a lack of balance. First and foremost, Drax himself lacks a specifically British form of "tact." He may be admirable for "his know-how and his drive and his dedication," but he is also a rough wag who cheats at cards and shows a complete lack of decorative taste (96, 101). Appropriately, the men who work the silo are depicted as efficient automatons, an army of "robot-like Germans" with few distinguishing characteristics and decisively uncommunicative eyes. And yet while their heads are close-shaven to improve efficiency, they each maintain an extravagantly different beard. This organization, in other words, also functions to manage extreme libidinal energies, but the system is at once too egotistical and too repressive, too violent and too rigid. Not surprisingly, the missile silo is described as the interior of a gun, and the missile itself is just barely restrained from mass destruction (113).

But if corporate society is always paradoxical or, more likely, ambivalent, it is best approached through the experience of the subject. In fact, the social transformation I have outlined here all too easily mirrors the psychic transformation of the postwar subject; the paradoxes of the former are the neurotic symptoms of the latter. Following Perkin, we can trace both transformations through the changing concept of property. For the professionals, capital is always human capital, a form of trained expertise that is valued in terms of its social usefulness (2–3). Consequently, property itself, with the rise of professional society, is reconceived in terms of its contingent, social dimensions. Professional society understands property not as "an object or credit interest, which are just its outward signs," but "in its major meaning of power over resources," as "*a right to a flow of income*" (7). In other words, professionals are not opposed to property as such, but to functionless, irresponsible property; hence, they redefine ownership as dependent upon a wider social network (123). This redefinition signals a far-reaching ideological shift as it initiates an organized assault on entrepreneurial identity and the social relations founded upon entrepreneurial ownership. For if property is conceived as the right to a flow of income, ownership itself is "capable of being divided and diverted into a myriad [of] channels and therefore sustain an infinite congeries of relationships" (377).[6] Indeed, Fleming's résumé of public and private service must be understood in this context, as it provided a rigorous training in the management of all sorts of commodified flows. In particular, his extensive training in communications technology led him to see himself as a "convenient channel for confidential matters," and the efficiency he practiced in this field provided the working model for his now famous prose style (Lycett, *Ian Fleming* 103). Fleming's attitudes toward money, which he extends to Bond, were similarly professional. As a friend explained, "To Ian [money] was more a medium of freedom from the material grind. The realities of business bored him. There had to be movement, excitement and glamour" (91). In his novels, Fleming combines this decisively anti-capitalist outlook with a more admirable professional ideal. Readers are reminded again and again of Bond's meager pay and his refusal to accept laurels or rewards for his service. In fact, Bond's main financial ambition is "to have as little as possible in his banking account when he was killed," and his obsession with gambling and expenditure attests to a related, and similarly non-egotistical, desire to keep money in circulation (*Moonraker* 9).

As we can now come to expect, Fleming lends his villains similarly professional attitudes and traits in order to highlight their potential abuses. It is safe to say that, even at their worst, Blofeld, Goldfinger, and Co. typify nothing more than a professional relation to property, and their criminal activities are often held up with admiration, if not envy. Tellingly, most crimes in the fiction involve an abuse of access; Fleming's evil masterminds corner the myriad flows of the market only to siphon off their power for purely selfish ends. Drugs, diamonds, gold, information, nuclear warheads—nobody owns these entities in the novels or even uses them, but they are the focus of intense international squabbling and control. More than anything else, Bond's missions are systematically focused on the reappropriation and restoration of these flows. His professional knowledge is put, again and again, in the service of a decisively corporate nation seeking to restore the most lucrative channels of material flow. Blofeld, whom we have already mentioned, rose to professional prominence much like Fleming himself, by mastering communications. He realized early on that "fast and efficient communication lay, in a contracting world, at the very heart of power" and that "knowledge of the truth before the next man, in peace or war, lay . . . behind every correct decision." Blofeld uses this knowledge first to attain and sell top secret messages between rival nations and then to develop a spy network called TARTAR. Importantly, though, this growing network has no political dimension; in fact, Blofeld is at first incapable of reading the content of the war transmissions he passes along. Unlike Fleming's work for the

Special Branch of the Navy, Blofeld's business practices are excessive precisely because they have no ideological restrictions; his talents are devoted to nothing other than making a profit by controlling an apparently meaningless flow of information (*Thunderball* 44–46). The professional control of limited resources is also central to the plot of *Goldfinger*, in which the title character has successfully managed to tap into and siphon off an international flow of gold. Much of the intrigue centers on the fact that it is difficult to impugn Goldfinger for his manipulation of the market; he is known as "quiet, careful, law-abiding and with the sort of drive and single-mindedness we all admire" (*Goldfinger* 063). As the narrator reminds us again and again, the power he wields is decisively professional: "the magic of controlling energy, exacting labour, fulfilling one's every wish and whim and, when need be, purchasing bodies, minds, and souls" (*Goldfinger* 184). The problem, perhaps, is simply the egotism and excess with which he pursues his aims. The manner in which Goldfinger seeks access is distasteful, for he upsets the standard channels of flow and hordes that which should be flowing. Again, though, there is nothing illegal about these practices, and so, consequently, Fleming has to invent for Goldfinger a series of related yet more explicitly asocial traits: he carries around huge amounts of gold blocks, he cheats at cards and golf, and, perhaps most importantly, he suffers from constipation (*Goldfinger* 020, 038, 120).

Fleming's fiction proves most insightful when it explores the way in which this redefinition of property impacts the subject and the psychodynamics of pleasure. Here, it is important to read Bond in his specifically mid-century British context, as "a neutral figure—an anonymous blunt instrument wielded by dolts in high places" (*Live Twice* 172). Kingsley Amis, for example, argues that Bond is little more a "Medium-Grade Civil Servant" (11), and Tony Bennett and Janet Woollacott smartly show that Bond's most intense moment of popularity coincided with his embodiment of "a new, meritocratic style of cultural and political leadership, middle class and professional rather than aristocratic and amateur" (34–35). Undoubtedly, for Bond, this professional bearing is the source of much anxiety and alienation. His "lean, hard face" bears a "hungry, competitive" sneer (*Moonraker* 26; *Casino* 50–51). His thinking is cold and crafty, "half-mechanical, half-intuitive," and his body is an efficient machine, ready for brutality or cold love at a moment's notice (*Casino* 41). Indeed, despite his modernist pretensions, Fleming consistently fails to portray Bond's interiority. When our hero isn't working, he either stares blankly or falls asleep: at one point in *Moonraker,* "He stood for a moment, thinking," but this so-called stream of consciousness ends here (27). Yet, at the same time, Fleming seems to revel in Bond's dehumanization as it seems to embody an anti-entrepreneurial ethic and its concomitant, a somewhat arch post-humanism. Indeed, despite Bond's fame in a postwar consumerist arena, he is, at least in the fiction, a surprisingly modest figure and a barely personalized one. Alongside his decisive unconcern with the accrual of money, we may add his apparent lack of personal memory or even family history, his incessant fatalism, his mostly untroubled relation to killing others, and his utterly corporeal interaction with the phenomenal world. One is particularly intrigued by those limit cases—a staple in all modern adventure fiction—in which Bond loses consciousness and must fight intuitively, with his body alone: as in *Goldfinger,* when he undergoes extreme physical torture, or *Doctor No,* as he falls out of the mountain chamber and battles a giant squid (*Goldfinger* 175; *Doctor* 193, 202). With these instances, it becomes clear that Bond's world is one that consistently fails to value or fetishize the ego. The loss of direct ownership, the transition to a managerial consciousness, and, perhaps most importantly, the replication of managerial identity—these forces have created the unphenomenon of Bond and prepare the way for his identification-based popularity.

Ultimately, Fleming's hero—like modernism itself—remains caught between a dying entrepreneurial ideal of a seemingly bounded power and a rising professional ideal which is at once more dynamic and social. Insofar as he is the hero of the corporation, his ego has undergone a process of deterioration, but it seems to exist only partially open to alternative configurations of being and experience. Everywhere in Fleming's work, this transformation is incomplete, inadequate, and perhaps neurotic. As I hope to show, though, this incompletion accounts for the anxious ambivalence central to corporate life in general. The neurotic energy of the postwar subject is precisely what sustains the corporate structure of the postwar socius. What needs to be explored is how Fleming conceives pleasure under a corporatist regime. At first glance, his novels suggest that desire within the corporate structure persists in familial channels. As mentioned, the members of M's staff still live within a paternalistic network; the inherently sadomasochistic structure of the bourgeois psyche finds a comfortable expression of its desires in the corporate hierarchy.[7] There is also much to be said for the oedipal conflicts between Bond and M or the spanking fantasies that inflect the giving and taking of orders between Bond and his female comrades. The ideological work of the fiction is most apparent in the ways in which

Bond's desires overlap with the aims and motives of the Secret Service. Often, he must pimp for England, using sex to gain secrets, track down code machines, or seduce enemy spies. His body, indeed, belongs to the state, and without fail, he learns to align his personal desire with professional duty. We might even say that Bond's relationships are not simply corporate in intent, but in structure. The women he is attracted to— Vesper Lynd, Tatiana Romanova, his fiancée Tracy—appear to be composed, yet each trembles on the verge of sexual meltdown. Bond's desire is kindled by this paradoxical state, the push and pull of an icy desire, and he relishes the possibility of breaking down a tough professional façade in order to open up the flow of passion. Regarding Vesper, for example, he realizes that "he wanted her cold and arrogant body. He wanted to see tears and desire in her remote blue eyes" and to "draw her into his own feeling of warmth and relaxed sensuality" (*Casino* 92, 94). This is not simply an entrepreneurial desire to possess; rather, Bond seeks in his lovers an opportunity to tap and control a passion, to manage libidinal flow. Indeed, for Bond, these women do not have any egos to possess; they are best described as dynamic configurations of passion that have yet to reach their full capacity and thus call for a more efficient management. Ultimately, Bond's greatest love, for the neurotic Tracy, is decisively managerial: "In some way this girl had come to the end of her tether, of too many tethers. Bond felt a wave of affection for her, a sweeping urge to protect her, to solve her problems, make her happy" (*Her Majesty's* 32). In deciding to make this a lifelong commitment, he argues, "Above all, she needs me. It'll be someone for me to look after" (183).

But there are other kinds of pleasure on display in the novels that seem to extend beyond the oedipal. Importantly, insofar as these pleasures entail a kind of subjective dissolution, they seem to recall a specifically anal form of ego-constitution. In other words, if the order Fleming gropes toward is decisively anti-entrepreneurial, it is also non-phallic; despite the boats, guns, and girls, Bond's exploits point toward a pleasure that is anal in nature, as it entails an efficient binding and release of a powerful flow. In his "Three Essays on the Theory of Sexuality," Freud outlines a process by which infantile sexuality is mapped onto the various sites of somatic need. In this formulation, the anal zone serves as the site at which ego boundaries are established and managed. The anus performs a more or less efficient control of the self, as sensations of pleasure and unpleasure are experienced with the restraint and release of the bowels. For Freud, though, this activity is also always social in nature and, more importantly, economic: the fecal mass is a "gift" which is either granted or withheld. Through this alternating, bipolar activity, the subject learns to "express his active compliance with his environment and, by withholding them, his disobedience" ("Three Essays" 265–66). This dynamic—particularly in its commingling of tension and release, pleasure and unpleasure, active and passive engagement—provides the basic terms of Fleming's fiction. The narratives take place in a landscape that is anally ordered, and each plot is driven by an action that is anally focused. The cramped tunnels and blocked corridors, the rank sewers and mounds of feces, the brutal spankings, whether literal or figural, all capped by the titillating threat of a hot-geyser colonic at the hands of Blofeld—throughout, Fleming's world is organized on anal terms, and its heroes and villains must negotiate its blocked passages and uncontrollable flows. Freud's analysis of the anal character, in fact, culminates with a discussion of the relation between anal flows and economic flows. He notes how easily the original erotic interest in defecation gives way to an interest in money; a certain reaction-formation against the earlier obsession provides the terms of a new financial consciousness concerned with the management of an equally "dirty" money.[8]

Importantly, this continual production and consumption of the self would not be possible without a loosening of the ego-ideal. But this loosening in turn depends upon an at least residual presence of oedipal binding. As Freud explains, the "anal character" is decisively restrictive; it is characterized as a "reaction formation against an interest in what is unclean and disturbing and should not be part of the body." Always, anal identity rests upon a kind of prohibitive self-mastery, an obstinacy or constipation, against the very temptation of anal pleasure. More precisely, it represents the struggle of an ideal self over and against the recognition of an abject self and thus a desire to bind or brace that self against its inevitable corruption ("Character and Anal Erotism" 296).[9] Indeed, Bond and his professional enemies indulge in obsessive-compulsive pleasures that, when not explicitly anal, are anal in nature. Gambling, for instance, entails the continual management of an otherwise random flow of cards, money, and, of course, luck. The gambler tries to maintain his tenuous position within a social network and thus tap into a fluid resource; what passes for pleasure at the table is founded upon an experience that is at once braced and fluid, efficient and risky.[10] Driving, too, involves a pleasurable mixture of control and recklessness. Bond armors his body with a series of advanced mechanical prostheses, only to set them at high speeds and thereby challenge his ability to regain control. Eating also entails mastery in relation to a loss of coherence, as consumption and defecation literally disrupt the boundaries of the corpus. Bond's meals are often depicted as primitive, if not animalistic, yet they are also highly ritualized. More precisely, then, we might say that the anus and its analogues serve to manage a crisis that no longer solves itself solely by way of psychic identification and disidentification. The anus is undeniably an important site of ego-formation in an imaginary sense, but that formation is always supplemented by the decisively physical process of restraint and release. In other words, identity exists at this site in its dual aspect, as founded on both identification and incorporation, on both metaphor and metonym. For Freud, particularly in the case studies, it is most often a crisis of oedipal authority that initiates an obsessive-compulsive relay of anal mastery and release. A literal or symbolic death of the father stymies the son's entry into the phallic order, thus forcing the latter's retreat back into the anal, where identity is shored up by physical means. For neurotics like the Wolfman and the Ratman, passage to the phallic mode has been bungled, often by some failure on the father's part, thus forcing them to seek the perhaps more stable comforts of anal pulsation—the difficulty of gender is thus blurred over by the more tangible "sadistic and predominantly masochistic sexual currents" typical of the anal character (*Wolfman* 310).

Perhaps, then, under corporatism, the oedipal order has not been destroyed, but weakened, and thus released and diffused throughout a non-hierarchical, material network. In the corporation, the father figure is not absent, but replicated throughout the system. His power—both as authority and as license—saturates the field; it is apparent at each node of the structure, but never complete or constant in itself. Thus, power differentials exist throughout the structure, serving to halt and perhaps redirect the flows of capital, but these ultimately must also give way to those flows. Indeed, as Freud's work suggests, anal character serves to manage ambivalent feelings toward a father that is both powerful and degenerate. Every corporate manager is and is not a paternal figure— each represents mastery over the network as a whole—yet each must also renounce and release all power.[11] In this, the very ambivalence of the oedipal relation—the commingling of envy and hostility, of identification and rebellion—is splayed out along the network channels. The subject's conflicted desires to be the father and to kill the father, desires for self-mastery and self-dissolution, find a perfect outlet in the need to manage and submit to flows. Ultimately, reading Freud's *Totem and Taboo,* it becomes clear that the corporate network is in fact a totemic network, one in which the actual father-owner no longer exists except in the psychic relation each member has to the whole. The father, as a physical presence, has been banned from the corporate board, but this exclusion results in a productive ambivalence. Feelings of guilt and release are redirected toward the construction of a working order and the management of otherwise disruptive forces. Or, rather, the fraternal horde has ingested the power of the father in both its aspects—as authority and as license—and now directs its newly acquired skills to the maintenance of the whole. In fact, the very act of consumption here entails both mastery and release, authority and license, and thus becomes the central mechanism by which the corporate system is maintained (*Totem* 171, 173). Indeed, Freud claims that totemism in its late, degenerate form is best described as a kind of "co-operative magic," a "magical producers' and consumers' union." The ambivalent feelings toward the totem eventually lose their anxious energy and settle into a certain productive groove that guarantees the "plentiful supply of one particular article" (*Totem* 143, 145).

There are many examples of oedipal desire at play in Fleming's fiction. One could easily look at the relationships between M and the often rebellious Bond, Darko Kerim and his army of sons, or Mr. Big and his ensorcerated gang. Each book, in fact, contains at least one oedipal encounter that occurs in an office; it could even be argued that the most intense scenes of conflict involve nothing more exciting than two men strutting for domination across a desk. Importantly, though, in these examples, the conspicuous absence of any explicit depth psychology suggests the externalization of the Freudian model, its channeling into the economic world. In other words, if we want to look for "psychology" in the novels, we inevitably need to turn to larger, extra-humanist structures, such as SPECTRE, Fleming's most explicitly corporate creation. Under the direction of Ernst Stavro Blofeld, this corporate horde is run by an extreme efficiency that leaves no room for personal license or even intimacy. In *Thunderball*, for example, the men sit at a table where all are equal, but equally replaceable; they take their places at "numbers from one to twenty-one that were their only names and that, as a small security precaution, advanced round the rota by two digits at midnight on the first of every month" (43). Blofeld is quite clearly the leader of the board, but he too is represented here only by his number, and his particular position, at least formally, will also be replaced by another man. Blofeld does not command, but models a necessary commingling of restraint and license, of self-deification and self-abasement. In this, he is at once the emblem of corporate order and its enactment, providing the board with the terms of law and its first restriction. As he explains, in a telling rhetoric of power and its disavowal,

> We are a large and very powerful organization. I am not concerned with morals or ethics, but members will be aware that I desire, and most strongly recommend, that SPECTRE shall conduct itself in a superior fashion. There is no discipline in SPECTRE except self-discipline. We are a dedicated fraternity whose strength lies entirely in the strength of each member. Weakness in one member is the death-watch beetle in the total structure. (*Thunderball* 54)

Despite his obvious power, Blofeld presides over the group only as a specter, as a structural device, which each man in turn despises and adopts. In their turn, the men at the table practice a nervous self-restraint, but they hold no special or sincere commitment to Blofeld. They look up at their leader with "the sharpest interest," but their attitudes are not necessarily those of "obsequious respect" (43). As Freud's work suggests, their abstemiousness serves only to maintain order within the board itself. It protects against any excessive display of paternal power, checking the murderous license upon which the horde was originally founded and which continues to lurk in the background of its rituals. Tellingly, when Fleming first depicts SPECTRE, the group is meeting to discuss plans to steal two nuclear warheads from England, but most of the intrigue here concerns a young woman who was kidnapped by SPECTRE for a large ransom. Blofeld considers the operation only partially successful, as the girl was violated during her captivity, and so he seeks to exact revenge against one of his own men. Importantly, this betrayal is presented in oedipal terms, as it directly defied Blofeld's desire to return the girl "to her parents" in undamaged condition (54). In a somewhat excessive display of paternal power, Blofeld has the guilty man electrocuted at the board table. While this public display serves to establish Blofeld's authority, it is at once subsumed under the putative power of the board. By the end of the scene, the men have clearly taken the paternal injunction upon themselves; the moment of retribution becomes a model for their own behavior. "Blofeld always exercised his authority, meted out justice, in full view of the members," and they quickly adopt the view that his reasoning is "just, necessary" (56).

Ultimately, what links the pervasiveness of anal character in the twentieth century with the rise of corporate society is that both function as a kind of regression. The anal obsessive mode refers back to an autoeroticism that existed before the (failed) incorporation of identity under the phallic regime. Similarly, Perkin describes the triumph of corporate society as a return to subinfeudation, to the pre-capitalist practice that recognizes intermediate claimants on the flow of income (381). In both cases, modernity is the crisis, and management figures as its anxious, untenable response, as it tries to work through the contradictions of modern identity by restoring an earlier state. The subject, in response to increasingly contradictory paternal claims, caught in a neurotic bind between repression and release, purification and corruption, can only project his crisis outward, on to the physical world. He discovers a solution in the unleashing of his libidinal energy through the corporate channels that confound him, where that energy thus becomes static, reified. Indeed, the subject's psychic turmoil at once reflects and encourages the corporatization of the modern world; it seeks affirmation in the very structures of its manipulation.[12] This account, though, at once raises the issue of causality and exposes the difficulty of delineating the effective relations between economic and psychological transformation. But, perhaps more importantly, this crisis, which is at base a hermeneutical crisis, can be defined as that which enforces corporate order. In other words, it is at first tempting to read corporate society and corporate character symptomatically, as a neurotic response to material experiences that are inherently contradictory. Indeed, one can push this even further to claim that corporate society—in its mobilization of the vast machinery of public relations and advertising—serves to erect a phallic defense against the ever-present specter of economic anality. This certainly accords with our reading of Bond's adventures, in which the second-order pleasure of phallic coherence—in the form of hierarchical regimes and commodity fetishism—always masks a less secure order founded upon the ceaseless production and consumption of waste. However, as I am trying to suggest here, corporate society is best characterized not simply as a neurotic condition with its attendant symptomology, but as a productive disorder. Freud touches upon this phenomenon in *Totem and Taboo* when he describes the projective nature of thought. As he explains, the obsessional subject always reads its psychic ambivalence into the overdetermined structures of its environment. Seeking confirmation of his crises, he projects his ambivalent feelings out into a world that he simultaneously transforms: as Freud writes, these feelings are "employed for building up the external world" (*Totem* 81, 120–21). Ultimately, totemic society, and thus corporatism, entails a self-affirming confusion of willing and seeing. That is, it all too rigorously conflates the symbolic with the productive; or, more precisely, its signifying practices are also its productive practices. If this is an obsessional society, it is an active society, caught in a continual activity of appropriation that exists somewhere between processing of information and production. Moreover, this self-affirming activity must continually shift—like the obsessional neurosis itself—to new products, new subjects, and new markets (*Totem* 39–40). As Freud reminds us, the totemic meal must be repeated for it to retain its psychological power (*Totem* 171, 176–78).

As Dennis Allen's essay in this collection suggests, Fleming's writing is inherently superstitious; his anxiety saturates the entire social field, shadowing as it penetrates the deepest relations between economics, politics, and culture. In other words, a decisively anxious wish for order and efficiency always already governs his depictions of the apparently extensive and overdetermined relations of the corporate world. Here, though, I would like to trace the specifically productive dimension of this obsessional consciousness, which we see at work most clearly in his prose style. Indeed, if Fleming's work depicts corporate society as a fraught attempt to manage the conflicting energies of modernity, then we can read his style as an attempt to manage his attitudes toward modernist literature. Or, as we can now say, if his narratives express ambivalent relations toward totemic authority, his style everywhere wrestles with the legacy of its modernist precursors. On the one hand, Fleming was drawn to the modernist revolution in the arts and literature. His writing flirts with innovation in structure and description, and it is peppered throughout with references to moderns such as Eliot and Yeats, not to mention Dali and the Futurists. But this is more true of the earlier novels and, even then, one might argue, the early chapters of the first few novels. Opposed to this avant-garde bent, Fleming's style is also characterized by an almost arid order and efficiency. At times, character and suspense literally give way to textbook-like displays of professional knowledge—decisively non-narrative lists, definitions, and reports. Indeed, in this, one might say that his flat, lucid prose, with its economy of depiction, serves to manage the disruptive energies of modernist style as it is rooted in an excessive subjectivity. As the following description suggests, Fleming's ideal author was decisively anti-modern, if not anti-humanist, in his professional decorum:

> He must be a credit to his country and his newspaper abroad; he should be either a bachelor or a solidly married man who is happy to have his children brought up abroad. . . . He must know something of protocol and yet enjoy having a drink with the meanest spy or the most wastrelly spiv. . . . He must be grounded in the history and culture of

the territory in which he is serving; he must be intellectually inquisitive and have some knowledge of most sports. . . . He must have pride in his work and in the paper he serves. (Lycett, *Ian Fleming* 171)

In this, though, Fleming's work mimics another, countervailing tendency of the modernist period. His economy of style—with its emphasis on structure, depersonalized objectivity, and encyclopedic knowledge— is also part of the modernist heritage. Eliot, for example, similarly argued for the depersonalization of poetry, and Wyndham Lewis called for an externalist approach to combat the excesses of interiority advanced by modernist fiction writers such as Joyce, Woolf, and Lawrence.[13] As we have mentioned, though, the corporate order is decisively paradoxical in its handling of modernist paradoxes. Fleming's prose is both rigid and charged, both ritualized and disruptive—in this, it embraces as it resists the contradictory energies of a specifically modernist totem. Indeed, Freud's description of obsessional reading practices aptly describes Fleming's ambivalent (not to mention ritualized and repetitive) attempts to regulate modernist style: "Whatever other unconscious phantasies and operative reminiscences may be present in the patient force their way to expression as symptoms along this same path, once it has been opened, and grouped themselves into an appropriate new arrangement within the framework of inhibition upon movement" (*Totem* 120–21).

But, even if Fleming's prose bears all the tensions of the order it opposes, further analysis reveals what exactly distinguishes it from its most immediate literary past. Kingsley Amis provides an intriguing point of access in his description of the "Fleming Effect" (109). Amis, writing at the time of Fleming's death, praises him for his ability to construe the fantastic in precise, realistic terms. Fleming's prose allows us to swallow the outrageous, the extreme, and the heroic because of its persistent emphasis on real-life science, contemporary inventions and products, and its constant display of Bond's logic and forethought. Readers suspend their disbelief because the unbelievable is packaged in a soothing web of incontrovertible, common facts. But Amis further suggests that, for Fleming and his readers, a certain pleasure is evinced in the very conveyance of facts, in the tracking, organization, and sharing of specialized or particularized knowledge (113). Indeed, Fleming displays his professional knowledge with relish, as if compelled by some professional demon, and at these moments the narratives threaten to solidify into a series of professional reports, memoranda, and lists. In this, Amis almost realizes that Fleming is never primarily interested in the action, but in the facts themselves. In other words, our description of the "Fleming Effect" needs to be inverted: Fleming does not present fact in order to help us swallow the action; rather, he presents the titillating action in order to help us swallow the facts. The spectacular nature of the action serves to enliven the facts, to teach us how to know and appreciate professional knowledge. Bond's work, caught as it is between the archive and the battlefield, shows us how to activate understanding and how to understand action. Most importantly, though, this activity reflects back on the dynamism of modern literature. The main features of the earlier movement are effectively managed by the "Fleming Effect," as the static, encyclopedic bent of high modernism is put into action, made practical, and the radical energy of the avant-garde is tamed according to the needs of the corporation. Importantly, though, these extremes are managed materially, on the surface of the postwar socius. The modernist tension of public and private, self and other, is flattened or perhaps exteriorized, so its dynamism becomes purely physical. The psychic conflict of the earlier period, particularly as it is characterized by an illusion of depth or at least hierarchical structure, is splayed out into a vast, multidimensional network that is perhaps more fluid, but no less neurotic.

This is perhaps the greatest distinction between modernism proper and Fleming's moment: the former movement—in all its radical contradictoriness—has become, like the modern socius itself, incorporated. In this, modernity itself may lose some of its vital energy and critical edge, but it may also advance beyond its disappointing mid-century endgame. It may relinquish its most aggressive energies and revolutionary angst, but it may reconfigure its libidinal flows in ways that are truly disruptive. As I have been trying to argue, this ambivalence is typical of the period insofar as it is typical of a corporatism that adopts and adapts earlier social ideals. This ambivalence, in other words, is not simply psychological or economic, but overdetermined and deeply historical. Fleming's moment, which is still our moment, both reinforces and dissolves the mechanisms of control by which modernity sustains itself. The significance of his fiction is that it matches this overdetermination point for point and thus initiates an essential process of critical interrogation.

NOTES

1. For the most forceful expression of the former claim, see Michael Denning, "Licensed to Look: James Bond and the Heroism of Consumption" (1992).

2. The analysis of modern corporatism begins, of course, in the second and third volumes of Marx's *Capital,* and finds its most coherent expression as economic theory in Rudolf Hilferding's early twentieth-century work. I have chosen to focus on Perkin primarily because he contemplates the ideological coordinates of a specifically mid-century English brand of corporatism. See particularly Karl Marx, *Capital,* vol. III (Chicago: Charles H. Kerr, 1915), 516ff.; Rudolf Hilferding, *Finance Capital: A Study of the Latest Phase of Capitalist Development,* ed. Tom Bottomore (London: Routledge & Kegan Paul, 1981), chapter 7.

3. This emerging corporate order, we might add, was given a big boost by the Second World War. Corporate mergers were officially sanctioned by wartime governments in need of greater rates of production. Moreover, the ability of the corporations to respond to these demands granted them a certain ideological credit, making solid the connection between economic greatness and national might. Indeed, as Paul Addison remarks, the postwar consensus in England was not a political consensus at all, but a managerial one and thus cemented the triumph of the professional ideal: "First of all the consensus historians do not define consensus in terms of agreement *between the parties.* They define it as a measure of agreement *between civil servants and ministerialists of both parties*" (259).

4. Much of this theory of modernity's contradictions and the ideology of corporatism has been culled from the work of the Frankfurt School and the post-Marxist tradition. See particularly Max Horkheimer and Theodor W. Adorno, *Dialectic of Enlightenment;* and Gilles Deleuze and Félix Guattari, *Anti-Oedipus: Capitalism and Schizophrenia.*

5. Ian Fleming, "If I Were Prime Minister," *The Spectator,* October 9, 1959, 466–67. Andrew Lycett aptly defines Fleming's political stance as a kind of "anarcho-tory populism" (*Ian Fleming* 213).

6. Marx similarly remarks on the "[t]ransformation of the actually functioning capitalist into a mere manager, an administrator of other people's capital, and of the owners of capital into mere owners, mere money capitalists. . . . This result of the highest development of capitalist production is a necessary transition to the reconversion of capital into property of the producers, no longer as the private property of individual producers, but as the common property of associates, as social property outright" (*Capital* 516ff.). Hilferding, like Perkin, argues that corporatism reveals the "social" nature of all property: in the corporation and on the stock exchange, "capitalist property appears in its pure form, as a title to the yield" (149). He, too, sees in this revelation a certain revolutionary potential: "only in this way are they integrated into society and enabled to share in the aggregate social product which has to be distributed among them" (29).

7. See the Frankfurt School theorists on authoritarian character and the hierarchical structures of fascism. Theodor Adorno's work, in particular, shows how the identificatory practices and libidinal investments of a deeply ambivalent bourgeois subject help to cement the hierarchical structures of the modern world. See his "Freudian Theory and the Pattern of Fascist Propaganda," in *The Essential Frankfurt School Reader,* 128.

8. See Sigmund Freud, "Character and Anal Erotism," in *The Freud Reader,* 296–97.

9. I am primarily interested in these anal metaphorics as they shape a certain productive activity, and by no means am I here advancing an argument about the critical value of homosexuality or the homosocial. However, I should mention that Freud's theories of anal character and the obsessional neuroses, insofar as they wrestle with the dynamics of identification, can be very fruitfully referred back to current debates about homosexuality and its political valences. For Freud's notoriously self-

contradicting discussions of homosexuality, see his "On Narcissism: An Introduction," in *The Freud Reader,* 559, 562; *Group Psychology and the Analysis of the Ego,* trans. and ed. James Strachey (New York: W.W. Norton & Company, 1959), 40, 51–52, 73; Sigmund Freud, *The Ego and the Id,* trans. Joan Riviere, ed. James Strachey (New York: W.W. Norton & Company, 1960), 34, 41–42.

10. Walter Benjamin's work also explores the structural relations between certain forms of modern entertainment, particularly gambling, and the psychodynamism of modern labor. See particularly Walter Benjamin, "On Some Motifs in Baudelaire" in *Illuminations,* 176–77.

11. Hilferding argues that this psycho-social dynamic is built into the economic structure of corporatism: "As a result of the transformation of property into share ownership the rights of the property owner are curtailed. The individual, as a shareholder, is dependent upon the decision made by all other shareholders; he is only a member of a larger body, and not always an active one. . . . At the same time, this limitation of property gives the majority shareholders unlimited powers over the minority, and in this way, the property rights and unrestricted control over production of most of the small capitalists are set aside, and the groups of those who control productions becomes even smaller" (127).

12. This theory draws upon Adorno's description of fascism as a kind of "psychoanalysis in reverse," in which the fascist demagogue and his followers each turn their unconscious desires "outward" in order to fuel the productive mechanisms of the nation. Indeed, as early corporatism is the foundation of fascism, at least in Italy and Germany, this correlation is not simply figural or even metaphoric, but deeply historical. See Adorno, "Freudian Theory," 133.

13. See, for example, T. S. Eliot, "Tradition and the Individual Talent," in *Selected Prose of T. S. Eliot;* Wyndham Lewis, "Mr. Wyndham Lewis: 'Personal-Appearance' Artist," in *Men Without Art* (1987).

2 "Alimentary, Dr. Leiter"

ANAL ANXIETY IN *DIAMONDS ARE FOREVER*

DENNIS W. ALLEN

Whether one focuses on the anality or the anxiety, it is difficult to know where to begin discussing *Diamonds Are Forever* since the film is so replete with both. Starting with the early scenes in which Bond dispatches several imitation Blofelds by drowning them in some very cloacal-looking mud—which even cascades, in one instance, from a sphincter-like device—*Diamonds* is both obsessed by the anal and suffused with a subtle but insistent panic about masculine identity, which are, of course, ultimately related. In this essay, I would like to address these anxieties and investigate their relationship in order to uncover certain assumptions and premises that underlie the Bond universe.[1] These premises, in turn, can help to explain the continuing popularity of 007 even after the sociocultural milieu from which the novels and early films derive has evaporated, a shift in the zeitgeist that was evident as early as 1971, when *Diamonds* was released. Even then, the fading of Cold War paranoia and a growing ambivalence about technology as well as traces of a post-*Batman* self-consciousness within the film itself indicate a world shaped more by the counterculture than by the Camelot White House. Now, certainly, Bond's longevity derives in part precisely from such mutability, his use over time to signal changing cultural and ideological values.[2] Thus *Diamonds* presents a lighter, more comic Bond, nicely suited to an era of international détente and of growing cynicism about the hegemonic values of the 1950s.[3] Yet, I would argue, beneath such surface changes, including the film's almost complete lack of fidelity to the novel, *Diamonds* seems to retain at its core a certain essence of the

Bond world, an essence that—as much as or more than Bond's protean nature—explains his enduring appeal. Finally, then, this essay will attempt to define that essence, arguing that it derives from the construction of the Bond universe according to an obsessional logic that is one of the defining characteristics of Western culture in the postwar period.

"My Clone Sleeps Alone"

We can begin then with a related question of essence, the essence of masculine identity. Bond is, of course, an avatar of masculinity, the perfect imago for the male spectator of *Diamonds*. Even if we weren't fully aware of this before the film began, the pretitle credits sequence leaves no doubt about it. Spanning the globe in his search for Blofeld, in the space of thirty seconds Bond roughs up a Blofeld associate in Japan, punches another in Cairo, and simultaneously seduces and threatens Marie, the woman who, we infer, can finally tell him where Blofeld is. Thus presented as the epitome of traditional notions of masculinity (tough, invincible, irresistible to women), Bond also represents masculinity's transcendental self-presence.[4] Even when pretending to be someone else, Bond is always thoroughly, confidently, and unmistakably Bond, at least insofar as the audience is concerned. It is this fact, I think, that underlies the enduring appeal of the celebrated tagline "Bond . . . James Bond," always delivered at the moment of (self-)introduction by the man who would seem to need none. If the traditional logic of the phrase is a movement of progressive particularization within a field of options—"Bond" as opposed to another surname, "James" as opposed to some other Bond, this one individual as opposed to any other—in Bond's case, the formula becomes, in effect, recursive. "Bond" is enough to establish identity so that what follows ("James Bond") seems to serve not as further information but as a repetition and intensification. Thus the phrase, like Bond himself, traces masculine self-presence as a perfect circle, a whole, and thereby confirms the self-presence of masculinity itself. The only problem with this example of self-evidence is that it also hints that the self may not be quite so evident, if only because Bond does in fact have to introduce himself in the first place.

A certain doubt about self-evidence, a fluid play with identity, is intrinsic to the genre of the spy thriller, central to the very idea of espionage. It does not surprise us, then, when we learn that Tiffany Case's Amsterdam apartment comes complete with built-in fingerprint-verifying equipment, or that part of Bond's impersonation of diamond

James Bond (Sean Connery) with Blofeld clone drowning in mud bath in *Diamonds Are Forever* (1971).

courier Peter Franks involves being equipped by Q with fake fingerprints, or that, having later killed Franks, Bond should pass the corpse off to Tiffany as that of Bond himself (by planting his wallet, which contains his Playboy Club membership card, on the body). The film seems to overdo the motif of impersonation, not merely by having Blofeld utilize a device that allows him to duplicate the voice patterns of Howard Hughes–like recluse Willard Whyte in order to take over Whyte's empire, but also by having Bond employ a similar device to impersonate Whyte's assistant, Bert Saxby. Aptly enough, one of the more high-concept parts of the film is Blofeld's multiplication of indistinguishable doubles of himself. Now, what is striking about this conceit is how irrelevant it is, diegetically speaking. Granted, it allows a continual renewal of the climactic scene in which Bond disposes of the film's villain, a possibility that it necessarily frustrates, of course, and I suppose one could argue that, conceptually, it suggests something like the protean and ineradicable nature of evil. Yet, precisely because we are never provided with any motivation for Blofeld's pioneering work in "plastic transformation" and because it is largely incidental to the plot of the movie, I take it to be, finally, a symptom of a certain anxiety about masculine identity that underlies the film.

As doubles, Blofeld's clones invoke that familiar uncanny logic in which their very similarity reveals that they must somehow be different. As such, the *frisson* that is produced each time it becomes clear that this particular Blofeld is not, after all, *the* Blofeld has a deeper resonance since it raises doubts about the validity of masculine self-presence that it is part of Bond's job to exemplify. Take, for example, the scene in which Bond confronts two Blofelds in Willard Whyte's penthouse and has to decide which one is "real." Bond kicks Blofeld's cat and then shoots the Blofeld that the cat leaps to, only to discover that there are two cats, and that this particular cat is itself, apparently, a double. "Right idea," says Blofeld. "But wrong pussy," says Bond. This statement resonates with a comment made by Blofeld much later in the film when he has retreated to an offshore oil rig to extort money from America, Russia, and China with his laser satellite. When his chief scientist expresses anxiety about an approaching plane, Blofeld is unconcerned. Some show of military force was to be expected, he notes; it's just "the Great Powers flexing their muscles like so many impotent beachboys." In other words, what appears virile may not be, and one of the anxieties underlying *Diamonds* is the realization that, just as not everyone who looks like Blofeld is Blofeld, not everyone who looks like a man is really a man. Some of them, it turns out, may actually be "pussies."

This anxiety is literalized when Blofeld dons drag in order to slip out of The Whyte House unnoticed on his way to the oil rig. Strikingly, what attracts Tiffany's attention to the she-Blofeld in the first place, revealing the disguise, is that he is carrying his cat, which the camera helpfully frames in a medium shot for the sake of the audience. This incident is normally read as an indication that Blofeld might be gay, and while the film certainly ties anxiety about masculinity to anxiety about homosexuality, a point I will discuss in a moment, I find it more helpful to read this scene as concerned primarily with gender rather than with sexual orientation, and to argue that the appearance of "Miss Blofeld," rather than provoking further anxiety about gender identity, actually works to resolve such anxiety.[5] If Bond clearly represents male virility throughout *Diamonds,* then it is in this scene that any difficulty in distinguishing the real men from the wimps is definitively exorcized. Just as it is impossible to imagine Bond disguising himself in drag, it is perfectly apt that Blofeld should do so, aligning himself with the "impotent beachboys" who look like men but who are not by making himself one of those men who look like women but who are not.

In short, Blofeld's transvestism signals—as if the audience hadn't known it from the start—that he will eventually prove "impotent," his attempt at world domination thwarted by the more masculine Bond. Even more significantly, by literalizing Blofeld's inherent femininity, making it externally visible as drag, the film implicitly insists that it is in fact possible to distinguish between real men and ersatz men, that even-

Mr. Kidd (Putter Smith) and Mr. Wint (Bruce Glover) in *Diamonds Are Forever* (1971).

tually any doubts will be cleared up. After this point in the narrative there are no more Blofeld clones since we now know who is the real Blofeld and who Blofeld really is. Even more comfortingly, the scene also implies that, had we paid close enough attention, there would never have been any doubt in the first place. The fact that Blofeld's metonymic signifier is a cat and that this cat allows us to recognize him here suggests that, had we been thinking about it, we would have known all along that Blofeld himself was a "pussy." In other words, the film is able to insist that both the essence and the absence of masculinity are, finally, visibly distinguishable, obvious on the surface.[6]

If I've been arguing that the film invokes and resolves an anxiety about masculine identity, what keeps this interpretation from being completely far-fetched, I hope, is that the film also features Mr. Wint and Mr. Kidd—the first gay villains to appear in a Bond movie and two of the first openly gay characters to appear in any Hollywood film—and it is in relation to homosexuality that anxiety about masculine self-presence is played out most fully and most problematically in *Diamonds*.[7] As Lee Edelman has noted in an argument that should now begin to seem familiar, one of the problems with homosexuals is that they very often look like "real" men. As such, they represent an intensified version of the anxiety that we've already seen operating in relation to gender identity: the possibility that, within a category ("men") where everyone appears to be the same, there is, in fact, difference, so that the integral wholeness and self-presence of the category of the masculine turns out to be illusory.[8] The corollary to the recognition that not all men are really men is the additional implication that the apparent self-presence of any individual man may be equally illusory. In other words, the homosexual raises the possibility that one may simply have repressed or not yet acknowledged one's own latent homoeroticism (162–63).

According to Edelman, one response to the anxiety produced by homosexuality is to insist on a certain textualization of the gay man, to argue that there are signs, external signs, by which one can tell who is really a man and who is not (9). What is striking about *Diamonds,* however, is that, as we have just seen, while it raises questions about masculine self-presence through its proliferation of Blofelds and then resolves those questions by presenting Blofeld in drag, it rather strikingly refuses the similar consolation of textualizing its gay characters by depicting them through a series of familiar cultural and filmic codes—in short, gay stereotypes, including various tropes of effeminacy—in order to clearly demarcate them as gay. Simply put, in the film, Wint and Kidd are literally played straight, the sole exception being that Mr. Wint tends to overuse his cologne. Instead, the sexual orientation of the characters is signaled by having them walk off holding hands after blowing up a helicopter, which is apparently how gay dates were conducted in the 1970s, and by having Mr. Wint glare at Mr. Kidd when the latter remarks that "Miss Case seems quite attractive . . . [beat] . . . for a lady." If you happened to be out in the lobby getting popcorn during these two brief moments, Wint and Kidd would be indistinguishable from the straight men in the film. I will return to the masculine anxiety that this sort of gay "passing" is likely to produce, but, for the moment, I'd like to digress to a related point, noting that it is not accidental that Blofeld's self-duplication process involves an entirely unclear use of that cloacal mud, since the flip side, if you will, of the movie's concern about masculinity is an obsession with anal vulnerability.

Of Mice and Men

> "Your problems are all behind you now."
> —Bond to Tiffany (as he slips the
> cassette that controls the satellite into
> the back of her bikini bottom)

Diamonds Are Forever is the story of a smuggling "pipeline," and the film relentlessly pursues this metaphor and its analogies. If this pipeline begins with South African miners hiding diamonds in their mouths, which are then shipped via the canals of Amsterdam, it only makes sense that, by the time they reach the United States, they should be strategically concealed within Peter Frank's corpse, motivating the exchange that provides the title of my essay. Impersonating a customs agent, CIA operative Felix Leiter says to Bond, "I give up. I know the diamonds are in the body, but where?" to which Bond responds, "Alimentary, Dr. Leiter." If the pipeline thus parallels and invokes the alimentary canal, the film's attention finally seems to focus primarily on the end of it. In other words, the movie is a bit anally obsessed, to say the least. I've already mentioned that mud of Blofeld's, and it's perfectly in keeping with the logic of *Diamonds* that, lowering himself through the ceiling of Willard Whyte's penthouse, Bond should find himself sitting on Whyte's toilet. In addition, as Ed Comentale has pointed out, Fleming's fiction is set in an "anally ordered" landscape of cramped tunnels and blocked corridors, and *Diamonds* may very well be the Bond movie that is truest to the novels, at least in this respect. Many of the jeopardies that Bond faces in the film take place in narrow, enclosed, rather rectal spaces— elevators, a coffin, and, most notably, his being buried alive within a literal oil pipeline. In other words, the film's anally ordered landscape is also the site of a certain anxiety.

As Lee Edelman has made clear, the rectum can be such a source of anxiety because it is an "overdetermined opening or invagination within the male," "an internal space of difference within the body" that threatens the idea of masculine integrity (162). A hole that undermines the illusion of masculine wholeness, it is a reminder both of the possibility of difference within and of the threat of penetration, the threat exemplified by the homosexual, who is either inclined to it or, worse yet, inclined to like it. Needless to say, all of this is implicitly suggested within the film. The first time they appear on the screen, Wint and Kidd eliminate the dentist who is one of the links in the smuggling chain, a goal they accomplish not by anything so straightforward as shooting him but rather by putting a scorpion down the back of his shirt.[9] The undercurrent of anxiety about anal vulnerability in the scene becomes even more overt later when Bond, who has been gassed, awakens to discover himself buried within the pipeline. This would seem to be dilemma enough, but, almost immediately, Bond is confronted by a motorized mechanical device that is aimed straight for his backside. And just in case the implications of this aren't clear, the scene even includes a rat, which, in this context, can't help but invoke Freud's celebrated analysis of the Rat Man in *Notes upon a Case of Obsessional Neurosis* (1909).[10] As you'll recall, the Rat Man was tormented by a pervasive anxiety that manifested itself in obsessional thoughts, actions, and fantasies, most notably a fantasy of punishment in which the victim is anally penetrated by a rat. Freud attributed this to the Rat Man's ambivalence about—his love/hate relationship with—his father, which itself involved the Rat Man's latent tendency toward homosexual object choices. Not surprisingly, then, one of the meanings of the rat fantasy is the analysand's repressed desire for and anxiety about anal eroticism, which Freud traces through a number of metonymic and metaphoric linkages, most notably the symbolic equation of rat and penis, so that, rather obviously, the rat becomes a central symbol of anal intercourse. But Bond is not the Rat Man, and one of the functions of the scene is to show the ease with which Bond triumphs over the film's symptoms of anal anxiety. Just as Bond has no trouble disarming the mechanical device, the rat, encountering him, seems to become immediately tame.

The film's conclusion plays off of this scene, and the anxiety it invokes, by having Bond definitively align and then completely eliminate the threats of homosexuality and anal vulnerability. Wint and Kidd, posing as waiters, prepare to attack Bond and Tiffany with a variety of weapons, including a bomb. Bond is able to see through their disguises and determine their true identities, however, even though he has never actually seen them (he was unconscious when they transported him to the construction site and left him in the section of pipe to be buried alive). In an elaborate plot device, as Wint and Kidd put Bond into the trunk of their car, Wint's cologne bottle falls into the trunk and shatters, dousing Bond with perfume. As a result, when Bond awakens in the pipeline and encounters the rat, he is initially unable to tell which of the two of them smells, as he puts it, "like a tart's handkerchief." When Bond later meets Wint posing as a sommelier at the film's end, he is thus able to recognize him by his cologne, or, as Bond puts it, "I've smelled that aftershave before, and both times I've smelled a rat."

Just like Blofeld's pussy, then, the rat becomes Wint and Kidd's metonymic signifier, nicely aligning and condensing the threats of homosexuality and anal vulnerability. Moreover, Bond's play on words ("I've smelled a rat") adds another layer of meaning here, suggesting that the "something wrong" with these men that the phrase implies is not just villainy but homosexuality itself, that they are wrong not only morally but as men. As such, the scene resolves any lingering anxiety about the possibility that gay men could pass as straight, that the boundaries of heterosexual masculinity might be porous. As with Blofeld, the film suggests that Bond—and by extension the audience—can always distinguish false men from true men by paying enough attention to details. Not too surprisingly then, the film concludes with a scene the Freudian undertones of which are difficult to miss, with Bond definitively distinguishing the rodents from the real men and reducing the threat posed by homosexuality by repositioning it, associating it not with phallic potency and the threat of anal penetration but with anal vulnerability, not with wholeness but with hole-ness. Bond finishes off Wint by pulling Wint's arms between his legs in what is very clearly an emasculating maneuver and then, attaching the bomb to Wint's coattails, flings him over the side of the ship, where he explodes. As Bond puts it, "He certainly left with his tails between his legs."[11]

A Woman Named Plenty

Freud's analysis of the Rat Man's obsessional neurosis can do more, however, than simply explain the relevance of Wint and Kidd's metonymic signifier to the anal anxiety that suffuses *Diamonds*. I could, for example, pursue a standard Freudian analysis and argue that the Rat Man can enhance our understanding of the Oedipalized landscape underlying the entire Bond corpus. If, beginning with Kingsley Amis, scholars have recognized that the Bond world is populated with fragments of the father, with M representing the "stern but loveable," empowering paternal figure and the villains representing the castrating father, then the Rat Man adds to the complexity of that picture.[12] Freud focuses his attention on the Rat Man's identification of the father with sexual prohibition, arguing that the Rat Man experienced a profound ambivalence because of his conflicting desires to follow his (heterosexual) erotic impulses and to obey the paternal injunction against them. Yet, even though Freud does not develop the point, an additional factor in both the Rat Man's anal anxiety and his ambivalence would have to be his repressed desire for and sexual anxiety about the father himself, a literal albeit unconscious love/hate relationship with Dad. In the case of *Diamonds,* this allows for an expanded reading of the film as a psychomachia of Bond's (and perhaps every man's) relation to the father, so that, beside M as the good father and Blofeld as the bad father, we have to place Wint and Kidd as the threateningly erotic father. Moreover, in such a reading, the multiplication of Blofelds serves nicely as a literalization or surface manifestation of the splitting of the idea of the father that underlies the construction of the text itself. Finally, to follow the standard Freudian reading, the repressed homoerotic desire for the father concealed beneath the fear and anxiety about anal vulnerability signified by Wint and Kidd would represent precisely the sort of fracturing or self-division within masculine identity and heterosexual desire—in the cases of both Bond and men in the audience—that the film goes to great lengths, exactly for that reason, to exorcize.

While such a reading is useful in understanding the Bond universe, I would like instead to pursue a slightly different line, following the lead of psychology itself, which has, in the hundred or so years since the Rat Man underwent analysis, moved away from an attention to the Oedipal specifics of the case to focus instead on the mental operations the Rat Man evinced. Remembering that the Rat Man was Freud's exemplary case history of obsessional neurosis, I want to suggest that the anal anxiety of *Diamonds* is primarily important not as a textbook illustration of the Rat Man's particular obsessions, but as a surface trace of a deeper phenomenon. I'd like to argue that the Bond universe is premised on a certain obsessive-compulsive logic, but a logic that can more profitably be understood as Althusserian and ideological rather than as simply Freudian and psychological, a logic that is less about regression to infantile sexuality than about the hopes and anxieties spawned by postwar culture.[13] I will explain this in more detail, particularly since I think it can help us understand why the Bond phenomenon has survived for some fifty years and may be more popular today than it was at its inception. First, however, in order to understand what we might call cultural obsessionality, we will have to look at a couple of instances of this logic at work in *Diamonds,* namely the use of motivated names and the trademark Bond gadgetry.

Example One: Like most Bond films, *Diamonds* relies on a use of motivated names, such as Tiffany Case, the diamond smuggler; Morton Slumber, the mortician; and Shady Tree, the nightclub comic cum minor criminal. It is to be expected in such a universe that, standing at the craps table, Bond should encounter a woman named Plenty:

> Plenty: Hi, I'm Plenty.
> Bond: But of course you are.
> Plenty: Plenty O'Toole.
> Bond: Named after your father perhaps?

Since Plenty doesn't demur, the audience is led to assume that, in fact, she was.

Example Two: Bond films are, of course, famous for their gadgetry, which is usually taken as an illustration of postwar optimism about and fascination with technology (Amis 134). Because *Diamonds* omits the standard expository scene with Q so that we encounter many of the gadgets for the first time as Bond uses them, an inherent principle of Bondian technology is clearer here than it usually is: Bond always has precisely the device necessary for the situation he encounters even if there was no way of knowing in advance that such a situation would occur. Thus, although Tiffany's fingerprint scanner comes as a surprise, it turns out that the fake fingerprints Q thought "might come in handy" are in fact exactly what the situation requires. More mundanely, when Bond is searched for weapons by one of Blofeld's henchmen early in the film, it turns out that his shoulder holster contains a rather gory hand trap, as if, dressing for the operation, Bond knew in advance what was going to happen. The corollary of this perfect synchronicity between preparation and event is that, as Pat O'Donnell has pointed out, typically all the gadgets that Bond is provided with during his scene with Q are used in the course of the film in a sort of phantasmatic ideal of efficient government planning.

In order to understand these features of the Bond world, we can return to the classifications provided by contemporary psychology. Read through the lens of psychoanalysis, the Bond corpus would most obviously seem to reflect, at least at its inception, an atmosphere of Cold War paranoia (Bennett 25–28). And, if we understand paranoia to be an epistemological or interpretive mania—a conviction that the (hidden) truth is out there and that we can make sense of everything if only we try hard enough—its applicability to the Bond universe seems undeniable. As I've already suggested, however, this universe might also be understood as operating according to an obsessional logic. Although the exact definition and characteristics of what is today called OCD (obsessive-compulsive disorder) are a matter of some dispute, the general view is that the obsessional neurotic responds to the anxiety produced by unwanted thoughts or premonitions of disaster by resorting to superstitious or magical thinking, compulsively arranging his environment or performing ritualized activities or mental acts (handwashing, repeating verbal formulas) to neutralize the perceived threat.[14] In short, obsessional logic can be characterized, in part, as a desire for order and a compulsive conscientiousness that attempts to anticipate and ward off potential harm.

Keeping this definition in mind, I would argue that under the surface chaos of the Bond world, behind or beneath the realm of accident in which—to take *Diamonds* as the example—Mafia goons throw women out of windows and police cars slam into each other during car chases, the underlying premise of this world is the obsessional fantasy that it is always already ordered. This is signaled by the use of motivated names, since linguistic motivation reflects a perfect, in fact inevitable, fit between word and thing, between the Symbolic Order and the Real, so that, ultimately, meaning is transparent because the thing *is* its name, is what it is. In effect, the motivated name reveals the underlying organization of the cosmos, the assurance that everyone and everything are in exactly the right place. To put it another way, this is a world in which it is inconceivable that Morton Slumber could have chosen a career as a rodeo clown or that a diamond smuggler could be called something other than Tiffany Case. In fact, the explanation for Tiffany's name provided within the diegesis, that she was born on the first floor of Tiffany's, reflects precisely the overdetermined, recursive nature of obsessional thinking: Tiffany's entire identity is—must be—predicated on a relation to diamonds.

In other words, this world is very highly organized, which I also take to be the meaning of the gadgets. As I've already suggested, their appeal finally derives less from their status as marvels of technology (fake fingerprints! a moon buggy!) than from the absolute aptness of their deployment. They represent an obsessional's fantasy of conscientiousness taken to an almost unimaginable degree of perfection: one is always perfectly prepared for exactly what happens and not prepared for what doesn't, and everything is always in the place that it will be needed when it will be needed without anything extraneous to clutter up the landscape, an ideal organization without any waste or excess. In short, the obsessional fantasy that shapes the film is not only that violence and chaos are merely a superficial—and transitory—disruption of an underlying order that is already, and always, there, but that Bond, as the audience's Ideal-I, will have anticipated virtually every contingency and be so thoroughly equipped for disaster that, despite a momentary setback or two, no real harm can ever come to him.

Bond Will Return . . .

"As usual, Mr. Bond, you're absolutely right."
—Blofeld to Bond

What I'm saying, in other words, is that *Diamonds,* like most of the other works in the Bond corpus, is itself a symptom, a compulsive "mental act" that is, and here I'll quote the *Diagnostic and Statistical Manual of Mental Disorders, 4th Edition,* "aimed at preventing or reducing distress or preventing some dreaded event or situation."[15] What, then, is the source of this distress? On one level, as we've already seen, the anxiety displayed across the surface of the film is about masculinity, about homosexuality and anal vulnerability, an anxiety that is resolved in the film's content not only by Bond's active abjection of these threats, but also by Bond himself as the unshakable symbol of male wholeness. Yet I take this particular anxiety and its resolution to be essentially a surface phenomenon, a synecdoche of a larger concern, and I would like to argue that the very form of the film (or, perhaps, the film as symptom) points to and attempts to counter a deeper source of distress. Simply put, this deeper anxiety is the fear, we might even call it the recognition, that the world is not really ordered but that it is actually random and chaotic. In contrast to paranoia, which insists that there's a truth that is hidden from us, this is the fear that there may be no deeper truth, no sense, at all. It is an anxiety about accidents, both in the sense of haphazard harm and of surfaces that may cover over not a hidden essence, but chaos, the absence of any essence at all. In short, this distress is an anxiety about the existence of the Real.

Within *Diamonds,* the Real is condensed into homosexuality, exemplified by Wint and Kidd and constituted in the film as a threat to masculinity, and hence, implicitly, to that locus of patriarchal meaning, the Symbolic Order. But homosexuality is only one aspect of Wint and Kidd's larger significance within the film, which is to represent a certain absence or failure of meaning in general. To begin with, they seem to kill without purpose. Although their ostensible function is presumably to wipe out the links in the smuggling pipeline once Blofeld has received all the diamonds he needs, this role is never clearly stated in the movie, adding a sense of random malice to their actions. In any case, after Blofeld has been defeated and his scheme for world domination has been foiled, Wint and Kidd nonetheless make a final attempt to kill Bond and Tiffany, although this attempt can now have no discernible justification, particularly since the two villains are so flatly drawn that there is no suggestion that this action derives from any personal motives. Deprived of any interiority except a vaguely defined "homosexuality" or any clear diegetic function at the end of the film, Wint and Kidd would seem to represent, finally, simply the possibility of inexplicable, unmotivated harm.[16]

All of this, I think, helps to explain why Mr. Wint and Mr. Kidd are the only characters who have no first names. The point is not simply that, reduced solely to their surnames, Wint and Kidd are deprived of the possibility of the sort of recursive self-evidence—the "Bond . . . James Bond" moment—that is the province of true maleness. Beyond this ultimate sign of their incomplete masculinity, the absence of Christian names for Wint and Kidd has an additional implication. Because Wint and Kidd are inadequately or incompletely named, the possibility that we could decipher their names as the motivated signifiers that would indicate their essences and thus their place in the world is radically restricted, just as if we had only been told that Shady was named Mr. Tree. Thus, those missing names signal an absence, an incompleteness in the Symbolic Order. Like the meaningless violence that the pair unleashes at the end of the narrative, this particular failure of eponymous meaning is singularly apt, since, finally, what Wint and Kidd really represent, their real essence, is precisely the threatening possibility that essence does not exist, that language and the Symbolic do not reflect the order of the universe but are merely artificially and imperfectly imposed on a deeper chaos that cannot, finally, be ordered.[17]

Bond defeats Wint and Kidd, of course, making the world make sense, and since, as I have already suggested, the obsessionality that the film represents is not individual but cultural, I will now add that the anxiety I've identified seems to be a pervasive, even central, feature of modern Western culture, which can thus help to explain the enduring appeal of the Bond oeuvre. On the larger level, then, the film needs to be seen as just one of a number of cultural assertions of the existence of order itself: that disaster is not random, that chaos could have been averted, that someone is responsible, those illusory notions of sense and control that are the contemporary legacy of Enlightenment rationality and of the ideology of technological and scientific progress. It is the same kind of fantasy as the logic underlying our persistent belief that events like the shootings at Columbine or the *Columbia* disaster could have been avoided if there had not been some failure of "intelligence" or action, that we should have—we did—know the future but failed to be conscientious enough to employ the means necessary—human or technological—to prevent tragedy.

To illustrate this point, I'd like to make a final juxtaposition between two narratives that represent, in radically different ways, the cultural persistence of this fantasy. The first narrative is part of the story of September 11th as articulated by the congressional committee that published in December 2002 the following finding about the terrorist attacks on New York and Washington, D.C.:

> Although relevant information that is significant in retrospect regarding the attacks was available to the Intelligence Community prior to September 11, 2001, the Community too often failed to focus on that

information and consider and appreciate its collective significance in terms of a probable terrorist attack. . . . Some significant pieces of information in the vast stream of data being collected were overlooked, some were not recognized as potentially significant at the time and therefore not disseminated, and some required additional action on the part of foreign governments before a direct connection to the hijackers could have been established. For all those reasons, the Intelligence Community failed to fully capitalize on available, and potentially important, information.[18]

To put it in simple terms, this is the worst nightmare of an obsessional culture. September 11th could have been prevented, the report insists, if only we'd been conscientious enough, had paid enough attention to the "relevant information" and "capitalized" on it, an assertion of the possibility of complete control that overrides all the suggestions within the text itself that such control is impossible. Thus, somehow, despite the vastness of that "stream of data," the tens of thousands of bits and fragments of information suggesting literally millions of possible events and futures, the report insists that we could have (we should have) known an outcome that, realistically speaking, can only ever have been fully evident "in retrospect." Moreover, and most significantly, the report assumes the inevitability of the September 11th plot, which is understood as potentially avoidable but as nonetheless bound to unfold even if we had finally made it fail, an assumption, I would argue, that retroactively imposes the coherence we give to the past onto the chaotic uncertainty of what was then the future. It is a final bit of insistence that the universe has a meaning and writes a story, a repression of the possibility that the future could be random, that, given a slightly different concatenation of events, September 11th could just as easily not have happened, regardless of anything we did or did not do.

We can compare this with another story about the "Intelligence Community," although this one, of course, is part of the larger narrative of *Diamonds*. Wint's cologne aside, what alerts Bond to Wint's identity in the film's final scene and thus signals the threat he poses is that, in response to a question from Bond, it becomes clear that this particular sommelier does not know that Mouton Rothschild is a claret. Wielding a vast store of information, attentive to the telling detail, Bond is the figure implicitly posited by the congressional report, able to defeat Wint and Kidd precisely because he incarnates the completely conscientious imago of an obsessional culture, thereby providing much of the comfort that we continue to seek from the Bond corpus. But this comfort does not lie only in the figure of Bond. It derives equally from the depiction of the Bond universe, in which even the bad things have a place and make sense. Thus, I would argue, despite their construction as representations of the Real, Wint and Kidd are finally also part of our dream of meaning, if only because, being literally scripted, they are bound to act as they do. In other words, the attraction of the Bond corpus comes in no small part from its implicit insistence that even random malice or the threat of harm or the possibility of chaos turns out to be, after all, part of a deeper (narrative) order.

I could multiply other examples of what I have called our cultural obsessionality—the explosion in the last three decades of negligence lawsuits, the continual implicit suggestion that if we do just the right things and not the wrong things, we can somehow ward off death itself—but I'd like instead to make one final point. In the world of the obsessive-compulsive, which I've been suggesting is our world, the preventive actions or thoughts never really reduce the distress. You have to repeat the verbal formulation or the counting or the handwashing again and again and again since it might not have really been effective the last time. And if, as I hope I've shown, the works of the Bond corpus can be taken as symptoms of the same sort, this might explain one final reason for their continued appeal—like all compulsive formulas, Bond must be repeated. The point is not simply that each new Bond film will provide the comforts of genre by being already familiar and, vastly more importantly, predictable, but that it will be so in an overdetermined, almost ritualistic way. One knows in advance that there will be gadgets and Bond girls and M and Q and familiar taglines ("Bond . . . James Bond") and directions for the proper way to mix a martini, all of which will implicitly but definitively ensure that there is an order to the universe. No matter what nefarious plot is afoot and no matter what blows up, the spectator is thus always guaranteed that, while she may be stirred by the film, her conviction that the world is meaningful will never be shaken.

NOTES

1. In this essay, I focus primarily on *Diamonds Are Forever* (dir. Guy Hamilton, Danjaq Productions, 1971) and the Bond films, which students of Bond seem to

universally agree mark something of a departure from, and evolution of, the Bond of the novels. See, for example, Jeremy Black, *The Politics of James Bond: From Fleming's Novels to the Big Screen,* 91–103.

2. Tony Bennett and Janet Woollacott, *Bond and Beyond: The Political Career of a Popular Hero,* 19.

3. James Chapman, *Licence to Thrill: A Cultural History of the James Bond Films,* 151; John Cork and Bruce Scivally, *James Bond: The Legacy,* 126.

4. Compare Toby Miller, "James Bond's Penis," in *Masculinity: Bodies, Movies, Culture,* ed. Peter Lehman (New York: Routledge, 2001), and reprinted in Christoph Lindner's recent volume *The James Bond Phenomenon,* in which Lindner takes the Bond of the films as an example of "weak commodified male beauty" and specifically argues, rather surprisingly, that Sean Connery was considered a "wuss" in the 1960s (244, 248). For a more complex view of Bond as a representation of masculine ideals, see Bennett and Woollacott, who argue that Bond's various incarnations over time negotiate changing conceptions of gender roles, gender relations, and sexual norms from the 1950s through the 1970s (35–39, 241–42).

5. See Chapman (*Licence to Thrill* 159) and Black (107), who view Blofeld as camp, which they seem to understand, entirely unproblematically, as synonymous with both homosexuality and drag. Although the conflation of gender identity and sexual orientation was certainly a feature of early 1970s conceptions of masculinity and of its discontents, I find it helpful to follow Queer Theory's theoretical distinction of gender and sexual orientation for analytic purposes. For a discussion of the distinction, see Judith Butler, "Imitation and Gender Insubordination," in *The Lesbian and Gay Studies Reader* (1993). In any event, the conflation of camp, drag, and homosexuality seems to be an inaccurate and critically unhelpful approach to any of these three concepts (or practices), as a few moments' reflection on the relation or lack of relation between Milton Berle, Octavia St. Laurent in *Paris Is Burning,* any of the films of Baz Luhrmann, and the gay men who populate the online personals at Bigmuscle.com should suggest. As far as camp is concerned, Chapman is much closer to the mark when he identifies *Diamonds* itself as camp because of its interrogation of "restrictive sex roles," Las Vegas setting, and attention to ostentatious visual spectacle (159).

6. As Pussy Galore in *Goldfinger* suggests, both Fleming and the Bond filmmaking team have never been afraid to invoke the general currency of "pussy" as a slang term for the female genitalia. As such, while I wouldn't insist on the point, one could argue that, in this context, Blofeld's cat further reduces the castration anxiety produced by the recognition of sexual difference, the anxiety that underlies the concern about masculinity in the film. If the idea of masculine self-presence is constructed in relation to an idea of female lack, and if this anxiety derives in part from the idea that the female genitalia present nothing to see, Blofeld's pussy functions, precisely, as a fetish, simultaneously signifying his castration and denying the very possibility of castration by providing the audience with a visible, materialized presence that represents the "absence" of the female genitalia. In other words, that cat is a lack that can be seen.

7. The classic study of representations of homosexuality in film is Vito Russo's *The Celluloid Closet: Homosexuality in the Movies,* Revised Edition (1987). According to Russo, the abolition of the Hays Code in 1968 paved the way for more overt depictions of lesbians and gay men in movies during the late 1960s and early 1970s (163–70), and *The Boys in the Band,* a watershed film due to its exclusive focus on the lives of a group of gay men, opened in 1970, a year before *Diamonds.* Russo consistently notes that such increased visibility is not to be confused with positive portrayals of gay men. For his specific (and sometimes factually inaccurate) comments on *Diamonds,* see 156.

8. Lee Edelman, *Homographesis: Essays in Gay Literary and Cultural Theory,* 4.

9. The script originally called for Wint and Kidd to kill the dentist by putting the scorpion in his mouth, which is particularly apt given that we are still at the beginning of the smuggling pipeline cum alimentary canal at this point in the film. Concerns that this might prove too gruesome for some viewers led to the substitution of the current scene, latent anal anxiety presumably being more palatable to a family audience. For the anecdote, see Cork and Scivally, 131.

10. See Sigmund Freud, *Three Case Histories* (New York: Touchstone, 1996).

11. In the case of Mr. Kidd, Bond douses him with alcohol so that he is set on fire by the burning kabob skewers with which he is menacing Bond and Tiffany, eliminating the phallic threat those skewers represent. I'm not certain the filmmakers had it in mind, but Bond thus literally turns Kidd into a flaming queen.

12. Kingsley Amis, *The James Bond Dossier*, 60. See also Chapman (*Licence to Thrill* 33) and Bennett and Woollacott (129–34).

13. An alternate reading of the film would stress its function as a response to contemporary cultural concerns, specifically the rise of the Feminist and Gay Liberation movements and the anti-authoritarian stance of 1960s subculture. Andrew Sarris's review of the film in the *Village Voice* explicitly discussed it as a negotiation of the challenge to heterosexual norms and to traditional gender roles represented by the first two social movements (quoted in Chapman, *Licence to Thrill* 162–63). In the third instance, one of the underlying ideological conflicts that the film has to resolve is the clash between countercultural rejections of (masculine, patriarchal) authority and the fact that Bond's identity is ultimately premised precisely on such authority. Thus Tiffany at one point refers to Leiter and his CIA agents as "pigs," and the film contains those staples of 1970s anti-authoritarian film: the dim-witted sheriff who is made a fool of and the car chase which consists largely of police cars crashing into each other. *Diamonds* negotiates this by positioning Bond as an anti-hero who nonetheless represents the Law. Note that it is Bond himself who is making fools of the police in the car chase sequences.

14. In *Theoretical Approaches to Obsessive-Compulsive Disorder* (1996), Ian Jakes notes both the current controversy over the exact definition of OCD (26) and provides a list of symptoms (14–18). General clinical practice distinguishes between obsession (the unwanted thoughts about possible misfortune) and compulsion (the physical or mental acts designed to ward off harm) (5–7). In non-psychiatric usage, of course, the two terms are often used interchangeably.

15. *Diagnostic and Statistical Manual of Mental Disorders, 4th Edition* (DSM IV) (Washington, D.C.: American Psychiatric Association, 1994), http://www.psychologynet.org/ocd.html.

16. Seen from another angle, it could be argued that Wint and Kidd's final attack at the conclusion of *Diamonds* simply reflects the generic conventions of the Bond film, which typically stresses action over character development (and sometimes even over coherent plot) and which requires a final climactic confrontation after the denouement. Yet, I would argue, those conventions themselves encode an obsessional anxiety about the nature of the universe since the basic narrative structure presents one final threat that has no logical explanation, that erupts without warning into the order ostensibly established at the film's end.

17. This would also explain why the film fails to clearly textualize homosexuality through familiar stereotypical representations, thus depriving homosexuality itself of any stable meaning.

18. Report of the Joint Inquiry into the Terrorist Attacks of September 11, 2001—By the House Permanent Select Committee on Intelligence and the Senate Select Committee on Intelligence. S. REPT. NO. 107-351 107TH CONGRESS, 2D SESSION H. REPT. NO. 107-792. December 2002. http://news.findlaw.com/hdocs/docs/911rpt

Lesbian Bondage, or
3 Why Dykes Like 007

JAIME HOVEY

It is accepted as common wisdom that the American cinema is overwhelmingly male and heterosexual. Vito Russo's classic analysis of homosexuality and film, *The Celluloid Closet,* not only concedes that "[h]omosexuality in the movies, whether overtly sexual or not, has always been seen in terms of what is or what is not masculine" (4), but also concludes: "In celebrating maleness, the rendering invisible of all else has caused lesbianism to disappear behind a male vision of sex in general" (5). Judith Halberstam suggests that this monolithic male heterosexual representation has broken down somewhat with recent popular cultural interest in "the fag hag role" and the "influence of lesbian drag king cultures on hetero-male comic film," but she maintains that relations between lesbians and straight men remain for the most part "submerged and mediated and difficult to read" (453). Yet reading the relations in popular culture between lesbians and straight men, or between gay men and heterosexual women, has gotten easier in recent years because feminism and queer theory[1] have questioned the self-sufficiency of such mutually constitutive subject positions as male and female, heterosexual and homosexual, normal and queer. Although the cinema may appear overwhelmingly male and heterosexual, the structural and discursive reliance of both these terms on women and homosexuality means that lesbianism may not only not be erased by "a male vision of sex," but may in fact be present in a "male" version of sex to the extent that lesbianism actually defines it.

Indeed, the mutual imbrications of heterosexual and homosexual as self-consciously present in mid-century as well as in contemporary cultural texts suggests a deep reliance by heterosexual masculinity on lesbi-anism, and lesbianism on heterosexual masculinity. This essay considers the queer gender and sexual dynamics of that most heterosexual of mid-century masculine heroes, James Bond—especially the Bond of Ian Flem-ing's *Goldfinger* in both his novel and film incarnations—in order to explore what about Bond might be lesbian, and what "old" Bond might offer contemporary lesbian culture. More specifically, this essay looks at exaggerated, polarized gender and its relation to the art of seduction—including lesbian seduction—in these Bond texts. *Goldfinger* is especially appropriate in this context because there are lesbian characters in the novel as well as the film version of Fleming's story, and their sexuality both foils and entices Bond. The queer aspects of Bond films more generally that I address here—qualities that also and paradoxically form the core of Bond's rakish sexual appeal—include excessive, highly styl-ized gender; heat between equals; conversion through better seductive technique; and finally, public sexuality. These "queer" aspects of Bond suggest that gender and heterosexual sexual expression in Bond novels and films are stylized to the point that they actually resist heteronor-mativity and respectability, constituting a recognizable queerness. Once gendered qualities define character almost exclusively, as they do in the early Bond films, both gender and character are marked by excess, sig-nifying something other than authenticity or the merely natural. At the same time, when these gendered qualities are displayed in the context of lesbians and lesbian sensibilities, as they are in *Goldfinger* and *From Russia with Love,* they suggest a homosexual kinship between Bond and his girls. Bond's masculinity responds not only to the challenge of their mannishness, but also to that mannishness itself.

James Bond movies have always been about gender. An exaggerated, nearly parodic fantasy of a powerful and irresistible western masculinity in the Cold War era, the James Bond character in the early films as played by Sean Connery epitomized a suave seductiveness, a boyish indifference to sentimental feelings, and a competent, even brutal efficiency around women, most of whom found their "true" femininity when they finally succumbed to his charms. Indeed, the most notable feature of Bond films has been the way they have mapped shifting gender roles in the wake of the women's movement. As the decades have passed, Bond movies have struggled to remain sexy even as the exaggerated gender polarities of the early films have been muted and mutated. A man's man whose sadistic misogyny in the films of the early sixties mirrored the self-contained masculinity of the era, Bond became much more of a woman's man in the more comic later films of the post-Vietnam seventies, one where the ironic self-presentation of Roger Moore and—to a lesser degree—Timothy Dalton suggested deep cultural misgivings about the correlation of machismo with heroism.

In the new century of Bond films such as *Die Another Day,* the powerful and untrustworthy femmes of the early sixties have become boyish sex buddies. The fact that Bond's sexuality has grown less hostile, if no more friendly, to women in the fifty years since his creation by Ian Fleming would suggest that women would find him more palatable in his kinder, gentler form than they ever did in Sean Connery's suavely brutal phallicism. The proliferation of gadgets, the ever more autonomous and physically dexterous girls, and the casting of the innocuous Pierce Brosnan in more recent Bond films has completed James's transformation from murderously efficient prick to stylishly accessorized dildo, and should by rights make for greater appeal to women—especially feminists and lesbians—than ever before. But this is not the case. Connery's electricity with women and *sprezzatura* on the job make him much more appealing both as a man to identify with and as one to desire. Why is this? If, as Halberstam and others have argued, Bond incarnation Austin Powers's parodic and "prosthetic" masculinity appeals to the drag king coterie in queer culture (442), why is it that the blander Bond of recent 007 movies doesn't? Have we forgotten feminism, or is there something about the exaggerated gender and sexual prowess of the Connery films that feels, well, dykier?

Stylized Gender and "Rules of the Game"

The film starts. A white dot becomes an iris, which opens to enclose a figure in the dark gray suit, tie, and short-brimmed hat of early 1960s masculine street clothes. He takes three steps, turns, and fires at the viewer. His walk is loose, his stance is balanced and assured, the drawing and firing of his weapon is without awkwardness. We know this is a man immediately because of these clothes, this hat, and this bodily comportment. Hat and suit signify male; gun and action signify kind of male— violent, reactive, graceful, and fascinating.

The film proceeds. A crime occurs. The scene switches to a private club where tuxedoed men surround an elegantly dressed woman playing cards. She is dark, powerful, and feminine. She is also losing. A man's voice tells her that he admires her courage. She retorts that she admires his luck, and they exchange names. Just before we hear her opponent identify himself, we see him for the first time. He is dark to the point of swarthiness, his hair carefully, tastefully slicked back. But his most important gesture is the way he lights his cigarette before giving her the satisfaction of an answer. "Bond, James Bond." Music plays behind him as he gives his name—the same music that introduced the figure in the iris in the opening credits of this film, *Dr. No,* where Bond appears for the first time. The link is established between the ideal signifier in the credits—masculine equals traditional gender "readability," as well as qualities of strength, action, reaction, violence—and this elegant, slightly brutal gambler with the quizzical sneer we see before us who answers a woman when he's good and ready.

Here, in the opening sequences of *Dr. No,* masculine style is worn as stylized masculinity, one where gender is signified by its exaggeration. Only the most expensive, the most formal clothes will do for him; only the most suave, self-contained gestures will convey his personality. A man of few words and decisive actions, Bond's economy is one of minimalism, an economy that serves as the classic masculine counterpart to the baroque feminine display of his opponent at cards. Both their genders are highly stylized, conventional, and opposite from each other to the point of excess. The early Bond films were made in the 1960s, not the 1950s (though Fleming produced the first novels in the 1950s), but you wouldn't know it watching *Dr. No* in 1962. Pussy Galore's unconventional career as a pilot may remind viewers that *Goldfinger* appears as late as 1964, but Bond's formal clothes, machismo, and insistence that Pussy eventually adopt a more conventional femininity seem more in tune with 1959, the year *Goldfinger* was published. While other films of the era could be equally conservative about gender—Hitchcock's lesbophobic 1964 *Marnie* is a case in point—Bond's retro masculinity in the early Bond films is dated enough to call attention to itself as stylized rather than "natural" or even contemporary gender. His butch is a classic gender, as is the femme gender of the women who will fall for him; if a Bond girl is not all that femme before he seduces her, she almost always is after he takes her to bed.

Bond's gender is not so much an individual quality as it is a social semiotic, something akin to what Dick Hebdige terms the "form of refusal" that signifies revolt against the status quo, where style and gesture refuse to take up the values of bourgeois normative society (2). In Bond's case, this refusal is signified by the cigarette, the evening clothes, and the good manners that are always deployed with the faintest trace of disdain, accentuating Bond's alienation from the very forms of the culture he serves. Framed in relation to dangerous and emancipated women, these gendered gestures of refusal make up a masculinity that tends mostly to obey the outward forms of heterosexual chivalry yet signifies its unwillingness to be domesticated by those forms. When Bond lights his cigarette before he answers a lady's question, he delays the proper response to her inquiry by just a beat—long enough to reveal himself as a bad subject, a subject who resists interpellation, who resists giving his name.

Such resistance wears masculinity, wears its wearing of masculinity as style rather than essence, as persona rather than person. Such comportment suggests a resistance not only to the masculine style that must bow to femininity, but also to masculinity and heterosexuality itself as they are dynamically configured in mainstream culture. This resistance operates as both imitation and gender insubordination (to paraphrase Judith Butler). And indeed, de-naturalizing the naturalness of gender through imitation and exaggeration is usually a queer strategy, as one that has traditionally been adopted by gay men and lesbians as part of their resistance to heterosexual gender roles. During the Cold War a stereotypically polarized masculine-feminine pairing style—one not dissimilar from the exaggerated masculinity and femininity I have described in the opening of the film *Dr. No*—seemed to appeal to heterosexuals as well as lesbians. Historian Lillian Faderman writes of U.S. lesbian culture: "It is not surprising that butch-femme was in its heyday during the 1950s, when not only were the parent-culture roles exaggerated between men and women, but the Hollywood values of dash and romance served to inspire the fancy of the young, especially those who were at a loss about where to turn for their images of self" (170). Faderman's observation suggests that an excessively conventional gender was seen as normal at this time, as heterosexual, and thus could have proliferated among lesbians as both a strategy of belonging and a strategy of queer visibility, in the same gesture.

Noting similar trends in Britain, Emily Hamer points out that in this era, "femme"—a feminine gender style adopted by some lesbians that can on occasion appear indistinguishable from conventional heterosexual womanliness—emerges as counterpart to "butch" for the first time: "While there have always been mannish lesbians who made their lesbianism clear through a rejection of femininity, there is little indication before the 1950s that the mannish lesbian needed a 'femme' partner" (149). Hamer's observation privileges the prior existence of "butch" as a form of lesbian identity, but it may also be true that "femmes" desired greater queer visibility in this era, and thus chose "butches" with greater frequency than before as their escorts and accessories. Excessively conventional gender differences identified the couple as a couple, no matter whether they were opposite-sex or same-sex.

The rise, fall, and recent revival of butch-femme gender style among lesbians has led to debates as to whether stylized lesbian gender imitates heterosexuality or not, with some lesbian theorists maintaining, as does Sue-Ellen Case, that butch-femme is a uniquely lesbian style of gender. Others, like Judith Butler, render the question moot by characterizing all genders as copies, while still others such as Judith Roof suggest that butch-femme both copies the terms of heterosexuality and points out the artificiality of those terms. In her book of essays on lesbian identity in the 1950s and 1960s, activist femme Joan Nestle writes, "The [lesbian] butch-femme couple embarrassed other Lesbians (and still does) because they made lesbians culturally visible, a terrifying act for the 1950s" (101). She points to the importance of gendered clothes as signifiers of resistance to gender norms: "None of the butch women I was with, and this included a passing woman, ever presented themselves to me as men; they did announce themselves as tabooed women who were willing to identify their passion by wearing clothes that symbolized the taking of responsibility. Part of this responsibility was sexual expertise. In the 1950s this courage to feel comfortable with arousing another woman became a political act" (100–101).

Like the man in the suit with a gun at the beginning of Bond films, in the lesbian bar of the 1950s the signification that gendered style enacts constitutes the meaning of gender itself. Nestle emphasizes that the resistance butch-femme couples offered to gender norms was not merely in terms of their appearance, but in the sexual resistance more deeply signified by their clothes: "My understanding of why we angered straight spectators so is not that they saw us modeling ourselves after them, but just the opposite: we were a symbol of women's erotic autonomy, a sexual accomplishment that did not include them" (102). Such resistance was signified as a style of comportment as well as a costume. Nestle writes, "I loved my lover for how she stood as well as for what she did. Dress was a part of it: the erotic signal of her hair at the nape of her neck, touching the shirt collar; how she held her cigarette; the symbolic pinky ring flashing as she waved her hand" (104). Lillian Faderman finds evidence that such comportment was regarded more seriously than theories characterizing it in terms of parody or defiance account for: "The roles might be merely the rules of the game that you followed if you wanted to be one of the players—or as J. C., who was a Texas 'butch,' phrased it, 'I looked around and thought, if that's the way you get to belong, I need to do it as good as they did, so I made myself remember to open car doors and light cigarettes and all of that' " (171). Faderman finds masculine and feminine roles in lesbian communities of the 1950s operating as a commonly held semiotics of gender, the "rules of the game" that can be read as defining how one gets to play the game of romance, rather than defining who gets to play.

Conversion through Better Technique

If excessively gendered or—as I will refer to it—"stylized" gender behavior paradoxically shifts the rules of romance away from the players to the game itself, then stylized gender also becomes a function of the game, the competition. Part of what defines the rules of the game is prowess, not only at the chivalry that stakes out the social tension between masculine and feminine players, but also at seduction itself. The Texas butch wants to play by the rules of the game; she also wants to play them one better, to compete in the sexual market on its terms, to challenge her exclusion as a lesbian from its norms. This ability clearly signifies sexual prowess, but even more importantly, it represents sexual fantasy. It is not only men that wish those jeans, that underwear, those bras and stockings and zippers and belts and socks that are sometimes fun to fumble with, but often not, could disappear when necessary. If clothes mark sites of resistance to seduction because the consciousness that seduction is taking place is brought to the fore by the awkwardness of undressing, getting rid of clothes quickly and easily makes the question of women's role as guardians of their own virtue a far less pressing, far less conscious matter. Plenty of women don't want to think about what they might be doing that they are not supposed to do; plenty of women, indeed, desire the simple cessation of consciousness around issues of monogamy, fidelity, abstinence, and normativity. They want to lose control; they want, for once, to have someone else in charge.

As Susie Bright writes of the million women who responded to Nancy Friday's *My Secret Garden,* the chronicle of women's sexual fantasies from the 1970s choc-a-bloc full of rape scenarios and forced sex, "Either we were a million perverts clutching our grimy handbooks in shame, or these sexual fantasies were as normal as apple pie" (39). Bond's prowess with women's clothes signifies his virility, but it also speaks to women's fantasies of seduction by a powerful, determined, and accomplished lover. James Bond's ability to compete in the game of seduction is exaggerated in Bond films to the point of self-parody; the mere proximity of Bond to a woman's clothing usually causes zippers to fly apart, dresses to fall, bras to snap magically off their owners. Here excess flips his gender into something that exceeds masculinity alone.

Moreover, the hilarious exaggeration of some scenes—the Velcro quality of Plenty O'Toole's disappearing cocktail dress as she and Bond kiss in the foyer of his hotel room in *Diamonds Are Forever,* for example—suggests the comedy of the zipless seduction, as well as its desirability. It is the moment where heterosexual social comportment finds its contradiction: the gentleman is supposed to be a little less gentlemanly, should pretend it is all his idea, if the lady so desires. Zipless dexterity in this case both foregrounds the double standard of female sexual behavior and helps cover it over. It allows a woman to have her forbidden desires met while putting the responsibility for those desires squarely in the, er, lap of the person unzipping her.

This particular kind of seduction—a woman's fantasy of seduction—operates as the chief factor that turns the tide of the power struggle between good guys and bad guys in a Bond film toward the good guys. Indeed, the seduction that turns women who serve the enemy into willing allies best illustrates one of the most important recurring maxims in the Bond universe, and the one that is perhaps most important for lesbian and queer Bond fans: good sexual technique will always convert enemy women to your side. One of the favorite themes of lesbian novels in the twentieth century is the seduction of the heterosexual or married woman away from her husband and lifestyle by another woman. From Radclyffe Hall's 1928 *The Well of Loneliness* to the lesbian pulps of the 1950s such as Ann Bannon's *Odd Girl Out,* from "serious" novels of the period such as Patricia Highsmith's *The Price of Salt* to later lesbian classics like Jane Rule's *Desert of the Heart* and Katherine V. Forrest's *Emergence of Green,* turning a woman's sexuality from boys to girls, or being the woman thus turned, forms a central part of the lesbian narrative of what it means to "come out" into a lesbian identity. Like the lesbian who enters a man's territory to find a woman lover, Bond's sexual conquests make enemies and strangers into friends.

This can happen because—like the bored women in many lesbian conversion stories—Bond women are often found in the service of men who employ them for jobs that do not include sexual favors. Pussy Galore is a pilot, Jill Masterson helps her boss cheat at cards, Tiffany Case directs smuggling operations, Bambi and Thumper are bodyguards.

While Bond might bypass kindness altogether in favor of force, he often is able to overcome the resistance of these women because it is his job to employ the whole woman, to offer her more on-the-job satisfaction than she has been used to receiving, to recognize and engage all her skills. Pussy Galore in *Goldfinger* is not only a bad guy who plays for the other team, she is, as she puts it, "immune" to his charms: indifferent, hostile, and—as the film suggests by her all-consuming pleasure in her all-girl flying squadron—a lesbian. Helga Brandt, the beautiful SPECTRE agent who interrogates Bond in *You Only Live Twice,* seems a cruel torturer who will not hesitate to use a plastic surgeon's scalpel to slice off bits of Bond's skin—not to mention other parts of him—in the quest for information. Like Pussy Galore, she too succumbs to the Bond kiss, foreshadowing the ultimate defeat of their betrayed employers. When the police ask Bond why she helped him, he coyly responds, "I must have appealed to her maternal instincts." Pussy Galore is especially satisfying because her conversion to the good guys is uncertain throughout the film, finally resolved only when Bond rescues her by forcing her to parachute with him out of a crashing plane to safety. We know she is on his side, finally, when she gratefully ceases trying to signal a rescue helicopter and instead accepts his invitation to join him for love in the sand: "This is no time to be rescued."

Heat between Equals

Indeed, Pussy Galore is the hottest seduction in all of Bond precisely because she refuses to completely give in until the final moments of the film, insisting on her intellectual, physical, sexual, and gender equality, and her status as foil and competitor to Bond in every endeavor, including the seduction of women. In the novel she inexplicably decides to side with Bond against Goldfinger because, as she tells Bond later when they are in bed together, "I never met a man before" (263). In the film, Pussy Galore—despite her name—is anything but, not only in her refusal to accept Bond's sexual and business propositions, but also in her many attempts to discipline him as well. In their wrestling scene that takes place in a horse barn, he tries to cajole her back to the right side of the law, but she tells him to skip it. When he persists with "What would it take for you to see things my way?" the language of business deals prompts her withering response: "A lot more than you've got." "How do you know?" he asks tenderly, turning the discussion from business back to pleasure, indicating his mastery of the movement be-tween those registers through the mere tone of his voice. "I don't want to know," she insists.

Bond finally attempts to placate her by occupying a subservient role, one resembling the traditionally chivalric position taken by gentlemen toward ladies: "Isn't it customary to grant the condemned man his last request?" At this point she's had enough of his flirtation, and she throws him over her shoulder down into the hay. He knocks her down in turn, she tries to retaliate, and he knocks her down again. At this point he has acknowledged her as a worthy opponent. She has taken him on phys-ically, on a man's terms, and he responds by taking her seriously as an adversary. "Now let's both play," he says, and proceeds to throw her down, pin her with his body, and win the match with a kiss that begins with his force and ends with her eager response. In spite of his physical domination of her and her resistance, they both clearly enjoy the com-bat; the heat between them is in large part created by their position as physical, mental, and strategic equals.

By contrast, the 1959 novel version of *Goldfinger* attempts to keep sexual difference "straight" by turning Pussy into a subservient girl whose resistance melts in the face of Bond's cruel mastery. Some readers see in Pussy's surrender the ideology of the bigger dick writ large: Eliz-abeth Ledenson reasons that "the very phallic Pussy succumbs to the even more phallic James Bond" (422). Tilly Masterton, also a lesbian in the novel, is incapable of this shrewd discernment of phallic size, consis-tently rejecting Bond's attentions and offers of help. As a result, when she decides to rely on Pussy rather than Bond for her personal safety, she gets her throat cut by Oddjob's lethal flying hat. It could be that Pussy was never a lesbian at all, but merely—as she maintains—a sexually abused girl who had never met a man before. But the novel implies something much more complicated and interesting than mere masculinist fantasy. Both Bond and Pussy appear to be playing highly stylized parts:

> Bond said firmly, "Lock that door, Pussy, take off that sweater and come into bed. You'll catch cold."
>
> She did as she was told, like an obedient child.
>
> She lay in the crook of Bond's arm and looked up at him. She said, not in a gangster's voice, or a Lesbian's, but in a girl's voice, "Will you write to me in Sing Sing?"
>
> Bond looked down into the deep blue-violet eyes that were no

longer hard, imperious. He bent and kissed them lightly. He said, "They told me you only liked women."

She said, "I never met a man before." (263)

Pussy has many voices—gangster, lesbian, girl. But this number of personas means that none of them is authentic, or all of them are. Her role as femme to Bond's butch is simply that—another role, one that suits her for survival at that moment. And although Bond seems stereotypically masculine in his brutal seduction of her, bringing his mouth "ruthlessly down on hers" in the closing lines of the novel, it is part of his demonstration of "TLC," the "Tender Loving Care Treatment" he defines as "what they write on most papers when a waif gets brought in to a children's clinic" (264). His role will be that of a doctor, or sex therapist, or mother, to hers as abused child. And despite these parent-child and butch-femme roles, it is her phallicism that is verified in the text, constituting her as a physical equal and counterpart with her boyish, muscular body and prominent erectile tissue: "Bond's right hand came slowly up the firm, muscled thighs, over the flat soft plain of the stomach to the right breast. Its point was hard with desire" (264).

When Bond seduces women who are not his equals—Honey Ryder in the film version of *Dr. No* is a good example—things are not nearly so interesting. Although Honey has a history of bestowing black widow spiders as presents on men who have crossed her, she's basically a dumb, sweet blonde, a daddy's girl in need of love and protection who offers no real challenge to masculine supremacy. The same is true for Tiffany Case in *Diamonds Are Forever,* who offers an interesting challenge to Bond as a competent drug smuggler but who becomes far less compelling—as does the film—when she turns into a plaintive, lobotomized bimbo running around an oil rig in a bikini. Stylized gender—and stylized gender play—serves the purpose not of exaggerating the differences between masculine and feminine sexual positions, but rather of rendering both as powerful, and equally so. Stereotyped gender, on the other hand, because it emphasizes inequality, is often just plain boring.

Public Sex

Perhaps the most important thing that the mixing of business and pleasure suggests is sexuality as a public, rather than a private, form. Sexuality seals the deal, makes allies out of enemies, converts people from bad to good, makes pleasure out of business, and makes women necessary actors in international politics. The notion that women should be de-sexed in their jobs is shown as ridiculous; if women have sexual power, they might as well use it, along with all their other talents. It is important that none of the compelling Bond girls is merely sexual; all of them are intelligent, well-trained operatives of some kind who match wits with Bond, who often succeed in thwarting his efforts, and who usually triumph when they are underestimated by either Bond or someone else because they are women. Because these are business deals, they elevate sex to the level of business; because sex is public, it is neither conventionally respectable nor heterosexually gendered, in the sense that it is supposed to take place in the private realm of love and family. When the nurse finds Bond strapped to a traction table set to kill him in *Thunderball,* for example, he bargains with her by offering his silence in return for sex with her in the steam room. Here, sex is queer—anonymous, public, coerced, for pay, for power, the kind of sex that "crosses the line" of the normal, as Gayle Rubin argues in her essay "Thinking Sex": "According to this system [of hierarchies of respectability], sexuality that is 'good,' 'normal,' and 'natural' should ideally be heterosexual, marital, monogamous, reproductive, and non-commercial. . . . Bad sex may be homosexual, unmarried, promiscuous, non-procreative, or commercial. It may be masturbatory or take place at orgies, may be casual, may cross generational lines, and may take place in 'public,' or at least in the bushes or the baths" (280–81).

It is this aspect of Bond, I should like to suggest in closing, that may plant him most firmly in the sexual politics of the sixties he seems otherwise to escape, a figure of resistance to the political and domestic order symbolized by the government he serves with such clear, such repetitively foregrounded ambivalence. A suave spy whose exaggeratedly masculine character emerges from the Cold War as one fashioned to resist both national and feminine domestication, his rakish bad-boy refusal of interpellation, a refusal signaled by his mobilization of his gender as if it signified subcultural resistance, makes his gender and sexuality subcultural, aligning him with other figures of subcultural masculinity, such as butch lesbians, whose gender is also worn as a style that signifies resistance. And this, in the end, may be why dykes like Bond: because the man who wears gender as a style rather than an essence, effects conversion to his side through better technique, thrives on heat between equals, and provides women the thrill of sex unprotected by heterosexual privacy and respectability, could, in the end, just turn out to be a woman.

NOTE

1. See Judith Roof, *A Lure of Knowledge: Lesbian Sexuality and Theory* (New York: Columbia University Press, 1991); Judith Butler, "Imitation and Gender Insubordination," in Henry Abelove, Michele Barale, and David Halperin, eds., *The Lesbian and Gay Studies Reader* (New York: Routledge, 1993), 307–20; Jonathan Ned Katz, *The Invention of Heterosexuality* (New York: Penguin [Plume], 1996), among others.

4 James Bond, Cyborg-Aristocrat

PATRICK O'DONNELL

In the United States, the early years of the seventh decade of the twentieth century can be viewed, without exaggeration, as the period in which the nation began its conversion from short-lived empire into security state. While the Cold War was reaching its apogee with the Cuban missile crisis of October 1962, the main players were transforming themselves from conventional to technologically advanced war machines, in part via the Cold War proxy of the "space race." Between May 5, 1961, and May 16, 1963, the six flights of the NASA Mercury space program took place; astronaut Wally Schirra had completed an orbital flight of nine hours, thirteen minutes on October 3, 1962, just a matter of weeks before President Kennedy initiated a naval blockade and quarantine in the Caribbean of Soviet vessels sailing to Cuba with weapons and missile parts. The U.S. space program had been accelerated in these years in direct response to the single-orbit flight of Soviet astronaut Yuri Gagarin on April 12, 1961. Scientifically, the success of Gagarin's flight in *Vostok 1* posed a threat to the destinal narrative of the nation in that it clearly signaled the technological superiority of the USSR over the United States; symbolically, the spectacle of Russians circling the earth in rockets suggested that they were winning the race in the evolution of the new security state subject—a self-enclosed and entirely-self sufficient cyborg in a space suit, the heroic man-machine of the future negotiating inhuman climes by means of a technology that surrounded him and that he had also internalized.

Both in the United States and in the USSR, the astronauts became images of the future of humanity as embodiments of Cold War warriors who had transcended earthly constraints in ascending to the status of "space men." The security of the nation thus became wedded to its utopian aspirations in the formation of subjects that were—as the photographs of suited-up astronauts in their capsules conveyed—machinic assemblages[1] who possessed special powers to slip "the surly bonds of earth."[2] As Tom Wolfe portrays them in *The Right Stuff* (1979), they are technological marvels who have survived the tortures of being converted from man into machine, and yet who, at the same time, retain the quintessence of their humanity by possessing "the right stuff" that transforms them from mere mortals into the post-human elite:

> A career . . . was like climbing one of those ancient Babylonian pyramids made up of a dizzy progression of steps and ledges, a ziggurat, a pyramid extraordinarily high and steep; and the idea was to prove at every foot of the way up that pyramid that you were one of the elected and anointed ones who had *the right stuff* and could move higher and higher and even—God willing, one day—that you might be able to join that special few at the very top, that elite who had the capacity to bring tears to men's eyes, the very Brotherhood of the Right Stuff itself. (19)

Portrayed as the high priests of the national security state, the astronauts are a contradiction in terms: at once robotic and the idealization of "the human," at the same time (merely) technological prostheses and, yet, super-men, inculcating the divine in their humanity. Paradoxically, it is the very dependence of this cyborg subject-formation upon technology that reveals its vulnerability, as the human body can become the transcendent encapsulation of "the right stuff" only when it is properly connected to the right technological stuff. This complex and overdetermined image of the subject in the national security state (a state maps its destiny in terms of a triumphant response to threats from within and without[3]) finds one of its most compelling avatars in the figure of James Bond as he emerged for the film audiences of the Cold War sixties in the West. Bond is doubly revealing in the Bond films of these early years of the sixties in that he is the idealized embodiment of what I will term the "cyborg-aristocrat" and, at the same time, entirely vulnerable to its wrenching contradictions. The cinematic constructions of Bond across the early, formational 007 films were crucial, symptomatic elements in the more general conceptualization and reception of the evolving national security state subject at a critical historical juncture. Bond on film clearly had "the right stuff"; scrutinizing him will allow us to comprehend more fully the complicit relation between human and machine in the development of a "Cold War machine" founded upon the contradiction of its own human origins.

We begin, however, not with James Bond, but with Hugh Hefner, who had a big year in 1963, the same year that the second Bond film, *From Russia with Love*, was released.[4] The June 1963 issue of *Playboy* featured an extensive pictorial entitled "The Nudest Jayne Mansfield" accompanied by "behind-the-scenes clips from the low-budget movie *Promises, Promises.*" Subsequent to the publication of the issue, Hefner was arrested by the Chicago police on obscenity charges; the trial resulted in a hung jury which voted 7–5 for acquittal. In that same issue there appeared "Part 7" of the emerging "Playboy Philosophy," which equated frequent heterosexual activity and multiple partners with a healthy lifestyle, as well as the third of three parts of Ian Fleming's eleventh Bond novel, *On Her Majesty's Secret Service* (the previous two parts had been published in the April and May 1963 issues of *Playboy*). And in 1963, Hefner moved his working offices from the building housing Playboy Enterprises to his bedroom in the seventy-room mansion located on Chicago's Gold Coast, thereby materializing that element of the Playboy Philosophy which states that work should feed play, play should feed work, and both should involve plenty of sex.

The June 1963 issue of *Playboy* marks a symptomatic moment in the formation of the cyborg-in-process that lies at the essential center of the Bond character. This figure, as I will explicate it, is a contradiction in terms: on the one hand, it instantiates a fully incarnate, passionate, highly intelligent, powerful heterosexual male that might be considered the end product of secular humanism—a recuperation of all that is threatened by capitalism's conversion of the heightened individual into mass subject; on the other hand, this figure is machinic and prosthetic. The early Bond films laid the foundation for the cinematic representation of this figure, which will recur throughout the Bond films and with significant variations beyond to the plethora of century's-end cyborg films, all the robocops, terminators, matrix-dwellers, and citizens of dark cities who stand for both the overdetermination of "the human" (gendered male) and its sundering. Hefner was clearly attracted to this figure in modeling his own lifestyle and identity, and the philosophy, workplace, and collective imaginary generated in the pages of *Playboy* reflect dual investments in an aristocratic past and a cybernetic future. This image of the cyborg is, to be sure, not that of Donna Haraway's revolutionary cyborg, though it bears some of those marks. It is, rather, a retrogressive figure representing a last-ditch effort to salvage "the human," or in another register, to save the phallus in the cybernetic age. Thus, both Hefner and the Bond films I discuss here exhibit a kind of pathos, as well as a pathology, in that, in the mode of repetition, they assert the anachronisms of class and the totalized subject as identity-in-the-future. This cyborg as prosthesis is directly contrary, yet bears an eerie similarity to the revolutionary cyborg formation Haraway marks out as "oppositional, utopian, and completely without innocence . . . [n]o longer structured by the polarity of public and private . . . [defining] a technological polis based partly on a revolution of social relations in the . . . household . . . [n]ature and culture . . . reworked; the one . . . no longer . . . the resource for appropriation or incorporation by the other" (151).

Ever-clothed in his trademark pajamas and smoking jacket, Hefner is often portrayed in a capacious bed, surrounded by beautiful women and centerfold stills, the sultan in his palace, the king in his castle, wenching and working his way round the clock. One of the FAQs on the Playboy.com website is the following: Does he still wear pajamas? The answer:

> Unless he has to venture outside the Mansion, Hef can usually be found wearing pajamas. In *Playboy*'s early years, Hef worked around the clock getting the magazine out, so he didn't bother getting dressed. During the Seventies, when he was working and living in the Chicago Mansion, he realized there was no need to change at all. He now puts on a fresh pair of pajamas each morning—usually gunfighter black—and changes to another color at night. If he has company, he puts on a smoking jacket.

The 1998 A&E *Biography* of Hefner portrays him in the Los Angeles Playboy Mansion describing how he organizes his life around work and play, always dressed in those same pajamas. Each "evening" begins precisely at the same time; each night of the week is dedicated to a different purpose: Monday is new movie night, Wednesday is poker night with the boys, Friday is party night, Sunday is vintage movie night, etc. In these self-made images, Hefner reduces himself to a prosthesis, the same phallus (or the phallic order of the same) everywhere, 24/7, a living sex machine whose obsessively ritualistic lifestyle reveals a kind of self-imposed programming. Not accidentally, this figure has been associated in *Playboy* with technology and gadgetry since the early days of its publication. Alongside the frequent fictional entries by science fiction luminaries such as Isaac Asimov and Arthur C. Clarke, the progenitors of cyberpunk, one finds in *Playboy* since its beginnings articles on the latest hardware for he who wishes to pursue the Playboy lifestyle, the hippest and most expensive gadget to prove that he has successfully converted capital into prosthetic attachment, the metallic *ding-an-sich* that makes him into the perfect man.

The cinematic image of James Bond forged in the first five Bond films, all starring Sean Connery and all but one directed by Terence Young—an image promulgated and reflexively imitated to the verge of self-parody in the successive Bond films—bears remarkable resemblance to the image of Hefner carefully manufactured across the issues of *Playboy* and numerous Hefner-centered television series and specials. Hefner would become his own self-parody in these vehicles as various avatars emerge, from that of the pipe-smoking pascha sitting cross-legged in the center of a huge, circular bed surrounded by photos of naked women, to the Hefner cartoon and voiceover on the *Playboy* website who gives browsers a tour of the Los Angeles mansion grounds, complete with nude *Playboy* centerfold gardeners and pool cleaners. Both the overwrought visual manufactures of Hefner and Bond appear to be sexually omnipotent: both are given over to signature, robotic rituals (Hefner's pajamas; Bond's taglines) that define them as "unique" identities; both are surrounded by gadgets and technology upon which they are completely reliant; both are phallic and prosthetic as they bear class pretensions via their dress, demeanor, and habits.[5] Indeed, given the simultaneity of the emergence of Hefner as sexual cyborg-aristocrat and the years during which the cinematic Bond image was founded, it is difficult, on some level, to tell the two apart. Both exist as coterminous symptoms of the cultural ideal of manliness, becoming, as it were, both more and less manly (that is, heterosexually omnipotent, but increasingly prosthetic) at the height of the Cold War in the early sixties. The period which saw the premiere of *From Russia with Love* and the publication of "The Nudest Jayne Mansfield" is bookended by the Cuban missile crisis in October 1962 and the Kennedy assassination in November 1963. The anxieties attending what can only be seen in retrospect as the posthuman formation of the Cold War male subject are everywhere reflected in the early Bond films, where, on a superficial level, Bond's body becomes the "answer" to the seeming impotence, celibacy, or gender ambiguity attributable to many of the films' cybernetically enhanced villains.

Despite the binary politics of the Cold War, this subject is unified and self-mirroring, a subjectival totality without borders, as any number of "spy stories," from le Carré's complex psychological portraits to *Mad* magazine's "Spy vs. Spy" strips—where "them" and "us" are identical— tell us. Yet notwithstanding its totalization, it is at the same time schizo- phrenic, both human and robot, communist and capitalist, the "im- moral" avatar of justice and salvation with "a license to kill." Like Hefner, Bond becomes himself in his performance as prosthetic agency—a per- formance by means of which the human is framed as proscenium and aftermath, and one which is a matter of sheer repetition. In other terms, the image of Bond manufactured by the early films produces a logic whereby Bond is bound over to the human as its own anachrony, to use the Derridean term for the historical subject originating in and haunted by its own displacement in time. Derrida writes that, in the contempo- rary moment where the present is experienced as a series of proleptic anachronisms in the mode of "back to the future," the "living ego" or the totalized subject doubles back on itself and is split between its "human" past and its "cybernetic" future:

> To protect its life, to constitute itself as unique living ego, to relate, as the same, to itself, it is necessarily led to welcome the other within (. . . differance of the technical apparatus, iterability, non-uniqueness, pros- thesis, synthetic image, simulacrum . . .), it must therefore take the immune defenses apparently meant for the non-ego, the enemy, the opposite, the adversary and direct them at once *for itself and against itself.* (141)

In regarding the image of Bond generated in the early films, we can assess the intricacies of this subject produced within the context of a geopoliti- cal conflict (and contributing to its public representation) that pitted the free subject, the "unique living ego" of democracy against the putatively robotic subjects inhabiting socialist states. Yet the (male, capitalist) ideal- izations of the "living ego" produced through the imaging of James Bond are, in part, cybernetic. This contradiction, embodied in Bond, demands further attention as it lies at the foundation of the binary logic of Cold War culture, and thus is the confounding, self-refuting "origin" of that logic.

One might intuitively turn to the Bond villains as providing the primary intimations of the prosthetic subject I have described: after all, Dr. No's human hands, destroyed in a scientific experiment, have been replaced by gloved metal parts capable of crushing a rock or a skull. Auric Goldfinger's bodyguard, Oddjob, uses his hat, complete with a razor-sharp metal insert in the brim, to decapitate enemies and innocent statues. Goldfinger himself cheats at cards via remote control, using his secretary/companion, Jill Masterson, as the prosthetic projection of his own eye—later, in the role of perverse Midas, he "appropriately" kills her by covering her with gold paint, thus turning her into a statue, just as he melts down gold bars and converts them into part of the exterior of his Rolls-Royce in order to smuggle the goods. His gold fetish, as well as his name, reveals a desire to be as closely identified with gold as possible—in effect, to be gold, metallic, if only by means of substitution, which is equated of course with the megalomaniacal desire to be the sole repository of all gold, to be a complete, totalized embodiment of it. SPECTRE no. 2, Emilio Largo, casts himself as a Hefner-like playboy, but with only one eye, yet as a form of overcompensation he is equipped with a multitude of technological devices that aid him in the attempt to establish worldwide domination, including the *Disco Volante,* a yacht that jettisons part of itself and converts to a hydrofoil during the climactic moments of *Thunderball.*

And then there is SPECTRE no. 1 himself, Ernst Stavro Blofeld, before *You Only Live Twice* only a voice or a limb coming into the camera's view, yet here seen by Bond full-face for the first time as he is magnificently played by Donald Pleasence, a Frankensteinian assemblage of scars attempting to run the world by remote control. Collectively, the early Bond villains appear to represent everything Bond is fighting against, shadowing everything he is trying to preserve: They are inhuman monsters, mired in manners and rituals, isolated in their fantastic laboratories, concealed islands, and hidden caverns, attempting to dominate the world through the projections and extensions of aristocratic, scarred, robotic identities, while Bond, corporeal (often enough with his shirt off), equally aristocratic in manner, but passionate and sexual, seems to be their obverse as the last man standing, always the final human barrier before the reign of the human accedes to the reign of the cyborg. If the Bond villains are on one side of the divide Derrida describes as the "other within" the "living ego," by which he means the subject living in the present composed of a future contending against a past, then Bond would appear to be on the other as the fullest remnant of "the human," whole and complete unto himself, the perfect body gazing into the mirror to shave an aquiline jaw or catch a glimpse of a beautiful woman unclothing herself in his room.

Yet this is to instantiate a binary that these films undermine or collapse in every conceivable register, most notably that of the political. It is not unusual to view the Bond films and, as I have mentioned, any number of the plethora of espionage and spy films that populated the Cold War cinematic landscape from the sixties through the nineties, as thinly veiled political allegories marking the confrontation between East and West, democracy and communism, these binaries themselves often articulated in terms of the liberal human subject vs. the robotic total-itarian subject. There is no doubt that the early films I consider here can be adequately read in this light, or that the audiences viewing them in theaters would have had little trouble equating Bond with freedom, the West, and democracy, and the Dr. Nos, Goldfingers, and Blofelds with Khrushchev or Mao, totalitarians with grand technological and social schemes, rapping their shoes on the summit table or gesturing fanatically at the multitudes. The logic here seems irrefutable: Bond represents democratic freedom, vigorous manhood, mobility, life; the villains rep-resent totalitarian bondage, machinic entropy, paralysis, death.

Countering this easy set of oppositions which appear, as it were, on the surface of the Bond films, Bond can be seen at one remove as merely the obverse of his arch-enemies, and thus in many respects their mirror image. Yet viewing Bond in this fashion only offers a certain reinscription of the Cold War binary in seeing it, like all binaries, as an imaginary bifurcation of the Same. Thus, the villains have their gadgets, and Bond has his. The increasing functional importance of the Q section and the technology it produces for Bond's use is reflected in the ever-enhanced gadgetry and sheer amount of film time given over to its production and use as the films evolve; the "deepening" of Bond's subjectivity as we move through the early films is concomitant with the elaboration of the tech-nology associated with his exploits. One can see this process at work in the evolution of "Q" as a character across the first three films: in *Dr. No*, his name is revealed to be Major Boothroyd, but he is referred to as "the armourer"; in *From Russia with Love*, he is referred to as the "equipment officer" and is played for the first time by Desmond Llewelyn, who would have the role of Q in seventeen Bond films; by the time we get to *Gold-finger*, he is hereafter referred to only by his code letter, his agency entirely collapsed into his function, and that function increasingly im-portant as he becomes something of Bond's sidekick, following him to exotic locales where he can demonstrate on site the latest gadget in the arsenal. And what Q makes for Bond are technological extensions of Bond, or in the Derridean language, cybernetic "defense mechanisms" whose purpose is both to protect and to meld with the "living ego" of 007. The infamous Aston Martin DB5 introduced in *Goldfinger*, for example, is clearly just a prosthesis for Bond himself: briefed only once by Q on the car's elaborate controls, in the film's car chase scene Bond instinctively moves from gadget to gadget in foiling his pursuers, but perhaps most importantly, he uses all of them. On one level, we might say, of course he does: true to the dramatic unities, if in the opening scenes of the film Q introduces a device that will produce an oil slick or eject a passenger, that device will most certainly be used in a car chase. But as Bond becomes one with the car, or the mini-helicopter, or the fashion accessories concealing knives and explosives, it is as if the totality of these resources and his expertise must be deployed in order for him to achieve totality *as* Bond. He is, no less than any of the villains, on the way to becoming a cyborg, if we conceptualize this retrogressive formation of the cyborg as the merging of the human and machinic in the total subject.

Yet, just as the plots of these films unfailingly introduce into the self-mirroring binary of the Cold War a third or mediating element—most notably in the figure of the arch-villain himself, who is neither pro-Soviet nor pro-U.S., and is only interested in employing Cold War rivalries and nuclear politics to his own ends—so, too, Bond serves as an embodied, sundering mediation of the relation between the cyborg and the human. In this respect, as a subject, he is both proleptic and nostalgic; more precisely, he embodies the anxiety of the human on the way to becoming a cyborg—an anxiety founded precisely on the recognition that the essence of "the human," in the most conservative or retrospective notion of that concept, depends upon its becoming increasingly cybernetic.

What is Bond? What are his symptoms, the marks of his presence, his customs and habits? Cinematically, he is both a mode of repetition and a representation of corporeality: across twenty films, the same character with a different body (often enough, partially unclothed, or rigged out in some kind of special gear) attached to the name of various actors, hence the game of who is the best Bond, the one who conforms to our image of who Bond should be. Many regard Sean Connery as the original Bond, in the sense that he was not just the first, but also the most "authentic." Connery's Bond, in the early films, is a constellation of ritualized habits and gestures, suavity and aristocratic manners, emanating a so-called "rugged individualism" marked by the actor's rugged good looks, hirsuteness, and calm agility in the action sequences. I have already remarked on how Bond in these films takes on some of the cybernetic characteristics of his antagonists, but he is also differentiated from them, and thus from the human-cyborg binary by the parodic, cross-marked assimilation of both cyborg and human elements in his character. For example, we can scrutinize the notion of Bond as sex machine: what would seem to be a sign of his hu-manliness—his ability to get it up at a moment's notice, his ability to satisfy any number of women under any set of circumstances, including engaging in a covert version of public sex on the canals of Venice at the conclusion of *From Russia with Love,* on rafts, in hot air balloons, underneath parachutes—is at the same time a sign of his cybernicity, his status as projectile or prosthesis. Either way, Bond is, in effect, oddly both overdetermined and underdetermined as human and as machine: no human male could possibly perform in this repetitive mode under all countervailing circumstances, no machine or cyborg-in-process could possibly be so hairy—and this double effect constitutes the parodic mode of Bond's mediate subjectivity.

In a slightly different key, we might note how utterly boring and predictable Bond is, caught up as he is in the manneristic rituals that define him, apparently reproduced best, or most authentically, or originally, by Sean Connery—an originality that from the beginning reproduces itself as a mode of repetition. Bond's innate identificatory conservatism and aristocratic style, reflected in all the familiar taglines ("shaken, not stirred"; "the name is Bond—James Bond"), seem both at odds with and aligned to his generic status as action hero. Bond must be both full of surprises—gadgetary and phallic—and able to meet a sudden turn of events with unflappable calm and technical precision; at the same time, he is repetitively machinic, not just in his sexual conquests, but in all of his performances: recall again the technology of the Aston Martin of *Goldfinger,* each gadget (and all of them) deployed in a precise fashion, the chaos and sudden turns of the car chase punctuated by Bond's robotic engagement with the car's prosthetic attachments. Bond seems bound in these ways to a carefully circumscribed, ritualized identity (the identity of the human survivor, the last man standing) that is at once all too human given the plethora of devices that must shield the body from its own mortality, and all too cybernetic given that what defines its humanness are the conservatory mechanisms and behaviors which are increasingly, and predictably, autonomic.

To complicate a comparison made earlier, the critical difference between Bond and Hefner lies precisely in what I have described as the parodic mode of Bond's subjectivity, which enables the negotiation between a corporeal humanism (marked as a form of masculinity) and a retrogressive cybernicity. Hefner is a figure of mere repetition, a Peter Pan whose hair grays and whose face wrinkles but who is always surrounded by the same bevy of blonde, tan twenty-year-olds, whether he is thirty or seventy; Hefner's is always the one, same body. He is a pure, mere robotic assemblage, though one which ironically ages. Bond, on the other hand, is more complex at multiple levels: he is, of course, literally multiple in that there is not one but several screen Bonds in a kind of eternal return of the same that is always more notable for its variation from the original than its replication of the first Bond, even if all the gestures and taglines remain intact across several films and several Bonds. We have watched Hugh Hefner age over the last four decades, and as he does so, the bevy of buxom twenty-year-olds that constantly surround him—contrary, we can be sure, to his intentions—makes the fact of his mortality increasingly visible. But because Bond is replaceable, because the cinematic representation of him across forty years is truly an assemblage, his mortality remains both visible, as his body is always at risk, and hidden within, while constituting the need for the shell of gadgetry, habiliment, and ritual that constitutes the Bond character. More importantly, Bond is a moving target, constantly mediating between the human and the cyborg, slipping out of a dinner jacket and into a wetsuit arrayed with gadgetry, and above all engaging the issue of mortality in ways that Hefner/Pan never will. For Bond can die; he can be replaced by 008, just as Connery can be replaced by Roger Moore. In fact, more than one Bond film begins with the simulation of Bond's death as a ruse to his enemies. Through his death, he gains greater agency; licensed to kill, he can be killed, really or virtually, and the Bond films in general are replete with Bond passing into unconsciousness, not really dying, and dying, at times, seemingly for real. The omnipresence of mortality in the Bond films as a continuous backdrop is what lends to his mediating and mediated subjectivity its parodic capacity to serve as symptom of and commentary upon the status of the human becoming cyborg, portending the temporality and death of both.

Bond will never die, Bond can die; in fact, he can die twice: this is the contradiction subtending his character that limns the particular qualities of this representation of a conservative humanism recognizing its potential—its future and, thus, its mortality—in the image of cyborg-in-process. As Derrida suggests, the subject in the contemporary present of anachrony—the "present" of late capitalism that extends from the end of the Second World War to the end of the twentieth century—incorporates into itself, as "other," the "difference of the technical apparatus," which he views as a "figure of death" (141). This contradiction, the death-in-life of Bond's human/cyborg subjectivity, undoes the logic of binary that constitutes it, for if the cyborg is envisioned as a permanent and immortal replacement for the human, the death of the human "part" of the cyborg renders the need—the narrative—of the cyborg meaningless. In a reversal of the common notion or anxiety about technology eventually rendering humans irrelevant, with Bond's subjectivity—the assemblage of an anachronistic human identity formation (the aristocrat) and of machinic prostheses—Bond's human death would portend the irrelevancy of the cybernetic.[6] If one of the more evident "purposes" of the Cold War was to enact a battle between superpowers over technological superiority, then the cyber-aristocratic identity formation of James Bond, one of the most cinematically visible representations of the "cold warrior," would seem to be symptomatic of the contradictions inherent in the Cold War binary which asserts the self-mirroring "differance" of contending social orders in order to ensure, via technology, the superiority and immortality of the state. Bond symptomatizes, or secretes within his identity, the subversion of this binary logic, for his mortality is, contradictorily, the *sine qua non* of the human/cyborg identity-in-process he becomes; just as surely as the gadgetry, his being subject to death serves as the guarantor of his survival as a cinematic subject upon whom box office profits can still be made across nineteen films. It does not seem too far a leap to suggest that what the superpowers called MAD (the doctrine of "mutually assured destruction" that accompanied the rapid development of nuclear weapons and the drive to technological dominance during the Cold War, which putatively served as a brake to any "first strikes" either side might contemplate) offered a similar recognition that the mortality of masses subtended any fantasies of national superiority based on the space race, the arms race, or any other competition whose progress was somehow marked in the conversion of the human into the machinic.

In a different register, the Bond movies continuously insist that, while impermanent and permeable, the human will survive on the verge of the apocalyptic, technology-ridden future that is inevitably "ours": this is the logic of the films' nostalgic affect. As I have suggested, with his manners, rituals, and aristocratic demeanor, Bond is a throwback to an earlier era, even if these are also coded as robotic; he is constantly placed in "foreign situations" and third world countries where his iconoclastic identity—from his height and accent to his stunning looks, clever wit, and sexual potency—causes him to stand out from the crowd. In other terms, there's never much secrecy to Bond's "secret agency"; he is the ego as it was, and as it could (impossibly) be again if we limit technology to the role of providing us with accessories and not allow it to take over the world as it will if one of the many cyborg-villains Bond confronts succeeds. And yet, for "Bond" as a collective narrative and cinematic assemblage spread across dozens of books and films to continue, just as he must always be on the brink of death, so too the villains must always be on the brink of succeeding; technology must always be on the brink of overtaking "the human." Thus Bond is suspended between the (human) past and the (cybernetic) future, as the point of contact between them. Across the novels and films that he inhabits as identity construct, the unresolved contest between "humanity" and "technology" is played out as if they were two different historical progressions taking place in one body, one narrative. Yet the elements of this dialectic are by no means balanced, for while "the human" is ridden with nostalgia and the knowledge of its own mortality, the "technological" is invested with determinacy, indicating that it will dominate the future and that we are all becoming increasingly cybernetic. Given the interdependency of the human and the cyborg as represented in the Bond image assemblage, however, this "determinate" future (along with any representations of what constitutes the cybernetic) paradoxically arises as a construction of human identity that perforce conceives of the future as the site of historical death. Bond's mortality, writ large, is our mortality, and we continue to be attracted to 007 because he so imperfectly represents, as a cultural projection, both the "living human ego" and "the other within," the counterpart of "technical apparatus, iterability . . . prosthesis" that we fear will one day become the totality of "us" and to which, in our flight from mortality, we are inexorably driven.

NOTES

1. The phrase "machinic assemblage" derives from Deleuze and Guattari, *A Thousand Plateaus*, where it is defined as "the precise state of intermingling of bodies in a society, including all of the attractions and repulsions, sympathies and antipathies, amalgamations, penetrations, and expansions that affect bodies of all kinds in their relations to one another" (90). In this discussion of the machinic assemblage I term the "cyborg-aristocrat," the relation to other bodies is signified primarily in the relation between the individual subject and the technological bodies that surround and interpenetrate him—the astronaut's gear, Bond's cars and gadgets, etc. As I will argue, this set of relations also marks the social hierarchy established between individual subjects, such that those who attain aristocratic status in the machinic class system are those who "remain" human, vulnerable subjects with corporeal bodies,

but who have symbolically mastered the interiorization of technology that, paradoxically, protects and occludes their "human-ness."

2. The phrase comes from the first line of the poem "High Flight," written by Canadian Air Force pilot John Gillespie Magee as a tribute to pilots. Magee was killed in 1941 during combat over Britain, and his poem—unpublished at the time of his death—was widely circulated (see http://www.qunl.com/rees0008.html for a web page devoted to the history of the poem). It is one of those cultural artifacts that has attained an iconic status, widely read on many occasions related to flight and space travel, serving as the text for the end of broadcast day sequences for television stations, and cited by President Ronald Reagan in a speech following the *Challenger* catastrophe in 1986.

3. I explore further the "destinal logic" of Cold War subjects in *Latent Destinies*.

4. Both *The Rough Guide to James Bond* (67) and the "Art of James Bond" website (http://www.artofjamesbond.com/playboy) trace the relation between Fleming, Bond, and *Playboy* magazine from the mid-fifties to the present.

5. Of note is the distinction to be drawn between the characteristics of the cyborg-aristocrat I am attributing to Hefner and Bond, and the more "proletariat" cyborgs represented by the robocops and terminators of later vintage, often dressed in leather gear and employing street talk. While I am not primarily interested in eliciting them in all of their variations here, the traces of social race, class, and gendered categories to be found in cyborgs-in-process reveals their foundation in "the human"; for a compelling discussion of the gendering of cyborgs, see both Haraway and Byers.

6. It is interesting that movies such as *The Matrix* and its sequels begin with the premise that the machines have won and control reality, and that the only reasons humans are any longer necessary are to fuel the machines; but this projection of a "total cybernicity" runs aground of a human remnant whose purpose is to remind human subjects—one by one—that they are not machines, and, thus, subject to death within the machinic reality constructed for them.

Ian Fleming
and Style

5 Living the James Bond Lifestyle

JUDITH ROOF

In 1999, Paul Kyriazi released a ninety-minute self-help tape titled *How to Live the James Bond Lifestyle.*[1] Along with helpful tips for über-suave wannabes (such as driving a fancy car, carrying a lot of cash in a money clip, wearing stylish clothing, and copping a can-do attitude), the tape made evident a curious conflation of Bond, Frank Sinatra, and organized crime kings. Although given the dialect of the speaker I was not surprised by the helpless admiration for Sinatra as the pinnacle of mafiosi sensibility, the association between Bond and Sinatra was a bit more provocative. In learning how to tip car valets with aplomb, I gleaned insight into how these figures have merged and why. The confusion of Bond and the Godfather suggests that for the last fifty years the Bond figure has served as the nostalgic champion of an older order, a Law that is slowly disappearing in favor of another, more diffuse, less hierarchical order. The Bond figure's performance of stylistic efficacy, mummified retroaction, and homeopathic opposition enact and salvage the Law of the Godfathers, securing those things—certainty, identity, history—we seem to have lost.

Arche-Bond

There is no factual or "historical" origin for the Bond figure, even if we confidently trace the figure back to the character created by Ian Fleming. Whatever Bond began as—and continues to be in the novelistic universe sustained arguably now by Bond films—is no longer what the figure Bond has become. The Bond figure has transmuted into a collection of representations, media, and commodity links, and the collection has shifted fractally from any original Bond character, which, like all other manifestations of the Bond phenomenon, now swirls endlessly around a rolling Bond that always gathers moss. In this sense, the figure of James Bond has accrued rather than evolved. The difference between accruing and evolving is the difference between mythic connotation and history, but it is also the difference between efficacious intervention and near tragedy. The Bond figure's floating collection of traits and associations can act without the constraint of personal causality. The character Bond must negotiate a series of choices involving loss and pain. The latter may be more characterologically satisfying, but the former can intervene more directly and effectively. The Bond figure does not have an ever-maturing and traceable trajectory over which historians of the "fact" can mull (and if they do so mull, it is always an effort to correct the rift or detour the Bond figure has taken). Rather, Bond's history is a non-history or the history of not having any history except a veiled link to the most basic Arche of all—the Law of the Father.[2] Thus, instead of evolving in response to selective pressures and presenting to us in one excessively sagacious (if not well-aged) individual the results of fifty years' learned experience, the Bond figure appears each time as if anew, like a myth constantly, but timelessly, regenerated from the same time-honored spore.

We might think that this "spore" is Ian Fleming's protagonist in the series of novels he wrote between 1953 and 1964. Fleming's Bond character does evolve; he reacts, learns, carries with him the lessons of his own traumatic history. The *Doctor No* Bond remembers painfully *Diamonds Are Forever*'s Tiffany Case. Bond's body and mind become increasingly scarred; his experience makes him reluctant at times, less foolhardy at others. We can go back to the character and series of novels again and again. The literary character James Bond, however, is not coterminous with the cultural Bond figure, much as Fleming fans and historical purists would like to constrain the figure to some species of referential accuracy. Bond has proliferated through culture primarily as the cinematic Bond, a figure who has crackled away from the novelistic, following a new trajectory and chronology whose relation to history is one of updated repetitions.

As a cultural brand—as a signifier that circulates with a large degree of recognition through Western culture—the Bond figure does not share the complex developmental shadings of its literary progenitor. A creature of almost pathological consistency, which would seem itself to be a side effect of Bond's constant cinematic rejuvenation, the Bond figure appears as if it always already knew everything—as if it was spawned with skills intact and little memory of past tortures which have no cumulative effect on him. Each Bond always knows everything already and is equally able (well, except the Roger Moore Bond, who is always equally unbelievably able) as all other Bonds. Bond's syntagm, if you will forgive recourse to a lexicon of semiotics, is almost always the same. Diachronically, however, the Bond figure snowballs through cultural consciousness, accruing layers and associations—the actors, the villains, the technologies—that are at the same time equally dissociable from the thing we understand to be Bond. What characterizes the Bond figure, then, is a resistance both to narrative notions of history as a series of cause-effect relations and to the archival search for a true source in favor of a species of performative iteration, which, as we shall see, is an iteration of an efficacy operated through style and associated with the phantasmatic order of a Mosaic (Law meted through the Father) past.

The obvious example of the inharmonious intersection of the Bond figure and history is the phenomenon of the changing Bond player. Through the willing wink of millions, Bond has been transmuted decade by decade into a younger, now Scottish, now English, now Irish bloke careening through a series of formulaic films. Rejuvenated in each impersonation, the Bond figure gains a series of associations completely alien to Fleming's Bond project, including associations made through actors' résumés—the Brosnan Bond is helplessly linked to Remington Steele and Thomas Crowne, for example—the cultural valence of the various songsters who provide the films' title music, the currency of the "Bond girl," and the increasingly shameless product links. In addition, the films themselves have their own, very-out-of-Fleming's-order history, and they all relate to and signify the cinematic milieus within which they were produced.[3] All of the films (with the exception of *Casino Royale* and *Never Say Never Again*) were made by the same production company and designed by a sequence of associated film production personnel.[4] Appearing sometimes sporadically, each of the films also stands by itself; that is, none depends upon the audience knowing a particular history (not like the *Star Wars* series, for example). Yet at the same time, the films and their protagonists spur constant comparisons among the various Bonds, the films' technologies, the attributes of villains, and the films' levels of frivolity. The industry of Bond trivia, anxieties about the proper or "real" Bond, and comparisons to the Fleming novels all embody both nostalgia and some worry about the history that is elided in favor of something else. If the Bond figure's dissemination evades narrative history, what version of existence through time might define the Bond phenomenon, and what does that version tell us about how the Bond figure is operating culturally?

Instead of signaling progressive stories of evolution or development, the figure of Bond presents an archaeology in both the anthropological and the Foucauldian senses of the word. Archaeologies, literal and metaphorical, present layers rather than lines, associations rather than causalities. Material may be linked or unrelated, but it all characterizes a particular place, which resonates what it has gathered. In the figurative anthropological archaeology of the Bond figure, texts jiggle and resonate, appearing to provide some labyrinthine textual trail as films derive from books and books from historical precursors. Somewhere in the Bondian substrata, for example, persists the prose fictional Bond, who has a history made up of changes in attitude and experience accounted for by the cause-effect pattern of his episodic assignments. This Bond is archaeologically imagined as subtending the cinematic Bond, who of necessity both deviates from the "original" and imports his own sets of characteristics. These characteristics, in turn, are imagined to relate to the contemporaneous conditions of each Bond production, and so on. Each manifestation of the common signifier we call Bond can be accounted for by his context, the conditions of film production, and the political tenor of the contemporaneous environment. In this archaeology, Bond is always an antidote or compensation, two reactionary modes of relation that situate Bond as a product of his various ideological environments.

Certainly, a figurative archaeology of the spy has already been achieved by several cultural historians who trace the substratum of the literary James and track the cultural debris that has piled atop him, including the multi-year versions of the cinematic Bond, the actors who play him, and the unchanging threats of world disaster.[5] Some such anthropologies have argued persuasively for understanding Bond as a creature of a particular context. Embedded, for example, in the detritus of the Cold War, Bond is newly historicized as a Cold War defense mechanism, a fantasy of potent superiority in troubled times.[6] More recent cinematic Bonds are assumed to correspond to newer scenarios of world power as would befit the proper and predictable relations among texts and their conditions of production. Significantly, the Bond enemy never really changes, at least in the films, fixed as a morphing transnational crime organization headed by an evil quasi-corporate genius with an odd taste in subordinates and a perverse fondness for totemic pets. In this archaeology, Bond represents a fantasmatic compensation for cultural powerlessness.

The historicist archaeologies of Bond contrast with a more Foucauldian archaeology, which eschews historical causality and contextual exegesis in favor of a more systemic spinning of ideas, structures, and multiple manifestations of power. Bond has never been either singular or linear, but has always and ever increasingly been a moving collection of projections, defenses, and compensations, coexisting through time, portrayed through a same-yet-always-different version of the solitary, inventive hero who is licensed to break the law in order to enforce a higher law and a greater good. In this archaeology, Bond is less an effect than a magnet who never leaves anything behind. Every scrap, word, image, take-off, knock-off, version, and copy sticks to the Bond phenomenon like glue, not so much layered as perpetually intermixed, like a large punch bowl to which people keep adding different ingredients. What might at the beginning have been an elegant champagne punch becomes a witch's brew still called "punch" only by virtue of its being located in the same receptacle. And the point to this rather unpotable metaphor is that its identity both as punch and as some version of the original concoction depends upon a persistent habit of retroactively resignifying all changes, no matter how brutal, as champagne punch—or Bond. The effect is a figure who grows and changes and still retains the illusion of its original character. The advantage is that such a snowball is well able to respond to and compensate for almost any trauma, emergency, loss, insecurity, suffered by populations in changing times. And the way this response occurs is not as much through the character's simple narrative efficacy—he is able to dispose of any threat—but rather through the fact that he is able to dispose of the threat *with style* that changes and yet always manifests the same inevitable reference to an *ab original* power. And like the punch, his style is always retro, always carries with it the efficacy of nostalgia as a nostalgia for efficacy. The Bond figure's power resides in his ability to embody an arche-history without having a history at all.

This "arche" is the sense of an ab original empowerment, as if the Bond figure carried with it the moment of the commencement of the Law of the Father. This sense of aboriginality or ancientness is precisely what gives such power its feeling of authority. I call this Law "Mosaic" in the sense that Bond, like Moses, embodies a Law whose only precursor or history is divinely paternal. Such Law is in itself absolute and requires no

James Bond (Sean Connery) emerging from protective gear in *Goldfinger* (1964).

debate, decision, or introspection. Such Law connotes the beginnings of history while its claim is to timelessness. The Bond figure, as I will discuss later, enacts this Law of the Father, this combination of agelessness and timelessness, through the somewhat odd vector of style. In this sense, the Bond figure is always a creature of paradox, in its juxtaposition of the Mosaic and the trivial, in its totally dated agelessness, and in the temporal layering always at play in its consumption.

We can never, for example, really look at any Bond who *was* except through the lens of the Bond that *is*, even if we don't like this newer Bond so much or think him unfaithful to the original. This figure of the efficacious soldier cum detective cum potent womanizer is a complex compendium of cultural grafts, arranged more like a mummy than a hydra, traits, identities, theme songs, actors, villains, all wrapped around a figure still evoked by its nest of lint, dropping shreds and associations with every move, never not conveying the Bond within, but unable these days to exist in any pristine aboriginal Bond form. This more Foucauldian notion of a Bond archaeology suggests that the tracing of cause, effect, character, and history is more or less impossible since our version of then is now and Bond's now is then and our tracings are always retro in the several meanings of the word. Explications of Bond are like unraveling a ball of yarn as it is being wound. His contexts are multiple,

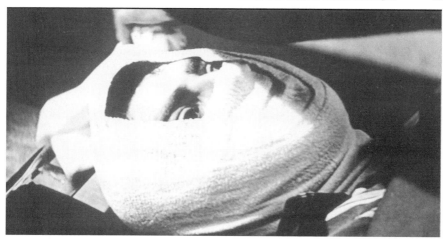

Postmortem Major Derval (Paul Stassino) in *Thunderball* (1965).

layered, and shifting, both diachronically and synchronically and both at the same time.

This Bond mummy has been mustered as a potent but human weapon in more than apprehensions of Cold War politics, appearing in fifty years of fantasies of competing versions of the Law—government versus government sometimes in the novels, legal nation versus extra-legal organizations in the films, whose threat, rather than being merely world destruction or epic material gain, is the specter of a law more efficacious (and older and more basic—more Mosaic) than the bumbling goodwill of democratic governmental organizations. As more than sim-ply an artifact whose placement in history unmasks his mystery, Bond is a figure who succeeds both narratively and culturally for three reasons beyond the simple effects of compensation, fantasy, or the conditions of production: (1) Bond represents a potency enacted through style, a style which seems to change as Bond goes from Aston Martin to BMW (and back to Aston Martin?), but in changing doesn't change at all—a style which, it turns out, is the substance, itself the fount of efficacy in a system where the signifier finally catches up to the signified, or at least is de-signed to provide the illusion that it does. (2) Bond is a mummy, figura-tively speaking, whose license has always already been, wrapped and layered in reference to what was, not the originary Bond who might himself be traced to Sherlock Holmes and Maugham's Ashenden, but to the imaginary time of the rule of absolutist paternal law. (3) Bond's mummification (represented in many forms in the Bond films) is ho-meopathic; that is, Bond can battle the evil that threatens because he works like the evil that threatens. He is a taste of their own medicine, and he can do this because he is both relevant and eternal at once, a mummy slave to style.

The Mummy Returns; or, The Style of the Living Dead

Bond's style signifies. It is actually performative in the sense that it does what it is in so being. The completely natural extension of his being, Bond's style is the correctly innate, thoroughly appropriate vestige of the alpha male. Style gives Bond authority; Bond's style is the word that enacts Law. But Bond's style is never style alone; it is the signifier of a being whose existence equals authority. Bond's style enacts a perpetual return to a mythic moment when the Law was the word and the word was uttered by the Father in a hierarchical vision of order and emplacement. Bond's style is always retro, mummified. Bond's style itself returns the past to the present, even, and especially, in its most futuristic moments, and it is in this constant temporal inter-referentiality that Bond can make style work as Law.

To read the Bond figure's style, we might begin with the most ham-fisted instance of style. A semiology of Bond's haberdashery—one of the qualities in which Kyriazi seeks to instruct us—reveals nattiness, propriety, versatility, careless wealth, and, in the case of the Connery Bond, an acre of leg proudly displayed. See, for example, Bond padding through Goldfinger's Miami hotel in his very brief beach holiday outfit. Carelessness, implied by all of these qualities, is the key tone—not a carelessness akin to sloppiness, but carelessness in not having to think at all about impeccability. This carelessness translates to a naturalness or innate capacity for self-presentation which itself bespeaks confidence, security, and mastery, not as attributes gained through hard labor or study, but as intrinsic to Bond. Bond does not have to worry about what to wear, or even, apparently, about what to pack. Rather, he always has the proper clothing for any occasion—clothing sometimes mysteriously supplied, and always cared for. When Bond returns from the casino or removes the jumpsuit from atop his tuxedo, he always scrupulously hangs his jacket, tosses it folded properly upon his bed, and adjusts his bow tie. Bond has two modes of dress: formal and coordinated casual, the latter less evident as his adventures seem always to require at least a sports jacket and tie.

But consider the meaning of this sartorial propriety. The Bond figure accomplishes the most challenging tasks while dressed up. This isn't simply about some historical formality of dress we have lost of late. Even in the sixties and very early seventies, when the Connery Bond was fashion-plating his way across the Alps, the golf course, or the high-rise Vegas penthouse (to which he mountaineers in a tux), other manly heroes (Steve McQueen, Clint Eastwood) were accomplishing their tasks in a more leisure-suited, off-the-rack ambience. Only the Rat Pack is as natty as Bond, and that fact, as we shall see below, is one significant connection between them even though they are less action heroes than conniving lounge lizards. This whole tendency toward the informal only increases, so that lately the be-tuxed Bond is even more unusual, the ubiquitous evening clothes operating as an even more pointed reference to class, suavity, and savoir-faire (especially in relation to the Vin Diesels of the world).

The clothes, however, are not the only thing that makes the man. Add this sartorial sense of security to a semiosis of carriage—Bond never hesitates, looks as if he feels out of place, or seems not to know what to do socially—synecdochized by the way Bond deploys his eyes and shoulders (the Connery Bond and perhaps the Brosnan Bond, but only sporadi-cally the Moore Bond, whose overplay of the cynical occasionally regis-ters as a kind of simpering insecurity), and the effect is efficacious pres-ence. Bond is the man who is most in place where he is out of place, the man whose style says he belongs, the man who belongs by virtue of not belonging—by virtue of his not having even to master the rudiments by which mastery itself is signaled. In other words, Bond's physical style signifies mastery in the ways in which it conveys the sense that mastery has never even been an issue. He has always had it, or to put it another way, it was always already there.

The two arenas where this efficacious style is made spectacularly manifest are the gambling tables and the bedroom—two sites not as unrelated as they might seem. Bond approaches gambling—or under-takes its challenge—without even flinching, just as he undertakes the bedroom duties thrust upon him as a British agent. Gambling is a figure of the same natural mastery as Bond's haberdashery. Bond need not worry about luck since he is always already lucky. He never loses. Gam-bling is also a figure of Bond's relation to male adversaries. With the stakes on the table, Bond dominates effortlessly precisely because he never flinches. In the battle of the lowering horns, Bond never even bows his head. In Bond films, gambling is always the gauntlet, tossed down to draw out his adversary, a little preliminary showdown of raised gen-tlemanly hackles. The first movie scene in which Bond appears is at a gambling table in *Dr. No,* where he bests his first adversary and sexual conquest, Sylvia Trench. Bond often reveals himself as a gambler who is more dangerous than he looks as he plays the fool beside Plenty O'Toole in *Diamonds Are Forever* or stares down Emilio Largo in *Thunderball.* He even outcheats the cheaters as he takes the golf match from the ponderous Goldfinger by cheating better than he. Bond's filmic connections to casinos are so plentiful that it is difficult to avoid the obvious gambit of taking the casino as an allegory of Bond's existence: he risks, he prevails since he has the luck. His venues are opulent; his opponents are gamblers wealthier than he, whose danger, like his own, is always hidden beneath a veneer of good manners and upper-class sportsmanship.

Just as he is poker-faced at the baccarat table, so he also can always bring a poker to the dutiful sexual liaisons with duplicitous women who can never resist his advances. In fact, both the speed and ardor of their capitulations signify Bond's irresistible magnetism, the potency of the Bond kiss (even if these amorous occasions are really business deals, as Jaime Hovey argues). The Bond girls' satisfied coos attest to Bond's unerring instincts—his real manhood in an age of eunuchs who pet cats or lose their girl Fridays to Bond's advances—rendered all the more impressive by Bond's occasional protestations about the arduous nature of his job. He is the man who can do it well even when he doesn't want to. Like gambling, cuckolding is one of Bond's modes of rearing up, threatening, needling his adversary when he isn't simply on a fact-finding mission. It is also a way of getting to his enemy as he takes on the female minions of adversaries. He seduces Goldfinger's bikinied rummy spy and his trusted pilot, Pussy Galore. He tantalizes both Largo's girl Friday and the avenging sister of the slain pilot in *Thunderball.* He totally wins over Tiffany Case in *Diamonds Are Forever* and succeeds in making the dutiful Russian agent his passionate friend in *From Russia with Love.* For Bond, women are tools wielded by a master whose instant irresistibility undermines his opposition.

Bond's without-even-lifting-a-little-finger gambling luck and venereal mastery are reduplicated in his carefully orchestrated multifunctional accessories—the lighters, watches, pens, cufflinks, briefcases, shoes, and cigarette cases—which quite literally get him out of any tricky situation as a most literal operation of style. If Bond employs women as tools, he employs his prosthetic accessories as prostheses of prostheses. His gadgetry, brainchild of the almost immutable Q, provides Bond with a longer reach (magnetized watches, tracking devices carried in the heel), hidden strengths (the hand trap carried in his inner pocket, the cutting lasers in watchbands, exploding pens, portable underwater breathing devices), and means of communication (the telegraphic wristwatch). That these tools are disguised as accessories shouldn't fool any intelligent adversary, but Bond's style is so thorough and naturalized that all but his most savvy enemies (such as Dr. No) are taken in.

Bond's most potent accessory is usually his car. If we want to consider Bond's automobiles as some sort of manly metastasis, they are not so much phallic compensations (an Aston Martin or BMW? Please. No Dodge Vipers?) as they are yet another extension of his stylistic mastery. The only openly phallic vehicle Bond ever drives is Tiffany Case's souped-up Mustang, and the situation is one in which Bond enacts a clear homeopathy by beating the rube Vegas police at their own game on their own terms and in a car they can clearly understand. Bond's cars are understated, which, as we all know, bespeaks wealth and quality, and in Bond's case also hides a lethalness. Accessorized with a series of turning panels, Bond's autos transform their fenders, lights, exhaust systems, and hubcaps into machine guns, oil slick spreaders, revolving blades, and rocket launchers, not themselves particularly delicate devices, but subtle as equipment on an automobile. As in his gambling and romance face-offs, cars offer Bond one more site of understated challenge, often linked with sexual seduction, as he races the gilded Jill Masterson's sister through the Alps in *Goldfinger* or withstands the challenge of the suicidal speedster Fiona Volpe in *Thunderball* or outguns and outruns a series of black-sedaned henchmen or even helicopters. Although the chase scenes are exciting, Bond's driving skill, superb equipment, and luck enable him to dominate on the road as in the bedroom or the casino.

Bond's style, however, is also retro in the sense that even in the 1990s it hints at the clean-lined casual formality of classic 1960s suavity. This style is not uncoincidentally associated with Frank Sinatra and the Rat Pack, and with romanticized seventies renditions of American mobsters, especially *The Godfather,* which itself refers to an earlier post–World War II, pre–RICO (and pre–leisure suit) mode of dress, completely ensembled if not formal, jaunty in a sportster fashion. If mobsters are depicted as tasteless natty dressers (as they are today in such vehicles as *The Sopranos*), Sinatra's Rat Pack was the dapper version of that. The slim-lined sport coats, glaringly shined shoes, and slicked hair merged the West Side Story hood with the smooth operator in a suggestive relation to the mobster. This slide from street to paneled room is a glide from crude muscle and standoff bravado to the subtle, hidden, but threatening manifestations of the veiled and powerful paternal will. And the Bond figure, too, slides through a series of associations with British spies such as Maugham's Ashenden, and with his earlier, more literary self, moving toward and crossing the moment of sixties casino machismo, which marks Bond forever with a scent of the underworld and a sense of their conjoined and charismatic power. If Bond is "always already" in more ways than we can count, most post-sixties filmic renditions of Bond also inevitably refer to the six classic sixties Bond films. These films, whether expressions of Terence Young's personal style or not, resonate with Frank Sinatra's 1960 gang caper film, *Ocean's Eleven,* itself a vehicle for style mingled with the casino ambience of Las Vegas. This retro inter-referentiality exists not only because the film texts are contemporaneous, but because both Bond and Sinatra refer to an older order, the lurking and veiled Law, evoked at the moment it was obviously lost, and not for the first time.

Bond's various effortless masteries, including his mastery of the self-reflective prostheses of his profession, signifies mastery itself, and a mastery rarely gained through visible effort. Bond's mastery is innate. It is and always has been. In Bond's case, the clothes (or accessories) do not make the man, nor the man the clothes, but rather, the evident symbiosis between Bond and style is a *fait accompli,* a given that is always already natural. What Bond is, he always was. The always-already-thereness of Bond's style, which is also the always-already-thereness of his mastery, is also always retro in the sense that it always refers to a previous untrackable, ab original time. Like the figure of the mummy which appears again and again in the Bond films, Bond is mastery returned. And just as a mummy's form is both metaphorical (in its gilded ceremonial container painted as a stylized version of the body within) and a quite literal extension of the body itself, which once and still does exist, so Bond brings with him the ancient primeval mastery of Man, which once and still does exist. Just as mummies look like mummies because they literally are the bodies they signify, so Bond is exactly what he conveys. And just as the signifier mummy equals its signified as body grounds mummy, so Bond, too, is what he looks like: his mastery of style and his style of mastery are finally mastery. And like the mummy, Bond's style always was.

Perhaps this retro inter-referentiality (Bond equals mastery equals Bond, mummy equals body equals mummy) accounts for the surprising number of mummy images appearing in Bond films. Unwrapping the bandaged figure in *Thunderball* resembles Bond peeling away the wetsuit in *Goldfinger,* which looks like Bond emerging from the desert pipeline, emerging from the water ball, and unwrapping himself from parachute shrouds in *Diamonds Are Forever*. Even the gilded girls of *Goldfinger* resemble mummies. The cinematic recurrence of this motif of uncanny unwrapping suggests both the constant revelation of an unconscious past and the iteration of the relation between a signifier of occlusion or containment (the wrapping, pipeline, shrouds, etc.) and a signified of hidden mastery always revealed, which is Bond himself.

One way to read the evocation of the mummy is as an evocation of the drama of unveiling, where what is unveiled is the primal signifier itself. One could go so far as to read this as a specifically Lacanian drama—and indeed it fits completely. Bond is the Phallus who works best when veiled, whose power comes not in his unveiling but in our thinking we know what is behind the veil. What is important is not that we might read Bond as the Phallic signifier of desire (and Law), but that the figure of Bond always in itself plays out the flirtation of veiling in such a way that we know that the Phallus and Law are there. Bond is, in effect, about the dynamic of not reducing the mummy to the body or the Phallus to the man, but about what kind of Law subsists in our knowing mastery is indeed there, veiled and signified at the same time. As the obverse of a fetishism which would know mastery is absent but believe it is there all the same, this drama of Phallic veiling (and suggestive unveiling, which never gets us quite there) is the figuration in another register of the ways Bond himself signifies mastery and Law by never needing to bare all.

Homeopathy Begins at Home

Bond's style as itself efficacious is a sleight-of-hand which produces the illusion that the signifier-style equals the signified-potency. Like Sinatra and the Godfather (or actually his more lethal son Michael), Bond conveys hidden power, a power conveyed by a style of always seeming to have something in reserve, of being calm when all others panic. This produces the illusion of control and a belief in the figure as a site where the signifier and signified of potency coincide. The sense of reserve and the ability to perform efficaciously when called upon links these characters suggestively to an older notion of Law as a set of absolutes, whose very appearance makes them efficacious. In this Law, first delivered by Moses, prohibitions are enforced by on high, the erroneous crowds corrected by a power who delivers the Law again. This Law, though it can be disobeyed, is a notion of Law in which the signifiers of law produce a signified that betrays no slippage. "Let there be light" is one way to put it, or the old performative "I do," or the best example would be the deed to property which creates ownership on a piece of paper. The relation between this piece of paper and ownership of a piece of property is a metaphorical relation that works like language itself. The word is the deed that produces the deed.

This notion of law is itself retro in the sense that it represents an order in which the father's word was the law in a hierarchical discipline of absolute rules. "Thou shalt not." It is an older form we associate with older forms, and its weight and authority reside in part in our sense of this kind of law as older. It is the Law that fundamentalists and Promise Keepers pine for; it is the law that animates sentimental tales of Sicilian mobsters with their protective godfathers and code of *omerta*. It is a law in which the word was efficacious if uttered by the primary signifier himself, always veiled nonetheless, whispering to his *consiglieri* or closeted in a soundproof room. This law is spread without airwaves or infection, without the possibility of being overheard, and executed without failure or slippage. This Law subtends all of our various and scattered laws, which are mere distant copies and which all resort in one way or another to a nostalgia for the absolute and efficacious. Law is absolute. Petty laws remark their constant failure at absolution.

The retro associations of Bond's style exploit and perform this nostalgia for Law, but as a measure of homeopathic resistance. Bond's efficacious style is a version of the same absolutist efficacy as that practiced by all world nemeses, who are themselves singular Mosaic figures delivering the word from on high. Unlike governments—even the Soviets—who administer rule through a series of interlinked functionaries where it is never clear from whence the Word is issued, evildoers work both efficaciously and absolutely. Their word, like Bond's style, is Law. Vestiges of an older order, they sit, like Gods above their minions (or Godfathers above their capos), passing judgment and meting out punishment. Their ambitions are also from an older order: ultimate dominion. Their threat, perhaps paradoxically, is the reinstallation of absolute Law in their dominion over world resources. This is exactly like the alternate hierarchical order romanticized by our fantasies of the Mafia, headed by a farseeing, ruthless, but benevolent paterfamilias. We yearn for the Law of the Father.

What the Bond figure does, then, is combat this older order with his own enwrapped version of it. Although Bond takes orders from functionaries higher up, when he is in the field, he becomes his own law. This law is the same as the more absolutist law of his adversaries; Bond's

A mummified Bond floats in the ocean in *You Only Live Twice* (1967).

power of life and death represented by his "license to kill" renders him a homeopathic version of the threat he is sent to quell. He can only vanquish because he plays by their rules, because his quality of efficacy matches theirs. And while the power of those who aspire to world domination is manifested in secret compounds full of high-tech equipment manned by scores of drone soldiers—a kind of futuristic industrial style of mechanical efficiency—the Bond figure's power derives from his explicitly retro style which reveals in its hiding the fact that power lies within. The interplay of Bond's veiling is an interplay between the present (or future) and the past that survives despite change, a past represented by the potent, victorious, and uncomplicated man. Bond's style is always retro because the Bond figure always refers to its entire fractured history, a refraction which can't help but be retro. And thus, style operates an older law, which is also the enemy to be warded off. The question finally is why this older form of law is such a threat if it is also intrinsically nostalgic. Why are we afraid of a familiar, patriarchal, hierarchal order if we view that order as purer and more just than contemporary compromises?

The answer the example of Bond shows us is that order is ultimately the effect of a temporal dynamic, a layering through time. Like Bond's mummitude, the kernel of efficacy exists only through the dynamic interplay of signifiers in which one signifier—the one that seems to equal its signified—moors the set of shifting empowerments represented precisely by the sense of change and advancement through time—through what we might call civilization. In this sense the mooring law becomes both nostalgic and primitive, a residue of cruel propensity that must be quelled by distributing power among men and things, by democratizing

James Bond (Sean Connery) emerges from water-walking balloon in *Diamonds Are Forever* (1971).

and technologizing so that the source of the law is obscured by multiple lines of distribution. In all of the Bonds, the modern man becomes the repository of brute patriarchy, the only force that can stem the always rising specter of an old father never put to rest.

NOTES

1. In addition to *How to Live the James Bond Lifestyle,* Kyriazi has recently released *The Complete James Bond Lifestyle Seminar,* the tape in book form. The book's self-description claims: "This Complete seminar Book won't make you 007, it will make you YOU, the real you, the individuality that is you. A you that will enjoy the style, confidence, and the resort experiences of James Bond. A you that will continue your education and make thing [*sic*] happen in your life. To not dream it, but be it. After all, you're on the planet too. Why should James Bond have all the fun?"

2. The "Law-of-the-Name-of-the-Father" is psychoanalyst Jacques Lacan's formulation of the system in which the name of the father is both order and authority for prohibitions.

3. For example, Ian Fleming's first two Bond books were *Casino Royale* (1953) and *Live and Let Die* (1954). The first two big-screen Bond films were *Dr. No* (1962) and *From Russia with Love* (1963).

4. These films were produced by a group including producer Albert R. Broccoli and directors Terence Young, Guy Hamilton, John Glen, and Lewis Gilbert.

5. See, for example, James Chapman's history of Bond in *Licence to Thrill* (2000).

6. Bennett and Woollacott's excellent analysis of the function of the Bond figure goes beyond simple Cold War politics, however, in *Bond and Beyond: The Political Career of a Popular Hero.*

6 James Bond, Meta-Brand

AARON JAFFE

> People don't live by bread alone; they live mostly by catch phrases.
> —George Creel, 1917

In what follows I analyze "James Bond" as a brand name, a unique selling proposition moving through a public reality inhabited by other, often only slightly less nuanced propositions. This way of reading Bond, I want to argue, is one of the few that can help account for all his versions: first order and second order, literary and cinematic, authorized (Fleming), under-authorized (Cubby Broccoli, the post-Fleming serialists), and unauthorized (the sundry popular appropriations and commercial uses). It addresses the continuity of the brand, the startlingly predetermined 007 pattern that spans very different cultural domains. It is a pattern in which the bizarre Bond villains serve as so many failed agents of commodity culture—in effect, clumsy, careless consumers and overzealous advertising men—and thus perfect nemeses to Bond and the PR ideas that prop him up. Their real crime—the central difference with Bond—is dereliction of duty to the values of the bourgeois world of commodities. In contrast to the metonymic command offered by adversaries like Doctor No, Bond represents the ultimate yes man, a charismatic, deterritorializing, and metaphorizing sanction of consumption.[1] In other words, on levels of both form and content, Bond is the apotheosis of consumer throughput. The pattern is there from the first Fleming novels. It goes beyond the literal and figurative "death of the author," because, in effect, Bond the meta-brand serves as the ultimate self-authorizing agent, with no fixed textual armature required.

I

> An authentic period piece. Absolutely, sixties perfect. Wild, trendy, jet-set fun culled from *Playboy* magazines: tailored suits, crazy furniture, sexy girls, champagne, drinks, fondue. Populuxe. Celebrating the cars, the costumes, it's really just about cocktails and grooming and wardrobe and style.

Why is it that this chain of associations inevitably leads to "James Bond"? Strictly speaking, the words come from the production commentary of the "extras" DVD accompanying Steven Spielberg's *Catch Me If You Can* (2003), the "true story" of Frank W. Abagnale (Leonardo di Caprio), boy check-forger on the lam in the early sixties, cut loose from a broken home, passing forgeries, passing himself off as a pilot, a doctor, and a lawyer, until he finds a surrogate father in the hangdog G-man (Tom Hanks) pursuing him. So what makes "Bond" such an obvious referent for a movie that's more E.T. than M.A.D.?[2]

As the cast and crew hold forth on furnishing the script with an operational language of periodizing style associations, the *mise-en-scène*, the name they're compelled to repeat most often is "James Bond." "There's something about this early jet-set age," one comments:

> Literally, Boeing 707s and Pan Am World Airways. James Bond movies. To me, it was the highlight of glamour. The colors looked cooler. Everything was very bold. Everything was very stylish. It was a time of [. . .] this whole brand new way of melding of rock n' roll music and media images that really did permeate us as a society, and I think it was really the beginning of merchandising not just of cool product but also of ideas.

Just as the name "James Bond" punctuates the language, the term "jet-set" spans it: people distinguished by their superfluity, literally, the ease, frequency, and rapidity with which jet-propelled air moves them through the sky. The fantasy is one of leisure as frictionless movement, ceaseless getting-there.[3] For all the cast and crew's talk about creating a distinct period piece, the phrase "early jet-set age" emphasizes period continuity. Now presumably being the late jet-set age, the style points still hold sway. Notice, moreover, the immanence of branding even in this seemingly naive account. What else is the whole brand-new way of melding, permeating, merchandising, moving, easing product and ideas into bodies and space other than a sense of the historical appearance of meta-branded goods? It's here in particular that "James Bond" enters the picture as a resource for establishing the continuity from what was emergent then to what is dominant now.

And, as if to shore up his infiltration of the paratext, Bond makes a decisive cameo in the movie as well. It's decisive, because it entails Spielberg dynamically cutting parts of a Bond film into his own. Tellingly, this happens the very moment the protagonist learns of his emergence as a kind of brand name. The measure of his transition from neophyte identity thief to superhuman counterfeit is conveyed by a montage that begins with him being described as "the James Bond of the sky." Immediately after this is uttered, the Bond theme music is cued, followed by a cut to the opening of *Goldfinger:* Bond in baby blue terry cloth, the words "Bond, James Bond." Binoculars lower to Goldfinger on the patio below, addled, fiddling with his earpiece. Then, a movie theater. Spielberg's protagonist is sitting in the back, watching *Goldfinger,* or, more exactly, watching Pussy Galore giving Bond the once-over: his silver-gray three-piece suit, white shirt, narrow black tie. Next, a tailor's shop, the protagonist in a mirror, trying on the suit:

> "Hello, Pussy," he intones, purposefully, his best Connery impersonation.
> "You're sure this is the suit?" he asks the tailor.
> "Positive. It's the exact suit he wore in the movie."
> "I'll take three."
> "Certainly, Mr. Fleming. Now all you need is one of those little foreign sports cars that he drives."

Finally, cut to a silver-gray Aston Martin rocketing through the city: transformation complete.[4]

More is going on here than the familiar drama of James Bond identification. True, Spielberg's protagonist plays 007 dress-up, but only after others (the newspapers, the cast and crew) cast him for the role. Bond's insertion is semiotic shorthand for mastery of associative liquidity. For Bond's part in both the *mise-en-scène* and montage, the message is one of brand association (catch phrases, as it were): "James Bond of the Sky"; "Bond, James Bond"; "Hello, Pussy"; "You're sure this is the suit?"; and "Certainly, Mr. Fleming." Insofar as *Catch Me if You Can* is an obvious parable of professionalism, it is a parable of professionalism as the performance of branding: sartorial savoir-faire will travel.[5] Bond provides Spielberg with a point of condensation for distinguishing his fake professional from that of the "real" pilots, doctors, and lawyers he so easily outperforms. Professionalism in any particular domain of expertise drops out of the picture, replaced—or else emptied out—by the competence of competence as such.[6]

One remarkable thing about James Bond is that for an agent of shadowy regimes of secrecy and security, everything about him is so much frictionless associations, jet-set common knowledge. This is the sense of Bond first appearing in blue terry cloth in a hotel room (not in a dinner jacket at the card table), our introduction to something with which we're already on familiar terms. He is, in Umberto Eco's phrase, "already known" to all, well-established, public domain from the start. Often, 007 simply introduces himself using his name—"Bond, James Bond"—signs hotel registries, checks in at airports, makes his name conspicuous to others with spectacular feats of baccarat, golf, bridge, and so forth. Even the code name 007 serves as common currency; villains are always proffering it back to him. As *Goldfinger* begins, Bond, waiting in an airport, gets outed as a "kind of intelligence operative" by a "civilian" bystander witness to his gambling exploits in *Casino Royale.*

If his claims to proprietary, well-established brands make Bond who he is within the narrative machinery—and if Bond's own name brand is itself always well-established, always preceding him, always making introductions perfunctory—then this property is also what ends up easing Bond out of the machinery into the circuits of PR. The brand name represents what's "already known" as its basic precondition, and the dictates of what comes automatically irrespective of provenance comes packaged with a promise of freedom, namely, individuality *qua* consumer choice. What's more, it comes with a promise of freedom in tow even more radical in its existential extension: this promise is no less than the vitalism of meta-branding, absolute fungibility on the level of PR. This is not a promise of subjectivity beholden to and organized by brands but brands in motion, always beholden to and organized by the agency of the name of yet another, more potent brand, the meta-brand.[7]

Allowing for inevitable disagreement among historians about the causes of PR's appearance as culturally dominant, we could say, generally, that the relevant divergence at stake is the shift from the subjective hard-sell of earlier advertising techniques to the objective soft-sell of modern public relations: compensatory substitutions of desirable brands for desires for agency, the cult of throughput, the cunning of corporate logic strung along paradigmatic chains of association, the isolated individual standing before a crowded marketplace, public reality as the vast promotional matrix called lifestyle, and that this divergence occurs by repetition and degree over the long march of the twentieth century.[8] I propose to read the entrance of Agent 007 in mid-century as a distinctive point of consolidation of this shift, a telling point of no return for our now dominant charismatic public reality of objective soft-sell.

II

That the Bond thrillers shoehorn a macro-cosmos—the geo-politics of the Cold War—into a micro-cosmos—popular, identificatory genre fun—is perhaps the most familiar of the "already known" inter-pretations. My contention is that the displacement moves in a particular direction, "throughputting" immanent concerns of the free world by processing them through Fleming's fictionalized sketch of the east bloc.[9] The best the Fleming reader can hope for, then, is world historical short-hand. The shorthand is instructive, because it rewrites the clash between modes of affiliation ("civilizations" may be a bit too ambitious for the transformations of capitalism and socialism at play in the Fleming nov-els) as a contest between hard-sell and soft-sell.

My hunch is that it's always something other than strict accounting of bad guys' evil plans that makes these bad guys so bad. Think of the centrality of the supplemental meaning that 007 invariably provides for the villains' seemingly exorable plans. "Does the toppling of missiles compensate for having no hands?" he asks Doctor No pointedly in the film version. On one level, Bond's pro forma interpretation draws atten-tion to the villain's embodiment of a kind of monstrous automatism. Yet, this form of embodiment has less to do with the consumerist fantasy of cyber-incorporation (*pace* the monstrous automaton or accessory-as-subject in the readings of Patrick O'Donnell and Craig Owens, respec-tively) than with the following PR crime: Bond villains are made to bear monstrous feats of metonymy. Bond the wild analyst reads Doctor No's filching of missiles as a kind of monstrous mechanical substitution, a pro forma compensation for pro forma castration. Just as having mechanical limbs—being relentlessly teased about them, being separated from them through token industrial mishaps—is of one piece with Doctor No's particular form of acting out—hijacking ICBMs—so too, being named Doctor No is of one piece with his doctoring a negation of the free world. Bond villains fail, as their brand names fail; their brand names fail as so many rigid designators—a phrase I'll return to shortly.

This idea of a nominalist shortcoming being an immanent critique of the east bloc is not so far-fetched as it may sound. In a recent obituary of the KGB spymaster Rem Krassilnikov, the demise of the deceased—both the man and "his" system—is put down to this very thing: that Krassilnikov "was literally fixed at birth with the stamp of Lenin's dream," because his first name is "an acronym for the Russian phrase meaning 'world revolution.'" The obituary reports that, in good communist form, Krassilnikov "married a woman whose parents had named her Ninel—Lenin spelled backwards."[10] What is it with these "evil-doers" and their names? Acronyms. Anagrams. It's this question, above all, that is the organizing preoccupation that connects obituaries for Krassilnikov appearing in the *New York Times* and Fleming's rogue's gallery. The now-defunct so-named head of counter-espionage of the now-defunct "world revolution" must have world-historical things to answer for, right? In other words, Comrade World Revolution, why did *you* do it? More to the point, the triumphal question, why *didn't* you? Metonymic expectations are built in, it seems.

That Lenin's name stands as a symbolic clearinghouse behind this is apparent enough: the husband-acronym bears the stamp of his dream, the wife-anagram bears the mirror image of his very name. Matrimonial union equals Soviet Union, consecrated under a revolutionary pseudonym, the arch sign of self-effacement as political self-discipline and revolutionary single-mindedness. Describing Lenin as the superhuman metonym in *Pravda* in 1920, Stalin tells readers that Lenin "happily combines the experience of a good practical worker, a theoretical education and a broad political outlook." It is "Lenin, and no one else," he writes, "who is today the leader of the strongest and most highly steeled proletarian party in the world."[11] And it was Stalin—the original man of steel—whose speech on Lenin's death in 1924 described the hard revolutionary ego-ideal most famously: "We Communists are people of a special mould. We are made of a special stuff."[12] Revolutionary in, revolution out: impossible metonymic feats of compression and extension follow suit up and down the supply chain.

Slavoj Žižek points to Stalin's statement as a linchpin of the obscene logic of the subject under totalitarianism, and it could equally be put down as the offending property in the nomenclature of James Bond villains. It's not "Stalin" the empirical individual who is "inexorable, steely," Žižek reminds us. "[W]hat is really inexorable and steely are the laws of historical progress, the iron necessity of the disintegration of capitalism and of the passage to socialism in the name of which Stalin, this empirical individual is acting—the ['inexorable, steely'] perspective from which he is observing and judging his activity" (*Sublime Object*

145). "Stalin" is what Žižek calls a "rigid designator," rigidly designating a putative certitude that claims to signify "in *all* possible worlds, in *all* contrafactual situations" (145). The special stuff comes into play at the point of symbolic identification, the monstrous powers of metonymic compressing and extending that steel the quotidian to the world-historical. That bizarre late moment in the Bond plot when the Bond villain lays his cards open to Bond, exposing him, in ridiculous detail, to all the workings of his evil plans (all the better for foiling them later), is Fleming's version of this logic. That Doctor No claims "I never fail" is more than classic literary hubris; it's the zero-sum game of his nominal ontology.

So, it's metonymic overkill that's the problem. In other words, the proposition is that Doctor No's name—like Stalin's or Rem Krassilnikov's or Red Grant's—fails on the level of PR, as an objective hard-sell. To wit, once the named inexorable thing proves questionable, dubious, mendacious—and it's "already known" that it will—special stuff becomes obnoxious stuff, the point of identification repulsive. More to the point, the perspective Bond occupies is that there is no objective hard-sell left, only the right objective soft-sell (i.e., the corporatist PR of finance capitalism) or subjective hard-sell (i.e., the liberal humanist advertising propositions of monopoly capitalism). And it's the monstrous metonymic thinking of the hard-sell (either the east bloc's objective version or the liberal humanist's subjective form) that is answerable for its impossible feats. Promise a unique selling proposition, and you'll have to answer for it. You say world domination. I say inept PR.

Let's compare this formulation to the "already known" charge about once-existing communism; namely, that the ultimate evidence of its villainous inhumanity is its erstwhile affective deficiency—its demand-side shortcomings. A cognate text, arguably drawn from the same cultural moment, is Robert Heinlein's *Puppet Masters* (1951), the science fiction apologia for McCarthyism. The parasitic slugs turn the citizens of the free world into affective sleepwalkers with "no emotion . . . except the contentment that comes from work that needs to be done." At one point, the novel's protagonist says the following: "I wondered why the [slugs] had not attacked Russia first: the place seems tailor-made for them. On second thought, I wondered if they had. On third thought, I wondered what difference it would make" (40, 108).[13] "You must be working for the East with your disregard for human life," says movie Bond to Doctor No. The disregard for human life pertinent to Bond is the annihilation of surplus affect—no affective excess, no demand-side metaphoric slide—

that's not put down to inhuman over-identification with the cause. "World domination. That same old dream." Along these lines, it's the intergenerational gift of the name "Rem"—Krassilnikov's first name—that's so unsettling to his obituarists. When you've named your child "world revolution," you've not only limited its career choices, you've fully instrumentalized its affect—killed affect by simultaneously over-internalizing and over-externalizing it. Once again, Doctor No is relevant. Because his unique selling proposition has been tied to a notion of its own inexorable futurity, that *same old dream*, it fails on all three of its key terms: it ceases to be unique, it ceases to be selling, and it ceases to be a proposition. Above all, and here's where Bond provides the contrasting position, it ceases to provide a quantum of sartorial solace in the surplus affect that comes packaged as brand choice.

III

> Bond verified that his room had been searched [. . .] by an expert. He always used a Hoffritz safety razor patterned on the old-fashioned heavy-toothed Gillette type. [. . .] The handle of a safety razor is a reasonably sophisticated hideout for the minor tools of espionage—codes, microdot developers, cyanide and other pills. That morning Bond had set a minute nick on the screw base of the handle in line with the "Z" of the maker's name engraved on the shaft. The nick was now a millimetre to the right of the "Z." (*Man* 86–87)

Classic Fleming formula: Bond lingering over some harmless found object, here one for the most quotidian of human activities, grooming. Not only does the object prove to have secret properties recommending it for the work of espionage, but it also turns out to be already inscribed in a narrative frame of world-historical contest. Ordinary razor? Hardly. It's a "tell," a secret language, spoken by agents of counter-espionage who use the minutiae of branded goods as so many calling cards. We see here what Michael Denning means when he describes Fleming's novels as less "guides to consumption, 'how-to' books" than exhibits of consumption redeemed, ideological dreamscapes where "the trivial contests" of leisure time are invested "with global intrigue" (*Cover Stories*, 100–101). Here, beating Hugo Drax at bridge is just as significant, more intricate, and perhaps an even more gratifying narrative than foiling his rocket caper.

Denning is right; Fleming is writing a romance of killing time. This project follows from the idea that brand choices—selections from the shelves of the world of commodities—live with a kind of existential, world-historical vitalism. The ideological work of Bond, his "cultural meaning and power," is in his dream that bourgeois time off really matters. Idle downtime—in the bathroom, before and after work, on the commute, in hotel rooms on business trips, at the casino, on the links, at the restaurant, in the airport lounge—turns out not so idle after all. Not only is it completely circumscribed by world-historical plotting, but it is also time punctured by a vector of radical freedom. The cultural operator here—the master agent, as it were—is none other than the brand name itself. The dream of Bond rests *not* on the idea that the hero of consumption could be you or me, not that Bond is some kind of ideal ego. Rather, it rests on the idea that the secret agent of consumption—the vital id-like force beyond the dictates of determinism—is that brand. It's the "Cardboard Hero" on the front of Solitaire's packet of Player's cigarettes that takes on a life of his own.[14]

Commodities choose you. A well-known nibble of James Bond ephemerata: the secret agent's ubiquitous marker—"The name's Bond, James Bond"—is first a found object, lifted from the spine of a book on Fleming's bookshelf, one *Field Guide to Birds of the West Indies* by the American ornithologist James Bond. It was, Fleming said, "suitably dull and anonymous."[15] However improbably, Fleming's "James Bond"—like Orwell's "Winston Smith," that other civil servant and cipher of the Cold War's corporatist imaginary—is selected for blandness and impersonality. Bond's name is selected for a requisite lack of associative feedback in psychic interiors, a suitable quality for a name that is to become a machine of meta-branding.

Perhaps, then, it's not too surprising to find much of the appeal of Fleming's bestsellers keyed to the exaggerated, often superfluous presentation of named goods. Kingsley Amis calls this the "Fleming Effect."[16] Amis's argument is that the science of Fleming's "science-fiction" depends on the fastidious detail with which he embroiders Bond's objects—the Hoffritz safety razor, the Rolex Oyster Perpetual watch. Extrapolating from Amis a bit, 007 is a hero of a form of fictionalized reality, real insofar as it is defined by detailed attention to brand-name commodities and their consumption. To return to the language of PR, 007 is the hero of the objective soft-sell—the challenge and game of Bond is to posit lifestyle as a reality where premium brands hold as the *sine qua non* of high living. To be "already known" as a high liver, that's the thing. Everyone knows this about Bond. It's his tell. Not everyone realizes, however, that it's about the brands. When the Russians brainwash Bond in *The Man with the Golden Gun,* they know that it will be high living that will authenticate him, allow him back from the cold into Special Branch so he can assassinate M. What exposes the brainwashed Bond is his missing brand loyalties. The Russians have forgotten to supply him with his trademark cigarettes—specially prepared, three gold bands, etc. (apparently no one read the SMERSH dossier on him included in *From Russia with Love*).

Normally—from Bond's cover (i.e., Universal Exports) to his signature drink recipes, from his Bentley to his Beretta—his world is fully dominated by brand loyalties, brand loyalties that are tells: drinks, cigarettes, watches, razor blades, perfume, cologne, other assorted toiletries (all of which villains variously misuse). Recent paroxysms about the collusion of advertising and content in the newest Bond movie are compulsively oblivious to this. The cultural property's existence depends on the invention of "lifestyle" not as a repository of branded goods but as branding machine *par excellence*. It's no accident that, from the first reviews, Fleming's signature style is held, for better or worse, to be his surfeit of commodity name-dropping. In the movies, tastes are more rigid: vodka martini, with Smirnoff, shaken, not stirred. In the novels, the tab is more eclectic: *gin* martinis, for starters, gin and tonics, old-fashioneds, Jack Daniels, Löwenbräu, Miller High Life. Marking the variance between the rigid brand naming in the movies and its slipperiness in the novels is central for unwrapping the natural history of the Fleming Effect and the Bond brand. Nevertheless, for self-described "purists" recently complaining on-line about shifts in 007's established brand loyalties—the supposed sacrilege of Finlandia edging out Smirnoff as Bond's vodka of record—this genealogy is lost.

Why find 007's switching vodka so vexing when so many other improbabilities and inconsistencies go down so smoothly? After all, from his first predilections for Smirnoff in the movie *Dr. No*, the auction house of cinematic Bond's tastes is no state secret. It's public knowledge that when it comes to brand loyalties, cinematic Bond is a kept man. Crudely, the "real" meaning of the brand switch is no more subtle than that, in the latest Bond movie, *Die Another Day*, a record $120 million was laid out by a variety of Universal Exports brands *quid pro quo* for labels prominently displayed on screen and for rights to set Bond's name to work.[17] The rationale for the new alliance with Finlandia boils down to that favorite tautology of PR, brand synergy: "No other man exemplifies the essence of style more than the suave, daring agent 007, and no other vodka but Finlandia could represent the sophistication and poise of such a world-class hero."[18] Just like James Bond, so, too, is

Finlandia Vodka: Bond's favorite from promotion of *Die Another Day* (2002). Photo courtesy Finlandia Vodka Worldwide.

Finlandia a "top premium," up-market brand: "James Bond is only associated with the best things in life: the best cars, the best women, and the best vodka. . . ."[19] Up-market brand, meet up-market brand, it's been expecting you. Understandably rankling to true believers in the fiction of Bond as brand-man, the heroic connoisseur, yet, sub rosa, absolutely characteristic of brand ideology.

Note to the formalists: Finlandia is no magic potion. It doesn't augment Bond's powers like Popeye's spinach—however tempting it may be to read it this way when Bond gets "tight" to prepare for bridge with Drax (*Moonraker* 47). It *is* what he is. The endgame of Bond's relationship with goods is his homology with them. As the latest ads put it, "007's Vodka of Choice" *is* "Pure James Bond."[20] What rankles true believers, then, are intimations of brand fickleness, yet this response and its presumption of Bond's extra-textual agency make up another tell. Bond is never fickle on the inside, in the course of the movie itself. We never see what I want: Bond sending back a disappointing Smirnoff martini, requesting Finlandia. No, the switch happens between movies, on the "outside," in *Advertising Age,* as it were, in multiform stories about new brand alliances picked up in a stunning number of business pages. That's where "Bond" truly goes to work as a hero of consumption, to return to Denning, the well-heeled, fully detached brand defining the outer world that purports to define his inner one. Here, public reality comes to resemble Bond's unique selling proposition—his vitality as a well-heeled, completely portable name emplotted in Manichean contests for domination, specifically brand domination, waged on a global scale.

Today, "Smirnoff" is owned by Diageo, the multinational superpower that controls a cosmopolitan rogue's gallery of brands: Gordon's (favorite gin of novel Bond), Johnnie Walker (also a Bond drink), J&B, Crown Royal, Captain Morgan, Jose Cuervo, Tanqueray, Hennessy, Guinness, Red Stripe, and Bailey's Irish Cream. "Finlandia" is owned by a rival hegemon, Brown-Forman, which possesses a bullpen nearly as impressive, if a bit down-market: Jack Daniels (another Bond favorite), Gentleman Jack, Early Times, Southern Comfort, Pepe Lopez, Canadian Mist, Appleton Estate Jamaican Rum, Fetzer, Bolla, Korbel.[21] Imagine these names on place cards around the table in Blofeld's secret lair or in Goldfinger's ready room. Cinematic Bond puts Smirnoff on the map, the vodka martini as synthesis of jet-set superfluity and uprooted provenance. Smirnoff represents the storied name in exile, the excess of Russian provenance saved from the socialist purge. It had its day. Finlandia—its provenance, entirely prefab—is this logic perfected. Invented expressly for the American marketplace in 1971, it demonstrates that the brand name represents provenance in exile from itself characteristically.[22] Provenance distilled into hype. "Finlandia Vodka consists of the best elements the country of Finland can be proud of: untouched nature and pure glacial spring water, high technological skills, the midnight sun and internationally renowned design. On top of everything, it cherishes the name of the country."[23] Whatever this product consists of, then, it carries the brand montage that really matters: the metaphorical chain of deterritorialized signifiers, repackaged up and down a paradigmatic axis of associations, slid down the discursive conveyer belt.[24] The point by now is—to the chagrin of Smirnoff-drinking loyalists—whether Finlandia or Smirnoff makes any difference. They are now all so many interchangeable "James Bond" branding machines, pseudo-provenance-generating circuitry. One ad for Finlandia includes a recipe for "the James Bond perfect martini": "2 parts Finlandia Vodka, A whisper of vermouth, Shaken not stirred until cold, Serve in frosted martini glass, Proceed to break bank of casino at baccarat table."[25] The recipe's implied reader is addressed simultaneously as Bond's drink, as its server, and as Bond's proxy at the gaming table, and it's here that the apparatus of posing orders to oneself turns its ideological squeaky wheel, because it shows here that the relevant interpellation in play does not involve activating your inner James Bond, but having your "license to be" activated and mastered by branding.[26]

Never mind Smirnoff. How did we get from Wolfschmidt—Bond's idiosyncratic vodka of choice in the novel *Moonraker*—to Finlandia?[27] One of the clues lies in Finlandia's martini recipe: *2 parts, A whisper of, etc.* How is it that its relational parts are to be measured? Against a whisper? Proceed to the next leisure fantasy. As Bond comments in *You Only Live Twice,* there must be "quick throughput" (107). "Like Vegas." For the brand to work it must be deterritorializing, prying the language of provenance from the conditions of production and context. Provenance jets with you, moves with your martini glass to the baccarat table— sinks with the pepper grains to the bottom of your vodka glass—even as you stand before the vodka display at the liquor store.

What's odd about the Bond novels—in contrast to the movies—is that product placement presses itself into service *pro bono,* unbeholden to the fiats of corporate lucre, and is at once more uncanny and more symptomatic as a result. The short story "Risico," from *For Your Eyes Only,* for example, gives us Bond in a bar. He's at work—on duty, so to speak—looking for a contact identified by yet another tell. The "secret recognition signal" is not to be one of "hoary, slipshod" clichés—"the folded newspaper, the flower in the buttonhole, the yellow gloves"—but crucially a particular mixed drink, an Alexander. Not a 007 drink, to be sure—a "creamy, feminine" one. Still, Bond admires the conspiratorial elegance. He eyes his quarry across the crowded room. "[O]n a corner table at the far side [. . .] flanked by a saucer of olives and another of cashew nuts, stood the tall-stemmed glass of cream and vodka" (102).

Let's note the obvious first: the classic Bond sexual intrigue plot structures even the most baseline of cocktail hour high jinks. Plotting down time—context apportioned to overt consumption off the job— characterizes Bond's up time, when he's up and running and available for use. And it's against this backdrop that Bond allows himself a quantum of solace in an absolutely superfluous gesture. In short, he orders a drink. "A Negroni. With Gordon's, please." No discretion for bartender allowed. "With Gordon's" is the salient bit of sartorial excess in an otherwise automatic set of exchanges. In effect, the gesture is all that remains of Bond, the unconsumed bit of affect manifested as brand loyalty proceeding in and through an otherwise highly prescriptive, formalized encounter, a "rendezvous" in which the operatives move as so many automata following orders. Without the Negroni with Gordon's, Bond is not really Bond.

When Bond, seldom given to introspection, reflects on consumer culture, the results are another tell. In fact, Bond's interiors—insofar as they exist—are invariably linked to such moments. *Live and Let Die* begins with him waylaid in a New York airport, suffering jet-set depredations in the (already) "notorious purgatory of the US Health, Immigration, and Customs machinery." Bond is caught in machinery in which he is "already known." Awaiting approval from shadowy channels in Washington, he thinks of his open dossier there: "A vital part of himself was in pawn, in the hands of others. Friends, of course, in this instance, but still . . . " Then, after clearance comes, during the car ride to his hotel, a rare moment of reflection.

> He was glad to keep silent and gaze out at his first sight of America since the war. [S]tart picking up the American idiom again: the advertisements [. . .]; the exotic pungency of the road signs: SOFT SHOULDERS—SHARP CURVES—SQUEEZE AHEAD—SLIPPERY WHEN WET; [. . .] the Civil Defence warnings: IN CASE OF ENEMY ATTACK—KEEP MOVING—GET OFF BRIDGE; the thick rash of television aerials and the impact of TV on billboards and shop windows[. . . .] [A]ll the [. . .] impressions that were as important to his trade as [. . .] bent twigs to the trapper in the jungle. (4)[28]

Through Bond, Fleming focalizes New York sprawl circa 1954. There's an elective affinity in what he sees, a secret sharer in the phenomenological iconography of New York by car. His movement through space is relativized and aestheticized as commodity and advertising throughput. This sequence anticipates architect Robert Venturi's *Learning from Las Vegas,* the landmark 1974 manifesto of postmodernism celebrating the iconography of the sprawl as viewed from a moving car.[29]

What's the phenomenon of Bond itself? Precisely an advanced specimen of Venturi's *cause célèbre.* In Fleming's collection *Thrilling Cities,* the piece called "007 in New York" depends on this very proposition. The pattern is familiar: first, depredations in airport customs; next, the machinery at work on Bond's name; then, at last, James Bond at rest—allegedly, at least—taking in the spectacle of American consumer society. "James Bond sat back and lit one of his last Morland Specials. By lunchtime it would be king-size Chesterfields. . . . Bond liked the Times Square jungle—the hideous souvenir shops, the sharp clothiers, the giant feedomats, the hypnotic neon signs, one of which said BOND in letters a mile high. Here was the guts [. . .], the living entrails" (127). There's a conspiratorial wink here, as if to say, we all know why Bond is really making a cameo appearance in Fleming's otherwise unrelated nonfiction venture. Why? Because he's the "already known" brand name "in letters a mile high" that guarantees the whole sprawling thing from on high. Thus, Bond in his work as meta-branding machine not only plays the ultimate yes-man to commodity throughput, but also anticipates the lesson of Las Vegas, the charismatic, self-deterritorializing sanction, re-organizing sprawl under the brand sanctions of consumption.

What's next for 007 in New York? The most exquisite form of American-style throughput, "a brief shopping expedition":

> brief [. . .] because nowadays there was little to buy in the [American] shops that wasn't [also in] Europe. [. . .] The drug-store first for half a dozen of Owens incomparable toothbrushes. Hoffritz on Madison Avenue for one of their heavy, toothed Gillette-type razors, so much better than Gillette's own product, Tripler's for some of those French golf socks made by Izod, Scribner's because it [had a] salesman [. . .] with a good nose for thrillers, and then to Abercrombie's to look over the new gadgets and, incidentally, make a date with Solange (appropriately employed in their Indoor Games Department) for the evening. (127)

And the drink he foresees? "A couple of dry martinis—Beefeaters with a domestic vermouth, shaken with a twist of lemon peel."

IV

The fact and tremendous duration of James Bond's popularity are cultural commonplaces. The language of this popularity is not just "already known," it's spoken fluently in marketing and publicity departments of the various corporations that own and license the Bond/Fleming properties. Furthermore, it's spoken in the 007 fan cells that mimic marketing theory, albeit with less spectacular pecuniary incentive. In constantly theorizing and retheorizing brand success, they follow semiotic expediency, akin to something Raymond Williams calls Plan "X" in another arena.[30] Should 007 go monogamous? More gadgets or fewer? Can "M" be a woman? Can Bond consumers handle CGI? Should Bond be sent to North Korea this time? Is Pierce Brosnan showing his age? Did Halle Berry upstage him in the cargo plane fight? Anything to learn from Vin Diesel? Is it time to take the BMW to the Ford dealer to trade in for another Aston Martin? Are there ever too many product placements and tie-ins? Can we cut more dialogue for the foreign markets? Are they ready for Chow Yun-Fat as Agent 007?

In his report on the Indiana Fleming symposium in the London *Times,* Andrew Lycett cites Jeremy Black's contention that theoretical approaches to 007 at the meeting "veered too far from Fleming's work to offer much illumination," lamenting "the inevitable divide [at the symposium] between participants who knew Bond in book form and those familiar with the films."[31] I find it curious that the same could be said of the Bond theories circulating in marketing and fan culture, which veer far from Fleming's work *sine qua non.* The issue isn't simply that we're all too ready to cast Fleming aside, forgetting his role as author-originator.[32] What complicates this narrative with its familiar fall from textual rigor to visual frivolity are the remarkable forms of continuity between the experiences of the "writerly" novel-text and the "readerly" film-text, the ways the "writerly" novels efface "Fleming" and cross the divide, conveying the charismatic, deterritorializing agent upward and outward. As we've seen here, the Fleming novels themselves put high stakes in processing Bond as throughput, stripping Agent 007 out of his fictional world. One thinks of the prominent billing of Bond's name on the novels' covers, overshadowing Fleming's, in effect competing with it for authorial credits.[33]

Bond's obituary, which appears at the end of *You Only Live Twice,* is the *locus classicus* for this process. M has falsely presumed Bond's demise. In truth, 007 is an amnesiac in Asia and will reappear brainwashed and mis-branded in *The Man with the Golden Gun.* Between these two last novels, "Bond" inhabits a space between two deaths (and between two novels) for a second time under Fleming's watch (the other being between *From Russia with Love* and *Doctor No*). That "Bond" lives on undead in between them is further evidence of his "already known" meta-branding. In M's obituary we don't find the usual litany of consumer habits and brand affiliations, the stuff of covert dossiers in shadowy bureaucracies on both sides of the espionage game. The ruse of *The Times* obituary is its nominal status as both Bond's first and final public presentation. M's letter promises no less than Bond's long-deferred *curriculum vitae,* his provenance as an agent of state secrets distilled for a thirsty public.

To take Bond seriously, let's take this obituary seriously. Why does M say Bond's name is worth public commemoration? It's not parentage: Bond's is unremarkable aside from his father's employment in the armaments trade. Not his academic career either: he left various brand-name

schools "undistinguished." Not surprisingly, it's Bond's military service in an overt war, the Second World War, upon which he makes his
name, albeit cryptically, satisfying superiors on unnamed secret missions, ensuring postwar promotion to yet more secret service with Special Branch. And yet here, too, Bond performs for an unnamed, covert
public. In the end, reports M, even the nature of Commander Bond's
special duties must remain classified. To the deceased's credit, M notes
that the unnamed duties were performed with "outstanding bravery and
distinction" if marred occasionally by a "streak of the foolhardy." Even in
demise, the importance of the special agent's work must be accepted on
the credit of M's assertion of its "extreme importance to the state." For
the voracious public's daily sustenance, all this is wholly insubstantial.
According to M, the only decisive, fully disclosed reason Bond merits
public consumption—an occasion of a *Times* obituary—is his status as
role model for the protagonist of prurient thrillers by a certain undisclosed hack:

> The inevitable publicity, particularly in the foreign Press, accorded
> some of [Bond's] adventures, made him, much against his will, some-
> thing of a public figure, with the inevitable result that a series of
> popular books came to be written around him by a personal friend and
> former colleague of James Bond. If the quality of these books, or their
> degree of veracity, had been any higher, the author would certainly
> have been prosecuted under the Official Secrets Act. It is a measure of
> the disdain in which these fictions are held at the Ministry, that action
> has not yet—I emphasize the qualification—been taken against the
> author and publisher of these high-flown and romanticized caricatures
> of episodes in the career of an outstanding public servant. (202)

James Bond is now not only a reluctant hero inside, he's the reluctant
hero outside the very novels that make him worth knowing anything
about at all. On the one hand, there's the "real" James Bond, agent of
undisclosed exploits, elliptically invoked. On the other, there's the fictional "James Bond," "mere" character in fictional micro-cosmos. Yet it's
"his" high-flown, high-living adventures that in fact author the preter-
natural and macro-cosmopolitan vitalism that's the mark of the Bond
name. No doubt, both "James Bonds" are fictitious, but if taking all this
"as if" way too seriously is part of the fun, the reading work at issue can
also lead to a theoretical conclusion very different from the familiar story
about what's often called aesthetic distance. Instead of the idea of art as
radical artifice leading to a heightened sense of reality, the Bond brand

effect leads to a heightening of further artifice, the consumerist artifice of extra-textual reality, not aesthetic distance but brand reality as aesthetic quickening. It doesn't so much confuse art and reality as it, like PR itself, closes the gap between them. In the same way that automobiles—or jet planes, for that matter—dream that they're rocket ships, consumers placed before the world of commodities dream that they're closing the gap between artifice and reality by their choosing from the shelves.[34]

NOTES

1. The point has been made that the act of consumption is metonymic because it involves the consumer's figurative ingestion and incorporation of consumer goods. My point has to do with the productive power of consumption—the way that the consumption of one thing both depends upon and entails the consumption of something else—and is thus metaphoric in the sense that it brings radically different things together and to us in the guise of overcoming their otherness.

2. It's no accident that Spielberg spent so much time on the set wearing his E.T. cap. Once more, he finds a story arc in the broken home and parental absenteeism, and resolution is suburbia regained, surrogate father restored, with the benevolent G-man (Tom Hanks) stepping in for the sensitive extraterrestrial.

3. However "dated" this fantasy seems given the endless deprivations and humiliations of post-9/11 air travel, it's worth noting that the jet set (of the mind, at any rate) is scarcely affected. They don't fly coach. They don't spend much time in airports. They're always free to move about the cabin and the VIP lounge.

4. Then, in the hotel scene to follow, Abagnale outprostitutes the prostitute, conning the celebrity call girl (Jennifer Garner) of her remuneration.

5. In this sense, it's consonant with the professional class's management of flows of cultural capital. Cf. Edward Comentale's reading of Bond's purchase on the ethos of professional society.

6. This is the sense of the hero choosing "Fleming" as an alias; it aligns him with the uncanny powers of the authorial imprimatur, the classic sign of competence of competence that is simultaneously the mark of the rule of counterfeit competence. For this particular aspect of the author-function, arguably in effect since Flaubert's "Madame Bovary, c'est moi," see my *Modernism and the Culture of Celebrity* (Cambridge: Cambridge University Press, 2004).

7. My understanding of the cultural history of PR broadly follows Stuart Ewen, *PR! A Social History of Spin* (New York: Basic Books, 1996).

8. The contrapositives, objective soft-sell and subjective hard-sell, are commonplace in advertising, marketing, and PR discourse. The latter refers to the hamhanded techniques of old-style advertising, whereas the former designates the nimbler entreaties of the PR game. The objective/subjective distinction refers to the site of consumer engagement—whereas the soft-sell/hard-sell distinction speaks to its affective texture. Marshall McLuhan's remark about the death of the salesman portending the birth of the PR man is relevant here. For McLuhan, the advent of PR entails a transformation of objective reality into a "nonstop ad," a "massive platform

and [. . .] mandate for sales promotion as a way of life" that "shatter[s] the individualist hard-sell salesman and the docile consumer," according to McLuhan, *Understanding the Media*, 205–206.

9. Could it be otherwise? Even if Fleming were the consummate insider of British intelligence—his Moscow junket circa 1933 notwithstanding—it's altogether too much to ask for a "Fleming," or any outsider, for that matter, to prepossess a subtle, insider's critique of Soviet communism.

10. James Risen, "Rem Krassilnikov, Russian Bane of C.I.A., Dies at 76," *New York Times*, March 24, 2003, sec. D7.1.

11. Joseph Stalin, from *Pravda*, April 23, 1920, quoted in "Stalin on Lenin," http://neptune.spaceports.com/~stalin/stalin_1.htm (accessed May 15, 2003).

12. Stalin, "On the Death of Lenin," January 26, 1924, quoted in "Stalin on Lenin," http://neptune.spaceports.com/~stalin/stalin_3.htm (accessed May 15, 2003).

13. These connections draw on the excellent discussion of Heinlein in Thomas M. Disch, *The Dreams Our Stuff Is Made Of* (1998), 85–86.

14. See the chapter called "Cardboard Hero" in *Thunderball* for Domino's discourse on "the story of Hero," the brand picture on Player's cigarettes, her one, "true love," as well as for 007's interpretation. The connection is completed when she describes Bond in these terms (see 201, for example).

15. This phrase is among the most circulated and embroidered anecdotes associated with Fleming's authorship of the Bond novels. For a fascinating treatment, including correspondence by Fleming, and written by the wife of the ornithologist ("James Bond *authenticus*," in her account), see Mary Wickham Bond, *How 007 Got His Name*, 16–24. Particularly resonant here is her final invocation of the model of Baker Street Irregulars, the Sherlock Holmes fans, whose "one rigid rule" is never to utter the name of Holmes' creator: "if he *must* be referred to, it can only be as Dr. Watson's literary agent" (62).

16. See Kingsley Amis, *The James Bond Dossier*, 98ff.

17. Jeff Chu, "A View to a Sell," "Forty Years of Bond: The Man with the Golden Run," *Time Europe*, November 3, 2002, http://www.time.com/timge/europe/bond2002/gadget.html (accessed June 15, 2003).

18. This quotation originates with Scott Reid, global marketing director of Finlandia Vodka Worldwide, and is part of a press release blitz leading up to the *Die Another Day* release. As such, it can be found verbatim on numerous news and business websites. A readily accessible example: "James Bond Selects Finlandia Vodka: Super-Premium Vodka Celebrates 30th Anniversary With Bond's 40th Anniversary," *Canada News Wire*, September 19, 2002, http://www.newswire.ca/en/releases/archive/September2002/19/c6446.html (accessed September 15, 2003).

19. Again, Reid, quoted in an editorial on trade website just-drinks.com, October 2002, http://just-drinks.com (accessed September 15, 2003).

20. "Finlandia 007: Pure James Bond," Finlandia.com, http://www.finlandia.com/007/bond_index.html (accessed May 1, 2003).

21. Bloomberg.com, http://www.bloomberg.com (accessed May 1, 2003).

22. "Finlandia History," Finlandia.com, http://www.finlandia.com/facts/history.asp (accessed May 1, 2003).

23. "Finlandia Heritage," Finlandia.com, http://www.finlandia.com/facts/heritage.asp (accessed May 1, 2003).

24. In other words—even though, as Owens points out, "vodka" is a decidedly odorless referent—it's the vehicle, not the tenor, that counts most.

25. "Finlandia: 007 Pure James Bond." Notice the use of "James Bond" as an attribute to modify "perfect."

26. In the Bond novels, when it comes to drinks, orders are to be given, not taken. In *Thunderball*, Felix Leiter—the novel's main martini man, incidentally—dresses down a bartender for slipping him an olive. In *Casino Royale*, when Bond and Leiter first meet, Bond does the instruction, trumping Leiter's order ignominiously with his own recipe: "Three measures of Gordon's, one of vodka, half a measure of Kina Lillet. Shake it very well until it's ice-cold, then add a large thin slice of lemon peel. Got it?" (45). The tutorial lies in Bond's meta-branding, rebranding the brand: Not just Haig-and-Haig but Haig-and-Haig *on the rocks.*

27. The idiosyncratic preparation of his "real pre-war Wolfschmidt vodka from Riga" in *Moonraker,* for example: "Bond took a pinch of black pepper and dropped it on the surface of the vodka. The pepper slowly settled to the bottom of the glass leaving a few grains on the surface which Bond dabbed up with the tip of a finger" (48).

28. This quotation is slightly altered from the Penguin edition. Following earlier editions I have substituted "billboards" for "hoardings."

29. See Robert Venturi, Denise Scott Brown, and Steven Izenour, *Learning from Las Vegas: The Forgotten Symbolism of Architectural Form* (1977).

30. See Raymond Williams, *The Year 2000* (1984).

31. Andrew Lycett, "Lesbians and 007: A License to Deconstruct," *The Times,* June 8, 2003, sec. 3.8, 8.

32. An approximation of a popular sentiment voiced at the symposium: "Don't forget that if it wasn't for Ian Fleming, we wouldn't have the consumer culture we so enjoy here today."

33. A point well illustrated by Tony Bennett and Janet Woollacott in *Bond and Beyond* (1987), 46ff.

34. This connection of automobiles and rockets alludes to Disch's book.

7 The Bond Market

CRAIG N. OWENS

Distilled Spirits

Consider vodka, the distilled beverage that characterizes the peculiar tastes of the filmic Bond, if less famously (and less consistently) those of his novelistic prototype. Colorless, flavorless, and odorless, distilled from a variety of starches, Russia's quintessential *little water* produced throughout the world, vodka is the most common liquor in cocktails, whether sweet or dry, high-class or common, sipped slowly or taken in gulps. Vodka, then, as a thing in itself, is a kind of ontological blank, which, according to *Mr. Boston*, "will graciously assume the characteristics of whatever it is mixed with" (129). In these signature cocktails, vodka, it appears, performs primarily secret service. But, unlike blended scotches or whiskeys, vodka's versatility comes from its simplicity and consistency. The blankness that constitutes it is not just nothing, but a placeholder for the something—the anything—vodka is capable of becoming. To formulate an identity theory of vodka, then: it is nothing, and that nothingness constitutes its thingness.

The garnishes and mixers it merges with in the martini, greyhound, gibson, gimlet, screwdriver, cosmo, bloody mary, Russians (black and white), collinses, and the v and t, seem to disguise it, making vodka the bartender's analogue to the many villains Bond himself encounters: Le Chiffre, the cipher, without character but for his idiosyncratic and over-determined consumption of *art nouveau* furniture alongside antique credenzas and a servile cane carpet-beater; Dr. No, mixed and without origin, his name, like Le Chiffre's, suggesting a blank at the center of his identity; Ernst Stavro Blofeld, the mind behind the omnipresent, mercenary, ghostly SPECTRE, apparently capable of physical shape-shifting and vocal transmutations that make him adaptable to every criminal situation he encounters, though he is incapable of tracing his lineage beyond his paternal great-grandfather's generation. Like vodka, these spectral villains do not travel under their own names; indeed, they are known less by name and more by a series of effects they are capable of producing. Moreover, each seems entirely identical not to his body or his past, but to a single-minded present desire; unencumbered by principles or beliefs or philosophies, these villains can be bought. The entire being of each is malleable, capable of mercenary redirection at a moment's notice. These villains do not suffer from moral compunctions, qualms, or reservations; they are never conflicted. For their identities seem to rely less on some deep interiority and more on the ends they maniacally pursue. Compared to these villains, Bond, the spy who travels under his own name and seldom uses disguises, according to the early pages of *From Russia with Love,* would appear the stable, self-identical, heroic male subject.

Auric Goldfinger's disquisition on the lush life would seem to strengthen this analogy's suggestion that Ian Fleming's villains tend to disappear, to lose their subjective consistency, while, complementarily, Bond grows more dense, more filled-in, more wholly *there.* During his dinner with Bond, Goldfinger makes clear that he strives for a mental and bodily purity that borders on asceticism—an asceticism he shares with Blofeld. Goldfinger explains,

> "I don't myself drink or smoke, Mr Bond. Smoking, I find [. . . .] a vile practice. As for drinking, I am something of a chemist and I have yet to find a liquor that is free from traces of a number of poisons, some of them deadly, such as fusel oil, ethylacetate, acetaldehyde and furfurol. A quantity of some of these poisons taken neat would kill you. In the small amounts you find in a bottle of liquor they produce various ill effects most of which are lightly written off as 'a hangover.' " Goldfinger paused with a forkful of curried shrimp half way to his mouth. (126–27)

Goldfinger's advocacy of personal purity, however, segues here quite neatly into pointing out the lack of restraint that threatens to corrupt Bond:

> "Since you are a drinker, Mr Bond, I will give you one word of good advice. Never drink so-called Napoleon brandy, particularly when it is described as 'aged in the wood.' That particular potion contains more

of the poisons I have mentioned than any other liquor I have analysed. Old bourbon comes next." Goldfinger closed his animadversions with a mouthful of shrimp. (127)

That the text describes these pronouncements as "animadversions," turnings of the mind (or soul), suggests the profound link between Goldfinger's *animus* and what he consumes. Being and doing for Goldfinger are unproblematically bound by a credo of purity.

If the Bond villains seem ghostly, spectral, and, in such tales as *Thunderball, Live and Let Die,* and "The Hildebrand Rarity," a little watery themselves, the objects of pursuit share—and reinforce—this perception: gold, guano, deteriorating elements, a deciphering machine, a cache of explosives, a cashier's check, or the colorless, flawless diamonds blown by Blofeld into orbit. These objects of pursuit, like the villains striving for them, are valueless except inasmuch as they are inscribed within a network of social desire.

This spirited analogy posits the villain, like the prize, as a somehow illusory lure in comparison to which Bond emerges as the stable, unified, fully self-aware masculine subject, filled in and corrupted by experience, "aged" in the field, the fairway, and the "wood[s]" that line the Canadian-American border in *For Your Eyes Only.* But such an analogy is itself a lure diverting our attention away from the pathways along which the Bond films and novels construct desire. That is, the easy conclusion that the objects of desire in the Fleming *oeuvre* are structured as blanks (*à la* Jacques Lacan's seminar on Poe's "Purloined Letter") fails fully to account for the way desire emerges from various readings of the Bond films and novels. And, as the perfect reader, the interpreter of transparent meanings, and despite the manifestations of nothing at the end of the chases, the real cipher is Bond himself.

Bond's response to Goldfinger's dinnertime disquisition offers at least partial confirmation of this claim. For, while Goldfinger has marked himself as pure by his avoidance of distilled liquors, Bond appropriates the mark of purity (an oxymoron, I know) in his riposte. He explains that, because of the impurities contaminating other distilled liquors, and despite his formerly broad range of tastes in booze, he himself has "recently taken to vodka." Then, matching Goldfinger ephemeron for ephemeron, he adds, " 'They tell me its filtration through activated charcoal is a help.' Bond, dredging this piece of expertise out of dim recollections of something he had read, was rather proud of having been able to return Goldfinger's powerful serve" (127). Goldfinger's startled reaction to Bond's apparent expertise suggests that Bond has bested Goldfinger.

And he has. For in pledging his allegiance to vodka, Bond establishes his purity—I might almost say his *transparency*—in three ways: first, his loyalty to a single liquor seems to match Goldfinger's quest for pure gold; second, in claiming vodka as his signature drink, Bond appropriates its aura of purity—after all, it's not "curried shrimp"; and, finally, by admitting that he has only "dabbled" in chemistry, Bond confirms the text's suggestion that he need not rely on a uselessly erudite store of trivia in order to perform his identity. Bond is uncorrupted even by the information that would confirm the extent of his own purity.

Being and Nothingness

I should pause here, momentarily, to address the apparent slippage in my use of the terms "purity" and "blankness" interchangeably. For, on the one hand, I have claimed that Bond's villains represent a kind of purity—a clarity, refinement, and essential coherence—because of their often mixed ethnic identities: No, Drax, and Goldfinger, as individuals, and SPECTRE and SMERSH, as organizations, are marked by their mixed racial and national heritages. This very mixing, I want to argue, erases their origins, allows them an international and silent ubiquity, and protects them from being traced. These mixed backgrounds, however, provide advantages similar to those of purity. For the diamonds and gold and radioactive elements, in their global exchange, also evade tracing. It seems, then, that the extremes of the purity spectrum provide the same kind of cover: a loss of positive identity that makes positive identification impossible. More importantly, they bracket a middle, where Bond, the middle manager (as Edward Comentale argues in this volume) of middle-class life, can emerge as the ideal masculine subject: scarred, sunburned, well-dressed, and well-groomed—but unmarked.

The intersection of the mixed with the pure, the doggedly single-minded with the irretrievably corrupted, manifests itself in the boundaries of Bond's identity laid out by the films and novels as opposite extremes of the spectrum of purity. If Bond finally emerges as identical to his unmixed, undiluted essence in *Goldfinger,* in the films, his mixable, dilutible essencelessness seems to confirm the sense that he, and not his antagonist, is the real cipher. Portrayable by the Scots, the English, and the Irish, ageless in all but his clothes and his hairstyle, his own origins tantalizingly mysterious[1] until the later novels specify his Scots background as a nod to Connery's success in portraying the film Bond, 007 marks a position, not a subject, into which the right combination of various characteristics can be inserted. To clarify: Bond is not that collection of various characteristics; rather, he is the blank middle they fill in. He is an opening, a vacant, unclaimed potentiality, rather than an ontologically assignable identity. The apparent emptiness of the objects of pursuit, and of the villains against whom he strives, itself serves as a diversion, an anim*aversion* distracting the reading mind from the recognition of Bond's fundamental and constitutive blankness. And as long as his self-identity and blankness, which operates quite differently than a *lack,* are preserved, Bond remains a subject without desire. My argument, then, is that Bond, as the gentleman consumer of the middle twentieth century, offers a model of masculine consumption that depends upon a conception of desire accounted for by a hybrid of Marxian theories of commodity fetishism and Freudian conceptions of the psycho-sexual fetish. For the psycho-sexual fetish begins to provide the gentleman consumer the means by which to disavow the lack it fills, and thereby in turn to disavow the model of desiring consumption associated with Marxian analysis and stereotypically feminine orientations to the commodity.

Bibeo Ergo Sum

If desire is predicated on a perceived interior lack, Bond himself appears to be the subject outside of desire, not because his interior is always unified (despite buffeting and temptation), but because he seems to lack an interior at all. Bond knows himself as we know him: from the outside. He inhabits the surface of his own body, forever shrugging off doubts, hot-bathing his troubles away, swimming his way to mental acuity, cold-showering and shaving and napping himself to spiritual preparedness.

Bond's stay at Shrublands, a naturopathic health resort to which M orders him early in the novel *Thunderball,* alerts him to his mind/body singularity:

> And the extraordinary thing was that he could not remember when he had felt so well—not strong, but without any aches and pains, clear of eye and skin, sleeping ten hours a day and, above all, without that nagging sense of morning guilt that one is slowly wrecking one's body. (32–33)

The "guilt" about his "body," assuaged by the physical therapy and restricted diet to which he is subjected, signals the deeper connection Bond discovers between his body and his sense of identity:

> Was his personality changing? Was he losing his edge, his point, his identity? Was he losing the vices that were so much part of his ruthless, cruel, fundamentally tough character? Who was he in [the] process of becoming? A soft, dreaming, kindly idealist who would naturally leave the Service and become instead a prison visitor, interest himself in youth clubs, march with the H-bomb marchers, eat nut cutlets, try and change the world for the better? (33)

These questions, we are given to understand, are questions Bond asks about himself. Importantly, Bond seems to realize that who he perceives himself to be grows out of what he does and what is done to him. He is Hamlet's foil: against this 400-year-old example of interiority, Bond stands as the modern revision of the Cartesian subject, his identity entirely exterior: *I drink, therefore I am.* "Vices" are the product of international espionage, it seems, whereas "soft, dreaming, kindly idealis[m]" grows out of too many "nut cutlets." The directional nature of these two models of identity is worth noting. In the Hamlet/Goldfinger model, being—"that within which passeth show"—manifests itself in doing. However, in the Bond model, being is constituted by, and legible in, doing: wearing "customary [leisure] suits of solemn black," for example. These models of identity, then, are in fact modalities of being, suggesting a latent hermeneutic of object and interpretation. But both suggest a transparency of the sign—whether the act as sign of the self or self as sign of the act.

The modality of 007's identity, then, locates Bond's subjectivity not so much firmly within his bodily boundaries as upon them; his tastes and predilections, motives and desires, are always governed and deployed (or restrained) in response to his own perception of his physicality. Bond neither adverts nor averts his *animus* because—as he makes clear at Goldfinger's board—as near as it is possible to tell, he has no *animus* in the first place. Significantly, motoring through France in *On Her Majesty's Secret Service,* Bond imagines the letter of resignation he will write upon his return to London. The unwritten letter complains that M has consistently rejected Bond's "animadversions" on several occasions. But, as if to alert us eavesdropping readers that the *animus* in question here is a rhetorical device, he brackets his own self-congratulation for using the term, which he deems "[another good one!]" (11).

Correspondingly, whatever moments of existential depth, self-doubt, or subjective articulation Bond experiences fall flat in the texts—reading like canned hard-boiled detective schlock—and arise from assaults on Bond's body, such as his torture at Le Chiffre's hands. But with bodily recovery, Bond always recovers his self-assuredness too. For though the "training" Bond begins "under the critical, appraising eyes of Quarrel," in both *Doctor No* and *Live and Let Die,* starts as bodily training (*Live* 174), it ends up achieving metaphorical mental preparedness too: "[T]he scales of big city life had fallen from him" (177).

No Means "No"

The upshot of this kind of characterization is that Bond seems always to be reveling in a never-ending mirror stage. His body becomes a text proclaiming his subjective unity, a text *de*cipherable by Bond himself, as he stands shaving and dressing before the hotel room's literal mirror or savoring the feel of cotton, serge, and flax against his body's hyper-aware surfaces.

In the Lacanian logic, this reflected image of the body unified with and respondent to the will both constructs the subject and mystifies the subject's constructedness within a symbolic field external to it. The image in the mirror—the body made aware of itself by its contact with and reflection in the mediating surfaces of polished glass, cold water, and warm flannel—is a sign of the self misrecognized as the self as sign. Rather than perceiving itself as emergent from the reading of the sign, the apparently self-aware subject reads the sign as simply reflexive of and posterior to the reading self. Upon this misrecognition subjectivity is founded, according to Lacan, as anterior to and unified apart from the symbolic order (*Écrits* 2–3). The bond the symbolic forges between identity and text is an under-cover bond, attesting to yet denying the subject as emergent only in the text.

Literally "under cover," however, in *From Russia with Love*, Bond's mirror stage merges with the panopticon. Bond's body, in the "large mirror in a gold frame" that "covered most of the wall" behind the bed, during his first encounter with Tatiana Romanova (131) is duly photographed by the two SMERSH agents sitting "[a]bove them [. . .] behind the gold-framed false mirror [. . .] in the cramped cabinet de voyeur" (186). These preparations for blackmail lay bare the lie of the mirror stage: The unity promised by the apparent mind-body identity reflected in the mirror is only an illusion of unity masking the rift, the slash that splits the subject and compromises his identity.

Against the mirror's promise of unity, then, in the case of the male subject, is the threat of castration. And that threat inheres in bodily

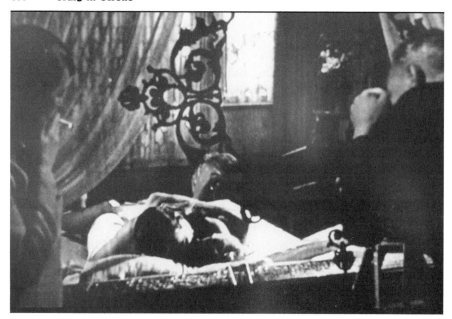

James Bond (Sean Connery) and Tatiana Romanova (Daniela Bianchi) observed in bed in *From Russia with Love* (1963).

mutilation and is attested to, in the Freudian conception, by the blank between mother's legs. As E. L. McCallum has explained Freud's conception, the mother's penis, imagined by the little boy, "is special because [before the boy's surprising realization] it had guaranteed the boy was like his mother, and because its loss promises that the boy could lose his" (18). If the mirror stage is the guarantee of sameness, the missingness of mother's penis is the mark of difference, of the otherness that reveals the object as other than the subject.

The threat of castration in the early Bond novels and films manifests itself variously. *Casino Royale*'s Le Chiffre follows his ball-busting torture of Bond with an attempt literally to castrate him, stopped short only by the timely arrival of a SMERSH agent. On the shores of No's reclusive hideaway, Honeychile Rider wards Bond off with a curved blade and later considers the possibility that he is "weak" below the waist (144). More obviously, the rockets launched over Dr. No's island fail to remain aloft. In the film version of *From Russia with Love*, Tatiana refuses to make love to Bond until she has fondled the labial gash on his lower back. And when she finally gives in to his advances, in the surveillance scene I mentioned above, the photography from behind the mirror alienates Bond's identity, figuratively castrating him by appropriating his virile dexterity for the sake of blackmail. The filmic Goldfinger's laser, which, he touts, can cut through solid "metal," stops perilously close to Bond's genitals. Finally, Bond's encounter with Judy Havelock in the title story of *For Your Eyes Only* elicits a response to the castration threat that hovers between arousal and fear: "Bond, his heart thumping, stared up the shaft of the steel arrow whose blue-tempered triangular tip parted the grass stalks perhaps eighteen inches from his head" (60). The "shaft" Havelock wields, with its "blue [. . .] tip," indicates that she has appropriated the penis even before she has removed it with the "hunting knife at her belt," which she may have borrowed intertextually from *No*'s Honeychile (62).

Castration anxiety, in the psychoanalytic field, is allayed by the fetish. The male subject, faced with mother's venereal testimony to the penis's vulnerability, fixates upon some convenient object of the mother's corpus, coiffure, or couture to stand in for her missing penis and to resurrect the illusion of sameness. Gilles Deleuze describes this transformation at the moment the boy "becom[es] aware of the missing penis" as a "return" to the "point of departure" which "enables him to validate the existence of the organ that is in dispute":

> The fetish is therefore not a symbol at all, but as it were a frozen, arrested, two-dimensional image, a photograph to which one returns repeatedly to exorcise the dangerous consequences of movement, the harmful discoveries that result from exploration: it represents the last point at which it was possible to believe . . . Thus it appears that fetishism is first of all a disavowal ("No, the woman does not lack a penis") [. . .]. (Deleuze 31–32)

Like the photograph, the fetish is worth a thousand words, and those words tell a story: the story of subjective unity. That story, if I may say so, is a stiff-cock tale, guaranteeing the male fetishist his masculine prerogatives to act in perfect accordance with his desire.

But the fetish always fails. That is, the story it tells is always just a story, a necessary fiction, the convenient lie that belies its own falsehood. For, as a supplemental mark, the fetish both allays the anxiety of difference the threat of castration evinces *and* attests to the potency of that threat in the first place. The fetish "doth protest too much." Therefore it oscillates between allaying and fueling the subject's anxiety. The fetish is, in this regard, a double agent.

I have just claimed that the fetish always fails. What I ought to have said, though, is that the fetish never fails to fail. That is, the preservation of difference under the sign of the same is necessary for the maintenance of subjective desire. It displaces desire's interior lack onto the body and preserves it as always potential, always a threat without ever becoming a fact. The failure of the fetish—and this is why a fetish is neither a penis nor a phallus—constitutes the subject's desire.

One of the most striking fetishes in the Bond novels is the Beretta, which M confiscates near the beginning of *Doctor No*. "Your gun got stuck," M reminds Bond, referring to his failed attempt to kill Rosa Klebb in *From Russia with Love:* "This Beretta of yours with the silencer. Something wrong there, 007." And then, significantly in my view, he asks half-rhetorically, "Would you prefer to drop [your double-0 number] and go back to normal duties?" It is easy, of course, to see the gun as a straightforward phallic symbol. But its failure, in this instance, is what arouses M's attention, and it prompts him to threaten Bond with "normal[cy]" if he does not give up the gun willingly (18). When M asks the Armourer's opinion of Bond's Beretta, he responds, "Ladies' gun, sir." Behind this dismissal, however, we can almost hear the unspoken indictment: "Ladies' stockings, sir." The gun, the Armourer explains, has "no stopping power. But it's easy to operate. A bit fancy looking too, if you know what I mean, sir. Appeals to the ladies." And, with a silencer, he goes on to explain, it would have "still less stopping power, sir. And I don't like silencers. They're heavy and get stuck in your clothing when you're in a hurry. I wouldn't recommend anyone to try a combination like that, sir. Not if they were meaning business" (18).

But, as every fetishist knows, one mustn't mix business with pleasure. And pleasure is what Bond's relationship with the Beretta has meant:

> He thought of his fifteen years' marriage to the ugly bit of metal. He remembered the times its single word had saved his life—and the times when its threat alone had been enough. He thought of the days when he had literally dressed to kill—when he had dismantled the gun and oiled it and packed the bullets carefully into the springloaded magazine and tried the action once or twice, pumping the cartridges out on to the bedspread in some hotel bedroom somewhere round the world. Then the last wipe of a dry rag and the gun into the little holster and a pause in front of the mirror to see that nothing showed. [. . .] Bond felt unreasonably sad. How could one have such ties with an inanimate object, an ugly one at that, and, he had to admit it, with a weapon that was not in the same class as the ones chosen by the Armourer? But he had the ties and M was going to cut them. (20–21)

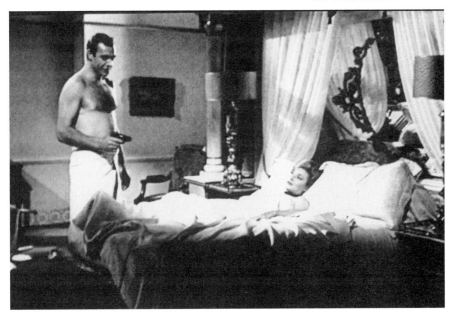

James Bond (Sean Connery) approaching Tatiana Romanova (Daniela Bianchi) at gunpoint in *From Russia with Love* (1963).

Indeed, it does not take confiscation to worry Bond about the Beretta. As early as *From Russia with Love,* Bond's protective relationship to his gun causes him to "fe[el] naked without it" (233). The gun becomes something he wears, something that completes him, provides him a sense of wholeness necessary to his self-conception.

Accessory to the Crime

The question arises at once, then: What allays the anxiety not of castration, but of defetishization? That is, when the fetishist is denied his fetish, when the "ties" he has to the "ugly bit," which he must strap on every night, his "unreasonable" fondness for which attaches to dismemberment, lubrication, and "pumping cartridges out onto the bedspread," are "cut," what object takes its place? What is the fetish of the fetish?

The first response to this question might be the commodity. For the commodity fetish seems to move the structures of fetishistic attachment beyond the realm of the shameful, the secret, the sexual. In the Marxian conception, the "secret" of the commodity inheres not in the desire it elicits; that desire is sanctioned quite publicly. The secret lies in the human labor hidden behind the social relations. In other words, the commodity fetish fails to stand in for the psycho-sexual fetish because, though the consumer reads her[2] own desire, that reading occurs, as it were, aloud, publicly, in full sight of, and sanctioned by, the consuming public sphere. In other ways, however, the Marxian commodity fetish works very much like the psychological fetish inasmuch as it oscillates between filling the lack and attesting to it; laying bare and mystifying its own origins. Most significantly, for my purposes, though, is that the commodity fetish and the psycho-sexual fetish operate as texts to be read. That is, they encode structures of desire to be decoded by the consumer or the fetishist. And these encoded structures once decoded always spell out the reader's name. In the ermine stole, Von Sacher-Masoch's protagonist in *Venus in Furs* reads his own subjective unity; in the commodity the consumer finds himself; in remembering the Beretta, Bond re-members (rather than dismembers) himself. Still, because the commodity fetish speaks to a public at large within a public sphere, it fails to maintain the secret, idiosyncratic encoding of desire that allows the psycho-sexual fetishist to imagine that his fetish speaks only to him.

In the act of decoding, reading, remembering himself uniquely in the fetish, Bond follows the fetishistic pathways of a desire—textual desire—that always emerges from a perceived lack or threat of loss, whether or not that loss is of a specifically sexual nature. In other words, Bond the consumer of commodities would be no less "abnormal" in his "work" than Bond the fetishist of the "ladies' gun." His abnormality, indeed, would be more widely sanctioned. But in the Secret Service, little value is placed on wide sanction. Notably, fetishism, predicated on the threat of emasculation, is explicitly coded feminine in *Doctor No* much as the consumption of commodities has been coded feminine in the popular imagination over the past half-century.

So the question remains unanswered: What is the fetish of the fetish? I want to suggest, temporarily, that the thwarted fetishist's fetish, the fetish that allays the threat of the cutting off of the fetish, is the accessory. In the Bond texts, these accessories take many forms: cufflinks and hair brushes, razors concealing secret compartments, wristwatch detonators and explosive pens, the attaché case exuding tear gas and ejecting throwing knives. Those of us who imagine ourselves Bonds in our own lives have only to visit the Sharper Image or Brookstone or *L'Occitane,* or to peruse the pages of *Gentlemen's Quarterly* or *Esquire,* to encounter a similarly spy-quality, if less deadly, array of men's accessories: the bullet-shaped nose-hair trimmer; the surgical-steel-bladed cigar clipper; the breast-pocket cognac flask with the retractable spring-loaded shot glass; the German-engineered corkscrew; the self-rinsing, self-draining, silver-tipped badger-hair shaving brush.

Despite the variety of accessories available to an agent of the Secret Service or to the middle manager at a regional accounting firm, the gentlemanly accessory is marked by three salient features. First, it makes explicit pretensions to utility. One *must* have a place to hide those documents; one *must* have a way of blowing a hole through that wall; one *must* have a means by which to hold one's cuffs together; one *must* carry one's cognac somehow. A second and perhaps more important feature is that the gentlemanly accessory is (like the fetish) a text that encodes the subjective unity of its possessor; but, unlike the fetish, that text is to be decoded not *by* the possessor, but by others. If the fetishist—of either the psycho-sexual or the commodity variety—reads himself through the structures of desire encoded in the fetish, the accessorist textualizes *himself* by means of the accessories out of which others read him as unified in taste and discretion. The way the accessory-as-text reverses the hermeneutic of the fetish-as-text becomes starkly clear at the beginning and end of *From Russia with Love.*

Our first encounter with Donovan Grant alias "Red" Grant alias Krassno Graniski (code name Granit) alias Norman Nash finds him sunbathing next to a small pile of personal accessories:

> To judge by the glittering pile, this had been, or was, a rich man. It contained the typical membership badges of the rich man's club—a money clip, made of a Mexican fifty-dollar piece and holding a substantial wad of banknotes, a well-used gold Dunhill lighter, an oval gold cigarette case with the wavy ridges and discreet turquoise button that means Fabergé, and the sort of novel a rich man pulls out of the bookcase to take into the garden—*The Little Nugget*—an old P. G. Wodehouse. There was also a bulky gold wristwatch on a well-used brown crocodile strap. It was a Girard-Perregaux model designed for people who like gadgets, and it had a sweep second-hand and two little windows in the face to tell the day of the month, and the month, and the phase of the moon. The story it now told was 2.30 on June 10th with the moon three-quarters full. (3)

That these accessories are the means by which "to judge" Grant "a rich man," that they are figured as "membership badges" which tell "a story," and that their utility is twice pointed out by the adjective "well-used" suggest the direction in which the accessory's message about its possessor travels. It is a message to be read by others in order to decode the identity of the accessorist.

By the end of the novel, however, the wristwatch serves as a means of distinguishing Bond's accessorizing tendencies from Grant's fetishizing ones. If, as I have argued, the fetish makes itself legible to the fetishist, then a familiar pattern of events repeats itself when, just as he is about *to read his own wristwatch,* Bond's intentions are thwarted; Grant deftly shoots the crystal from the watch face as a warning (235). Bond is denied the pleasure of decoding his own possession, just as he is denied the habit of doing so when M confiscates his gun. Grant's watch, on the other hand, remains importantly intact; for it is synchronized to SMERSH director Rosa Klebb's watch to ensure that they meet punctually at noon the next day. Grant/Nash's success as a spy depends on showing up precisely on time. Thus, in reading his own watch—in engaging in the fetishistic hermeneutic, in other words—Grant maintains his own subjective stability, otherwise threatened by his various aliases and national alliances.

But when, after killing Grant, Bond appropriates the wristwatch in order to ensure that he springs his trap on Klebb at precisely the right moment, Bond converts the fetish into an accessory. For he reads it as a sign not of himself, but rather of Grant, whose habits he must mimic in order to gain access to Klebb. That is, he reverses the hermeneutic by converting the watch from a text about the owner to be read by the owner into a text about the owner to be read by someone else, thus proving the maxim *one man's fetish is another man's accessory.*

This hermeneutic reversal appears·in *Moonraker* as well, when Bond deciphers Hugo Drax's cigarette case during a game of bridge. After several hands of cards, Bond discovers the means by which Drax cheats during his nightly games at Blades, the club to which M belongs. As Bond explains, Drax cheats

> [o]nly on the deal [. . . .] You know that silver cigarette-case he has in front of him, with his lighter? He never takes cigarettes from it. Doesn't want to get fingermarks on the surface. It's plain silver and very highly polished. When he deals, it's almost concealed by the cards and his big hands. And he doesn't move his hands away from it. Deals four piles quite close to him. Every card is reflected in the top of the case. It's just as good as a mirror although it looks perfectly innocent lying there. As he's such a good businessman it would be normal for him to have a

first-class memory. You remember I told you about "Shiners"? Well,
that's just a version of one. (41)

Drax's employment of the cigarette case seems to Drax himself to follow
the fetishistic hermeneutic. "Though it looks perfectly innocent" to others, as would a shoe or a mink stole to those for whom such objects were
not legible as fetishes, in it Drax reads the code of his own expertise as a
bridge player. For, though it would appear that in revealing the cards of
his fellow players, the cigarette case allows Drax to read *them* more
accurately, bridge demands primarily that one read his own cards correctly and value them *relative to the other hands at the table.* So, in
apparently reading the other players, Drax is, in practice, reading himself. His cigarette case makes his own position more legible to himself.

Once discovered, Drax's ruse prompts a disbelieving question from
Lord Basildon: "What the hell does he want to do that for? Bloody
millionaire. Rolling in money" (42). Though neither M nor Bond responds, Basildon's question highlights two fundamental features of the
fetish I have already suggested. First, the story the fetish tells it tells only
to the fetishist, whose fetishistic attachment to it is not fully legible to
outsiders; and second, the fetish always operates supplementally, as an
excess, an add-on seemingly unnecessary to the stable subject. But, perhaps more importantly, this attempt to win profits that, in comparison
to Drax's vast fortune, would seem small change, signals an excess of
desire. And, given the quite public nature of Drax's winnings at the
bridge table, together with the lengths to which he goes to hide his
scarred appearance, this excess marks Drax as anxiously feminine in
character. Bond's ability to read Drax's cigarette case allows him once
again to convert the fetishistic hermeneutic into an accessoristic one. In
reading the cigarette case as a sign of Drax's character, Bond makes
Drax's fetish Drax's accessory legible by an outsider as a "badge" of its
owner.

The third feature of the accessory, differentiating it from the fetish, is
that it truly never fails. Grant's watch does allow Bond to time his rendezvous correctly with Rosa; Drax's guilty glance at Bond, when Bond
bests him after the final stacked deal, confirms that Bond has read the
cigarette case correctly. Whereas the Beretta Bond carries is susceptible to
catching on his holster lip, the Smith and Wesson and the Walther with
which it is replaced are not. The cufflinks stay put, the nose hair trim-
mers will not draw blood, the cigar cutter will not mangle the natural-
leaf wrapper. The accessory, that is, does not oscillate. It betrays nothing.

It is trusty, foolproof, and univocal in its proclamation of its owner's discretion and control.

A Singular Character

Of course, the accessory does not really offer a way around psycho-sexual fetishism. It only pretends to. In the Bond novels and films, as well as in gentlemen's magazines marketing such accessories to the sophisticated consumer, it emerges as another fetish disguised as a safe loophole in the fetishistic semiotic. To illustrate this point, I want first to reexamine some of my earlier assertions about Bond's fetishistic tendencies, and then to turn to a particularly telling moment in the film version of *From Russia with Love.* For it soon becomes clear that Bond is not the average, garden-variety fetishist he appears to be at the beginning of *Doctor No.* Rather, Bond's subjectivity makes him, in some ways, immune to the fetishistic impulse by making him immune to castration anxiety in the first place. In this way, Bond takes shape as a radically different kind of man.

I have already said that threats of castration crop up frequently in the Bond novels and films. These threats, however, are usually veiled; most do not directly take aim at Bond's genital integrity. Bond coolly charms his way past Honey Rider's brandished knife and Judy Havelock's blue-tipped arrow. In more symbolic figurations of castration, Bond acts not as the victim of castration, but as the prophylactic against it. He thwarts Dr. No's missile-toppling enterprise; Goldfinger's laser does not elicit from Bond the silence of castration, but rather a surprisingly fertile stream of words; in fingering Bond's scar, Tatiana seems also to be pressing his buttons, turning him on, arousing his capacity for virile performance.

Even when faced with literal castration, Bond does not lose the subjective unity the intact genitals guarantee. Bond's reactions to Le Chiffre's torture are primarily bodily. As readers, we get the sense that behind the "body arched in an involuntary spasm" and the "face contracted in a soundless scream," Bond does not really fear what might happen to him (*Casino* 113). Indeed, he seems at ease with the whole process of being tortured, which, "he had been told by colleagues who had survived" it, ended with "a wonderful period of warmth and languor leading into a sort of sexual twilight where pain turned to pleasure" (115). This description suggests that the castration Bond faces will actually produce an effect quite like that of having fully functional genitalia.

But of course, the castration never occurs. On the level of the plot, a

SMERSH agent kills Le Chiffre at the moment he reaches for his carving knife. However, on the narrative level, the castration cannot occur: Where he would expect to find Bond's *genitals hanging* through the false seat of the chair to which he is bound, Le Chiffre would find only that "the *underpart* of his body *protruded*" (*Casino* 112; my emphasis). Under*part*? Bond's anatomy in this circumstance seems quite singular. What is this mysterious protruding part? After all, there is a certain plurality and diversity of underparts where castration is concerned; the castrator and the castrated must keep them straight if castration anxiety is to be evinced and if the castration is to prove effective. It seems, though, that the text conceives of Bond's nether region as a vague mass, a single part, an undifferentiated field of flesh. In protruding, moreover, this mass would seem smooth and rotund and turgid, not loose and creased and flaccid.

A similar genital abnormality surfaces in Fleming's late novel *You Only Live Twice* when Tiger Tanaka explains to Bond the sumo wrestler's uncanny ability to withstand assaults to his groin:

> Well, the *sumo* wrestler will have been selected for his profession by the time of puberty. Perhaps because of his weight and strength, or perhaps because he comes of a *sumo* family. Well, by assiduously massaging those parts, he is able, after much practice, to cause the testicles to re-enter the body up the inguinal canal down which they originally descended. (110)

Compared to the vague reference to Bond's "underpart" in the first 007 novel, this detailed description of the wrestler's plural parts, each so precisely named, seems striking in Fleming's later tale. While we might easily conclude that changes in social mores made such specificity more allowable in the later novel, I would argue that the difference in precision has less to do with relaxed conceptions of novelistic decorum and more to do with the difference between the sumo wrestler, who bears normal genitals, and Bond, who does not. Bond's response to Tanaka's explanation emphasizes this difference: "You mean he gets them right out of the way behind the bones of the pelvis or what not?" (110). The pronoun *them* without antecedent and the throw-away *what not* suggest that, as Tanaka claims, Bond's "knowledge of anatomy is [. . .] vague" (111).

What can account for so vague a knowledge of male genitals in a man so widely reputed as a womanizer? The frequent note of surprise and rapture in the way the women Bond beds describe his lovemaking offers a clue. For along with the question of Bond's ignorance of male anatomy is the question of his lovers' surprise at his expert lovemaking. What explains, though does not answer, both questions is that Bond has no genitals in the first place. Despite his often ballsy exploits, Bond, it would seem, is the man without a penis. In this, Bond bears a genital configuration similar to that other icon of sixties masculinity: the Ken doll.

In the film *From Russia with Love,* Bond's genital non-conformity is made strikingly apparent when he emerges from his hotel bathroom to find Tatiana lying naked in his bed. Over her head hangs the ornate mirror behind which cameras will roll to catch Bond *in flagrante delicto.* At the foot of the bed stands Bond himself, his gun drawn, his middle wrapped in a powder-blue bath towel. Against the predominant grays and blacks of this scene, and in contrast to the smooth silvered mirror and the satin sheets, the stark terry cloth towel appears as a gap, a blank spot, in the image. Though the scene suggests sexual tension, Bond's gun, which is visible—and not his genitals, which are blank—threatens the penetration. Gun, mirror, woman, and genitallessness: these are the elements that compose Bond's subjectivity.

If, therefore, as I have argued, M's removal of Bond's Beretta is a moment not of castration, but of defetishization, it is because Bond is the uncastratable male subject to begin with. Thus, the fetish for Bond is not the substitute for the penis, but the ground zero of his masculinity in the first place. With these accessories in constant supply, thanks to Q branch, Bond's invulnerability is guaranteed. Indeed, his timelessness in the popular imagination is partly due to this invulnerability, and partly confers it in the first place. The accessory, then, which stands in for the fetish really is the fetish of the fetish; for, like the psycho-sexual fetish, it stands in for the missing marker of masculinity, even though for Bond that marker is not a penis. Moreover, this fetish-once-removed allows for an overlap between the otherwise apparently incommensurable Marxian and Freudian notions of fetishism. If the accessory is *both* a psycho-sexual fetish *and* a commodity fetish, we can begin to understand the evolution of contemporary notions of masculinity symptomized in the Bond novels and films. For Bond stands as a figure of decentered masculinity; maleness moves from the interior of the enlightenment humanist subject to the surface of the Freudian subject, and thence to the commodity marketplace of the post-modern male subject. We always already know that Bond will survive intact; the promise of the marketplace—of the next novel or film or big-name actor to play the signature role—is, in fact, the final guarantee of Bond's immunity from castration. As a sexed subject, the consuming gentleman of the West exists in this last moment. He regards market share and purchasing power as the baseline guarantor of masculinity, but the genitalia are surplus luxuries, mere markers, compared to the market's monetary masculinity. In relation to this guarantee, discretionary, discriminating, refined consumption of accessories becomes two kinds of fetishism: commodity and psycho-sexual.

As a result, the consumption of accessories only appears to be consumption without desire. The accessory does not construct the gentlemanly subject, but merely extends his reach and expresses him. But this kind of consumption is, of course, an illusion, as Drax's and Nash's experiences suggest. It is the make-believe of a marketplace that must lure men into consumption without threatening castration. And it is make-believe made belief by gentlemanly consumers who themselves wish to partake of desiring consumption without acknowledging the fundamental lack (or by scholars who wish to mask their fascination with these lurid texts behind academic inquiries into Fleming's "cultural legacy"). The accessory is not the opposite of the feminizing mark, but rather the mark of marklessness. To return to the boozy world of Bond's late nights and early mornings at continental casinos, the accessory is the martini's olive, the gibson's onion, the vodka and tonic's wedge of lime. These garnishes seem mere markers of the drink in hand, its supplemental accessories. But, as every serious drinker knows, and despite Leiter's thunderous protestations to the contrary in *Thunderball*, the olive not only marks the drink, but makes it as well. Bond, therefore, and those gentlemen consumers who emulate him, though apparently made men, will also always be marked men.

NOTES

1. The later novels *On Her Majesty's Secret Service* and *You Only Live Twice*, however, make Bond's Scots origins quite clear, probably in deference to Sean Connery's popularity in the early films. Ursula Andress's appearance as a character in *On Her Majesty's Secret Service* seems to confirm that the film *Dr. No* influenced Fleming's conception of the fictional world of 007.

2. I use the feminine pronoun here advisedly, since the kind of public display of desire that commodity consumption invites has traditionally been coded feminine, and since this coding will become essential to my argument later in this essay.

Ian Fleming
and the
Global Imaginary

8 Bond and Britishness

JAMES CHAPMAN

> Bond J. is the last man in of the British Empire Superman's XI. Holmes, Hannay, Drummond, Conquest, Templar *et al* have all succumbed to the demon bowlers of the twentieth century, while The Winds of Change make every ball a googlie.
> —Durgnat 151

> [In] the context of "swinging Britain," Bond provided a mythic encapsulation of the then prominent ideological themes of classlessness and modernity.
> —Bennett and Woollacott 34

> If there were any question about assigning the story of Bond to an American Dreamtime, it would lie in the *universality* of Bond's appeal, and not in a parochial Britishness that . . . others have insisted on ascribing to him.
> —Drummond 128

In recent years national identity, an ideologically unfashionable subject during the heyday of high theory in cultural studies, has become respectable again. If cultural commentators no longer accept the nineteenth-century idea that national identity is a naturalized phenomenon, nor do they share uncritically the view of the intellectual left that national identity is an entirely false or irrelevant ideology promoted by ruling elites to encourage social cohesion and loyalty to the nation-state. Rather, following Benedict Anderson's notion of "imagined communities," the trend in recent scholarship is to regard most forms of identity as being "constructed"—constructed by history, by geography, by politics, by institutions, by ideology, and by culture. A characteristic of much recent scholarly work on national identity is the attention now being given to the role of popular culture in the construction of shared sets of ideas and values. For the majority of people, indeed, it is largely through popular culture that concepts of identity and nationhood have been formed, disseminated, contested, and reformed.[1]

The cultural politics of national identity have long been recognized as a factor in the popularity of James Bond. The Bond novels and films have become a focus of both popular and academic attention for their representation of the codes of nationhood, imperialism, class, and masculinity. Bond scholarship has tended on the whole to fall into two distinct schools defined by method as much as by content—on the one hand the theoretical/textual approach, on the other hand the historical/contextual approach—though central to both these paradigms are questions of identity and representation.[2] That Bond has become such a contested figure—claimed variously as an old-fashioned British imperial hero, as a classless modernizer, and even as an agent of American cultural imperialism—suggests that the question of national identity in the Bond novels and films is neither straightforward nor unproblematic. Indeed, the extent to which Bond has transcended his origins as the protagonist of a series of English snobbery-with-violence thrillers to become an international cultural phenomenon, as well as the basis of the most successful continuous film series in cinema history, raises questions of cultural capital and ownership that go to the very heart of the study of popular culture.

Bond is so indelibly associated in the popular imagination with a particular image of Britishness—the suave gentleman hero whose role, in the concluding words of the film *The Spy Who Loved Me* (1977), is one of "keeping the British end up"—that it might seem unusual to problematize the nature of that Britishness. Yet that is precisely what this essay seeks to do. My thesis is that there is, and always has been, a tension between the construction of Britishness in the Bond texts themselves (by which I refer to both novels and films) and in their reception by critics and academicians. The Britishness of Bond has never been as clear-cut as some commentators would allow. Yet, as Jeremy Black sagely observes, "As so often, criticism is self-validating. Classification in terms of a set of values is presented as readily apparent. . . . The clarity and conviction of such an approach can, however, be misleading, the classification invalid and the presentation flawed. That is the case with much of the criticism of the Bond persona and corpus" (202).

In fact, Bond is something of a paradox for the cultural historian in that he represents, on the one hand, a throwback to the "clubland heroes" exemplified by characters such as John Buchan's Richard Hannay and Sapper's Bulldog Drummond, but is also, on the other hand, an embodiment of the values of meritocracy and professionalism that helped to shape British society after the Second World War.[3] The notion of Bond as a modern version of Hannay or Drummond was apparent in early reviews of the books. The anonymous reviewer of *The Times Literary Supplement*, for example, described *Casino Royale* as "an extremely engaging affair, dealing with espionage in the 'Sapper' manner, but with a hero who, although taking a great many cold showers and never letting sex interfere with work, is somewhat more sophisticated" (*TLS*, April 17, 1953, 249). The Bond novels divided critics, as has been well documented, but something that has generally been missed is that what critics disagreed about was not the quality of Fleming's writing but rather his representation of traditional themes and archetypes. Thus, on the one hand, Simon Raven liked *Casino Royale* (except for its "too monstrous to be excused" torture scene) because it combined the pace and excitement of the modern thriller with certain old-school values: "All honour, then, to Mr Fleming for taking the best elements of the Cheyney method (speed, controlled savagery, a pungent and skeptical idiom) and yet combining them with the more spacious and gracious atmosphere of old-style international intrigue—monocles, medals and milordos. Mr Fleming is a Cheyney with a Sandhurst accent" (*Listener*, April 23, 1953, 695). On the other hand, however, Paul Johnson's notorious attack on *Doctor No* condemned Fleming for much the same qualities Raven had admired: "There are three basic ingredients in *Dr No*," Johnson averred, "all unhealthy, all thoroughly English: the sadism of a schoolboy bully, the mechanical, two-dimensional sex-longings of a frustrated adolescent, and the crude snob-cravings of a suburban adult" (*New Statesman*, April 5, 1958, 431). It seems that what is at stake in these contrasting and contradictory reviews of Fleming's books is the very issue of national identity itself. To what extent did Fleming's Bond represent traditionally British (or English) values?[4]

To take the most obvious expression of Bond's national identity—his patriotism—we can see that he is very much an heir to the Hannay-Drummond heroic archetype. Bond is a conservative hero, a defender of the realm, a staunch patriot and, as the resonant title of the eleventh book asserts, an upholder of monarchy. It is true that in the first adventure Bond wonders whether "this country right-or-wrong business is getting a little out-of-date" (*Casino* 135), but that was following his torture at the hands of Le Chiffre and is entirely out of character with the books that follow. Bond is single-minded in hunting down the enemies of his country. In the short story "For Your Eyes Only," for example, Bond goes to Canada on an unofficial mission to exact rough justice for the killers of a British couple who had been personal friends of Secret

Service chief M. The mission is not officially sanctioned, but all Bond needs to justify it is to remember that "these men were as much enemies of his country as were the agents of SMERSH or of other enemy Secret Services. They had declared and waged war against British people on British soil and they were currently planning another attack" (*Your Eyes* 69). Bond's patriotism, indeed, is integral to his work as a secret agent. When he is in danger of "going to pieces" following the death of his wife at the hands of arch-villain Blofeld, Secret Service neurologist Sir James Molony describes him as "a patriotic sort of chap" and suggests that what he needs to jolt him from his depression is an assignment "that really matters to his country" (*Live Twice* 17).

The social politics of the Bond novels are essentially conservative. Thus, *The Times* is "the only newspaper that Bond ever read" (on one occasion he buys the equally conservative mass-circulation paper the *Daily Express*), and he has a sentimental attachment to the old five-pound note, which had been "the most beautiful money in the world." When he thinks about his country (usually referred to as "England" rather than "Britain") his mental image is drawn from a picture postcard: "His mind drifted into a world of tennis courts and lily ponds and kings and queens, of people being photographed with pigeons on their heads in Trafalgar Square" (*Doctor* 224). And Bond dislikes the consequences of social change, on one occasion taking an instinctive dislike to a taxi driver whom he considers "typical of the cheap self-assertiveness of young labour since the war" and on another suggesting that lesbianism was "a direct consequence of giving votes to women and 'sex equality' " (*Thunderball* 9; *Goldfinger* 222). Yet despite such occasional moments of skepticism, Bond is quick to stand up for his countrymen against Johnny Foreigner. A recurring theme of the books is the misconception of England and the English by foreigners who really should know better. "You underestimate the English," he warns Goldfinger. "They may be slow, but they get there" (*Goldfinger* 254). Crimes against the Queen's subjects must be avenged in order to prevent further atrocities: "If foreign gangsters find they can get away with this kind of thing they'll decide the English are as soft as some other people seem to think we are" (*Your Eyes* 46–47). Even allies who have formed a poor impression of the British are not immune from rebuke. When Tiger Tanaka, head of the Japanese Secret Service, tells Bond that "I, and many of us in positions of authority in Japan, have formed an unsatisfactory opinion about the British people since the war," Bond retorts that "there's nothing wrong with the British people—although there are only fifty million of them" (*Live Twice* 79, 81).

For all his patriotic fervor, however, Bond himself is not the quintessential English gentleman hero that the metaphorical comparison of him to St. George in *Goldfinger* would suggest. Bernard Bergonzi, an equally trenchant if less hysterical critic of Fleming than Paul Johnson, disputed Bond's links to the earlier generation of clubland heroes, complaining that the novels "have an air of vulgarity and display which contrast strongly with those subdued images of the perfectly self-assured gentlemanly life that we find in Buchan or even Sapper" (Bergonzi 222–23). Bond is emphatically not part of the comfortable clubland world of the upper classes: "Doesn't look the sort of chap one usually sees in Blades" (*Moonraker* 34). Indeed, Bond represents a significant shift away from the model of the English gentleman hero epitomized in popular fiction by characters such as Phileas Fogg, Allan Quatermain, Rudolph Rassendyll, Sir Percy Blakeney, Raffles, Beau Geste, Simon Templar, Hannay, and Drummond. The traditional English gentleman hero is typically characterized as decent, chivalrous, courteous, humorous, sporting, and patriotic (Richards 4–5). Probably only the last of these characteristics could be ascribed to Bond. The adjective used most frequently to describe Bond is "cruel." Bond may have some of the external trappings of a gentleman (he knows the right drinks and the right food), but quite often his behavior more closely resembles that of a cad (a true gentleman would never have resorted to cheating at cards or golf even if his opponent did so). As one contemporary critic remarked, "It is the fact of his not being a gentleman—both in this sense and in the chivalric meaning of the word—which immediately differentiates him from Buchan's Richard Hannay" (Price 69).

Fleming is at some pains to portray Bond as a modern, to some extent classless, hero. Bond, a civil servant who "liked anonymity," exemplifies what Harold Perkin has called "the rise of professional society," namely one "that is structured around career hierarchies rather than classes, one in which people find their place according to trained expertise and the service they provide rather than the possession or lack of inherited wealth or acquired capital" (Perkin 359). Bond is, above all, a professional secret agent whose attitude toward his job is in stark contrast to talented amateurs like Hannay and Drummond, for whom saving English civilization from the ambitions of diabolical criminal masterminds was a part-time occupation in between hands of bridge or hearty games of rugger:

> It was part of his profession to kill people. He had never liked doing it and when he had to kill he did it as well as he knew how and forgot about it. As a secret agent who held the rare double-O prefix—the

> licence to kill in the Secret Service—it was his duty to be as cool about
> death as a surgeon. If it happened, it happened. Regret was unprofes-
> sional—worse, it was death-watch beetle in the soul. (*Goldfinger* 3)

The many examples of Bond's professionalism in the books include his
reading up on card tricks before his meeting with Sir Hugo Drax (*Moonraker*), his meticulous preparation for his masquerade as an expert on
heraldry (*On Her Majesty's Secret Service*), and the rigorous physical
training routine he undertakes before setting off for Crab Key (*Doctor
No*). The ethos of professionalism that inflects the characterization of
Bond clearly differentiates him from the prewar school of English popular fiction.

The most striking difference between Bond and his generic pre-
decessors, however, is to be found in his attitude toward sex. In complete
contrast to the chastely romantic Hannay, Drummond, and Templar,
Bond enjoys a string of casual affairs and sexual encounters.[5] When not
on assignment, Bond spends his evenings "making love, with rather cold
passion, to one of three similarly disposed married women" (*Moonraker*
9). Bond has a different relationship in each of the books, moving from
one girlfriend to another between adventures, rarely forming anything
resembling a romantic attachment (Vesper Lynd in *Casino Royale* and
Tracy di Vincenzo in *On Her Majesty's Secret Service* are the two main
exceptions).[6] It is true that some commentators have seen Fleming's
heroines as examples of a more liberated postwar womanhood than the
dutiful wives of Hannay and Drummond on account of their taking a
more active role in the narrative: Tiffany Case (*Diamonds Are Forever*)
and Tracy (*On Her Majesty's Secret Service*) both come to Bond's rescue
at crucial moments, and it is Domino Vitali rather than Bond who kills
the villain Largo in *Thunderball*. Against this, however, must be set the
fact that "the girl" in the stories is invariably described in terms of her
physical appearance (especially her "fine breasts"), while the parodic
names invented by Fleming (Honeychile Rider, Pussy Galore, Kissy
Suzuki, Mary Goodnight) suggest that their role in the stories is one of
titillation and (male) fantasy fulfillment. The Bond novels need to be
seen in the context of a period when British society was gradually breaking free from the prurient Victorianism which had, depending on one's
view, acted as either a straightjacket or a safety valve for the previous
century. Although the "permissive society" did not fully emerge until the
1960s, changes in sexual attitudes were gradual and the seeds of change
were sown in the 1950s. As Christopher Booker has argued:

[The] new prominence of sex in the late Fifties was not just a concern with the realities of sex; even more, it was a preoccupation with the idea of sex, the image of sex, the written word, the visual image, the image that was promulgated in advertisements, in increasingly "daring" films, in "controversial" newspaper articles and "frank" novels; the image purveyed by the strip-tease clubs and pornographic book shops that were springing up in the back streets of Soho and provincial cities; and the image that, mixed with that of violence, was responsible in the years after 1956 for the enormous boom in the sales of Ian Fleming's James Bond stories. (Booker 42–43)

It is important here to acknowledge the influence of America. It is significant, if entirely coincidental, that it was in the same year as Bond's first appearance in print that *Playboy* magazine was launched in the United States. The Bond books embody the *Playboy* ethos of easy, free, open sexuality, emphasizing sexual pleasure (for men) and a lack of guilt about the sex act itself. As Bond reflects after his night of train-compartment passion with Jill Masterson: "Neither had had regrets. Had they committed a sin? If so, which one? A sin against chastity? . . . There was a quotation for that too, and from a saint—Saint Augustine: 'Oh Lord, give me Chastity. But don't give it yet!' " (*Goldfinger* 48).

Historical context, indeed, is essential to a proper understanding of the Bond novels. Bond "is a man of his time: he belongs to the England of Macmillan and Clore and Hughie Green" (Price 69). This is apparent on so many different levels in the books that it is beyond the scope of this essay to mention them all, but a select list would include the politics of the Cold War (Bond's enemies in all the books written during the 1950s, barring *Diamonds Are Forever,* are either Soviet or Soviet-backed), the decline of Britain as a global power, the "retreat from empire" that accelerated in the late 1950s and early 1960s (Tiger Tanaka taunts Bond that "[y]ou have not only lost a great Empire, you have seemed almost anxious to throw it away with both hands"), and the shift in Britain from a culture of austerity to the beginnings of affluence (exemplified in Bond's habit of conspicuous consumption and his penchant for brand-name goods with snob value). It is surely no coincidence that the popularity of the Bond books began to take off in the later 1950s, when the sort of lifestyle Fleming described for his hero (if not the actual goods themselves) was becoming more attainable at a time when, in the oft-misquoted words of Prime Minister Harold Macmillan, "most of our people have never had it so good." By the end of the decade, indeed, there was much evidence to support Arthur Marwick's contention that "the reality for the vast majority of British people was that at last the country seemed to have emerged into the kind of high-spending consumer society long familiar from American films" (110).

Bennett and Woollacott identify 1957—the year that *From Russia with Love* was serialized in the *Daily Express* and when a "James Bond" strip cartoon began in the same newspaper—as "the first stage in the transformation of Bond from a character within a set of fictional texts into a household name" (24). It is far too often overlooked that sales of the Bond novels were increasing before the production of the films and that the advertising campaigns for the early films placed much emphasis on the books. The theatrical trailer for *Dr. No,* for example, asserted that it was "an exciting new motion picture . . . from Ian Fleming whose brilliant action filled books have entertained millions of readers." The U.S. film trade press believed there was a ready-made audience for the films due to the popularity of the books: "The vast numbers of people in this country, not to mention those overseas, who have read avidly, hungrily and expectantly every story of intrigue and excitement written by Ian Fleming . . . form a wide, waiting and ready audience for the first of the films based on the James Bond stories" (*Motion Picture Herald,* April 3, 1963, 785).

That said, however, it was the success of the films—which in turn boosted sales of the books—that "both significantly broadened the social basis of Bond's popular appeal in Britain and extended the horizons of his popularity internationally" (Bennett and Woollacott 29). The conventional explanation for the success of the films is that they remodeled Bond into a classless hero more in tune with the ethos of the 1960s, though, as I have argued, there was already an element of classlessness in the books. Moreover, the first of the films, *Dr. No,* was redolent with the remnants of British imperialism and the class system that sustained it. Durgnat, for one, considered that the colonial location of this particular narrative (Jamaica had in fact become independent on August 1, 1962, between production and release of the film) represented nothing more than "Edwardiana in modern drag . . . The British Raj, reduced to its Caribbean enclave, lords it benevolently over jovial and trusting West Indians and faithful coloured police-sergeants, the Uncle Toms of Dock Green" (Durgnat 151).[7] A rather more convincing explanation for the success of the Bond films, however, especially given the political economy of the film industry, is that they made Bond into something more than a purely British hero.

Sarah Street observes that the Bond films are "fascinating as examples of texts that crossed cultural boundaries" (*Transatlantic Crossings* 183). The Bond films represent the combination of American finance (United Artists) and British cultural capital (the source material). They use a British production base (Pinewood Studios) and British technical personnel—an important consideration in the decision to make the films in Britain was that they qualified for the Eady Levy, which provided a subsidy for British productions, distributed according to the box-office success of the films—and are imbued with a sense of Britishness in terms of both content and performance. At the same time, however, this is a Britishness packaged for the international market. With their American backing, the Bond films could afford the level of production values and visual gloss usually associated with big-budget Hollywood films. Richards attests that the formula of the Bond films was "an unbeatable blend of conspicuous consumption, brand-name snobbery, technological gadgetry, colour supplement chic, exotic locations and comic-strip sex and violence" (Richards 163). While this is certainly correct, these elements were all present, to a greater or a lesser extent, in the books. What was it about the films that made them substantially different from the books?

The narrative differences between the books and the films are relatively superficial, especially in the early films that remained closely based on Fleming's stories (from *Dr. No* to *On Her Majesty's Secret Service*, with the exception of *You Only Live Twice*, the plots of the films are recognizable as only slightly modified versions of Fleming's). It is true that the films detached Bond from the Cold War background of the 1950s novels and instead adopted the device of an international crime syndicate as Bond's main antagonist—thus the removal of SMERSH from the first three films and its replacement in the first two by SPECTRE—but this was merely utilizing a device that Fleming had written into the books with *Thunderball*.[8] While the later films have abandoned Fleming's plots entirely, they have tended to refashion the plots of earlier films: *The Spy Who Loved Me* bears many narrative similarities to *You Only Live Twice*, for example, while *A View to a Kill* is a reworking of *Goldfinger*. Most of the narrative possibilities of the Bond films, indeed, were established in the first three films—science fiction (*Dr. No*), taut thriller (*From Russia with Love*), master criminal (*Goldfinger*)—which were closely based on the Fleming originals. The differences between books and films, therefore, are not to be found in their narratives.

It was in the characterization of Bond himself that the films parted most substantially from their source material. The Bond of the films is a more humorous and ironic character: the throwaway one-liners that director Terence Young and star Sean Connery introduced had not been present in the books. The code of patriotism is downplayed, and when there are references to nation and duty, they tend to be ironic rather than serious.[9] And Bond's attitude to authority is different in the films: whereas Fleming's Bond was fiercely loyal toward M, Connery's Bond has a rebellious streak that suggests a less deferential attitude toward his chief. This aspect of character and performance was probably influenced by the "angry young men" of British stage and screen—characters such as Jimmy Porter (*Look Back in Anger*), Joe Lampton (*Room at the Top*), and Arthur Seaton (*Saturday Night and Sunday Morning*), who were abrasive, brusque, and defiantly anti-authoritarian. It was here that the casting of Sean Connery was most adroit. Connery's style of performance, his unique combination of brawny physicality and graceful movement on screen, had little in common with previous British male stars like Ronald Colman, Robert Donat, and David Niven, with their gentlemanly poise and polite vowels, and owed more to the rugged masculinity and physical presence of American stars such as Gary Cooper, Clark Gable, and Humphrey Bogart. Connery's trace of a Scottish accent—not yet the exaggerated tone of his later career—has the effect of detaching Bond from the pukka-Englishness of Fleming's preferred choice for the role, David Niven, and making him, as Fleming had hinted in *Moonraker*, something of an outsider. What the films did, in effect, was to re-create Bond as what is generally termed a "trans-Atlantic" hero, a character whose apparent classlessness would appeal to American audiences while still maintaining enough of the character's British origins to satisfy audiences at home.[10]

It is a rule of thumb of the film industry that the North American market (meaning the United States and Canada) accounts for up to 50 percent of the total worldwide box office. In the case of the Bond films, the American market accounts for approximately one-third of the total box-office gross—testimony to the genuine international appeal of the films—but is still the most important single market. To this end the Bond films have been at pains to appeal to the American market. It is significant that the film that really marked Bond's breakthrough in America was neither *Dr. No* (set entirely within the British Commonwealth and featuring only a marginal American involvement through the presence of Jack Lord as Felix Leiter) nor *From Russia with Love* (set entirely in Europe with no American presence at all), but *Goldfinger* (set mostly in the United States and with the threat directed against America). *Gold-finger* took in $23 million in North America, compared to $6.4 million for *Dr. No* and $9.9 million for *From Russia with Love. Thunderball* (set in the Bahamas but with a threat again directed against an American target, in this case Miami) took in $28.6 million.[11] In both *Goldfinger* and *Thunderball*—and again in *Diamonds Are Forever, Live and Let Die,* and *A View to a Kill*—Bond acts in the interests of America, defending her from economic disaster (*Goldfinger, A View to a Kill*), nuclear blackmail (*Thunderball, Diamonds Are Forever*), and a massive influx of heroin (*Live and Let Die*). Whereas in the books Britain had been the dominant partner in the Anglo-American alliance—a quaint reversal of the real balance of power, reflected in the professional and personal relationship between Bond and his CIA colleague Felix Leiter[12]—in the films Britain and America are presented as equals.

The casting of Roger Moore in the role in the 1970s and early 1980s signified a return to "a comforting national stereotype" (Street, *National Cinema* 87) insofar as Moore's star persona was very much that of the English gentleman hero from his previous television career as Simon Templar in *The Saint* and aristocratic playboy Lord Brett Sinclair in *The Persuaders!* It is significant that Moore's very English Bond was less attuned to the tastes of American audiences than Connery's had been: Moore's first film, *Live and Let Die,* took in less in North America ($15.9 million) than Connery's *Diamonds Are Forever* ($19.7 million), and his second, *The Man with the Golden Gun,* had an even poorer return ($9.4 million). The most successful of the Moore Bonds (in all markets) was *Moonraker,* which took in $33 million in North America. This can be explained through a combination of the film's science-fiction theme, riding the wave of the sci-fi boom following the phenomenal popular success of *Star Wars* (1977), and its topicality, featuring the U.S. space shuttle as a plot device some two years before the first shuttle flight. In *Moonraker* Bond is again part of an Anglo-American alliance insofar as he is teamed with NASA scientist Dr. Holly Goodhead and a party of U.S. "Space Marines" who help to save the day.

Neither of the Timothy Dalton films (*The Living Daylights* and *Licence to Kill*) did especially well in America, even though the second featured a Noriega-like drug baron, Sanchez, who poses a direct threat to American security. Dalton, for all his occasional flat northern vowels, was probably too much the stage actor to be convincing as an action hero in the age of Willis, Schwarzenegger, and Stallone. However, the four Pierce Brosnan films to date (*GoldenEye, Tomorrow Never Dies, The*

World Is Not Enough, and *Die Another Day)* have all grossed over $100 million at the American box office. While this increase is due in no small measure to the effect of inflation, it also suggests that Brosnan's Bond has greater appeal to American audiences than his predecessor's did. British film critic Philip French felt that Brosnan, "a classless Celt, has a superficial resemblance to Sean Connery" (*Observer Review,* December 14, 1997, 12). The evidence would seem to suggest, therefore, that "Celtic" Bond (Brosnan of course is Irish) is more acceptable to American audiences than pukka-English Bond. The greater warmth of American audiences toward Brosnan also undoubtedly owes something to his previous television role as smooth gentleman detective *Remington Steele.* American audiences were already familiar with Brosnan and were predisposed to accept him as Bond.[13]

Bond's role as a virtual surrogate American hero in several of the films has led some commentators to claim him for American popular culture. Drew Moniot, for example, argues that Bond appealed to American cinema-goers in the 1960s because the films tapped into a mood of disillusion and disenchantment with the "corporate state" which had created a social climate controlled by a hierarchical, mechanical, dehumanized organization indifferent to the rights and interests of the individual. In this argument the 007 fan, "vaguely sensing a loss of identity and worth in the age of the corporate state, could vicariously experience a certain sense of triumph and relief when Bond struck a blow against SPECTRE" (30). It is an intriguing argument, though ultimately unconvincing insofar as Bond himself also belongs to what might be compared to a corporate organization (the Secret Service). Indeed, it was contested even at the time by one commentator who felt that Bond was "intellectually fraudulent" in the era of the Vietnam War and that "Spectre—that diabolical world organization of sin and corruption—seems less corrupt than Bond himself, not to mention his heartless superiors who license 007 to kill" (*New York Times,* February 1, 1970, S2, 19).

Perhaps the most absurd attempt to claim Bond for America, however, has come from media sociologist Lee Drummond, who argues that "the *story of Bond* . . . has become fully incorporated into the larger, ongoing *story of America,* the Dreamtime chronicle of that rich, gimmicky and bizarre land that is less a place than a state of mind" (128). Drummond's argument is that the Bond films were the first truly global media phenomena of the modern age, crossing boundaries of language, social background, ethnicity, and culture. To some extent, certainly, this is correct—there is a good case for seeing Bond as "the very first truly global media sensation"—but Drummond's argument falls down in its insistence that this necessarily makes Bond a product of American culture. If the twentieth century was, as is so often claimed, the "American century," then it was due not merely to the projection of American economic and military power but also to the spread of a mass culture originating from America. It is significant that the other examples of cultural icons Drummond cites (Luke Skywalker, Indiana Jones, E.T., Sue Ellen and J. R. Ewing, Rocky, and Rambo) are all American. For the American critic, it seems, Bond is part of the process that has brought about the "Coca-Colonization" or "McDonaldization" of global culture.

The argument that Bond represents a form of American cultural imperialism is highly contestable. It ignores the origin of Bond in a British historical and generic context, and it marginalizes the ideologies of Britishness that inform the Bond narratives. While the literary Bond is a uniquely British cultural and ideological construct, it is probably appropriate to regard the cinema's Bond as neither purely "British" nor wholly "American" but rather as an "international" construct. Bond in the films functions as a sort of international Mr. Fix-It who just happens to be British. An important difference between the books and the films is that rarely in the films has the conspiracy been directed solely against Britain (*From Russia with Love, For Your Eyes Only,* and *GoldenEye* are the only instances). In most of the films it is the Western world as a whole that is threatened, and Bond's role is therefore as a protector of Western interests. The most explicit statement of this role comes, oddly enough, from one of the films made outside the official Bond series (*Never Say Never Again*) when British comedian Rowan Atkinson, playing Our Man in the Bahamas, tells Sean Connery's 007 (returning to Bondage for the one film only), "M says that without you in the service he fears for the security of the civilized world."

It would probably be fair to say that James Bond has become something bigger than Ian Fleming ever intended. Bond was, or so Fleming claimed, "the author's pillow fantasy . . . the Walter Mitty syndrome—the feverish dream of the author of what he might have been—bang, bang, kiss, kiss—that sort of stuff" (Lane 15). Through his various incarnations in the cinema, Bond became more than just Fleming's fantasy *alter ego:* he became the world's foremost idea of what a British hero should be. The fact that Bond represents an imaginary notion of Britishness—a fantasy hero who could never exist in reality—is hardly the point, for popular culture more often than not reflects back what people want to see rather than what is really there. The continuing popularity of Bond is eloquent testimony to the enduring cultural potency of Fleming's creation and to the myth-making powers of the Bond filmmakers. It is also due in large measure to the ideological flexibility of the Bond character and the various forms of Britishness that it represents.

NOTES

1. The scholarly literature on national identity is immense. Anderson remains the pioneering theoretical study. Colley is the most influential recent account of the historical formation of a sense of nationhood in Britain. Heffer and Paxman exemplify the political investment in popular notions of Englishness, while the fruits of recent scholarship are represented from a historical perspective by Colls and Weight and from an interdisciplinary cultural studies perspective in Walton. The cultural representation of English/British national identity is investigated by Giroud and Richards.

2. The theoretical/textual approach is exemplified in the books by Bennett and Woollacott, Boyd, and Del Buono and Eco, which apply—respectively—a Gramscian, Christian moralist, and structuralist analysis to the Bond narratives. The historical/contextual approach, which assumes that the novels and films should be seen in relation to the political, social, and cultural conditions of the times in which they were produced, is exemplified by Black, Cannadine, and Chapman (*Licence* 1999). While I recognize that the paradigms of "theory" and "history" might not be accepted by all scholars, including some of the contributors to the present volume, there are nevertheless significant *methodological* differences within Bond scholarship.

3. See Usborne, Watson, and Denning (1987) for, respectively, a celebratory, a critical, and a scholarly account of this type of fiction. Richard Hannay was the hero of five novels by John Buchan: *The Thirty-Nine Steps* (1915), *Greenmantle* (1916), *Mr Standfast* (1919), *The Three Hostages* (1924), and *The Island of Sheep* (1936). Hugh "Bulldog" Drummond appeared in a series of novels by "Sapper" (pen name of Herman Cyril McNeile, an officer of the Royal Engineers): *Bulldog Drummond* (1920), *The Black Gang* (1922), *The Third Round* (1924), *The Final Count* (1926), *The Female of the Species* (1928), *Temple Tower* (1929), *The Return of Bulldog Drummond* (1932), *Bulldog Drummond at Bay* (1934), *Knock-Out* (1936), and *Challenge* (1937). After McNeile's death the series was continued by Gerald Fairlie.

4. Bond's "obituary" in *You Only Live Twice* reveals that Bond had a Scottish father and a Swiss mother and so was not strictly English at all. At the end of *The Man with the Golden Gun* Bond refuses a knighthood, citing as his reason that he is "a Scottish peasant" (180). It is significant, however, that both these books were written after Sean Connery had made his first appearance as Bond in *Dr. No.* The fact that Fleming would have preferred David Niven as Bond (Lycett, *Ian Fleming* 393) suggests that he saw Bond as an Englishman.

5. Hannay is married to Mary Marston, whom he met in *Mr Standfast,* by the beginning of *The Three Hostages;* Drummond married Phyllis Benton at the end of his first adventure; while Templar has a steady girlfriend in Patricia Holm.

6. In *The James Bond Dossier*—still the most accessible and astute literary study of the Fleming stories—Kingsley Amis suggested that Bond's sexual conquests were not excessive by the standards of the day: "Bond collects almost exactly one girl per excursion abroad, which total he exceeds only once, by one. This is surely not at all in advance of what any reasonably personable, reasonably well-off bachelor would reckon to acquire on a foreign holiday or a trip for his firm" (46).

7. However, see Baron for a more nuanced discussion of the representation of race and imperialism in *Dr. No*.

8. SMERSH is a contraction of *Smiert Spionam,* meaning "Death to Spies"; SPECTRE stands for "Special Executive for Counter-Intelligence, Terrorism, Revenge and Extortion." From *Casino Royale* to *Goldfinger,* with the sole exception of *Diamonds Are Forever,* the villain is either an agent or an associate of SMERSH. In the films of *Dr. No* and *From Russia with Love,* SMERSH is replaced by SPECTRE, necessitating an explanation in *From Russia with Love* that Rosa Klebb, formerly chief of operations for SMERSH, has defected to join SPECTRE. Goldfinger, in the novel the "foreign banker" of SMERSH, becomes a freelance operator in the film, backed by Red China.

9. A good example is in *You Only Live Twice* (1967) where Bond murmurs, "The things I do for England!" as he prepares to bed villainess Helga Brandt. The original theatrical trailer for *Thunderball* reveals that the line had been used in that film but cut from the release print. The comment recalls Charles Laughton's line in Alexander Korda's *The Private Life of Henry VIII* (1933) when the King pauses on the threshold of his bedroom following his marriage to Anne of Cleves and remarks, "The things I've done for England!"

10. Interestingly, reviewers of *Dr. No,* both British and American, had difficulty in placing Connery's accent, which several described as "Irish-American" (Chapman, *Licence* 86).

11. These figures are the "rental receipts," i.e., the amount received by distributors after exhibitors have taken their cut. For information regarding the box-office grosses of the Bond films, see *Variety,* May 13, 1987; *The Hollywood Reporter,* July 14, 1987; *Screen International,* December 5, 1997; and *Screen International,* November 15, 2002.

12. Amis was typically astute on this aspect of the books: "The point of Felix Leiter, such a nonentity as a piece of characterization, is that he, the American, takes orders from Bond, the Britisher, and that Bond is constantly doing better than he, showing himself, not braver or more devoted, but smarter, wittier, tougher, more resourceful, the incarnation of little old England with her quiet ways and shoestring budget wiping the eye of great big global-tentacled multi-billion-dollar-appropriating America" (90).

13. Brosnan, like Moore, was an established television star when he became Bond. However, Brosnan would have had greater visibility in America, as *Remington Steele* was a U.S. prime time network series, whereas *The Saint* and *The Persuaders!* were British-produced shows bought as schedule fillers by the U.S. networks. *The Saint* had initially been rejected by U.S. networks for being "too English," but had proved popular in syndication and was bought by NBC, which fully networked 32 episodes (of the 118 produced). *The Persuaders!* was bought by ABC but fared badly in the ratings and was taken off air after only 20 of the 24 episodes had been broadcast.

9 Shoot Back in Anger

BOND AND THE "ANGRY YOUNG MAN"

BRIAN PATTON

James Bond is widely regarded as a quintessentially English figure—or "British," perhaps, in the wake of the Scottish Sean Connery's seminal performances in the early films of the 1960s—but that famous "license to kill" was never validated for use on British soil. As Fleming's narrator remarks in *Moonraker,* "Abroad was what mattered. He would never have a job to do in England. Outside the jurisdiction of the Service" (34). Bond's violent craft is normally practiced in places like the United States, Japan, Turkey, French Guinea, various tropical outposts of the soon-to-be-eclipsed British Empire, and other locations abroad that would have appeared exotic to many of Ian Fleming's contemporaries. Indeed, with the exception of the late short story "The Property of a Lady," *Moonraker* (1955) is the only one of Fleming's James Bond adventures set entirely in England, and, perhaps more than any of those tales of Bond's foreign intrigues, this novel sheds light on the idea of England for which this very English spy is willing to kill or die—and on the surprisingly difficult relationship between Her Majesty's secret servant and his imaginary homeland.

At the time of *Moonraker*'s publication, the state of England as it emerged from the shadow of the war was being probed with some urgency among the nation's writers, especially in the work of a handful of newcomers often lumped together under the banner of the "Angry Young Man," a social type who seemed for a time to be everywhere: on stage, on the page, behind the typewriter, angrily tapping out more fictional versions of himself, and, by the decade's end, on the screen in the handful of "British New Wave" films adapted from the work of this group of writers.[1] An early manifestation of the type was Charles Lumley, the class-rebel at the center of John Wain's first novel, *Hurry On Down* (1953); a more famous one was Kingsley Amis's Jim Dixon, who appeared in *Lucky Jim* in the following year. Arguably the most genuinely *angry* young man, Jimmy Porter, first appeared on the stage of the Royal Court Theatre in 1956, in John Osborne's play *Look Back in Anger*. By the time Joe Lampton made his debut in John Braine's novel *Room at the Top* in 1957, the "Angry Young Man" was already a well-established, if foggily defined, cultural myth, so that when Ian Fleming wrote in 1963, "I am not an angry, young, or even middle-aged man" ("How to Write" 14), it would have been immediately clear to most readers that he was drawing a line between his own adventure stories for "warm-blooded heterosexuals" and other contemporary fictions supposedly more concerned with mapping the present state of the nation as viewed from the kitchen sink or thereabouts. That Fleming even felt it worth drawing that line suggests the contemporary popularity of angry-young-man spotting, a trend that saw some very unlikely candidates put forward for membership in the club. Prominent among these is Iris Murdoch, whose first novel, *Under the Net* (1954), bore some surface similarities to those of Amis and Wain, as a result of which she found herself having to point out what ought to have been obvious: that she was neither angry, nor young, nor a man.

In retrospect, it would appear that the widespread currency of the phrase "angry young man" was at best a mixed blessing for the writers who found themselves or their creations wearing it. No doubt the journalistic search for the next "Angry" drew welcome attention to the work of hitherto unknown writers, but it also had a homogenizing effect, obscuring the breadth of work and the variety of writers behind the eye-catching label. Even when they were in fact young and male, not all of the so-called "Angries" were angry in the same way or about the same things: the comically unambitious Jim Dixon and the venom-spitting Jimmy Porter, for instance, are hardly cut from the same cloth. And despite V. S. Pritchett's rather incongruous description of Amis, Braine, and a handful of others in a 1957 essay as "the Teddy Boys of Literature," hindsight fails to reveal an entirely convincing barbarian horde at the gates of the citadel. Still, Pritchett's invocation of the Teddy Boy is suggestive of an anxiety that was far from unique at the time of his writing. When gangs of Teddy Boys (also known as "Teds" or "Edwardians," owing to the cut of the jackets they favored) began to appear on British streets in the mid-1950s, they constituted a new phenomenon that has since become familiar: a highly visible youth subculture whose rebellion from perceived societal norms is signaled by a distinctive form of dress.[2] The Teds represented the *first* such subculture to gain national recognition, and, like the "Angry Young Men" with whom they were sometimes conflated, they appear to have embodied for many the threatening possibilities of a new postwar generation disdainful of the traditions of the old.[3] Commenting on *Lucky Jim* in the Christmas 1955 edition of *The Sunday Times,* Somerset Maugham noted an "ominous significance" in its representation of a "new class that has entered on the scene" at Britain's universities, men "who go there on a Government grant," who "do not go . . . to acquire culture, but to get a job, and when they have got one, scamp it." Worse still, Maugham warned, this rough beast of the welfare state would soon begin its inevitable slouch toward Whitehall: "Some will doubtless sink back, perhaps with relief, into the modest class from which they emerged; some will take to drink, some to crime and go to prison . . . A few will go to Parliament, become Cabinet Ministers and rule the country. I look upon myself as fortunate that I shall not live to see it."[4] Nearly fifty years later, the thought of Sir Kingsley Amis as a "Teddy Boy" is risible, but viewed through conservative eyes in the context of a nation and an empire so significantly reshaping itself, the connection is perhaps not quite so absurd. Myths, however fuzzily articulated, often arise for a specific cultural reason, and we might regard the media noise about "Angry Young Men" or Pritchett's "Teddy Boys of Literature" or, indeed, Teddy Boys themselves, as arising from attempts to imaginatively embody the *zeitgeist,* to discover the emerging creatures of postwar Britain.

The challenges facing Britain in the years after the war are familiar to students of the period. Abroad, the military victory of 1945 was quickly followed by a major fracture in the Empire when India, the celebrated jewel in the imperial crown, won its independence in 1947. In international affairs, Britain was being eclipsed by the now vastly more wealthy and powerful United States. While the Suez Crisis of 1956 is usually regarded as a watershed moment in British imperial history, that notorious debacle really only made plain what most observers had already recognized: the days of overwhelming British power abroad were finished. *Moonraker,* published in the year prior to Suez, already knows this well. At home, the Labour governments of 1945–51 set about implementing the radical social and economic reforms behind the "welfare state," with the national and local governments assuming responsibility for social security, housing, medical services, and education—a project carried on by Churchill's Conservatives when they formed the government in 1951. Of course, not all were pleased with this development. Toward the end of *Casino Royale* (1953), Bond himself remarks critically upon the postwar refashioning of British Conservatism that marked this extended period of political "consensus": "If I'd been alive fifty years ago," he says to his French liaison René Mathis, "the brand of Conservatism we have today would have been damn near called Communism and we should have been told to go and fight that" (135). Maugham's grim prognostication that "scum" would soon be running Parliament resonates with a widespread concern over the supposed dissolution of a long-established social hierarchy in which many, including the author of the James Bond series, had a considerable emotional investment.

The cultural landscape that gave rise to both James Bond and to the myth of the "Angry Young Man," then, was an uncertain one. And while the figures who wear the "Angry" label may not always bear obvious similarities to each other, they do share a sense of dislocation from the cultural landscape and disengagement from the social order and the institutions that they have inherited: they are creatures of a transitional time. Set in England in more or less its own present, *Moonraker* offers Fleming's fullest take on this transitional time. My aim in this essay is not to try to refute Fleming's denial and secure for either Bond or his creator a place in any supposed league of Angry Young Men. Rather, I wish to consider *Moonraker* as a product of this cultural moment and to trace some of the connections between Fleming's England and the disoriented nation portrayed in these other accounts of this transformational period in British history. *Moonraker* is an imperial thriller set rather awkwardly in a declining empire, whose hero works in the service of an idea of the nation that is passing out of existence. That Britain appeared at the time on the brink of a fundamental change is suggested by the novel's bipartite narrative structure. The contest between Bond and Drax is a game of two halves most obviously distinguished by their settings: the first, the bridge match at Blades, is redolent of an old, aristocratic, and imperial Britain; the second, the encounter at Drax's missile site on the Kentish coast, takes place in the shadow of an up-to-the-minute technological marvel, a huge atomic rocket whose presence unavoidably suggests the new postwar order in which late-imperial Britain is struggling to establish its place.

The eponymous Moonraker serves as a symbol of modernity, firmly locating the novel's action in a fictionalized version of its own present. As Jeremy Black has noted in *The Politics of James Bond,* at the time of

Fleming's writing, Britain had just become the world's third atomic power—in 1952, to be precise—and "the Joint Intelligence Committee warned that war with the USSR would lead to serious rocket attacks on London" (18). Furthermore, Black observes that the development of rocket technology itself spelled "the end of British invulnerability" (16). Britannia's famous boast was that it ruled the waves, but the development of air power and rocket technology over the course of the previous century greatly diminished the force of this claim. Certainly, less than a decade after the war, there was still plenty of evidence throughout Britain of the destruction that could be caused by enemy bombers and by rockets, such as the German V-1 and V-2, which carried only conventional explosives. More than just a symbol of modernity, then, the Moonraker is also a compelling symbol of the nation's newly discovered vulnerability. That Drax is secretly a German enemy-within further suggests that the plot of *Moonraker* may have arisen in part from Fleming's own concerns stemming from the debates of the early 1950s regarding the admissibility of West Germany into the NATO alliance. The book might be approached as a sort of literary intervention into the debate, with Drax and the German caricatures surrounding him embodying the potential for German treachery. In his closing comments, M offers a reading of the novel's events as a cautionary tale: "Well, we all knew there was plenty of Nazism left," he says, "and this will make the Cabinet go just a bit more carefully on German rearmament" (239). However hopeful, though, M's implication that the question of German rearmament was in the hands of the British Cabinet is deceptive. According to Black, "the British [especially the Labour opposition] were much less enthusiastic than the Americans" about the prospect of rearming West Germany, but it was ultimately the pro-German argument that held sway, and West Germany joined NATO in 1955, the year of *Moonraker*'s publication (Black 21).

England, as Fleming portrays it in *Moonraker,* is astonishingly vulnerable—in fact, the novel's implausible plot arises directly from this sense of vulnerability. As a scheme for the national defense, the Moonraker plan would appear to leave much to be desired: a virtual unknown, a man with no memory prior to the end of the war, has suddenly come into great wealth. He proposes to build a rocket carrying a nuclear warhead as a deterrent to enemy attacks on Britain. With the blessings of the Queen and Parliament, he establishes a relatively isolated coastal site for the project, where none are permitted entrance save himself, fifty bald and mustached Germans who worked on the rockets that devastated

Britain during the war, and a mere two representatives of Her Majesty's government. Fortunately, one of the two is James Bond; otherwise, one wonders who could fail to invade a nation so defended!

The plot is admittedly ludicrous, but it voices a genuine anxiety about military impotence and political desperation rooted in economic crisis at a time when the Cold War was sending shivers down spines. It is within this economically and militarily compromised Britain that Drax is able to operate so effectively. In the midst of a diatribe worthy of a villain who is part Nazi and part Soviet agent, Drax offers a description of the state of the nation that the novel itself never quite dispels: "I loathe and despise you all," he spits at Bond and his female accomplice, Gala Brand. "Useless, idle, decadent fools, hiding behind your bloody white cliffs while other people fight your battles. Too weak to defend your colonies, toadying to America with your hats in your hands" (210). Obviously, Drax is being made to play the evil foreigner here, an all too familiar stock character of the imperial adventure story[5]—but, significantly, a similarly humbling observation regarding British decline is made earlier, with far greater subtlety, by Fleming's narrator. As Bond and Gala stare out together over the Kentish coastline, the description of the landscape eases into a description of the historical resonance of that landscape: "It was a wonderful afternoon of blue and green and gold. . . . They stopped for a moment on the edge of the great chalk cliff and stood gazing over the whole corner of England where Caesar had first landed two thousand years before" (143). The subsequent paragraph extends their gaze imaginatively along the majestic coast toward Margate and the mouth of the Thames, but one detail disrupts the suggestion of a steady historical line that might be traced from Caesar through Vera Lynn to the present moment: the "Thunderjets [writing] their white scribbles in the sky" (143) are both modern-day symbols and agents of the defense of the realm, but they are not *British* jets but American. For Fleming, as for most other Britons at this time, recognizing a diminished British might did not require the exclamation mark that Suez was to provide in the months to come.

What seems to have opened the door for Drax in the first place, then, is that Britain stands desperately in want of an independent say in world affairs that it cannot have as long as those "American Thunderjets" are needed. The Moonraker promises a degree of made-in-England national security that would be unimaginable without the initiative and private sponsorship of this one man. Bond himself acknowledges that what Drax has done for Britain with his Moonraker project is "far beyond what any government seems able to do," adding (in a comment that would no doubt have added to V. S. Pritchett's despair) that "it's really extraordinary that they [the British public] don't insist on making him Prime Minister" (16–17). In the eyes of the common folk, Drax is a "national hero." This heroic status seems able to transcend the man's unavoidable physical deformities—the "shining puckered skin that covered most of the right half of his face," the mismatched ears and eyes, one of which he is unable to close completely, "the naturally prognathous upper jaw and a marked protrusion of the upper jaw and teeth" that both Fleming's narrator and Bond himself describe as "ogre's teeth" (38, 213). These physical deformities are married to Drax's usually appalling manners: he is a braggart, a bully, and a cheat—a grotesque caricature of a man, a bestial figure who "brays" and "barks" when he laughs (48, 117). Yet, in the face of Drax's Moonraker project—Britain's hoped-for salvation—not even the sum of all these negative qualities can dim Drax's apparent luster.

Significantly, this rapt admiration born of expediency is not limited to the common folk. The mandarins of the Ministry of Supply have been won over, as has the prime minister. Even Bond himself—*after* he has caught Drax cheating at cards in the holiest shrine of English gambling—has moments of rapture as he ponders the wonder of modern capitalism that is Sir Hugo Drax. In *Moonraker,* the villain's ability to infiltrate the political halls of power and the cultural haunts of the establishment is indicative of the social disjuncture arising from England's own attempts to negotiate the passage from its celebrated past to its uncertain future. England's social landscape has apparently shifted in such a way that a would-be destroyer, Drax, has gained a remarkably sure foothold on it, while those who ought to be defending the nation are all but oblivious to his presence. Having cornered the market in a valuable ore called "Columbite," Drax has earned a vast fortune in just a few years, and has made a gift of £10 million toward the development of (to quote Bond) "a super atomic rocket with a range that would cover nearly every capital in Europe—the immediate answer to anyone who tried to atom-bomb London" (20). In fact, the rocket is intended to destroy London itself—an impending test-flight threatens devastation if Drax's plot is allowed to proceed. The novel's plot, then, arises from a new sense of vulnerability not only to enemies abroad (Drax is eventually revealed to be an unreformed Nazi now in the service of the Soviet Union), but also to an enemy within.

Drax's successful infiltration of Blades is noteworthy because it indicates that, despite his obvious resemblance to an Ian Fleming super-villain, he has managed to charm his way not only into the hearts of the British public, but into the very heart of the British establishment itself. The episode at Blades that dominates the first half of *Moonraker* is at the center of the book's nostalgia for an imagined old and undiminished England. Fleming's narrator describes Blades as "probably the most fa-mous private card club in the world" (27), whose origins lie somewhere in the Regency period, when gaming clubs and coffee houses became the haunts of London's elite. He dwells admiringly on the architectural and decorative details of the place, most of which suggest its Regency ori-gins—from its "Adam frontage" and "the fine Lawrence of Beau Brum-mel over the wide Adam fireplace" (32, 35) to "the beautiful white and gold Regency dining room" and the "small gas-jet enclosed in a silver grille—a relic of the days before the use of matches" (45, 47). The club's apparently unshakable edifice is founded on a social hierarchy so fixed and harmonious that it borders on the feudal, a still earlier era suggested by "the old-fashioned porter's lodge ruled over by Brevett, the guardian of Blades and the counsellor and family friend of half the members . . . whose family had held the same post at Blades for a hundred years" (32–33). Like the white cliffs of Dover—another nationally symbolic site in which Drax has (literally, in that case) carved out a space for himself—Blades is a repository of English history, a remnant of the Regency London of the aristocrats and their hangers-on who populated clubs such as this one. In Fleming's account, through Bond's adoring eyes, Blades is anything but an anachronism—it is, rather, a vital, living rem-nant of a more elegant and decorous time, an oasis where Bond's ideal England is most fully realized, where each man, whatever his failings, is "invested . . . with a kind of aristocracy" (52).

The description of Blades reveals a telling split in the narrator's apparent understanding of the club's cultural significance. On the one hand, the gentlemanly ideal on display here is presented as the quintes-sence of Englishness. When Bond challenges Drax in the game of bridge, he is playing for Blades and, by extension, for England, defending the code of fair play against a dastardly cheat who would sully it. As Bond sits back in his chair, he imagines the ghosts of former members crowding around him, looking down approvingly on the "rough justice" he is about to administer to Drax:

> He sat back in his chair and for a moment he had the impression that there was a crowd behind him at each elbow, and that faces were

peering over his shoulder, waiting to see his cards. He somehow felt that the ghosts were friendly, that they approved of the rough justice that was about to be done.

He smiled as he caught himself sending this company of dead gamblers a message, that they should see that all went well. (63)

As readers—however dubious the "kind of aristocracy" we might ourselves embody—we are also implicitly invited into this approving circle, not only by virtue of our vicariously experiencing the drama of the bridge match, but also by way of Fleming's narrative sleight-of-hand, by which he works to insinuate the proper gentlemanly values into our understanding of the contest. As the bets reach their exhilarating peak, Drax commits a grave offense against decorum when he remarks to M, "I suppose your guest is good for his commitments," to which the narrator adds the cutting qualifier "Unforgivably" (56). This judgment is neither M's alone, nor Bond's, nor that of the living or ghostly members of Blades gathered around the table. Rather, it is the judgment of all good and true Englishmen, a body that has quietly engulfed us over the course of this passage.

Working against this deceptive normalization of the supposedly gentlemanly values on display at Blades, however, is the inescapably *exotic* quality of this episode, a quality emphasized in the narrator's careful and fascinated attention to detail. Fleming's instincts as a travel writer appear fully alert here, as he guides his readers through a slice of British life so far from most of their experiences that it must be treated as foreign. Even the suave James Bond, through whose eyes we see Blades, is a tourist here, and his attentive and admiring survey of the place serves as an important reminder of his own outsider status here in the inner sanctum. Indeed, Bond's entry into this normally hidden world of wealth and power bears an interesting resemblance to the episode in John Braine's *Room at the Top* in which the working-class Joe Lampton gains access to the local establishment haunt, the Leddersford Conservative Club:

> I felt a cold excitement. This was the place where the money grew. A lot of rich people patronized expensive hotels and roadhouses and restaurants too; but you could never be really sure of their grade, because you only needed the price of a drink or a meal or a collar and tie to be admitted. The Leddersford Conservative Club, with its ten-guinea annual subscription plus incidentals (Put me down for a hundred, Tom, if the Party doesn't get it the Inland Revenue will) was for rich men only. Here was the place where the right word or smile or gesture could

transport one into a higher grade overnight. Here was the centre of the country I'd so long tried to conquer; here magic worked, here the smelly swineherd became the prince who wore a clean shirt every day. (202–203)

Lampton's response to the Leddersford Conservative Club, mixing contempt with hungry approval, suggests that we are witnessing a collision of social worlds whose essential separateness is still generally assumed. The title of Braine's novel (like that of its sequel, *Life at the Top* [1962], and of Wain's *Hurry On Down*) points to one of the prevailing concerns of the texts featuring the "Angry Young Man": social mobility in postwar Britain. Like Gore-Urquhart in *Lucky Jim*, Lampton's soon-to-be-father-in-law, Brown, plays the role of gatekeeper here, opening for Lampton the door into a world of power and privilege. Unlike the aristocratically hyphenated Gore-Urquhart, though, Brown—with his working-class origins and his broad northern accent—indicates the extent to which the supposedly exclusive world of the establishment has already been compromised, revealing its openness to self-made men such as himself and (so Lampton hopes) Joe Lampton. Thus, while Lampton's crass materialism may suggest more of a kinship with Hugo Drax than with Bond, Lampton's covetous appraisal of this display of elegantly conspicuous consumption invites a reconsideration of the material realities of Blades, whose membership is not based *solely* on gentlemanly conduct.

Narrowing considerably the field of well-behaved candidates for membership at Blades are the requirements that each must also "be able to 'show' £100,000 in cash or gilt-edged securities" and either win or lose £500 a year or pay a fine (*Moonraker* 29). Of course, the unspoken code of Blades dictates that the only "new money" that properly belongs here is in the form of the uncirculated currency members always receive in change, a practice that rather underscores the hermetically sealed quality of this elegant world. However, as with the Leddersford Conservative Club, the apparent exclusivity is illusory: Hugo Drax is "new money"— *very* new money—and, like Joe Lampton, he cynically regards money as the solvent against the barriers standing between himself and his supposed betters. With some justification, he mocks the pretensions of the Blades set. "I spent a million," he tells Bond, "and London was in my pocket" (211). But there is more: "I knew that all I needed was money and the façade of a gentleman. Gentleman. *Pfui Teufel!* To me a gentleman is just someone I can take advantage of. Those bloody fools in Blades, for instance. Moneyed oafs. For months I took thousands of pounds off them, swindled them right under their noses until you came along and upset the apple cart" (210). During the encounter at Blades, Drax stands out like a big, sweaty bull in an elegantly appointed Regency china shop, suggesting that the distinction between "the smelly swine-herd" and "the prince who wore a clean shirt every day" is an unmistakable one. Yet Drax has been admitted to the club, both literally and metaphorically, despite his persistent failure to fulfill the demands of gentlemanly conduct.

The distastefully democratizing tendencies of the welfare state are suggested by the fact that Drax is not recognized as a foreigner at this early point in the book, but as a man who has risen from among the working class. In response to Bond's disapproval of Drax's "manner," M makes a halfhearted plea for indulgence on behalf of a man who has only recently exchanged his working-class "mates" for the more refined company on offer at Blades:

> "I know what you mean," said M. "But you may be being a bit hard on the man. After all, it's a big step from the Liverpool docks, or wherever he came from, to where he is now. And he's one of those people who was born with naturally hairy heels. Nothing to do with snobbery. I expect his mates in Liverpool found him just as loud-mouthed as Blades does." (49)

That M's comments here have "nothing to do with snobbery" seems, at the least, open to question, as does the depth of his insights into the likes and dislikes of Liverpool dockers. Nonetheless, those comments are helpful in that they highlight the critical importance of Drax's breaches of decorum in exposing his villainy. What truly sets Drax apart from his fellows at Blades—at least, until his plot is revealed—is precisely his "manner."

The first clash between Bond and Drax is prompted by the suspicions of M and the chairman of Blades that "Sir Hugo Drax cheats at cards" (21). This business of cheating at cards is on the face of it only one of the subtler crimes of Sir Hugo Drax against the laws of gentlemanly conduct, but it stands as the one damning fact in the eyes of the Blades set that leads to his exposure as the enemy within. That this one sin is deemed unforgivable suggests the extent to which Blades embodies that mythic notion of "fair play" that divides the true gentlemen from everyone else. Plainly, Drax himself represents the very perversion of this gentlemanly ideal. "There's no fair play down here," he later taunts Bond and Gala Brand. "No jolly good sports and all that. This is business"

(205). "Cheating at cards," M explains, "can still smash a man. In so-called Society, it's about the only crime that can still finish you, whoever you are" (22). And it turns out that in the fictional world of *Moonraker,* this test of character is a useful one: Drax's cheating at cards eventually renders visible his other, greater offenses. However, the narrator's approving description of Blades suggests that the place is probably well stocked with unsavory characters:

> It was a sparkling scene. There were perhaps fifty men in the room, the majority in dinner jackets, all at ease with themselves and their surroundings, all stimulated by the peerless food and drink, all animated by a common interest—the prospect of high gambling, the grand slam, the ace pot, the key-throw in a 64 game at backgammon. There might be cheats or possible cheats amongst them, men who beat their wives, men with perverse instincts, greedy men, cowardly men, lying men; but the elegance of the room invested each one with a kind of aristocracy. (52)

Unlike these other, more discreet villains invested with "a kind of aristocracy," Drax does not know how to conduct himself in an elegant room, and his boorish behavior in the temple of gentility inspires in Bond a passionate outrage so great that his later foiling of the Moonraker plot almost appears a mere follow-up to this earlier, apparently equally important contest. In the wake of Drax's "unforgivable" *faux pas,* all Bond wants is "to give this hairy ape the lesson of his life, give him a shock which would make him remember this evening for ever. . . . For all its importance, Bond had forgotten the Moonraker. This was a private affair between two men" (57). When Bond faces Drax at the card table, he does so as an agent of old money working to dispel the distasteful presence of new.

Standing in the sharpest possible contrast to his opponent, Bond fits in seamlessly at Blades: he knows how to conduct himself; he knows what to order; he recognizes "the delicate glutinous texture only achieved by Highland curers [of smoked Salmon]—very different from the desiccated products of Scandinavia" (48). However, Bond's effortless gentility obscures his true status at the club. Despite the apparent ease with which he negotiates the challenging waters of Blades, Bond is not a member, nor could he be. The £15,000 Bond wins from Drax is ten times his annual salary of £1,500, to which he adds "a thousand a year tax free of his own" (9). Like Joe Lampton and Jim Dixon, Bond too requires the assistance of a gatekeeper: he is admitted to Blades as a guest of M, but—

as Kingsley Amis protested in *The James Bond Dossier*—M's membership is as implausible as Bond's would be (29). In the midst of the drama around the card table, we are reminded that "M wasn't a particularly rich man" (*Moonraker* 36). Thus, the neat line that Fleming draws between this mythic notion of England and its others—between the gentlemanly Bond, M, and the living and dead members of Blades on the one hand, and the boorish Drax on the other—is somewhat deceptive. Bond is an outsider here—not a peer, but a (secret) servant whose role is akin to that of the loyal porter, Brevett, who once intervened in an election to block the admission of an unworthy candidate.

Nonetheless, Bond identifies absolutely with what he regards as the living tradition of gentility represented by Blades; when he vanquishes Drax there he feels instinctively a part of a community, gentlemen all. However, in the postwar world of Teds, Angries, and ungentle university students, the imaginary homeland Bond serves is an idea living on borrowed time. In the England of 1955, Blades is as much a relic as its gas jet enclosed in a silver grille, embodying an idea of the nation that is foreign to most English people—even, to a degree, to Bond himself. The approving ghostly circle Bond imagines at Blades could never actually include him, but this is the chimera he serves. When the novel's focus shifts from saving Blades to saving England from Drax's atomic rocket, there is no comparable community, not even a ghostly one, for Bond to embrace and be embraced by. When the threatened nation is imagined more inclusively—when, for instance, it encompasses the seven-man crew of the South Goodwin lightship munching their pork and beans as they listen to the Housewife's Choice on the Light Programme (*Moonraker* 124)—Bond simply does not seem to feel that same profound sense of connection. Gala Brand, by contrast, is very much at home here in post-Regency London. When she is Drax's prisoner, bundled in the back of his Mercedes under a rug, she is instinctively reassured by the familiar sounds of the city: of cars, bicycle bells, shouts, "the animal growl of an old klaxon, the whirring putter of a motor-scooter, a scream of brakes"—all these sounds remind her "that she was back in the real world, that English people, friends, were all around her" (191). What is to Gala "the real world" is to Bond the depressingly empty space between the deadly assignments that he expects will kill him before he reaches the statutory age of 45 (9). Thus, it is perfectly appropriate that the two turn from each other and "[walk] off into their different lives" as the novel closes. Gala can disappear back into the familiar noises of England, but Bond does not really live there; he has nowhere to go. For all his noble sacrifices in the cause of his country, Bond remains a homeless man in postwar Britain.

NOTES

1. There are numerous surveys of the phenomenon of the "Angry Young Man." Among the more useful are Blake Morrison's *The Movement: English Poetry and the Fiction of the 1950s* (1980) and Robert Hewison's *In Anger: Culture and the Cold War 1945–60* (1980).

2. See Paul Rock and Stanley Cohen, "The Teddy Boy."

3. The type of the Ted appears to have been a versatile tool, providing commentators of various political and class affiliations with a symbol of cultural decline. In his influential study of British working-class culture in the age of mass production, *The Uses of Literacy* (1957), Richard Hoggart famously portrayed "The Juke-Box Boys" as harbingers of cultural deterioration among the postwar working classes, whose self-created prewar culture Hoggart recalled with fondness (246–50). In the second chapter of *Thunderball*, Bond encounters a rather late-model Ted, a "foxy, pimpled young man in a black leather windcheater," behind the wheel of the taxi conveying him to Shrublands. Bond's initial assessment of the young man accords with the familiar depiction of the Ted as an embodiment of a nation shaken loose from its moorings: "The play with the comb, Bond guessed, was to assert to Bond that the driver was really only taking him and his money as a favour. It was typical of the cheap self-assertiveness of young labour since the war. This youth, thought Bond, makes about twenty pounds a week, despises his parents, and would like to be Tommy Steele. It's not his fault. He was born into the buyers' market of the Welfare State and into the age of atomic bombs and space flight. For him life is easy and meaningless" (9).

4. Maugham's comments are quoted in William van O'Connor's "Two Types of 'Heroes' in Post-War British Fiction," *PMLA* 77, no. 1 (1962): 171, 172.

5. Umberto Eco cites Fleming's repeated use of such stock characters as evidence of the author's reactionary politics: "The use of such figures (the Manichean dichotomy, seeing things in black and white) is always dogmatic and intolerant—in short, reactionary—whereas he who avoids such figures, who recognizes nuances and distinctions and who admits contradictions, is democratic." See Eco, 162.

10 Tropical Bond

VIVIAN HALLORAN

The exotic world of Ian Fleming's James Bond novels and short stories is shaped by the social forces of displacement, repatriation, immigration, defection, and decolonization which resulted in the mass movement of people and the reconfiguration of the geopolitical map in the post–World War II world. This new fluidity of the sociopolitical landscape, along with the ideological shift toward the two extremes of democracy and communism during the Cold War, polarized the way in which nations related to and perceived themselves and one another in the 1950s and 1960s, the time during which Fleming dreamed up his alter ego. While he actively participates in Cold War politics by covertly defending England from the Soviet threat presented by SMERSH, the fictional Soviet anti-spy organization, James Bond primarily wrangles with larger-than-life individuals, as Christoph Lindner discusses later in this volume. As a consequence, Fleming's creation of memorable megalomaniacal foils to his all-too-human secret agent demands a reading of the Bond texts that recognizes the battles between spies and/or criminals and law enforcers not only as ideological clashes, but also as tests of the authenticity and viability of individual identity construction.

Most important for my purposes, the Bond novels pit a self-styled and often racially hybrid criminal mastermind against 007's various ethnic/national and class performances of himself as a creole Jamaican millionaire or American businessman. However, while Bond usually blows his cover early in his interaction with the enemy, largely due to his often halfhearted performance of his assigned identity, the complex and individual cultural identity claimed by his various foes stays constant until their respective deaths. Rather than reading Bond's various battles with his foes as clear-cut examples of white Anglo-Saxon superiority over "mongrelized" races, in this essay I will contrast James Bond's own national doubleness as a representative of England with the racial hybridity or intermixing of his alienated and territorially displaced foes in the context of Fleming's invocation of the Caribbean as what Arjun Appadurai has called an "ethnoscape": the "landscape of persons who constitute the shifting world in which we live: tourists, immigrants, refugees, exiles, guest workers, and other moving groups and individuals [who] constitute an essential feature of the world and appear to affect the politics of (and between) nations to a hitherto unprecedented degree" (33). Fleming's repeated references to Nassau, the Cayman Islands, Haiti, Cuba, and Jamaica in the Bond fiction, as well as the region's history of European colonialism, enslavement of Africans, and economic immigration by Irish, Indian, Chinese, and Lebanese peoples, make the Caribbean the perfect ethnoscape for a discussion of the competing ethnic and national claims to authenticity and/or validity in Fleming's worldview.

The Caribbean in the James Bond novels becomes both a home space for European criminals (some of them ex-Nazis like von Hammerstein) and a base of operations for racially mixed villains such as Mr. Big and Dr. No, who reenact either of two predominant Caribbean tropes in their respective schemes to conquer the world: the plantation machine or the mythification of piracy. In his groundbreaking reading of postmodernism in the Caribbean, *The Repeating Island*, Cuban novelist and theorist Antonio Benítez-Rojo appropriates Deleuze and Guattari's concept of self-duplicating machines to describe the plantation economy that characterized the Caribbean region from the sixteenth until late nineteenth centuries as a basin-wide cultural, socioeconomic, and political phenomenon. Atlantic slavery affected both Africans and Europeans and gave rise to a new group of racially mixed creole, or island-born, peoples. Benítez-Rojo also explains that the

> mythification of piracy should be seen as an attempt to authenticate through the narration itself . . . an entire field of allusion, scarcely explored in literary criticism, which speaks of sackmaps, of the terrible black flag and of duels to the death, of coffers of jewels and pieces of eight, of the gallows and the plank, of galleons and fortresses, of muskets and culverins, of boardings and of ransoms, lookouts and alarm bells, of besieged cities and naval battles. (215)

Although Benítez-Rojo's catalogue refers specifically to "the theme of piracy and buried treasure" (214) in Caribbean folklore and literature, Fleming overtly employs these same tropes in his Bond fiction as the airtight alibis used by Mr. Big and Emilio Largo in *Live and Let Die* and *Thunderball* to answer any official query into their dealings in Jamaica. Indeed, a convincing case can be made for reading the Bond novels as modern-day pirate fiction.

Although gold bullion figures prominently in the plot of the two novels mentioned above, Fleming presents the modern equivalent of the pirate treasure chest in his discussion of the anonymity of the offshore banking institutions in Nassau, which afford a measure of economic security for Auric Goldfinger, who locates his financial headquarters there in *Goldfinger*. Dr. No, in the eponymous novel, brings the planta-tion economy back to life in his guano mines by exploiting his captive workforce and enforcing a strict breeding program, and the novel also uses a third trope often associated with sea journeys and, by extension, with the Caribbean region—the sea monster. Dr. No's use of a flame-spewing, camouflaged vehicle to scare intruders away from his island suggests his skill at manipulating the local inhabitants' superstition. By creating a seemingly natural or ecological threat, Dr. No achieves his desired privacy with a minimum waste of munitions or manpower. Like-wise, Mr. Big promotes the idea in Jamaica that he himself is a monster of sorts—the undead zombie of the voodoo deity Baron Samedi in *Live and Let Die*.

Through a detailed reading of the settings of Fleming's fiction, I want to demonstrate that the Caribbean constitutes the one physical and ideological space in which the displaced, racially hybrid characters—both villains and heroes—feel at home. Unlike the homogeneously white England and the racially divided America, the diamond-rich Africa, or even the exotic and dangerous Orient of Fleming's novels, comprising Japan, Macao, and mainland China, the various Caribbean islands con-stitute the actual "contact zones" (to borrow Mary Louise Pratt's term) between European, American, Asian, and African forces battling for global supremacy in the post–World War II world.

Bond's Racial and National "Whiteness"

While Ian Fleming's James Bond novels explicitly discuss race as an important component of a given character's makeup, his approach is unusual in its almost obsessive emphasis on racial hybridity and intermixing. Fleming's conception of mixed-race characters, however, does not allow for the actual combination of racial characteristics within one given individual. That is to say, Fleming does not address either the development of a "new ethnicity," to use Stuart Hall's term, as a result of miscegenation, nor does he comment at length on the possible ill effects of "mongrelization" or dilution of the national character within a mixed-race individual. In the world of the novels, biracial characters *combine* the qualities of each of their racial backgrounds without *blending* them. Mixed-race characters in the Bond fiction, such as the evil Mr. Big and Dr. No, but also the noble Cayman Islander Quarrel and the friendly Kerim Darko in *From Russia with Love,* son of a Turkish father and a British mother, are presented as more dangerous or enigmatic to Bond than people of more homogeneous parentage because 007 cannot ultimately decide whether their actions will be in keeping with one set of national characteristics and stereotypes or the other at any given time.

As Gerald Early notes in his discussion of *Live and Let Die,* Fleming "is fascinated by miscegenation" (157). However, despite, or perhaps because of, the prominent role that race and interracial sexual encounters play in the Bond fiction, we must be careful not to impose American standards and conceptions of racial identities onto the Caribbean characters who people Fleming's oeuvre. Although the plots of *Live and Let Die, Goldfinger,* and *Diamonds Are Forever* all mention or capitalize on the tense racial climate of the United States, they do so from an outsider's perspective—Bond's and Fleming's—not from an American point of view, Felix Leiter's good-natured banter notwithstanding.

British historian Jeremy Black regards Fleming's "approach to ethnicity" (12) as the product of racial tensions between black and white Britons in Cardiff during the early 1950s. However, despite the increasing presence of black Britons in Wales and England, they do not appear in Fleming's novels. Black therefore adopts an American-inflected view of Ian Fleming's portrayal of race when he quotes Eldridge Cleaver's wholesale dismissal of James Bond in *Soul on Ice* (1968). Black sums up the Black Panther's view of 007 as "the upholder of empire, and thus, the defender of white control" (12) without analyzing the context for or implications of Cleaver's comments about Fleming's character. Speaking from the perspective of a self-declared "Ofay Watcher, a member of that unchartered, amorphous league which has members on all continents and the islands of the seas" (65), Cleaver discusses the white race's loss of its heroes after the Second World War. Joining the fictional Bond among the number of white fallen heroes whom Cleaver considers "arch-villains" are historical figures and national leaders—George Washington, Thomas Jefferson, and Winston Churchill—who presumably share a comparable iconic value to that of 007. In this context, Cleaver declares:

> The "paper tiger" hero, James Bond, offering the whites a triumphant image of themselves, is saying what many whites want desperately to hear reaffirmed: *I am still the White Man, lord of the land, licensed to kill, and the world is still an empire at my feet.* James Bond feeds on that secret little anxiety, the psychological white backlash, felt in some degree by most whites alive. It is exasperating to see little brown men and little yellow men from the mysterious Orient, and the opaque black men of Africa (to say nothing of these impudent American Negroes!) who come to the UN and talk smart to us, who are scurrying all over *our* globe in their strange modes of dress—much as if they were new, unpleasant arrivals from another planet. (80–81)

Cleaver's attack on Bond as a representative figure of the white race's suppressed desires does not differentiate between the battle-scarred secret agent of Fleming's novels and the dapper superhero of Sean Connery's movies. Likewise, his juxtaposition of a fictional character with historical figures blurs the lines between popular culture and national myth without considering the contrasting political implications of each discourse. Cleaver's critique of European imperialism and American racist stereotypes of "oppressed peoples of the world" (70) suggests that he sees no difference between the history of European annexation and rule of foreign countries for extended periods of time and the global influence of American consumer culture. However, Cleaver assumes that even the most racially prejudiced, Bond-identified white person easily distinguishes between the "opaque men from Africa" and "those impudent American Negroes!"[1]

Another African American reader of Fleming, Gerald Early, echoes Cleaver's dismissal of Bond's role as an unrepentant colonial agent even as he notices that "we, as a culture, feel a need to renew Bond, not to dismiss him" (140). Like Cleaver, Early reads Bond as "a sort of last white guardian of colonialism," linking the European Cold War world with "the world of colonialism and non-white dependency on whites" (161). While Cleaver rejects Bond outright as a dangerous cultural icon and compares the negative impact of Bond on the white American (and presumably European) community to the damage that the popular stereotypical depiction of black docility in Harriet Beecher Stowe's *Uncle*

Tom's Cabin had on both slave and free American blacks, Early does not judge Fleming's portrayal of black characters by the American standard, the one-drop rule as the determining factor in black racial identity. Instead, he treats Fleming's fiction as a supplement to his reading of African American literature as a young man, especially the works of Richard Wright. Early comments on the unlikely resonance he finds between the two authors:

> What reading Wright simultaneously with Fleming did was make me more impressed by Wright's idea that blacks, rightly angry over having the nature of their humanity questioned by whites, respond by creating an ideology to prove their humanity to themselves which only more deeply traps them in the throes of their self-consciousness. Fleming opened up Wright for me in ways that probably would not have happened had I not read the two authors together. (152)

As a teenager, Early developed a new understanding of the national domestic racial dynamic within the black community in America through his reading of James Bond's adventures as the defender and enforcer of the British Empire. Whereas in *Soul on Ice,* Eldridge Cleaver denounces Bond as a harmful role model for impressionable young white Americans, Early chronicles his eager, though ultimately unsuccessful, attempts to pass on this legacy of self-discovery as an African American by encouraging his college-age daughter to read Fleming's novels.

Before scrutinizing Fleming's portrayal of racially hybrid characters, we should first confront the most pressing question suggested by Cleaver's attack on 007: Just how white is James Bond? The answer—Bond is whiter than he is English—brings together the three main components of the cultural hybridity of Fleming's characters: race, ethnicity, and nationality. The mystery behind Bond's family history and national origins is solved toward the end of the last Bond novel published in Fleming's lifetime, *You Only Live Twice,* where the secret agent's obituary, ostensibly authored by M, appears in London newspapers.

> James Bond was born of a Scottish father, Andrew Bond of Glencoe, and a Swiss mother, Monique Delacroix, from the Canton de Vaud. His father being a foreign representative of the Vickers armaments firm, his early education, from which he inherited a first-class command of French and German, was entirely abroad. (*Live Twice* 200)

Unlike Cleaver, who uses the racialized term "white" to encompass an undifferentiated group of European ethnicities together, Fleming always deconstructs any notion that racial whiteness signifies any particular cultural identity in his novels. James Bond's mixed Scottish and Swiss heritage and his upbringing abroad mark him as as much of a hybrid figure as any of the villains he encounters in his assignments. Further, his dual Scottish and Swiss heritage situates him, at least partially, as a colonial subject—he is not English, although his father's Scottish blood qualifies him as British. Thus, Bond's various impersonations of a white creole Jamaican millionaire while undercover abroad in *Casino Royale* and *Thunderball,* for example, ring true precisely because they are accurate performances of a colonial cultural identity rather than expressions of imperial entitlement.

Even when he inhabits the profoundly traditional English space of Blades, the exclusive gambling club to which M belongs in *Moonraker,* James Bond doubts that he can "pass" as English. The third-person narrator convincingly conveys this anxiety when he relates a rare instance of the spy's introspection: "Bond knew that there was something alien and un-English about himself. He knew that he was a difficult man to cover up. Particularly in England. He shrugged his shoulders. Abroad was what mattered. He would never have a job to do in England" (34). However, the narrator does not explain the source of Bond's uncanniness as an Englishman in the rest of the text. Only when we consider the novels together can we as readers fill in the gaps in Bond's personal history and appreciate the larger implications of enigmatic remarks such as these.

Even the settings of his overseas assignments, if not necessarily the cover stories he is required to perform in order to fool his opponents, make Bond feel like a racial outsider, displaced from any conceivable "home" space. As he waits in line to go through immigration at the airport in New York City early in *Live and Let Die,* Bond reflects: "Here in America, where they knew all about him, he felt like a negro whose shadow has been stolen by the witch-doctor" (2). The metaphysical dimension of the references to voodoo in this passage clearly invokes a Caribbean, rather than an American, context for Bond's self-identification as a "negro," despite his claim that he only felt this way "[h]ere in America." In this passage, Bond's declaration of a black identity, however affected, makes him sound more like the protagonist of Jack Kerouac's *On the Road,* a work Eldridge Cleaver praised for its sensitivity to the plight of blacks, than the white supremacist colonial enforcer Eldridge describes. While Kerouac's Sal Paradise walks around Denver "wishing I were a Negro" (72), Bond does not feel envy but rather empathy. Ironically, in this passage Fleming suggests that Bond felt like a "negro" because of his lack of anonymity—since the Americans "knew all about him," Bond cannot "pass" or pretend to be anyone else. Following this logic, Bond's biography is as undeniable as the blackness of the negro's skin, although neither an official file nor the epidermis can fully contain the soul or "shadow" that marks each person as an individual.

Fleming continues to complicate Bond's whiteness later in the novel when he describes the secret agent's efforts to read his body as he thinks others will interpret it in America. In this moment of physical and racial "transraciality," a concept developed by Michael Awkward to explain "the adoption of physical traits of difference for the purpose of impersonating a racial other" (19), Bond reinterprets the blackness of his own hair and the position of his cheekbones as signs of racial hybridity despite being assigned to pretend he's "a New Englander from Boston" (*Live* 22). As he shaves, Bond muses, "there was the mixed blood of America in the black hair and high cheekbones and Bond thought he might get by—except, perhaps, with women" (23). The regionally specific nature of the "mixed blood of America" on which Bond relies to carry out his cover successfully depends on a mix of races for its hybridity, whereas Bond's own mixed pedigree combines two distinct nationalities with the same racial characteristics. Susan Gubar argues in *Racechanges* that "the word 'transracial' should imply dwelling within racial borderlands" rather than a concrete effort either to "blend[] into or integrat[e] within the Other's community" or to "ridicul[e] the Other's mores" (248). Since Bond's mission is to impersonate a white American businessman to the African American associates of the Haitian Mr. Big, 007 thinks he can negotiate the blurry space of the American color line long enough for him to get to the source of the smuggled gold pieces he is chasing in *Live and Let Die*.

Because of his own status as the hybrid offspring of an interethnic or international marriage, James Bond shares Fleming's fascination with miscegenation, although with an interesting qualification.[2] At the beginning of *From Russia with Love*, M probes into Bond's personal life by asking about the seriousness of his relationship with the American girl Tiffany Case, the diamond-smuggling croupier introduced in *Diamonds Are Forever*. Bond brushes off the question easily, admitting that although the couple had contemplated marrying, they had since broken up over their respective cultural differences. Although according to Eldridge Cleaver's logic, both Bond and Tiffany Case are equally racially white, Bond himself cannot overlook the social and national differences between himself and his American ex-lover. He tells M that he has no regrets over the breakup and shares the wisdom he has gained from the ordeal: "Mixed marriages aren't often a success" (*Russia* 105). Bond's aphorism reveals that he considers a shared culture an important predictor of a couple's compatibility despite his personal predilection for a rainbow coalition of temporary lovers.

In the short story "Quantum of Solace," from the collection *For Your Eyes Only,* Bond rather arrogantly proclaims that because he values their subservience to men, the only women he would ever consider marrying would be either an airline stewardess or "a Japanese" (80). Later in the same story, Bond expresses his fear of impregnating any of his exotic mistresses. Speaking to the governor of Nassau at a private dinner party, Bond remarks, "The only trouble with beautiful Negresses is that they don't know anything about birth control" (*Your Eyes* 83). Although Bond does not have the opportunity to father children with the one woman he does marry, Tracy in *On Her Majesty's Secret Service,* he begets a child with the woman whose husband he pretends to be for an assignment, Kissy Suzuki. Because Kissy does not reveal to Bond the secret of her pregnancy, he unwittingly leaves behind a potential son whose racial makeup is even more hybrid than his own; this embryonic "son of Bond," so to speak, will be half Japanese, a quarter Scottish and a quarter Swiss.

Ironically, this future offspring is the result both of a more real "mixed marriage" than the one Bond had contemplated with the American Tiffany Case or entered into with Tracy, and of Bond's and Kissy's stylized *performance* of a traditional marriage between two Japanese nationals. Acting as both a cultural translator and a fellow secret agent, Kissy Suzuki informs Bond, whom she knows as Taro Todoroki, of their duty to act out stereotypical gender roles in public: "Come along, Todoroki-san. The *kannushi-san* says I am to treat you as a comrade, as an equal. But give me one of those two little bags to carry. For the sake of the villagers who will be watching inquisitively, we will wear the Oriental face in public" (136). Even as he acts out the role of a Japanese man, Bond's need to "pass" racially means that he must outwardly assume the passive or feminized role of a deaf-mute man while Kissy takes charge of the household duties as his wife. Privately, Kissy continues to be in charge, acting as a cultural, as well as a linguistic, translator for Bond. Although they strive to conform to the accepted norm, Bond's and Kissy's simulacrum of a marriage is always already a revisionist performance. The most real aspect of their fake union is the consummation of the marriage, which results in Kissy's pregnancy.

This is one of the few instances in which Bond changes his body in order to "pass" as a racial Other to provide the cover for his battle against Blofeld. Kissy Suzuki takes advantage of Bond's amnesia to convince him he is exactly who he was pretending to be, a Japanese fisherman, despite his inability to speak the language. This is yet another instance in which the simulacrum of Bond's and Kissy's marriage ends up being more real than his actual marriage to Tracy in *On Her Majesty's Secret Service,* which lasted only a few hours. Thus, when Bond leaves for Russia in search of answers at the end of *You Only Live Twice,* it is unclear whether he has fully reclaimed his white British identity or whether he still thinks of himself as Taro Todoroki. This ambiguity carries over into the posthumously published *The Man with the Golden Gun,* which opens with a Soviet-brainwashed James Bond trying to act as the "real" James Bond of old, going through the motions of what his Soviet handlers tell him he was in the habit of doing before he "died" in Japan. Since there is a profound disconnect between the "new" and "old" Bonds, it is impossible to ascertain when and if 007 fully regains the British identity that he once claimed. What better place to go sort out this crisis of identity than the Caribbean, then?

Racial Hybridity in a Caribbean Ethnoscape

By reconceptualizing geographical spaces and racial and ethnic characteristics, Ian Fleming firmly ensconces 007 within the cultural frame of reference of Caribbean multiculturalism and doubleness. Since the various mixed-race villains in the novels do not feel at home in either of their parents' nations of origin, they each emigrate to a neutral third space: Mr. Big to the United States by way of the Soviet Union, and Dr. No to Jamaica by way of New York. Bond's adversaries also try to hide their own racial hybridity, either by "passing" as other ethnicities or by associating with ethnically diverse Others.[3] I want to explore the choices of racially hybrid criminal masterminds like Mr. Big and Dr. No, and racially pure European SPECTRE agents Emilio Largo and Francisco Scaramanga, to establish their bases of operation in the islands of the Caribbean basin. The racial, cultural, and linguistic diversity of the region proves invaluable as an ethnoscape that accommodates tourists, travelers, and mixed-race individuals while its varied geography presents physical and supernatural challenges for Bond and his adversaries to exploit or overcome.

Bond's only "authentic" and long-lasting connection to the Caribbean in the novels is his friendship with Quarrel, the Cayman Islander who trains him and appears in both *Live and Let Die* and *Doctor No*. Like Kissy Suzuki in *You Only Live Twice*, Quarrel acts as a cultural translator by helping Bond decipher the local customs and traditions he needs to know to survive. Ironically, Quarrel's own authenticity as a guide to Jamaica and Nassau is a bit tenuous, since almost all the descriptions of this character emphasize his outsider status by emphasizing his national origin as a Cayman Islander instead of a Jamaican or a native of Nassau, as in his first appearance in *Live and Let Die*:

> This was Quarrel, the Cayman Islander, and Bond liked him imme-diately. There was the blood of Cromwellian soldiers and buccaneers in him and his face was strong and angular and his mouth was almost severe. His eyes were grey. It was only the spatulate nose and the pale palms of his hands that were negroid. (*Live* 168–69)

Some readers of the novel, like Gerald Early, have argued that Quarrel is a foil for Mr. Big since both characters are Afro-Caribbean men of mixed blood, and in their diametrically opposed ways each represents some of the exceptional qualities of the "negro races" which M praises to Bond during a briefing: "They've got plenty of brains and ability and guts" (*Live* 17). Both Quarrel and Mr. Big fit this description to the letter. However, I want to suggest a different reading of Quarrel as Bond's double. Bond's recognition of Quarrel's blood suggests that he views him as a kinsman. Further, both character's eyes are grayish—Quarrel's com-pletely so, while Bond's are described as "grey-blue eyes" (*Live* 23). Fi-nally, Quarrel's "negroid" features, his nose and light palms, are almost as few in number as the "mixed blood of America" that Bond hopes to read into his own hair and cheekbones, as I discussed earlier. In fact, Bond's earlier statement that he felt like a "negro" at the airport is the strongest declaration of a (imagined) racialized identity in the entire novel since Quarrel discusses race with Bond.

The Caribbean ethnoscape of the novels and short stories as a whole is an abstract space that includes not only the islands on the basin itself, but also the American states of New York, Louisiana, and Florida. These areas are linked by legitimate economic ties and travel routes as well as by more nefarious drug and casino dealings through organized crime gangs based in the United States. The threat posed to Bond by the racially hybrid criminals who operate within this expanded Caribbean landscape is magnified by their apparent inscrutability: their mixed racial heritage makes them almost impossible for a European opponent to "read." The racial mixture of his most formidable adversaries confuses Bond in *Live and Let Die* and *Doctor No;* he second-guesses whether to approach Mr. Big and Dr. No as either "Europeans"—French, German—or as "natives" of some Other place like Haiti or China. In contrast, the creole Honeychile Rider has no problem ignoring Dr. No altogether. She regularly defies his orders for outsiders to stay away from his island and goes collecting seashells at the local beaches without a care in the world. As a "native" inhabitant of a multicultural society, she does not find racial intermixing unusual or even remarkable.

For their part, Dr. No and Mr. Big encourage the creation of myths to maintain control over the local population of Jamaica and its surrounding islands—Dr. No exploits technology to promote a fear of the mysterious "dragon," while Mr. Big spreads the rumor that he is a zombie of one of the most powerful voodoo deities in the Haitian pantheon, Baron Samedi. Both criminal agents import outside cultural artifacts to heighten the sense of reality or plausibility of these myths: Dr. No modifies a vehicle by adding flame-throwers, while Mr. Big uses the rhetoric of Haitian voodoo in Jamaica, a country marked both by its Rastafarian theology and by the regional devotion to *obeah,* which H. P. Jacobs defines in *Ian Fleming Introduces Jamaica* as "sorcery" (92). The seeds for the success of these scare tactics originate within the bodies of each villain. The "grayish tint" of Mr. Big's skin, which the narrator of the novel explains away as one result of "chronic heart disease" (*Live* 18), eerily supports his grandiose claim to be "the Zombie or living corpse of Baron Samedi himself, the Prince of Darkness" (*Live* 19). Mr. Big in essence holds himself out as physical proof of the ideology he promulgates. Dr. No, conversely, stays far from the gaze of any curious onlookers. However, for anyone adventurous enough to have braved the mechanical "dragon's" fire, the sight of the doctor's "articulated steel pincers at the end of a metal stalk" (*Doctor* 146) would suggest he had lost his limbs to just such a legendary beast.

In *Doctor No,* the followers, rather than the leader, present the living spectacle of racial hybridity in Jamaica. M tells Bond that Dr. No is a "Chinaman, or rather half Chinese and half German" (*Doctor* 28). By contrast, his minions have stronger ties to the land in which they operate; they are the mixture of two races which arrived in the Caribbean because of the plantation economy in effect during the times of slavery—enslaved Africans, who were brought to the New World against their will during the Middle Passage, and Chinese laborers, who came under contract as indentured servants and worked as overseers in the plantations in places like Cuba. Yet another cultural translator, the colonial secretary of Jamaica, explains to Bond how this racial intermixing affects the non-white social hierarchy of the island:

> Finally there are the Chinese, solid, compact discreet—the most powerful clique in Jamaica. They've got the bakeries and the laundries and the best food stores. They keep to themselves and keep their strain pure. . . . Not that they don't take the black girls when they want them. You can see the result all over Kingston—Chigroes—Chinese Negroes and Negresses. The Chigroes are a tough, forgotten race. They look down on the Negroes and the Chinese look down on them. (57–58)

In Crab Key, the island he purchases to mine guano and sabotage American missile tests over the Atlantic Ocean, Dr. No reestablishes an exploitative plantation economy to administer the collection of organic material. Among his mad schemes, Dr. No engages in eugenics, selectively breeding his workers to produce the most docile and obedient workforce possible. In a twisted parody of the sugar plantations in Jamaica and Cuba during the time of slavery, Dr. No's underpaid and ill-treated captive labor force performs heavy physical labor shoveling ashy, malodorous bird droppings under the hot sun. No one is allowed to roam freely around the islands.

By contrast, Mr. Big does not have to genetically engineer a group of racially alienated followers because he operates largely outside of the Caribbean at the beginning of *Live and Let Die*. Mr. Big emerges as a highly efficient criminal figure who deploys the diasporic network of peoples of African descent to disseminate Bloody Morgan's treasure and fund communist revolutions with the profits. His business plan, although evil in its intent, is nothing short of brilliant in its execution because it exploits the racial tensions built into American society at the time—segregation and Jim Crow—to create a subversive, alternate economy. Like Quarrel, Mr. Big is a mulatto, as M tells Bond: "He's not pure negro. Born in Haiti. Good dose of French blood. Trained in Moscow" (17). This formulation implies that it is the "good dose" of French blood that makes Mr. Big unpredictable and ruthless instead of his diluted Negro-ness or incidental birth in Haiti.

Through his use of exotic locales, fancy restaurants, and exclusive casinos in the James Bond novels, Ian Fleming establishes his protagonist's exquisite taste and discerning eye. His penchant for ordering pink champagne, expensive caviar, and martinis indicates that Bond is a man who knows what he wants and how to get it. His appetite in women, although voracious, is nonetheless based on his own sense of quality; he prefers "real" blondes to the bleached kind, as we find out in "From a View to a Kill," and he appreciates the rich tailoring of women's designer gowns then in vogue, as we learn in *Casino Royale*. For a man with such clear standards and discriminating tastes, facing the racial hybridity of his adversaries' mixed heritage must have been tremendously frustrating. Thus, while Bond asserts the fundamental importance of small differences in the pursuit of the good life and the appreciation of life's pleasures, he finds an insidious evil in the haphazard racial mixing he reads in the physical appearance and murky cultural heritage of his antagonists.

Bond's efforts to decode and determine the exact genealogy and racial constituents of his opponents represent his own attempt to exploit his special knowledge to pass between social and cultural milieus of the modern world and bring it to bear on the Cold War and postcolonial struggles he faces. As the empire slowly retreats from the Caribbean islands, Fleming finds a cultural and environmental accommodation of racial difference but without the accompanying financial stability of more homogeneous first-world nations like England and the United States. Clearly fearing the stifling uniformity of communist ideology, Fleming pits his debonair secret agent against hyper-individualist criminal masterminds and implies that racial intermixing is at the root of the growing impulse toward globalization. Thus, although Bond explicitly tries to discriminate, or tell apart, which racial characteristics his foes employ to bring him harm, he also nonetheless believes in the fundamental superiority of "pure" races over mixed ones. But by simply writing James Bond off as a racist icon, we risk misunderstanding how a changing world requires the development of new rules for interaction and understanding across difference. So, in presenting racial hybridity as the new face of the world to come, Fleming may have wisely asked his readers to imagine a new world order.

The Caribbean: Geographical Hybridity, Doubleness, and the Marvelous Real

The Caribbean setting acts as either a physical foil to James Bond or a purgatory where M sends him to expiate his professional sins in *The Man with the Golden Gun, Thunderball, Doctor No, Live and Let Die,* "For Your Eyes Only," and "Quantum of Solace." In the Caribbean of Fleming's novels, Bond faces racial and geographical hybridity and intermixing which demand to be deciphered and read in contradistinction to a European framework of long-standing prejudices, adjacent ethnic enclaves, and a strict demarcation between natives and outsiders. More importantly, the doubleness of the Caribbean landscape and people in Fleming's Bond novels resonates with another leitmotif of spy fiction—the double agent—and thus colors the entire basin region as a foil for 007.

Fleming depicts this Caribbean doubleness in the novels by emphasizing the ostensibly punitive nature of M's chosen assignments for 007 and also by describing the islands themselves as sites of exotic danger lurking in the shadows or under water.[4] M usually sends Bond to the Caribbean to clear up administrative snafus, exact revenge, or expiate professional sins. In *Thunderball,* for example, the undersea landscape and the remoteness of Nassau from the British mainland come together to provide the almost perfect cover for SPECTRE's plan to extort money and demand recognition as an equal player with the nuclear nations. The coral reefs off the shores of Nassau provide natural camouflage for the stolen fighter jet and its cargo of nuclear bombs that the SPECTRE agents hope to wield as leverage to force the national powers to succumb.

While Bond eventually performs the dangerous feats of underwater exploration and battle, M engages SPECTRE directly by correctly second-guessing its "reading" of geopolitical space. Both M and the SPECTRE council (re-en)act the role of colonial absentee plantation owners when they plan from afar to use the resources available to them in an extended Caribbean region. As he tells 007, M breaks ranks with his superiors in order to test his own interpretation of the maps and the data available against the evil machinations of his new adversaries:

> It seemed to me that the only grain of possible evidence in this case was the DEW radar plot, a doubtful one I admit, of the plane that left the East-West air channel over the Atlantic and turned south towards Bermuda and the Bahamas. . . . [G]oing on these assumptions, and assuming that the plane could not have landed in America itself or off American shores—the coastal radar network is too good—I looked for a neighbouring area which might be more suitable. . . . I decided on the Bahamas, the group of islands, many of them uninhabited, surrounded mostly by shoal water over sand and possessing only one simple radar station—and that one concerned only with civilian air traffic and manned by local civilian personnel. South, towards Cuba, Jamaica, and the Caribbean, offers no worthwhile targets. (*Thunderball* 77–78)

M's insistence on the strategic location of the Bahamas as a site of operation for SPECTRE but not as a likely target for terrorism attests to his assumption that urban centers constitute the basis of powers for both nations and exilic criminals. The distinctions he draws between the populous Caribbean countries, identified individually as "Cuba" and "Jamaica," and the unpeopled isles of the Bahamas attest to the Antilles' in-between status as crowded, but not fully urbanized, spaces.

Bond himself embodies the trope of doubleness in *The Man with the Golden Gun* when he makes a tentative return to the Secret Service after suffering from amnesia and being brainwashed by the Soviets in the extradiegetic space after the ending of *You Only Live Twice*, only to make an attempt on M's life as mentioned earlier. Proving his skill at reading 007's body language once again, M effects a narrow escape from this unexpected threat by lowering a plastic screen to shield him from the cyanide Bond aims at him with a poison-spewing gun. As punishment for his Oedipal insubordination, M sends Bond to hunt down the most dangerous criminal on Her Majesty's Secret Service's casebook—Francisco Scaramanga in Jamaica. In both *Doctor No* and *The Man with the Golden Gun*, M waits upon the outcome of the Caribbean assignments he gives 007 to determine whether indeed James Bond has earned his trust anew. The Caribbean, then, is the only fit testing ground for Bond to atone for the sins he has committed on the European continent.

Even the fully European foes James Bond faces in the Caribbean basin either come from racially and ethnically charged geographical regions or else they embody hybridity by working as double agents. Although Francisco Scaramanga, the antagonist of *The Man with the Golden Gun*, is not himself biracial, he hails from Cataluña, a region in Spain that wants to assert its independence from the rest of the country.[5] Scaramanga operates between Cuba and Jamaica, much like von Hammerstein, the German criminal mastermind in "For Your Eyes Only." In the shorter text, the ambiguity surrounding the villain's name attests to his doubleness as a character—M tells Bond that no one is sure whether he is "a man called Hammerstein, or von Hammerstein" (*Your Eyes* 44). His background as an ex-Gestapo Nazi suggests that he was deemed to be racially "pure" by one of the most racist regimes to have ever governed. Both characters have found a safe haven in the "banana republics" (*Your Eyes* 44) of the Caribbean, where they can put their criminal skills and military training to the service of a communist revolution in Cuba and organized crime in casinos in Jamaica.

Besides their spotless European heritage and their emigration to the Caribbean, both villains share some of the same criminal affiliations: Scaramanga works for the Cuban secret service, and von Hammerstein plays the Batista and Castro forces against one another during his lengthy period of operation in Cuba. Each man launders large amounts of illegal money, and their business dealings involve travel to Jamaica. Their respective backgrounds affect the way in which these two villains operate in the Caribbean. Scaramanga's Spanish roots ensure that his business dealings in Cuba go smoothly because he speaks the language, whereas von Hammerstein remains a mysterious figure and never actually utters a word in the short story. Ironically, by virtue of working in Cuba, von Hammerstein finds himself in a society characterized by the racial intermixing between Spaniards and Africans, thus going against the ideology of racial purity of the German Nazi party to which he belonged. Francisco Scaramanga negotiates directly with Jamaican Rastafarians for the sale of marijuana, while the enemies Bond has previously fought in this particular island have all been foreign-born.

While Scaramanga prefers to do his own dirty work, thus earning the epithet of the novel's title, von Hammerstein chooses to stay behind the scenes where he can keep his identity a secret. He also works with the natives when he hires a Cuban thug named Gonzales to extort property owners, to launder money, and, when necessary, to kill.

Likewise, Scaramanga's national status as a Spaniard in an ex-Spanish colony, Cuba, parallels Bond's position as a representative of the old colonial power, England, while in Jamaica during his assignment in *The Man with the Golden Gun.* By working strictly with colonial officials like governors, police chiefs, and bureau directors or collaborating with American secret agents, the criminals themselves exploit the diversity of the Caribbean ethnoscape by blending in and working with local gangs, spies, or criminals, while Bond cannot shake his European identity when he is in the Caribbean.

Although he needs Quarrel's help to combat Mr. Big and Dr. No, by the time he faces Largo in *Thunderball,* von Hammerstein in "For Your Eyes Only," and Scaramanga in *The Man with the Golden Gun,* Bond has learned enough about the Caribbean to act by himself. Bond never sets foot in Jamaica during "For Your Eyes Only," yet he manages to avenge the death of M's creole friends, the Havelocks, with the unexpected help of their daughter, Judy. The surreptitious attack on von Hammerstein, the cold-blooded SMERSH agent, is facilitated by a distinct performance of racial or cross-racial drag, which Gubar defines as "crossing over racial demarcations" (248). First, Bond smears brown walnut oil on his skin as camouflage in order to avoid detection and comes out " looking like a red Indian with blue gray eyes" (*Your Eyes* 53). Already Bond had been accused of "playing red Indian" in the beginning of Fleming's first Bond novel, *Casino Royale,* and this story provides the first and only instance where Bond literalizes the metaphor by altering the color of his skin to disguise the telltale sign of his Britishness—his whiteness. 007 makes use of the natural resources available to seek cover and carry out his mission of revenge, thus acting very much the part of the hunter in pursuit of his prey in this story. His chance partner in this adventure, the Jamaican-born Judy Havelock, is out to avenge her parents' death through the use of a bow and arrow, weapons that are seemingly in keeping with the Native American theme of the story's climax.[6] However, because of Judy's fair skin and blond hair, which she only camouflages with gold-enrod, James Bond uses an English cultural frame of reference to read her as "Robina Hood" (*Your Eyes* 62) rather than as the more geograph-ically appropriate cultural referent, Pocahontas, the Native American princess.[7]

Although these three novels and two short stories are ostensibly set on various Caribbean islands, the action itself takes place away from the populated areas and in more rural, or secluded, spaces, which is why not one of the *Thrilling Cities* Fleming visits in the anthology of travel pieces of the same name is located in the Caribbean basin. Following the lead of Alejo Carpentier, the Cuban novelist who was Fleming's contemporary and who first proposed a theory of the marvelous real based on the inherent mystery and power of the Caribbean landscape in the context of Haiti, Ian Fleming imagines a tropical world in which voodoo, zombies, and monstrous animals are as real and influential in shaping daily life as are the various agents from the highly regimented criminal networks of SMERSH and SPECTRE. It is in this view of animals as swift dispatchers of justice and punishment that Fleming's novels most closely approxi-mate the marvelous real in Caribbean fiction such as Carpentier's *The Kingdom of This World* or Patrick Chamoiseau's *L'esclave vieil homme et le molosse.* The island featured most prominently in *Doctor No* is not Jamaica proper, but rather Crab Key, a privately owned islet where the eponymous villain operates a guano mine and secretly makes U.S.-launched missiles veer off course. And in his personal commentary, handwritten inside the front cover of his leather-bound edition of *Live and Let Die,* Fleming earnestly attests:

> All the settings are based on personal experience . . . The undertaker chapters are based on Cabritta Island, Port Maria, Jamaica, where Bloody Morgan careened his ships & which is still supposed to contain his treasure.[8]

Emphasizing his personal acquaintance with the satellite islands he describes as well as attesting to the verisimilitude of these marginal settings, Fleming in essence redefines Caribbean geography by familiarizing his readers with places not normally included in vacation brochures. Because they reveal otherwise "hidden" locales, Fleming's Bond novels act as a kind of treasure map for the reader, who follows along the spy's journey into an unknown, if not undiscovered, country.

The Caribbean in the James Bond novels and short fiction is neither *what* nor *where* it first appears to be. As he describes it, this region is as defined by the islet's (and American city satellites') peripheral relation to the greater Antilles as it is by the former island colonies' ex-centric relationship to the mother country, England. An ambiguously geographic ethnoscape, Fleming's Caribbean pits the ghosts of England's colonial past against the specters of international communism; it serves as a meeting point for Old and New Worlds as well as a place from which to articulate a hybrid cultural identity.

NOTES

1. In Cleaver's views, not only is race (defined as white vs. "oppressed" brown and yellow people) a determining factor in separating the privileged people of the world from those without means, but nationality also plays a role in marking a group of people as "exotic" and indecipherable (the "opaque" Africans), while another is simply described in negative terms (the "impudent" African Americans) because they presumably do not conform to the ideal quality of "Americanness."

2. Bond is always eager and willing to have sex with exotic damsels, from English roses like Gala Brand in *Moonraker* and Mary Goodnight in *The Man with the Golden Gun,* to brassy Americans like Pussy Galore in *Goldfinger* or Tiffany Case in *Diamonds Are Forever,* to Caribbean creoles like Solitaire in *Live and Let Die* and Honeychile Rider in *Doctor No,* to fearless Italians like Domino Vittali in *Thunderball,* to Soviet double agents like Tatiana Romanova in *From Russia with Love* and Vesper in *Casino Royale* and, finally, to capable Japanese spies like Kissy Suzuki in *You Only Live Twice.*

3. Mr. Big, the highly organized Haitian SMERSH agent in *Live and Let Die,* runs African American smuggling rings. Donovan Grant, the remorseless killer in *From Russia with Love,* who is half Irish and half German, immigrates to Russia and pretends to be British to get close to Bond. The paranoid and vengeful Count Lippe is half Chinese and half Portuguese and hides a Chinese Tong tattoo under his watch in the opening pages of *Thunderball.* The scheming Doctor No is "the only son of a German Methodist missionary and a Chinese girl of good family" (*Doctor* 163). Even Bond's archrival, Ernst Stavro Blofeld, is the offspring of a "mixed" union: he "was born in Gdynia of a Polish father and a Greek mother" (*Thunderball* 44).

4. The recurrence of immersion as a theme in the deaths of all these villains suggest that as a nexus for travel, movement, and displacement, the Caribbean island can literally absorb whatever evil comes its way without becoming contaminated by it. Von Hammerstein and Scaramanga each literally become one with the environment that surrounds them through their watery deaths. Emilio Largo's death in *Thunderball* involves both water and an angry woman with a phallic weapon: his ex-lover, Domino Vittali, harpoons him as he scuba dives in pursuit of James Bond. As was the case in "For Your Eyes Only," the female murderer, Domino, kills to avenge a personal tragedy inflicted by the villain—in this instance, the death of her brother, the pilot who stole the military plane for SPECTRE. Like Judy Havelock, Domino herself is not racially mixed—the latter is Italian, while the former is a white creole Jamaican. In *The Man with the Golden Gun,* Bond and Scaramanga have a shootout in a swamp, but only after the secret agent narrowly escapes death on a train. The Caribbean landscape literally swallows the two racially hybrid villains who square off against Bond, but the secret agent himself, not a woman, manipulates the forces of nature to bring about the killing: Bond dumps a ton of guano on Doctor No, thereby suffocating him with the fruits of his own harvest, and he blows up Mr. Big's boat just as shark fins surround it, paying the villain back in his own coin for the maiming of his friend Leiter.

5. In this fleeting reference to his villain's nationality, Fleming alludes to the sociopolitical phenomenon of internal colonization perpetrated by a European nation upon its citizens.

6. The only other white creole character to play a prominent role in the novels is Honeychile Rider, Bond's love interest in *Doctor No.* As I argued earlier, Fleming does not present a stable definition of a white racial identity in any of the Bond novels. This is a concept that only resonates within the American context of black-white racial tensions.

7. In an inverse parody of the Cupid myth, Judy Havelock kills the mastermind behind her parents' murders, von Hammerstein, by shooting him through the heart with the bow and arrow as he's diving into a lake. Bond, the professional spy with a license to kill, shoots Gonzales, the actual murderer of the Havelocks.

8. I consulted Fleming's own 1954 edition of *Live and Let Die* (London: Jonathan Cape), which can be found at the Lilly Library at Indiana University.

11 The Kennedys, Fleming, and Cuba

BOND'S FOREIGN POLICY

Skip Willman

In his biography of Robert Kennedy, Evan Thomas notes that both JFK and his younger sibling "shared a fascination with secret operations and spy stories" (119). Their interest was sparked as adolescents by the fiction of John Buchan and was cultivated as adults with the work of Ian Fleming. The Kennedys were also intrigued by Fleming himself, not just his fictional protagonist, James Bond. Henry Brandon, Washington correspondent for the *Sunday Times* and friend of both JFK and Fleming, observed that "Kennedy . . . was fascinated by the line dividing Ian's real life from the fantasy life that went into his books. He often asked me how such an intelligent, mature, urbane sort of man could have such an element of odd imagining in his make-up" (Pearson 298). Fleming actually met the future president at a dinner JFK gave in his Georgetown home on March 13, 1960, after scoring the invitation through a mutual friend of the Massachusetts senator, Mrs. Marion "Oatsie" Leiter. During this memorable evening, JFK solicited Fleming's views on how to topple Fidel Castro. Fleming "described how he would use 'ridicule' to force Castro out of office. Since the Cubans cared only about money, religion, and sex . . . fake dollar bills should be dropped on the island to destabilize the currency, as well as leaflets declaring Castro to be impotent" (Seymour Hersh 174). Fleming biographer Andrew Lycett provides a slightly less sinister account of this high-profile dinner, contending that Fleming had his "tongue firmly in his cheek" when he suggested that "the Americans should drop leaflets from the air, informing the Cuban people that their beards were a natural receptacle for radioactivity and would lead to their long-term impotence" (368). Amused by Fleming's banter, John Bross, a CIA official who was also in attendance, informed Allen Dulles, director of the CIA, about Fleming's proposals. Bross describes being "puzzled that Allen's amusement was not as hearty as he had anticipated" (quoted in Thomas, *Very Best Men,* 384 fn. 11). Unbeknownst to Bross, the CIA was devising psychological warfare schemes to overthrow the Cuban dictator at the time, and several resembled the ideas Fleming advanced at the party. More menacingly, as the Church committee publicly exposed a decade later, the agency was also concocting various plots to assassinate Castro, including the use of poisoned cigars and exploding seashells (Thomas, *Robert Kennedy* 153). The next morning Dulles tried to reach Fleming in order to discuss his "interesting ideas" on how to deal with Castro, but Fleming had already left Washington (Seymour Hersh 174).

This encounter between Fleming and Kennedy has been employed by various historians to underscore how out of touch JFK was with the reality of clandestine operations, while his obsession with the fantasy world of espionage conjured by Fleming accounts for his inexplicable romance with the CIA. Such accounts tend to reinforce a sharp distinction between fantasy and reality that the Lacanian psychoanalytic work of Slavoj Žižek disputes. According to Žižek, the experience of social reality is always already mediated by fantasy. Fantasy supports reality, providing it with meaning and coherence. The point of this analysis is thus not to rehash a condemnation of Kennedy for falling prey to the "pillow fantasies" of Fleming and allowing that unrealistic vision to shape foreign policy, but rather to examine the ways in which JFK's fixation on covert action to oust Castro was constituted through an underlying fantasy shaped in part by the work of Fleming.

The CIA encouraged Kennedy's James Bond fantasy as a way in which to advance its own agenda. However, the CIA's employment of Bond was not merely a cynical means of solidifying the position of the CIA within the Kennedy administration, primarily because the CIA itself was grounded in a fantasy of heroic action that the Bond novels reinforced. In other words, the CIA was as fully invested in the fantasy camp as Kennedy, despite their presumed knowledge about the harsh reality of espionage.

Those who construct a sharp differentiation between the fantasy of the Bond novels and the reality of the work of the CIA also do Fleming a disservice. For while he described his Bond novels as "pillow fantasies," he had a legitimate background in British intelligence working for the

Office of Naval Intelligence (ONI) in World War II. With this experience and his familiarity with the Caribbean, Fleming represented for the Kennedys what Jacques Lacan calls "the subject supposed to know," the "central axis, anchor, of the phenomenon of transference" (Žižek, *Sublime Object* 185). Fleming was presumed to possess knowledge of the proper way to handle Castro through covert means. Furthermore, the fascination of the Kennedy brothers with the world of espionage cultivated by their interest in the fiction of Fleming would make them highly susceptible to intelligence legends such as Allen Dulles, Richard Bissell, Edward Lansdale, and Desmond FitzGerald, who would play key roles in the development and execution of their Cuban policy. This Lacanian view also offers a way in which to describe the formative influence of James Bond on the identity of the Kennedys. Bond represented an ideal ego for both Kennedy brothers. More importantly, the fantasy figure of Bond shaped the expectations of the Kennedys regarding the possibilities of CIA covert activity in Cuba, even after the horrendous failure of the CIA-led Bay of Pigs invasion on April 17, 1961. The establishment of Operation Mongoose, a secret program of sabotage and harassment of Cuba, only months after this military and intelligence fiasco demonstrates how firmly entrenched the Bondian fantasy frame was within Kennedy's Cuban policy. His honeymoon period with the agency may have ended with the Bay of Pigs, but his rocky romance with the CIA endured even the Cuban missile crisis.

Transference: Ian Fleming as "the Subject Supposed to Know"

The relationship between Kennedy and Fleming can be illuminated by the Lacanian revision of the psychoanalytic theory of transference. According to Freudian convention, transference occurs when the analysand displaces onto the analyst feelings, emotions, and attitudes associated with another figure, typically a parent. Within clinical practice, then, the analyst subtly manages the framework of this transference to help the analysand work through whatever symptoms materialize in the course of the analysis. Lacan contends that transference entails a necessary illusion on the part of the analysand that the analyst possesses knowledge unavailable to him or her: the meaning of his or her symptoms. The analyst occupies the position of what Lacan calls "the subject supposed to know" (*Four Fundamental Concepts* 232), and this is the crucial feature of transference. This attributed knowledge is false, but the belief in the analyst enables the analysand to interpret his or her symptoms. Eventually, the transference dissolves when the analysand recognizes that the analyst does not possess this presumed knowledge, and that the analysand has produced the meaning of his or her own symptoms. Importantly, Lacan contends that this transferential relationship is not to be found only in the analytic situation: "Whenever this function may be, for the subject, embodied in some individual, whether or not an analyst, the transference, according to the definition I have given you of it, is established" (*Four Fundamental Concepts* 233). Žižek has perhaps gone further than anyone in taking this cue, developing the notion of "the subject supposed to know" into a cultural logic of sorts, a way in which to describe the causal mechanism of certain events based on the attribution of some knowledge (or enjoyment, belief, or desire, in his own revision of Lacan) to an imagined third party, a proverbial "they" or "them." Thus, Kennedy's training in spy fiction sets the stage for his transferential relationship with Fleming and several top CIA officials, whose mythology contributed to their status as "subjects supposed to know."

Fleming's claim to fame resides in the iconic success of James Bond, but his own experience working in British intelligence should not be overlooked as an important reason for his transferential relationship with the Kennedys. During World War II, Fleming rose to the rank of commander in the Royal Naval Volunteer Reserve, occupying a key bureaucratic position within ONI that offered him a privileged view of the espionage business. He served as the personal assistant to Admiral John Godfrey, director of naval intelligence (DNI). In this capacity, Fleming served as Godfrey's "liaison with the outside world," primarily "with other clandestine services" (Lycett, *Ian Fleming* 103), including "the Special Operations Executive (SOE) for sabotage and subversive activities in enemy countries, the Political Warfare Executive (PWE) for propaganda, rumours and information policy for enemy countries, and . . . the Secret Intelligence Service" (McLachlan 5). By all accounts, Fleming distinguished himself in the headquarters of the Naval Intelligence Division, the famed Room 39 of Whitehall. According to his colleague and historian Donald McLachlan, "His gift was much less for the analysis and weighing of intelligence than for running things and for drafting. He was a skilled fixer and a vigorous showman, and he seemed to transmit the energy and wide-ranging curiosity of his first chief by whom so much was delegated" (8). McLachlan also notes that Fleming's "real achievement . . . was to set a standard of independent, critical and forceful behaviour by RNVR officers which was of critical importance in a Division where civilians had such big parts to play" (10). While his job was almost exclusively bureaucratic, Fleming nevertheless did participate in some fieldwork. For instance, as France collapsed in June 1940, Fleming flew to Paris to coordinate several "British intelligence operations" (Lycett, *Ian Fleming* 114), culminating in the evacuation of Secret Intelligence Service personnel from Bordeaux as the Germans pushed south after overrunning Paris on June 14, 1940 (115). Later, Fleming participated in Operation Golden Eye, "a sophisticated NID plan to carry out limited sabotage and maintain essential communication with London if the Germans marched into Spain" (125). While this operation was never conducted, Fleming was clearly invested in the name "Golden Eye," since he later named his house in Jamaica after this clandestine operation. This experience with the Office of Naval Intelligence, along with his flair, bravado, and independence, would clearly enable him to project an image of authority, even in the midst of presidential candidates, famous journalists, and CIA officials.

The key to Fleming's status as "the subject supposed to know" involves his work with Admiral Godfrey in helping to establish the CIA. The story of the origins of the CIA is a legendary and contested one, with both the British and the Americans claiming the ultimate responsibility for its establishment. Shortly after the outbreak of World War II, with Britain reeling from a series of setbacks, Winston Churchill was anxious to enlist U.S. support, but the isolationist mood of America made that politically difficult even though President Franklin Delano Roosevelt was convinced that American involvement in the war against Germany was inevitable. In June of 1940, Churchill appointed William "Little Bill" Stephenson, the British agent code named Intrepid, to head up British Security Coordination (BSC), and sent him to New York to oversee various operations, from safeguarding supply shipments to Britain from sabotage to monitoring fifth column activities in the United States. The other task charged to Stephenson by Churchill was to lay the groundwork for the sharing of secret intelligence between Britain and the United States. Initially, this intelligence sharing occurred sub rosa between the FBI and BSC. Unfortunately, this arrangement quickly broke down, and the British were forced to look elsewhere for intelligence aid.[1]

The most pressing intelligence need for the British that led them to coordinate information with the United States involved German U-boat activity. Before America entered the war, British shipping losses in the Atlantic had reached a crisis level. The U.S. ambassador to Great Britain,

Joseph P. Kennedy, was unsympathetic to the British plight and believed that America should withhold its support since Britain's days were numbered against the vastly superior forces of Hitler. Churchill, the first Lord of the Admiralty and then Prime Minister after the resignation of Chamberlain, decided to circumvent Kennedy and the formal diplomatic avenues. Churchill enlisted Stephenson for this back-channel approach to acquiring American material and intelligence support. Stephenson, in turn, approached William P. Donovan, a war hero, lawyer, and one-time "private intelligence gatherer for [J. P.] Morgan" (Lycett, *Ian Fleming* 120), who, like Churchill and Stephenson, believed in the necessity of an American "integrated intelligence service" (120). Churchill and Stephenson also believed that "Wild Bill" Donovan would be the ideal man for heading up such an intelligence service, and the fact that he had the ear of FDR didn't hurt. In order to persuade the Americans to help them, the British invited Donovan to England to assess the British war effort, since "the Americans needed to be convinced," thanks in part to Ambassador Kennedy's grim prognosis, "that Britain had not only a cause worth fighting for but also the will to succeed" (120). This initial back-channel venture was successful. Donovan's "clean bill of health" led to the brokering of a deal between the two countries: America provided fifty destroyers and other military hardware to the British in exchange for a "99-year lease on British bases in Canada and the Caribbean" (120). The British courting of Donovan continued; the next year Fleming escorted him on a no-holds-barred tour of British military installations in the Mediterranean and the Middle East (124).

However, Fleming's most important mission was to come on May 25, 1941, when Godfrey and Fleming arrived in the United States to meet with President Roosevelt and make the British case for an American centralized intelligence service. Snagging an invitation to a private dinner from Mrs. Roosevelt, Godfrey finally managed to make his case to the president, and he was successful. On June 18, 1941, Roosevelt established the Office of Coordinator of Information under the direction of Donovan. The COI, as it was abbreviated, would be renamed the Office of Strategic Services on June 13, 1942, dissolved by Truman on September 20, 1945, after the end of World War II, only to be resurrected as the Central Intelligence Agency in 1947. While Godfrey returned to England, he left Fleming behind to help Donovan put the new intelligence service together. Fleming wrote several memoranda for Donovan during this stretch, and his efforts led to Fleming's exaggerated claim that "he had written the blueprint for the Central Intelligence Agency" (131). Despite the hyperbole, Donovan was grateful for Fleming's assistance and gave him a .38 revolver as a parting gift with the inscription "For Special Services," a trophy in which Fleming would take great pride. His experience working for ONI would provide Fleming with the necessary background for the James Bond novels, but it would also underwrite his authority and expertise in intelligence.

The Identification of the Kennedys with Bond

According to Lacan, identity is constructed through a twofold process of identification, which he calls imaginary and symbolic identification. The ego (as opposed to the subject, which is equated with lack) is a bricolage of internalized features from the subject's encounter with various individuals (the other) and society (the big Other or the symbolic order). Žižek distinguishes between imaginary and symbolic identification, between the ideal ego and the ego-ideal, in the following way: "imaginary identification is identification with the image in which we appear likable to ourselves, with the image representing 'what we would like to be,' and symbolic identification, identification with the very place *from where* we are being observed, *from where* we look at ourselves so that we appear to ourselves likeable, worthy of love" (*Sublime* 105). The crucial difference between these two forms of identification, then, is that symbolic identification proceeds on behalf of the gaze of the Other with the assumption of a symbolic mandate, a fantasy that enables the subject to locate and occupy a determinate position within the symbolic order.

The clues to JFK's symbolic identification may be found in his Pulitzer Prize–winning *Profiles in Courage.* In this sympathetic history of senatorial figures who showed courage in sticking to their convictions and voting against their constituencies in the face of enormous public pressure, JFK articulates his own symbolic mandate. As John Hellman points out in *The Kennedy Obsession: The American Myth of JFK,* the writing of *Profiles in Courage* "was as much a process of revising his self-image as it was of reworking the face he showed the public" (75). In other words, the cynical take on the book as a mere exercise to make the Massachusetts senator look more mature and presidential, while no doubt accurate, overlooks the way in which JFK's identity was shaped by the gaze of the public. Or rather, to express this idea in a more Lacanian fashion, *Profiles in Courage* articulates what JFK presumed to be his symbolic mandate, "a place in the intersubjective network of symbolic relations" (Žižek, *Sublime* 113). As Žižek notes, the assumption of a symbolic mandate involves an element of fantasy in the form of an answer to the question, "*Che vuoi?*" or "What does the Other want of me?" Hellman locates this fantasy of interpellation in one of the discarded openings for the book, in which the young, convalescing Kennedy is visited in his hospital bed by the ghosts of four United States senators from Massachusetts: "Their message to him is that he should retain his independent judgment and be prepared to one day defy the constituents of his state by voting his perception of the national good" (Hellman 3). While ultimately cut from the final draft of *Profiles*, this fantasy scenario reveals the gaze that structures his symbolic identification, the gaze for whom Kennedy strives to appear worthy, namely history. One of the key words of *Profiles* is "vindication" (in various guises as a noun and verb), a possibility offered only by the retrospective gaze of history, or as JFK writes, "the long-run judgment of the people" (Kennedy 245).

In one sense, the book may be seen as an indirect or distorted attempt to vindicate his own father's position against U.S. involvement in World War II as the U.S. ambassador to Great Britain. In this revisionist mode, Joseph Kennedy, Sr. adopted an unpopular position, one that cost him his diplomatic position, but the motivation for his decision was honorable and courageous, even though isolationism proved ultimately to be the wrong path. At the time, one must remember that the senior Kennedy's position on Germany was primarily criticized as being cowardly. In this way, JFK masks "the lack in the big Other," the inconsistency of the symbolic order, manifested in the fallibility and failures of his father. In yet another vein, the book may be an occasion to transform his family's outsider status among the Boston blueblood elite into a virtue. The Irish Catholic Kennedys lacked the pedigree to truly rub elbows with Boston's finest WASPs, and the alleged source of the Kennedy fortune in bootlegging or other unsavory activities only magnified the difficulties. In both of these cases, the motivation behind these narratives of courageous senators seems to lie in a compensatory fantasy that revises the Kennedy position within the symbolic order or explains away their social rejection.

According to Žižek, symbolic identification hinges upon "the identification of the subject with some signifying feature, trait (I) . . . in the symbolic order" (*Sublime* 104). Obviously, the single trait upon which JFK's symbolic identification proceeds is courage, and *Profiles* famously begins by invoking Ernest Hemingway's definition of courage as "grace under pressure" (1). Hellman articulates the cultural work performed by the invocation of Hemingway as JFK's attempt to navigate the tricky cultural divide between the "Eisenhower *ethos*" (66), associated with complacency, detachment, conformity, and security, and the "radical political and social critiques" of "younger writers, such as Norman Mailer" (67). By the mid-fifties, Hemingway, who had won the Nobel Prize in literature in 1954, had come to serve "as an exemplar of traditional American values of work and achievement" and "an authoritative representative of 'mainstream' ideology" (67). Hemingway comes to represent something of a mediating figure in much the same manner as James Bond; their supercharged masculinity serves as the antithesis to the stale fifties "organization man," although, as Edward Comentale points out in this volume, Bond may actually be the ideal "organization man."

Ironically, JFK first read the ultra-masculine James Bond novels while convalescing from one of his back surgeries in the fifties, offering yet another possible explanation for the appeal of Bond to Kennedy. JFK met Fleming in early 1960 when he was a presidential hopeful, but the link between Kennedy and Fleming was primarily established in the mind of the public in early 1961. The White House PR team was busy courting national publications, offering privileged glimpses into the daily life of the new president. In March of that year, *U.S. News and World Report* "devoted ten pages to photographs of JFK at work" (Seymour Hersh 223). On March 17, 1961, *Life* magazine published a story depicting Kennedy as a "voracious" reader and listing his ten favorite books, one of which was Fleming's *From Russia with Love*.[2] This list has garnered much critical attention, primarily as a way in which to understand the hidden workings of the mind of JFK. This critical task is not without merit, as these books do seemingly offer insight into the figures with which Kennedy identifies and, subsequently, the image of himself he would like to project, what Lacan would call Kennedy's ideal ego. Thus, in his analysis of the "Kennedy phenomenon," historian Gary Wills offers a highly critical look at JFK through the lens of another book on this list of favorites, Lord David Cecil's *The Young Melbourne*. Wills notes, "The Melbourne described by Cecil, a doting descendant, was all the things Kennedy wanted to be—secular, combining the bookish and the active life, supported by a family that defied outsiders" (73). However, Wills throws a humorous barb into this rather noble impression of the traits Kennedy admired about English aristocratic life: "From Cecil's *Melbourne* he seems to have derived his impression that English aristocrats have naked women emerge from silver dishes at their banquets (the moral *Time* magazine drew from the book)" (73). Seymour Hersh reaches a far more disconcerting conclusion, arguing that the appearance of *Melbourne* on this list of favorite books unwittingly reveals a "dark side." He notes the reaction of Hugh Sidey, author of the *Life* article, to describe the unfavorable light this list sheds on JFK. According to Sidey, JFK's favorite book, *Melbourne,* the biography of "Queen Victoria's prime minister and political adviser," was a tale of public service and private debauchery, and it offered incredible insight into JFK:

> It was the story . . . about the young aristocracy of Britain . . . who gave their lives in military campaigns, who held the ideal of empire and national honor above all else. But on the weekends, when they went to their country estates, it was broken-field running through the bedrooms. I mean they swapped wives, they slept with others. But the code of that period was nobody talked about it. And you didn't get divorced; otherwise, you were disgraced. (Quoted in Seymour Hersh 25)

Hersh takes Sidey's observation as confirmation of the underlying master narrative of JFK's entire political career, one that runs counter to the officially sanctioned myth of Camelot. The most important feature of the "dark side of Camelot" was sexual license, an intense drive that compromised the president on numerous occasions and degraded the office. Recent revelations that Marion Beardsley, a nineteen-year-old intern nicknamed Mimi, was hired specifically to service JFK sexually lend credence to Hersh's contention.[3]

Sexual license may be one way to formulate the basis for the imaginary identification of Kennedy with Bond. Journalist and JFK confidante Ben Bradlee observed that Kennedy's enjoyment of the Bond films entailed a fascination with that patented Fleming mix of sex and sadism, if not snobbery: "The movie was James Bond, and Kennedy seemed to enjoy the cool and the sex and the brutality" (quoted in Wills 25). Gary Wills notes that Kennedy's sexual license "led him to take political and personal risks . . . even his father and brothers thought foolhardy" (29). In some sense, JFK thrived on the danger of his sexual conquests; it was part of the thrill *à la* James Bond. However, JFK's identification with James Bond works because 007 is a public servant, albeit one smeared with the stain of private enjoyment. As Alan Nadel points out, sexual and political conquests are conflated and equated: "Kennedy was an acknowledged fan of the novels, and probably of the figure of Bond himself, who was in many ways the apotheosis of the kind of leader Kennedy most admired—one who furthered the cause of containment with unlimited license, whose sexual prowess . . . was testimony to his political fitness, whose amorality was a sign of goodness" (157). Interestingly enough, the womanizing of Joseph Senior, the Kennedy family patriarch, finds a rationale in the actions/seductions of Bond—screwing for the good of the country, promiscuity for the promise of a better tomorrow.[4] Bond as ideal ego provides a bridge between the public and private split in JFK that so infuriates critics of Kennedy, like Hersh, who view Camelot as a hollow myth, public idealism tainted by private immorality. Bond ennobles promiscuity: "For the good of England, James." Kennedy's favorite Fleming novel, *From Russia with Love,* represents the most brazen example of this theme of the spy as gigolo.

However, I want to suggest a possible alternative or supplement to what Nadel claims to be the basis for the imaginary identification of both John and Robert Kennedy with Bond. Žižek points out that "the feature, the trait on the basis of which we identify with someone, is usually hidden—it is by no means necessarily a glamorous feature" (*Sublime* 105). This specific trait may be uncovered if we examine what drew JFK to *From Russia with Love* in particular. Perhaps he identifies with the predicament in which Bond finds himself, namely becoming involved with a beautiful spy. During World War II, while JFK was stationed in Washington in the Office of Naval Intelligence, he had an affair with a Danish journalist on the staff of the *Washington Times-Herald* named Inga Marie Arvad (Seymour Hersh 82). Rumors swirled about Arvad's allegiances because she "had interviewed Hitler and briefly socialized with him and other leading Nazis in 1936, while covering the Olympics for a Danish newspaper" (82). With his love for digging up the sexual dirt on powerful people, J. Edgar Hoover became involved in the investigation in early 1942, placing Arvad under surveillance and accumulating "a large file of explicit tape recordings of the lovers at play" (83). Moreover, Hoover leaked the story to columnist Walter Winchell, who published a brief snippet on the affair on January 12, 1942: "One of Ex-Ambassador Kennedy's eligible sons is the target of a Washington gal columnist's affections. So much so she has consulted her barrister about divorcing her exploring groom. Pa Kennedy no like" (quoted in Seymour Hersh 83). This affair with someone deemed a security risk culminated in JFK's rather disgraceful exit from the Office of Naval Intelligence (Wills 21). However, his dismissal eventually led to his assignment in the Pacific, which would pay dividends when he became the celebrated war hero of PT 109. The allegations of espionage against Arvad were never proven and seem unlikely, but the entire scenario bears a resemblance to the plot of *From Russia with Love*. This type of scandal is precisely the fate that awaits Bond at the end of the villain Kronsteen's plan; the sexual misconduct of a British agent with a foreign spy would disgrace and compromise the British Secret Service. Initially, Bond is lured to Istanbul by a beautiful Russian "traitor" and tool of SMERSH, Tatiana Romanova, who promises him a Spektor cipher machine. One more odd coincidence between JFK's real-life affair and Fleming's fictional story is that Bond's initial sexual encounter with Tatiana, the Russian spy, is filmed by SMERSH for blackmail purposes in the novel.

More damaging allegations of a similar nature would surface in the spring of 1963 when JFK became involved with Ellen Rometsch, a professional "party girl" born in what became East Germany; she was also a former member of a Communist Party group (Seymour Hersh 387–88). Long aware of the possible security problems posed by his brother's sexual escapades, Bobby had warned his brother, "You've got to be careful about these girls. A couple of them might be spies" (quoted in Thomas, *Robert Kennedy* 255). Shortly after the initiation of this affair, Britain was rocked by the Profumo affair, in which the British minister of war was discovered to have had an affair with prostitute Christine Keeler, who was simultaneously having an affair with a Soviet naval attaché (Seymour Hersh 390). This scandal eventually led to the resignation of Prime Minister Macmillan. JFK was obsessed with the case, and for good reason; he was allegedly involved with Suzy Chang, one of the prostitutes implicated in the British scandal. This link was intimated in a story published by the *New York Journal-American* in its afternoon edition for Saturday, June 29 (394). Days later, on July 3, Bobby Kennedy was informed that the FBI was aware of his brother's illicit relations with Rometsch and that she had unsavory connections to Walter Ulbricht, the communist leader of East Germany (398). In order to suppress a possible American version of the Profumo scandal, Bobby Kennedy had Rometsch deported to Germany on August 21, 1963 (Seymour Hersh 399). Unfortunately for Kennedy, the threat of the scandal emerged yet again in October 1963 when an investigative probe of Bobby Baker for influence peddling was launched by the Senate Rules Committee (Thomas, *Robert Kennedy* 263). In addition to his official duties as secretary of the senate, Baker ran the Quorum Club, an establishment in which "senators and lobbyists caroused together" (Thomas, *Robert Kennedy* 255) with girls provided by Baker, one of whom was Rometsch. More importantly, Baker "allegedly provided

Rometsch for JFK's pleasure" (263), so the investigation threatened to reveal her amorous encounters with the president. As in the case of Arvad, no evidence was produced that Rometsch was a communist spy, but the mere appearance of a communist link was enough to initiate massive damage control by the Kennedys.

RFK was equally fascinated with Fleming and his work, although the basis for his identification with Bond appears to be slightly different. On June 1, 1962, he wrote a brief letter to Fleming on attorney general letterhead thanking Fleming for autographed copies of *From Russia with Love*. The typed letter included a handwritten inscription: "As you know you have many Kennedy fans. We all can hardly wait for your next contribution to our leisure hours. RFK." In his biography of RFK, Evan Thomas notes, in almost non sequitur fashion, "In Djakarta [February 1962], reporters saw him engrossed in a copy of the latest James Bond novel, *Diamonds Are Forever*" (166). This particular novel offers an intriguing possibility regarding RFK's identification with Bond, as his principal antagonists are the Spang brothers, the operators of a diamond smuggling pipeline. RFK presumably identified with this battle against the mob, since he was the chief counsel of the McClellan Committee, which investigated the infiltration of labor unions by organized crime in the mid-fifties. This legal work provided the basis for his book *The Enemy Within* (1960), and gave him a larger-than-life villain in Jimmy Hoffa. His prosecution of the Mafia continued when he assumed the position of attorney general. In an intriguing side note, Fleming wrote a letter to RFK in which he praised the attorney general for precisely this work: "Over here we are all watching with fascination your gallant attempts to harass American gangsterdom. If James Bond can be any help to you please let me know and I will have a word with M."

In February 1964, shortly after the assassination of his brother, RFK encountered Ann Fleming in London at a dinner given by Ambassador David Bruce (Thomas, *Robert Kennedy* 284). According to her, RFK was "obsessed by Ian's books" and "grilled her, in a 'humorless' fashion . . . for facts about her husband and his espionage intrigues" (284). After the conspiratorial speculation concerning the JFK assassination, it is perhaps no surprise that Kennedy would turn to Fleming for insights into the world of espionage, seeking his own answers to the mystery of who was behind the murder of his brother. Such a move, once again, demonstrates how Fleming occupied the role of the "subject supposed to know" for the surviving Kennedy.

From the Bay of Pigs to Operation Mongoose:
Bondian Provocation

Weaned on spy thrillers from Buchan to Fleming, JFK had what some have called a "romance" with the CIA that would prove costly to his presidency. During the first weeks of the Kennedy administration, the CIA's Richard Bissell claims he was asked by the White House to develop an "Executive Action Capability," a program similar to Fleming's licensed to kill "00" agents, that was subsequently code named ZR/RIFLE. The use of assassination in foreign policy was nothing new, although it was publicly disavowed. The Eisenhower administration had begun exploring these lethal options during its final summer against three possible targets: Trujillo in the Dominican Republic, Lumumba of the Congo, and Castro, who eventually learned of the U.S. designs on his life (Thomas, *Very Best Men* 220). In addition to ZR/RIFLE, the CIA approached and worked with the mob to attempt to whack the Beard. This disastrous collaboration with the Mafia, along with the development of an executive action capability (what LBJ called "a damned Murder Inc. in the Caribbean"), would later give RFK nightmares and provide conspiracy theorists with ammunition in the wake of the JFK assassination.

The most notorious failure early in Kennedy's presidency was, of course, the Bay of Pigs invasion on April 17, 1961. However, this ill-conceived plan by Cuban exiles undertaken by the CIA with the support of the U.S. military was not a Kennedy administration venture, but rather was developed by the Eisenhower administration shortly after Castro seized power in 1959 and his allegiance to Marxism became apparent. Why did JFK go along with the plan? Nearly every historical account of this event, whether penned by JFK hagiographers or Camelot debunkers, alleges that Kennedy mistakenly deferred judgment to the experts, the "subject(s) supposed to know." In particular, JFK relied upon the advice and experience of three figures: former president Dwight D. Eisenhower; the Director of the CIA, Allen W. Dulles; and the Deputy Director of Plans for the CIA, Richard Bissell. Seduced by the myths of these legends, JFK was persuaded by their recommendations for covert action against Castro. Regarding the influence of Eisenhower, for example, Arthur Schlesinger, Jr. suggests that backing out of a plan of invasion "organized and recommended by the supreme commander of the greatest amphibious landing in history," referring to Operation Overlord and the Allied invasion of Normandy, might have serious "political fallout" (8). Perceived inaction against the communist threat was also a powerful political liability. Kennedy himself had benefited in his 1960 campaign against Nixon from the alleged "missile gap" argument. Kennedy accused Nixon and the Eisenhower administration of being soft on communism for allowing the missile gap to develop. (Nixon was unable to counter Kennedy effectively and disclose that no such gap existed because such a claim would reveal the intelligence gathered by U-2 spy plane flights over the USSR.)

Deferring to Eisenhower seems like a reasonable explanation for a new president facing a tricky foreign policy decision, but why place so much faith in Dulles? It is important to note that Dulles was surrounded by a potent mythology as a "legendary" spymaster. During World War II, he worked for the Office of Strategic Services (OSS), the forerunner of the CIA, in Bern, Switzerland. The highlights of his adventures in this hotbed of intrigue and espionage are well-documented. For example, Dulles was in contact with a network of spies in Germany called the Black Orchestra, who opposed Hitler and sought to negotiate peace with the Western Allies after they assassinated Hitler. Dulles was also in contact with a German cipher clerk who passed him copies of numerous signals and orders being sent through the pipeline. The mythology of his mastery of the espionage business emerged from his experience in Bern, although some have questioned this mastery. For instance, Burton Hersh alleges that Dulles, as the not-so-secret U.S. representative of the OSS in the neutral Switzerland, was the dupe of German counterintelligence and manipulated by these "traitors" of the Fatherland (96–97). In other words, the spymaster was something of a charlatan; or as Lacan might say, the Master was an impostor. In this fantasy frame articulated by Fleming, Dulles occupied the role of M, the sage head of the Secret Service and James Bond's boss. Indeed, Dulles oversaw several successful covert operations as director of the CIA that contributed to his legendary status, most notably the overthrow of Arbenz in Guatemala in 1954. Operation Success, as it was known, provided the blueprint for the Bay of Pigs invasion.

The final piece in the transferential puzzle that awed Kennedy into submission regarding the Bay of Pigs invasion was Richard Bissell. Bissell's list of accomplishments was indeed impressive. He was instrumental behind the scenes in implementing the Marshall Plan. His managerial deft touch also led to the CIA's successful development of the U-2 spy plane (rather than the Air Force). During his watch, the U-2 remarkably came in under budget and proved to be enormously effective in its first few years of secret operation. This success paved the way for him to become the Deputy Director for Plans and heir apparent to Dulles as Director of the CIA. On November 18, 1960, shortly after Kennedy won the election, Bissell flew to the Kennedy winter home in Palm Beach, Florida, to brief the president-elect on intelligence matters. At this meeting, Bissell presented JFK with the Cuban invasion plans (Thomas, *Very Best Men* 241). This first meeting with Bissell evidently made a lasting impression on Kennedy, because when asked later by a member of his transition team if there was anyone within the intelligence community whom he trusted, Kennedy answered that he trusted Bissell (240).

The transferential relationship between Kennedy and Bissell was cemented in February 1961 when the CIA welcomed the Kennedy administration with a private dinner at the Alibi Club in Washington. Evan Thomas describes Bissell as the star of the evening, who cracked in his remarks that he was "a man-eating shark" (261). Thomas notes, "There was laughter across the thicket of glasses. It was just the right touch, a mix of bravado and self-mockery" (261). Bissell's appearance underscored the comedy of his comment: "He seemed like an incongruous spymaster—tall, slightly stooped, a little clumsy. But no one doubted his force of personality or intellect" (261). Kennedy evidently took this self-description quite seriously. Either that or the false modesty of this comic statement was compelling enough to convince Kennedy that Bissell was, in essence, lying in the guise of the truth, i.e., that Bissell was indeed "a man-eating shark," despite his gawky appearance. According to Arthur Schlesinger, the Kennedys and their top advisors were "transfixed" by Bissell: "They were fascinated by the working of this superbly clear, organized and articulate intelligence" (quoted in Thomas, *Very Best Men* 265). National Security Adviser McGeorge Bundy was also spellbound by Bissell, although he is harder on himself and the Kennedys in hindsight for not recognizing the danger of the invasion: "It was the stupidity of freshmen on our part, and the stupidity on their part of being wrapped in their own illusions" (quoted in Thomas, *Very Best Men* 245).

Kennedy deferred judgment on this first salvo in foreign policy to these "subject(s) supposed to know." However, with the failure of the Bay of Pigs, JFK recognized the transferential nature of his relationship to these figures, as he acknowledged that he attributed some special knowledge to them: "You always assume that the military and intelligence people have some secret skill not available to ordinary mortals" (quoted in Thomas, *Very Best Men* 266). The fallout from the Bay of Pigs was swift. Kennedy publicly accepted responsibility for the fiasco, but privately he felt betrayed by the CIA. He appointed Maxwell Taylor and

Robert Kennedy to head up an investigation of the failed invasion. They quickly reached the conclusion that the CIA was ill-equipped to handle large-scale paramilitary operations. He fired Dulles and Bissell and threatened to break the agency into a thousand pieces. Following the failure of the Bay of Pigs, Robert Kennedy made an offhand remark that betrays the fantasy frame that underlies their expectations for the clandestine operation: "Why couldn't this have happened to James Bond?" (Thomas, *Robert Kennedy* 123). Rather than discourage their efforts in Cuba, the fiasco fueled the Kennedy brothers' desire for revenge. Unfortunately, they still regarded the CIA as the primary tool for achieving the overthrow of Castro.

Within this fantasy frame, the *modus operandi* of Bond captured the imagination of the Kennedys and shaped their expectations regarding the work of the CIA in Cuba, namely provocation. The clearest articulation of this strategy is found in *Diamonds Are Forever*. Posing as smuggler Peter Franks, Bond waits in Las Vegas for possible additional work from the Spang brothers following his initial smuggling run, but he gets tired of waiting and decides to provoke the villains: "There were two ways of playing the rest of the game, by lying low and waiting for something to happen—or by forcing the pace so that something *had* to happen" (140, italics Fleming's). Thus, Bond departs from his convoluted instructions for his payment of $5,000 through fixed gambling at the casino owned by Serraffimo Spang; he gambles some more and walks off with an additional $15,000, the provocation that he hopes will force his adversary's hand. His strategy works, of course.

On November 3, 1961, RFK articulated a similar strategy of provocation in Cuba: "My idea is to stir things up on the island with espionage, sabotage, general disorder, run & operated by Cubans themselves with every group but Batistaites & Communists. Do not know if we will be successful in overthrowing Castro but we have nothing to lose in my estimate" (Thomas, *Robert Kennedy* 147; White 74). The Kennedy brothers "wanted 'boom and bang' on the island" and envisioned "raids that would produce tangible results, like blowing up bridges and factories" (Thomas, *Robert Kennedy* 151). The "objective" of this "Cuba Project" was "to help the Cubans overthrow the Communist regime from within Cuba and institute a new government with which the United States can live in peace" (White 88). Operation Mongoose, as the "Cuba Project" came to be called, planned to accomplish this goal through various means, but much stress was laid upon harassment and sabotage operations that aimed to hurt the Cuban economy and the Castro regime, such as bombing power plants, ruining sugar crops, and damaging shipments and machinery.

On November 30, 1961, Operation Mongoose was formally established and placed under the direction of Edward Lansdale (White 79), yet another "subject supposed to know" in this series of transferential relationships with intelligence figures. Robert Kennedy handpicked Lansdale because he had an impressive track record in counterinsurgency: his "covert machinations had been instrumental in suppressing a communist uprising and electing a democratic leader in the Philippines in the early 1950s" (Thomas, *Robert Kennedy* 148). Evan Thomas notes a curious and significant detail in Robert Kennedy's notes for the November 3 meeting that points to the source of his "too-easy infatuation" with Lansdale (149). Listing those in attendance, RFK adds in parentheses "the Ugly American" behind Lansdale's name (148). The nickname refers to the title of a bestseller from 1958, William Lederer and Eugene Burdick's *The Ugly American,* which was a "publishing phenomenon," spending seventy-two weeks on the bestseller lists (Freedman 154). More importantly, the book was "regularly referred to in debates over the course of American foreign policy" and "tellingly endorsed by Senator Kennedy" (154). Lansdale was the model for the book's heroic protagonist, Colonel Edwin Hillendale, who was fighting communist guerrillas in Southeast Asia. A less flattering portrait of Lansdale emerged in Graham Greene's *The Quiet American,* in which Lansdale was apparently the model for Alden Pyle, an idealistic menace of a CIA agent, although Greene publicly denied it (154). As Thomas sharply notes, the portraits of Lansdale in these novels were far from complimentary, "but the subtleties seem to have been lost on RFK, whose weakness for hero worship sometimes eclipsed his own discernment" (*Robert Kennedy* 148). The mythology of Lansdale, established through both his real-life exploits and fictional fame, clearly impressed RFK and translated into a transferential relationship: Kennedy assumed that Lansdale possessed the knowledge of counterinsurgency that would topple Castro.

Coincidentally, one of Edward Lansdale's most harebrained psychological warfare ideas for Operation Mongoose echoed a "spoof proposal for giving Castro the James Bond treatment" (Pearson 297) concocted by Fleming during his evening with JFK. Playing on the religious superstitions of the Cubans, Fleming playfully suggested, "Using the Guantanamo base, the United States should conjure up some religious manifestation, say a cross of sorts, in the sky which would induce the Cubans to look constantly skyward" (297). Lansdale intended to flood Cuba with rumors of the Second Coming, while painting Castro as the Anti-Christ. Then to "signify that The Hour was at hand, Lansdale wanted a submarine to surface off the coast at night and fill the sky with starbursts" (Thomas, *Very Best Men* 289). Skeptical CIA insiders derisively called Lansdale's plan for ousting Castro "elimination by illumination."

Knowing of the Kennedy fondness for the work of Fleming, Richard Helms, the successor to Bissell as the deputy director for plans, ironically selected William Harvey to be the commander of Task Force W, the CIA team that would carry out Operation Mongoose (Thomas, *Robert Kennedy* 150–51). Harvey was a colorful former FBI man and an experienced operative, having served as the Berlin station chief during the 1950s. His intelligence successes included tapping into the Soviet communications in Berlin through a tunnel and ferreting out Kim Philby as a Soviet agent (Burton Hersh 321). Yet he was an alcoholic and a loose cannon. JFK was evidently skeptical of Harvey upon meeting him in November 1961: "So you're our James Bond?" The overweight Harvey clearly didn't cut the same dashing figure as Bond. Later, frustrated at the apparent lack of progress in the effort to eliminate Castro, RFK castigated Harvey: "Why can't you get things cooking like 007?" (Thomas, *Robert Kennedy* 151). These comparisons illustrate how expectations for Operation Mongoose were framed by the fictional exploits of James Bond; the "pillow fantasies of the bang-bang, kiss-kiss variety" (Lycett, *Ian Fleming* 290) of Fleming's novels were translated into the "boom and bang" of Kennedy's desired covert Cuban policy.

However, the CIA took full advantage of the Bond image to sell itself both to the policymakers like Kennedy and to the public. Moreover, as much as the CIA was subjected to pressure from the Kennedys to produce instant results in its covert activities as in some Fleming plot, it relied on the fantasy frame of Bond to define itself, whether by contrast or correspondence. William Colby, the director of the CIA from 1973 to 1976, for instance, resorts to James Bond to discuss the image of the CIA prior to the Bay of Pigs fiasco in his memoir *Honorable Men: My Life in the CIA:*

> Until the Bay of Pigs—indeed, ever since the glory days of the OSS in World War II—the Agency had enjoyed a reputation with the public at large not a whit less than golden. After all, we were the derring-do boys who parachuted behind enemy lines, the cream of the academic and social aristocracy, devoted to the nation's service, the point men and women in the fight against totalitarian aggression, matching fire with

fire in an endless round of thrilling adventures like those of the scenarios in James Bond films. (180)

Colby goes on to say that the public image of the CIA was "essentially naïve and uninformed" (181), but he is primarily referring to the "dirty tricks" employed in this fight, the unsavory methods used to conduct clandestine operations that would appall the public. James Bond still serves as an appropriate model for what the agency is ultimately about. Bond had his fans in the CIA, not just in the White House. In his book on the CIA, Thomas counts Tracy Barnes, Assistant Deputy Director for Plans, as one such fan: "Tracy Barnes loved James Bond. At Thanksgiving he laughingly passed out copies of the Ian Fleming spy series to his family" (*Very Best Men* 207). Perhaps not surprisingly, given this odd conjunction of Fleming fans and Cuban operations, Barnes was placed in charge of assembling a team to oust Castro in the winter and spring of 1960 by Richard Bissell (204). Thomas also notes in a footnote that Allen Dulles and the Kennedys swapped copies of the James Bond novels (383–84 n.11). Dulles was also friendly with Fleming. In a letter to Fleming dated April 24, 1963, he playfully remarks, "I received and finished reading your latest 'On Her Majesty's Secret Service.' I hope you have not really destroyed my old friend and colleague James Bond, but I fear his bride has gone." Dulles also alludes to the Fleming-JFK link in the letter: "You have been much publicized here recently as being the author of one of the President's favorite books 'From Russia with Love,' which is also one of my favorites as in my old diplomatic days I spent a couple of fascinating years in Constantinople, 1920–1922."

Some historians claim that the clandestine efforts of Operation Mongoose to harass the communist regime in Cuba, coming on the heels of the Bay of Pigs invasion, forced Castro to seek the aid of the Soviet Union. Thus, Kennedy's aggressive Cuban policy of covert subversion precipitated the Soviet arms buildup in Cuba in the summer of 1962 and was ultimately responsible for the Cuban missile crisis. In fact, William Harvey enraged RFK and destroyed his own career by making precisely this claim during a dispute on October 26, 1962, with the attorney general over an ill-advised Mongoose guerrilla infiltration operation during the blockade (Thomas, *Robert Kennedy* 235). However, Harvey was probably only responding to intense pressure from Kennedy to get something done on the island. Earlier, on October 16, 1962, two days after nuclear missiles were detected in Cuba by a U-2 flight, RFK met with Mongoose officials and bemoaned the "lack of progress" and vowed to give the operation "more personal attention" (White 171). The resolution of this dangerous situation that brought the world to the brink of nuclear war was achieved through a very un-Bondian method of back-channel deals, in which the removal of the missiles in Cuba was exchanged for the removal of Jupiter missiles in Turkey. Furthermore, Kennedy pledged not to invade Cuba.

The Cuban missile crisis spelled the effective end of Operation Mongoose; however, JFK did not abandon plans for covert work in Cuba. Lansdale and Harvey were out, and Desmond FitzGerald became the head of the Special Affairs Staff, the revamped form of Task Force W, on January 25, 1963 (Thomas, *Very Best Men* 291). FitzGerald was one of the "real-life James Bonds" at the CIA that impressed the Kennedys: "Charming and smooth, wellborn and well-taught, [he] seemed to blend effortless grace and schoolboy panache" (Thomas, *Robert Kennedy* 119). By April 1963, many of the clandestine plans of Operation Mongoose to put pressure on Castro were back on the table. In a National Security Council meeting on April 23, 1963, Robert Kennedy proposed three studies on the problem of Cuba, including a "program with the objective of overthrowing Castro in eighteen months" (White 320). JFK also asked for revised contingency plans for an invasion of Cuba that month (321). On June 8, 1963, the CIA presented a paper detailing its plans to apply pressure to Cuba; their outline is almost identical to Lansdale's initial plan in Operation Mongoose with the caveat that the CIA plan assumes that "current U.S. policy does not contemplate outright military intervention in Cuba or a provocation which can be used as a pretext for an invasion of Cuba by United States military forces" (324–25). Presented with the CIA plans on June 19, 1963, President Kennedy evidently "showed a particular interest in [the] proposed external sabotage operations" (330) and approved the clandestine program. Under pressure from the Kennedys, FitzGerald pushed for results in this sabotage program, but the subsequent raids were ineffective and "twenty-five CIA agents, Cuban exiles recruited as commandos, were killed or captured in five raids on the island in 1963" (Thomas, *Very Best Men* 293). By November 12, 1963, JFK had his doubts about the sabotage program, wondering "whether it was worthwhile and whether it would accomplish our purpose" (White 341).

What these doubts in the last month of his life ultimately signify in regards to Cuban policy will never be known. Do they represent the waffling that spelled disaster at the Bay of Pigs when JFK refused to provide air support to the exiles? Or, more optimistically, do they repre-sent the misgivings of a man whose attitude toward communism had turned from hawkish to dove-like, as his famous speech at American University in the summer of 1963 seems to indicate? Fostered by admin-istration insiders, one of the enduring myths of the Kennedy presidency is that JFK learned a valuable lesson from the Bay of Pigs that would help him immeasurably in his handling of the Cuban missile crisis: prin-cipally, that he should be skeptical of the experts and trust his own instincts. What this analysis hopefully demonstrates is that JFK and his brother did not relinquish their faith in the experts, the "subjects sup-posed to know." They merely transferred their faith from one intelligence figure to another who presumably held the key to successful covert oper-ations, from Dulles and Bissell to Lansdale and then FitzGerald. In short, Kennedy never abandoned the Bondian fantasy of espionage as one pos-sible solution to his problems with Cuba.

Oswald, Kennedy, and Bond

James Bond would play an unlikely role in the tragic coda to the Kennedy saga. Less than a week after JFK's assassination, the *New York Times* ran an article documenting the books Lee Harvey Oswald borrowed from the New Orleans Public Library, noting that the alleged assassin and the victim were both fans of the James Bond novels. The bewildering accompanying volumes of *Hearings and Exhibits* of *The Warren Commission Report* reveal that Oswald checked out four Fleming novels between June 24 and September 19, 1963, beginning with *Thun-derball* (6/24/63), then *From Russia with Love* (8/22/63), *Goldfinger* (9/19/63), and *Moonraker* (9/19/63). (In addition, Oswald had taken out Kennedy's *Profiles in Courage* and *Portrait of a President* in July of 1963.) With all the publicity regarding Kennedy's predilection for the Bond novels, Oswald's reading them as well could be seen as some form of preparation for the assassination, a type of misguided identification between killer and victim that has become far more prevalent with con-temporary celebrity stalkers. In *Libra*, his novel of the JFK assassination, Don DeLillo elucidates the nature of this identification in the mind of Oswald, depicting this shared interest in Bond as a "coincidence" that taps into some "hidden principle" (172), a "connection" or "third line" that bridges the gap between two lives and "puts a man on the path of his destiny" (339). However, *Libra* offers a suggestion that provides a more intriguing rationale for Oswald's motivation for the assassination and establishes a potential connection to the Bond novels, in particular *From Russia with Love*. In DeLillo's novel, Oswald returns to the United States after his failed defection and two years living in Russia only to find more dissatisfaction. He subsequently contemplates defecting to Cuba. Of course, he finds that for an American citizen, access to Cuba is difficult. However, if he could bring something to the table, as he did in his defection to the Soviet Union with his knowledge of the U-2 spy plane operating out of Atsugi Air Base in Japan, then perhaps he would be welcomed into Castro's Cuba: "What would he have to give Fidel before they let him live happily in little Cuba?" (DeLillo 373). While conspiracy theorists tend to discount his interest in Cuba, Oswald did attempt to form a local branch of the Fair Play for Cuba Committee in New Orleans, although he was never actually granted official membership. He was also arrested for an altercation with anti-Castro Cuban exiles while handing out fliers for the committee, an event that some have spun as an attempt to establish his pro-Castro résumé.

Oswald no doubt found the covert world of James Bond exciting, as Kennedy did, and the novels perhaps served as a model for his own brand of intelligence work infiltrating the anti-Castro community in New Orleans. However, he may have found a more congenial figure for identification in Donovan "Red" Grant in *From Russia with Love*. Grant's defection to the Soviet Union mirrors Oswald's own in several ways, although it is completely successful, whereas Oswald deems his experience a failure. Grant defects to the Soviet Union as a motorcycle courier with sensitive documents as his offering to the Soviets. Oswald had worked at Atsugi Air Base and had information on the U-2 spy plane that he offered the Russians when he defected. Grant ultimately assumes an indispensable role as the top assassin in SMERSH, a position of importance to which Oswald clearly aspires. Oswald wants to be important within the Soviet system, but in a political way. His disappointment was keen when he was assigned to a radio factory in Minsk as a skilled worker. In other words, the Soviet career of Grant offered Oswald a fantasy of how his own defection was supposed to work. And perhaps Donovan Grant provided a model for his second stab at defection, this time to Cuba with the trophy of Kennedy's death as his gift to Castro. For both Kennedy and Oswald, then, fantasy and identification play a crucial role in the structure of their social reality and, consequently, in the vicissitudes of history.

NOTES

1. For a full account of the difficulties encountered by Stephenson in his work with J. Edgar Hoover and the FBI, see H. Montgomery Hyde, *Room 3603: The Incredible True Story of Secret Intelligence Operations during World War II.*

2. Kennedy's list of favorite books includes the following: *Melbourne* by David Cecil; *Montrose* by John Buchan; *Marlborough* by Winston S. Churchill; *John Quincy Adams* by Samuel Flagg Bemis; *The Emergence of Lincoln* by Allan Nevins; *The Price of Union* by Herbert Agar; *John C. Calhoun* by Margaret L. Coit; *Byron in Italy* by Peter Quennell; *From Russia with Love* by Ian Fleming; *The Red and the Black* by M. de Stendahl (Sidey, "The President's Voracious Reading Habits," *Life,* March 17, 1961, 59).

3. This recent revelation accompanied the publication of a new biography of JFK. See Robert Dallek, *An Unfinished Life: John F. Kennedy, 1917–1963.*

4. For an interesting examination of the relationship between Joseph Kennedy, Sr. and his sons, especially regarding their womanizing, see Gary Wills, *The Kennedy Imprisonment: A Meditation on Power.*

12 Wanting to Be James Bond

ALEXIS ALBION

In early 1966, as he witnessed the astounding success of *Thunderball,* the fourth screen appearance by fictional secret agent James Bond, Bosley Crowther of the *New York Times* appealed to his readers for enlightenment. "How could this comic-strip movie achieve such box office momentum on the strength of what it contains?" he asked. More than fifty-eight million Americans—about a quarter of the country's population—would eventually go to see *Thunderball,* and Crowther wondered, "How could so many foolish people be so excited and amused by a merely spruced up repetition of a collage of Superman and sex?"[1] Across the ocean, French critic Claude Mauriac was having similar thoughts. Still recovering from the onslaught of the previous Bond film, Mauriac was incredulous at the lines of fans who had waited to see *Goldfinger*—lines which were, according to one Paris cinema manager, the longest in living memory. "The critics, the specialists are discussing it," he assured readers of *Le Figaro Litteraire,* "They are trying hard to understand."[2]

Indeed, by the mid-sixties, commentators around the globe—from New York to Moscow—were trying very hard to understand. The intellectual challenge facing cultural critics such as Crowther and Mauriac at that particular moment had gone beyond the effort to comprehend widespread commercial success. Record-breaking box-office figures proved beyond a doubt what members of London's intelligentsia had determined as early as the late fifties: that people were more than willing to spend their money to escape the reality of their everyday lives into a fantasy of sex, violence, and brand-name snobbery.[3] Superlative sales of 007-related merchandise confirmed what Kingsley Amis, among others, had recently observed, that it was not self-identification—an identification with one that exists *outside* the self—but self-substitution—a desire to substitute another for oneself—that drove this fantasy: "We don't want to have Bond to dinner, or go golfing with Bond, or talk to Bond," as Amis pointed out, "we want to *be* Bond."[4]

But by the middle of the decade, some individuals wondered whether long lines of moviegoers and stellar sales of 007 pajamas were only the tangible, quantifiable effects of a current fascination. Underneath the statistics lay a deeper sociological meaning to something so ubiquitous and yet so indefinable that a new vocabulary had been invented to describe it: "die Bondomanie," in Germany, "il bondismo" for the Italians, and a commercial "Bond Wagon" or "Bondanza" in the United States.[5] At a certain point, a number of critics recognized that wanting to "*be* Bond" was no longer just about making money, but had become a social phenomenon and an intercultural experience. As Simon Raven noted in the *Spectator* in 1966, "[a] gigantic genie has been conjured and an explanation is called for."[6]

What I want to discuss in this essay, then, is a global historical moment of Bond in the mid-1960s—a moment when individuals in entirely different parts of the world were offering their explanations for why, as Crowther put it, so many foolish people seemed to be so excited and amused about what was really just a simple commercial formula of blood, bikinis, and Bollinger. Interestingly, by this time most critics no longer saw Bond as representing something expressly British. Back in 1958, when noted intellectual Paul Johnson famously found himself unable to put down one of Ian Fleming's increasingly popular novels (despite its purported lack of literary qualities), he described the Bond adventures as the indulgence of a postwar society expressing its repressed schoolboy fantasies. He added that Britain "is a soft market for Mr. Fleming's poison."[7] But it had not taken long to discover that Britain was by no means the only market susceptible to Mr. Fleming's toxins. Less than a decade after Paul Johnson explained away Bond's popularity as the expression of a British social condition, a worldwide interest in Bond forced critics to conclude that Bondomania was equally the expression of a French, American, Japanese, and Australian social condition.[8]

Moreover, contemporary commentators do not appear to have considered Bondomania as a particularly gendered phenomenon, but as an experience in which both men and women participated with equivalent, if not always identical, interest. As *Variety,* the American entertainment industry's trade paper, observed after a screening of *From Russia with Love,* "every man in the theatre will identify himself as the cool James Bond and every woman will spend a blissful couple of hours imagining herself the blonde seductress leading him to his doom."[9] If women did not aspire to *"be* Bond" themselves, they might well desire to be *with* Bond, and in this sense, to relate themselves to the same fantasy as men. At the peak of Bondomania, however, it can be argued that, at least in the West, the roles of Bond and the "blonde seductress"—the ambition to *be* and be *with* Bond—became almost inseparable with the emergence of "Jane Bonds," women with Bond-like skills and accessories, on film and television.[10] Bond's historical moment was, I suggest, a condition in which both genders were involved.[11]

For some social observers, Bond stood for something timeless and universal. "Since the first ages of humanity," Mauriac explained, "everywhere, always, the same representations manifest themselves that we do not see outside, but which we discover buried within ourselves," and 007 was the personification of Carl Jung's archetypal hero—a modern-day knight or Samurai—with Bondomania the expression of an eternal and cross-cultural, collective unconsciousness of mankind.[12] Most critics, however, saw Fleming's creation as far less mythic. The Bond phenomenon, they believed, belonged to the moment, an effect of either the social conditions or the Cold War politics of the 1960s. As we shall see, trying to understand the aspiration to "be Bond" was, more often than not, also a way of trying to understand this moment.

Many words have been written, both scholarly and non-scholarly, about the Bond phenomenon in the sixties, and none fail to mention the international component to that success. Yet few works give any real sense of just how internationalized Bond became during this period, or, in other words, the extent to which wanting to "be Bond" resonated with peoples from Boston to Zanzibar. One component of this was certainly the popular attention Bond adventures received around the world. Fleming's novels began to sell in translation as early as the late 1950s (though mostly in Western Europe), and when President John F. Kennedy added 007 to his top ten list of favorite books in 1961, millions of Americans too discovered a taste for James Bond.[13] But it was his transition from the printed page to the silver screen a year later that gave 007 truly global reach. Film audiences for Bond's colorful, exotic, sexy, and action-packed exploits could be found on every continent, and the opening of the latest Bond film invariably drew crowds. A near riot broke out in Boston in 1967, for example, when fans came to see a free performance of *Casino Royale* at four in the morning and found that 8,000 people were not all going to fit into the same theater. (The cinema's assistant manager valiantly kept the film running despite two fires in the seats and a broken fire hose that soaked portions of the audience because, he explained, "I was scared stiff to shut the projector down.")[14] But this was nothing compared to when the government of Zanzibar decided at the last moment to ban "the cultural event of the month" in March 1964: a screening of *From Russia with Love*. Local U.S. officials described the pronouncement as "the crowning blow to morale in Zanzibar."[15]

Beyond the doors of the movie theaters, the Bond persona also had enormous appeal, and once again it was something that moved easily between countries and cultures. In Tokyo, Japanese men put on a "007-style" topcoat if they wanted to look good, while in Paris, it wouldn't do to be without your secret agent underwear and James Bond shirt and cufflinks—unless, of course, your companion was wearing her gilded lingerie, inspired by *Goldfinger* and purchased from the "Bond Boutique" at *Galeries Lafayette*.[16] The attraction of Bond merchandise, as one East German newspaper noted, referring to the practices of its West German cousins, was that it offered a way to get closer to being Bond. "Just as primitive people once wore leopard skins around their shoulders—hoping to also possess the strength of the leopard," the writer remarked, "in such a way do many young men wear James Bond articles in the hope of resembling their idol."[17]

But some cultures went beyond wearing the clothing of James Bond and absorbed the character altogether, fashioning 007 in their own national form—as Derek Flint or Matt Helm in the United States; Jiro Kitami in Japan; Coplan, Secret Agent FX-18 in France; or West Germany's Agent 505.[18] Italy perhaps produced more of their own Bonds than any other country, turning out a stream of Italianized secret agent heroes in the mid-1960s who invariably demonstrated style, sophistication, and immense sex appeal in films such as "077 from France Without Love," "Kiss Agent 088 on Sight," and "007½ Mission Goldsinger," a spoof in which the Aston Martin is replaced by a baby Fiat, complete with shower and espresso machine.[19] In distinct contrast, Finnish writer Arto Tuovinen made his Bond a more somber, perhaps more Finnish, character in his three novels, published from 1966 to 1968. Boris Stolitsky is a misfit: he works for the KGB but has forsaken the communist cause; he drinks too much and falls too easily for Western decadence, but in the end he can be relied upon to be merciless in hunting down Nazis and arms merchants.[20]

What is so interesting to look for in these imitations is how cultures adapted different elements of Bond to suit their own current national concerns—reflecting, perhaps, what kind of Bond an Italian or a Finn might imagine himself to be. South Vietnam's Z.28 presents a fascinating example. In 1965, Bui Anh Tuan (using the pen name Nguoi Thu Tam) published the first in a series of immensely popular spy novels featuring Van Binh, or Agent Z.28 of Saigon's Secret Affairs Bureau, quickly becoming the most popular spy novelist in South Vietnam in the pre-1975 era. Z.28 likes to smoke, gamble, race cars, and love beautiful women, and he is also in demand by all the Western powers to help them maintain the balance of power against communism—no wonder, because he is not only the best agent in South Vietnam, he is the best agent on the planet. This is not just the opinion of the Vietnamese, for even his adversaries agree. "No one is as good as he," remarks top communist spymaster General H of SMERSH, adding, "Last year, at a general conference organized in Moscow, all important persons in the intelligence services of the socialist block admitted that Z.28 is the No. 1 secret agent in the world." The director of the CIA, Mr. Smith, can only concur; he remarks to one of his agents of Van Binh, "I wish we could hire him, but I hesitate about his fee."[21] Vietnamese readers would already have been familiar with Bond, both from translations of Fleming's novels and from film screenings, when Bui Anh Tuan first began writing about Van Binh; they surely recognized the modeling of Z.28 on 007.[22] And yet, in the highly uncertain political environment of South Vietnam in the mid-1960s, Van Binh must have offered his readers some comfort that it was not Britain's James Bond but a tough, virile Vietnamese—who could not be bought—who was the West's best defense against impending communist forces of evil.

That Bond was ubiquitous as a character of fiction and film throughout much of the world at that moment indicated for a number of commentators that he personified a set of ideas or values with a particular contemporary relevance. These ideas or values were alike across all cultures: independence of action; professionalism; open, guiltless sexuality; a license to kill; a certain insolence toward authority; technological proficiency; and so on—a standard of behavior and morality that many saw as being distinctly modern, perfectly in tune with the times.[23]

Indeed, so in tune with the times was agent 007 as to be able not only to epitomize contemporary masculinity, but to embody modern femininity as well, at least in the West. Appearing on TV screens at the height of Bondomania, the sensuous *Honey West* (ABC, 1965–1966) was the first female detective to take the central role in an American network television series. A Pussy Galore look-alike equipped with a lipstick microphone, radio receiver earrings, and a mean judo throw, Ms. West directly imitated the Bond ideology of a sexy, swinging, single, and independent professional—albeit a woman. (She in turn inspired other "Jane Bonds," such as superspy April Dancer in *The Girl from U.N.C.L.E.* and the feisty Agent 99 of *Get Smart*). At the same time, Britain's sleuthing adventurer Emma Peel, from *The Avengers,* achieved iconic status both at home and abroad with her dry wit, modern lifestyle, black leather cat suits, and karate kicks. These women characters were plainly cultural responses to the feminist movement. Yet, inasmuch as they explicitly found their persona as feminized Bonds—as "James Bond in skirts," as one commentator put it—they can also be characterized as products of Bondomania.[24]

For some cultural observers, embracing Bond as a reflection of the *Zeitgeist,* the epitome of modern man or woman, was being progressive. The *New York Times,* for example, observed that in the traditionally conservative Islamic society of Yemen, 007 was, in his own way, helping to transform archaic social customs. Yemeni moviegoers, the newspaper explained, were so enthralled by Sean Connery's appearances in the cinema, with audiences "shouting and whistling excessively during romantic scenes," that the government had forbidden the customary housewives' matinees, with the result that women were now allowed to attend films in "the foreign way," along with their husbands. Moreover, the films had contributed to a demand for consumer goods (such as beds and fitted dresses) as well as a gradual acceptance of dating—certainly all good things for bringing Yemen closer to a Western-style democracy.[25] In Britain in 1966, at least one intellectual wished for the same degree of Bondian influence on his countrymen. "[007 is] a projection of what every spirited and normal man would like to be," maintained Simon Raven in the *Spectator,* encouraging millions of fans to throw off the stale bonds of their conformist lives and be inspired by a more self-assertive Bond, someone who "believes in practical equity, in his own right to enjoy what he himself has earned . . . and, *above all,* in freedom." Raven argued, then, that if society wanted to move forward, it was not enough to want to "be Bond," we needed to *think* like Bond as well.[26]

Most critics, however, were far less certain that the Bond phenomenon was socially or politically constructive; if Bond was a mirror in which to discover an image of ourselves (male or female), that image was not actually very attractive. "That a fascist sadist, misogynist and racist, compensating for his intellectual insufficiencies with gunshots, has somehow become a model for the masses, that's what is surprising," wrote French critic Philippe Pilard in 1965.[27] Others agreed and thought Bond an extremely objectionable type of popular hero; as a reflection of modern values, he was, in fact, more suited to play the villain.[28] For Eldridge Cleaver, that villain was a racist, imperialist white man, a "paper tiger" hero, offering whites a "triumphant image of themselves."[29] For the Reverend Edward Rogers, he was a man who misused women in the context of a violence that bordered on sadism. "007 takes his women where he finds them and he finds them pretty well anywhere," the Reverend declared in his sermon at the World Methodist Youth Conference in Bath, adding, "There, in my judgment, is the measure of our contemporary standard of morality."[30] For Kansas City minister Lycurgus Starkey, Bond was a self-centered idolater who put love of country above love of God; delivering his warnings against Bondomania both on television and in print, Starkey warned, "We may enjoy the story, but the moral decay implied is not so funny."[31] And for Claudio Sorgi, writing in the Vatican City newspaper *L'Observatore Romano,* Bond was a slow-working poison, eating away at the humanity of his admirers. "[T]his is a really serious problem," Sorgi wrote. "He who dreams of being James Bond today, of doing what he does, of killing, of having the deviant experiences that for him are normal, is like a sick man." For these commentators, the harmful social effects of trying to "be Bond" might be with us for a long time, Sorgi cautioned: "Who knows how many years it will take before we can laugh this off?"[32]

These commentators saw the Bond phenomenon as indicative of the wider social ills of the sixties, with Bond acting as a visible and influential spokesman for such contemporary problems as racism, sexism, lack of faith, or general moral corruption.[33] And critics worried that the public's fascination with Bond connoted not only an endorsement of his values, but also active promotion of them. In this respect, one type of behavior displayed by Bond worried critics more than any other: violence. Ian Fleming's work had been charged with sadism since his first publication, but the elegant yet brutal killing performed by Sean Connery in the cinema made the realities of possessing a license to kill all too vivid, and for many, far too attractive. "Anyone who has attended a matinee and heard the screams of approval . . . at the sadistic torture—and brutal beating scenes—knows what this means," wrote Peter Schröder for the West German paper *Zeit* in 1964, and what it meant to Schröder was "the release of moral, ethical or other restrictions, the boundless anarchy of the individual, and its unconditional dissemination . . . as a model of our times."[34] West German film critic Andre Müller similarly argued that a film like *Thunderball* destroyed any sense of a moral compass guiding or limiting human action; the pattern of resulting behavior that he described must have been a particularly sinister one for German readers, all too familiar with the mistakes of their past. "Right or injustice have become obsolete moral terms," Müller declared:

> What James Bond does is right. Each murder, which he commits, is considered as necessary for the rescue of western civilization. Homicide is made palatable. A neofascist ideology is announced: the alleged threat justifies the murder.[35]

By contrast, audiences behind the Iron Curtain were not swept up in Bondomania. Although Bond novels and films no doubt made their way into Eastern Europe and the Soviet Union through unofficial channels, 007 was officially viewed as *persona non grata* in the communist world of the 1960s (and a Bond film would not be shown in the USSR until 1974).[36] Yet critics in the East were by no means unaware of the cultural preoccupations of the West, and in fact added their voices to the same discussion about Bond that was taking place among Western commentators. For communist observers, however, the political lens of the Cold War, rather than the sixties social scene, offered a more focused perspective on the contemporary significance of the Bond phenomenon.

As Western critics did, commentators in the East read Bond as an expression of contemporary Western values and behavior (sex, violence, consumerism). "An unreflective killer and partisan of violence guarding the interests of the proprietor class—that's the favorite hero of bourgeois society," wrote Yurii Zhukov in 1965, describing Bond to the readers of the Soviet newspaper *Pravda*. As a symbol of the bourgeois morality of a corrupt, imperialist system, Bond, quite understandably, should be embraced by the West; after all, "every civilization has the hero it deserves," Zhukov noted, and the veneration of someone like James Bond was simply proof that "the civilization of the bourgeois world is seriously and incurably sick."[37]

Once again, it was the violence practiced by Bond—the depravity of the license to kill—that communist critics seized upon as supremely indicative of the sickness of the West. Zhukov outlined for Russians the perversions of 007's world, as "a world where they write laws with the butt of a pistol, where violence and outrage against female honor is looked on as prowess, and murder, like an amusing game."[38] Grigor Chernev described for his Bulgarian readers how they might react to a James Bond film: "How many people killed on the screen! How easy all this is done! People just fall without tears, without any remorse. Human life is worthless, it doesn't cost even a penny." This type of indiscriminate killing, without attention to the value of human life, illustrated the dehumanization wrought by bourgeois society—a common socialist theme: "A human being stops being an enlightened person, a goal, an ideal, a ray of light," Chernev declared, "he becomes a suspicious figure with doubtful wishes and dark complexes."[39]

For communist commentators, there were direct parallels to be made between James Bond's fictional adventures and Western adventurism of the mid-1960s. As Chernev noted, "It's not just the director's desire to make a profitable movie . . . these things do exist so that they can be represented on the screen. And then the directors just add the little details."[40] Some critics highlighted the equivalency between the brutality with which 007 carried out his missions and the violence being committed by Western agents around the world—notably in Vietnam. "[T]he idolization of the killer Bond in a world where the use of napalm substitutes for persuasion and bombs drown out the voice of conscience is, to some extent, natural," Zhukov suggested, arguing that Bond not only reflected the culture from which he emerged but, in turn, helped shape the actual world around him: "A good number of [Fleming's fans] have cursed James Bond as they choked in blood on the ground in South Vietnam."[41] The East German communist youth paper *Junge Welt* in 1966 drew examples from reports in the Associated Press of murders supposedly inspired by 007: a young boy in southern Italy found dead in the apartment of a single woman, coated with gold bronze after the example of the victim in *Goldfinger;* an Austrian man who shot his young apprentice in a delusion that he was James Bond killing an enemy.[42]

For those on the other side of the Iron Curtain, therefore, the Bond phenomenon could only pose a threat. If millions of Westerners wanted to "be Bond," this was clearly a sign of the dehumanizing effects of bourgeois society, leading to increased aggression and the intensification of the West's opposition to the peace-loving people of the communist world. "What does James Bond represent?" asked the Soviet youth paper *Komsomolskaya Pravda* in 1966; he represented "a banner of anticommunism . . . and Bondism has become a symbol of moral deformity, antihumanism brought to paroxysm . . . and rabid anger against the Soviet Union."[43] For the East Germans, the presence of millions of Bondomaniacs right next door was especially alarming. "Is it a coincidence that the Bond wave strikes particularly high waves in West Germany?" *Junge Welt* asked its readers. And was it just a coincidence that the brutal methods of murder and attack being practiced in the Bond films were identical to the training of the soldiers of the German Federal Armed Forces? "Hand in hand with the creation of secret agent 007, who is being used to artificially manipulate public opinion," *Junge Welt* explained, "preparations are being made in West Germany for covert war against the GDR." The ideology of the Bond films, it appeared, corresponded exactly with that of the imperialists in Bonn.[44]

There could, perhaps, be no better way to neutralize at least the ideological threat of the Bond phenomenon than by challenging him with a strong rival. In 1965, Bulgarian novelist Andrei Gulyashki announced to the Western press that in his next book he intended to pit his well-known hero of several spy stories, Bulgarian Secret Service case officer Avakum Zakhov, against the best that the West could offer—the depraved 007. Zakhov is a loyal communist citizen and a skilled expert in counterintelligence with an analytical mind and a doctorate in archaeology from Sofia University. His superior mind is his weapon of choice and, as Gulyashki explained, the idea was therefore to set Zakhov's pure cerebral power of deduction against James Bond's ruthless, intuitive violence and see who would come out on top.[45]

When "Avakum Zakhov vs. 07" was published in 1966, it turned out that the fight was actually rather close. "07" is a formidable enemy who kills ruthlessly and without guilt. "Well what can you do?" he exclaims, after forcing a car that has been following him off the road and over a cliff. "A game's a game, and the most adroit man wins. Like in golf." But it is clear from the start that his motivations are weak, and he is no intellectual powerhouse besides. When 07 sets off on his mission to hunt down a Russian scientist who has invented a powerful new weapon, we get a good sense of what type of man he really is:

> To live in the present, and in particular to make use of the pleasant aspects of the present—that was in his blood. As for the future, it wasn't worth thinking about beyond what was necessary for his job. . . . Let students from Oxford and Cambridge spend their time on Nelson and Suleiman the Magnificent to get their diplomas; he was satisfied with having his number in the Secret Service, a check book in his pocket, excellent digestion, and, thank God, firm muscles, a true eye and not bad chances of success.[46]

In the end, 07's brutality and "live-for-today" attitude turn out to be no match for a man of Zakhov's intellectual and emotional complexity and depth. As a Soviet reviewer explained, Fleming's hero may be a fantastic spy, "but he has no concept of such things as humanity. He is a crude cynic, his romantic adventures are sickening."[47] Britain's *Daily Mirror* put the oppositional qualities in more stark terms. "Bond and Zahov [*sic*] . . . have about as much in common as the Kremlin and Buckingham Palace," and Zakhov is a "humourless intellectual" who "sits around a lot thinking about the social structure and the dignity of man," only managing to get to bed with one woman per book. "He seems about as sexy as a collective farm," the newspaper concluded.[48] The difference between what type of Bond the readers of the *Mirror* and the readers of *Pravda* might want to be could not have been clearer.

The idea of individuals all over the world participating in a shared cultural experience is something that is no longer new or surprising. Globalism—"the state of the world involving networks of interdependence at multicontinental distances"—has become a fashionable term for characterizing social and cultural realities in an age of cell phones and the Internet.[49] But it also seems an apt expression for what we can see taking place in the 1960s around James Bond, as critics and audiences on all continents, without the benefits of MTV and CNN, found connections through the figure of a fictional secret agent. This does not mean that they all held the same viewpoints or interpreted information in the same way; as we recognize nowadays, social globalism involves information *entering* global networks, but it is selectively filtered and modified within the contexts of national politics and local cultures.[50]

In the 1960s, how individuals ultimately understood both Bond and the Bond phenomenon similarly depended on their own social or political concerns, from Reverend Starkey in Kansas City to Bui Anh Tuan in Saigon. But whether they interpreted Bond within the context of sixties society or Cold War politics, as a social scourge or a political tool, there was an interconnectedness between these individuals in the same global historical moment of James Bond. In 1967, when a party of Soviet explorers dropped in at a remote American station in the Antarctic, for example, despite acute national rivalry, they soon found a common language with which to communicate with their hosts: 600 miles from the South Pole, the two groups of adventurers watched a James Bond film together.[51]

Does it really matter that we can identify a shared global consciousness in the mid-1960s through the figure of a fictional secret agent? I would posit that it does, if we believe that culture matters—that, as Akira Iriye has argued, international relations are also intercultural relations, and that within a world that is defined geopolitically and economically there also exists "a world of shared conceptions, dreams, and problems." Cultural stability can be an indicator of global well-being, along with such traditional indicators as the balance of power and economic activity.[52] This essay suggests, therefore, that a case can be made for a remarkable constancy in international relations in the mid-1960s that transcended national boundaries, political contentions, and economic systems, but instead took place on the level of conceptions, dreams, and problems—a constancy brought about by a global interest in being (or not being) James Bond.

Almost forty years later, are we perhaps experiencing another global historical moment of Bond? I ask this because it is arguable that James Bond now has a more prominent presence on the international scene than at any time since the 1960s. The success of Pierce Brosnan in the film role of 007 has brought the character renewed popularity, making the opening of each new Bond film since the mid-1990s once more an event on the cultural calendar.[53] And with this international popularity has come, once again, reflection on the character's enduring significance. Just in the past few years, for example, serious studies have been published about Bond as a cultural and political figure, and this volume itself represents the work of a diverse group of scholars discovering new meanings for James Bond.[54] What we are doing, of course, is exactly what intellectuals in the 1960s were doing: using the Bond phenomenon to explore a host of other political and social concerns. Some of this interest is no doubt due to the appearance of cultural studies, and popular culture in particular, as a fashionable focus for legitimate scholarly analysis. But I wonder whether it also indicates a new global relevance of James Bond—a sign that through 007 we might once again be able to better understand something about our own selves and our own times.

How else can we explain the North Korean government's official denunciation of the latest Bond offering, *Die Another Day,* than as an acknowledgment of the currency that Bond and his world of ideas and values are still perceived to have forty years after his first screen appearance? Opening in the last weeks of 2002, just as international tensions began to grow over North Korean leader Kim Jong Il's determination to restart its nuclear weapons program, it was perhaps not surprising that Pyongyang found the plot of the new Bond film just a little too topical:

007 chases down a crazed North Korean arms dealer who plans to vaporize sections of the planet with a powerful new weapon—beginning with an invasion of Seoul. And yet the main thrust of Pyongyang's censure was clearly *not* the oppositional relationship portrayed in the film between North Korea and the West. Rather, directing their remarks principally toward their brothers and sisters in the South, North Korean officials condemned the Bond film for requiring moviegoers to make a choice between "bad" Koreans in the North (whom Bond would inevitably defeat) and "good" Koreans in the South (whom he wanted to save). This was a choice that was simply unfair. After all, what chance could the North possibly have against the world's favorite secret agent?[55]

It is evident that Pyongyang saw *Die Another Day* as a political threat. The danger it posed, however, derived not from power politics but from the power to affect the consciousness of individuals and their attitudes toward culture, politics, and personal identity. In this sense, Kim Jong Il's denunciation of the film displayed an appreciation for the widespread appeal of wanting to "be Bond" (or be on Bond's side) that holds sway even in the twenty-first century. A similar understanding may have been behind the Royal Marines' decision to allude to the world of 007 in the recent war in Iraq. By naming their action in Basra "Operation James," with military targets code named "Goldfinger," "Blofeld," "Pussy Galore," and "Connery," British commanders surely aimed not only to "give morale a boost," but to inspire some of the heroism and brute force that goes along with being Bond.[56]

The most compelling argument for James Bond's new global relevance, however, is that the shape of the world around us appears increasingly to resemble that in which Bond operates. Indeed, as two political scientists have recently argued, the more diffused political environment of the post–Cold War era has shown a remarkable correspondence between the central plotline of the Bond adventures and our own national security concerns, with a move away from wars between states toward acts of violence being carried out by groups outside the established state system.[57] From the post-9/11 perspective, Bond's world looks even more modern: non-state-bound agents of terrorism, working through a well-funded, worldwide network—not so unlike SPECTRE—and headed by an elusive but clearly charismatic leader—not entirely unlike Ernst Stavro Blofeld—pose our greatest current threat to global stability.[58] We shall certainly need men and women with James Bond's experience and skills in order to prevail; but more importantly, we need to recognize that there are conceptions, dreams, and problems that we all share. We are, perhaps, ready for Bond to remind us of that once again.

NOTES

1. Bosley Crowther, "Neo-Realism and James Bond," *New York Times,* January 16, 1966, Sec. II, 1. The figure of 58.1 million U.S. admissions for *Thunderball* is lower than the 74.8 million usually cited and is taken from Cork and Scivally's *James Bond: The Legacy,* 87, 300. Regardless of which numbers one chooses, U.S. admissions for the Bond series reached a peak with the 1965–66 release of *Thunderball.*

2. Andrew Mulligan, "A France Fit for 007s to Live In," *Observer,* February 28, 1965, n.p. [from the British Film Institute's microfiche collection, hereafter referred to as BFI microfiche]; Claude Mauriac, "James Bond: Un Essai D'Explication," *Le Figaro Litteraire,* March 4–10, 1965, 24.

3. *Thunderball* became the highest grossing film of 1966, taking in $141.2 million worldwide and breaking house records on four continents. See *Hollywood Reporter,* November 2, 1995; Alan Barnes and Marcus Hearn, *Kiss Kiss Bang! Bang! The Unofficial James Bond Film Companion;* Cork and Scivally, *Legacy,* 87.

4. By 1966, manufacturers in Europe, Asia, and North America had signed contracts to produce Bond-related products; Chicago toy designer Marvin Glass and Associates, Inc., for example, speculated that their 007 line would result in business worth $40 million in 1965. See "The Bondanza," *Newsweek,* May 10, 1965, 92, 94; Austin C. Wehrwein, "James Bond Given New Mission: Toys," *New York Times,* April 27, 1965, 53; Kingsley Amis, *The James Bond Dossier,* 28. Italics are mine.

5. See, for example, "Die Bondomanie," *Film* (Germany) 4, no. 2 (February 1966): 38; as referred to in Claudio Sorgi, "Il caso James Bond," *L'Observatore Romano,* no. 13 (May 17–18, 1965): 3; Vincent Canby, "Climb on UA's Bond Wagon," *Variety,* June 2, 1965, 5, 25; "The Bondanza," *Newsweek:* "James Bond, it's like mythology," exclaimed toy manufacturer Marvin Glass. "He's the modern equivalent of the demigods of the past, Hercules and the Prometheus type. This is a Bondanza."

6. Simon Raven, "The Natural Man," *Spectator,* October 28, 1966, 552: "A phenomenon like this cannot just be pooh-poohed or laughed off."

7. Paul Johnson, "Sex, Snobbery and Sadism," *New Statesman,* April 5, 1958, 430. Johnson famously identified the essential ingredients of Fleming's success as "sex, snobbery and sadism," depraved fixations that he described as "all unhealthy, all thoroughly English." Bernard Bergonzi similarly located Bond's appeal within the British social order: "Fleming's fantasies of upper class life can only be a desire to compensate for the rigours of existence in a welfare state: they have an air of vulgarity and display." See "The Case of Mr. Fleming," *The Twentieth Century* 163, no. 973 (March 1958): 222.

8. It was not until the 1970s and 1980s that Fleming's spy fiction began to be seriously analyzed as part of a literary tradition, reaching back to the First World War era (first William le Queux and E. Phillips Oppenheim, and then the imperialist thrillers of John Buchan and "Sapper"), contrasting with the gritty "realism" of the inter-war period (Graham Greene and Eric Ambler), borrowing from the hard-boiled detectives of American crime fiction (Dashiell Hammett and Raymond Chandler), and inspiring a new generation of secret agent novelists (John le Carré, Len Deighton, Alan Furst). See, for example, Jerry Palmer, *Thriller: Genesis and Structure of a Popular Genre,* which draws generic conclusions from the author's analysis of Fleming and Mickey Spillane; John G. Cawelti, *Adventure, Mystery, and Romance: Formula Stories as Art and Popular Culture;* and Michael Denning, *Cover Stories: Narrative and Ideology in the British Spy Thriller.*

9. *Variety,* October 14, 1963, n.p. [from the Library of the Motion Picture Academy microfiche collection, Los Angeles, Calif.].

10. See my later discussion of Jane Bonds in this essay.

11. Decades later, Tony Bennett and Janet Woollacott have looked back on the sixties sensation of James Bond and interpreted the narrative ideology of the films as one that contributes to primarily male privileges—the license to look (at women) and to consume (cars, cigarettes, alcohol). Sixties Bond girls may be modern in the sense of being sexually liberated, but they ultimately obey the rules of the patriarchy, for they are fashioned to be "equal but yet subordinate." The conclusion is that the *implied* audience for Bond has been male; without supporting evidence from a gendered breakdown of cinema ticket or book sales, however, there is no reason to believe that the main audience for Bond in the 1960s was, in actuality, male. Indeed, to do so might well be to suppose historically inaccurate cultural assumptions as to how women in general, and women in different parts of the world, may have connected with Bond. See Bennett and Woollacott, *Bond and Beyond: The Political Career of a Popular Hero,* 247, 141, 242. Jeffrey S. Miller supports this same argument in *Something Completely Different: British Television and American Culture,* 52.

12. Mauriac, "Un Essai D'Explication," 1965. Mauriac cites directly from Jung throughout his analysis of Bond. Similar interpretations are made by Richard C. Carpenter in "007 and the Myth of the Hero," *Journal of Popular Culture* 1, no. 2 (Fall 1967); and Anne S. Boyd, who compares the Bond fantasy with the myth of St. George and the dragon in *The Devil with James Bond!* (1967).

13. Lewis Nichols, "In and Out of Books," *New York Times Book Review,* April 1, 1962, 8; "Ten Kennedy Favorites," "President's Reading," *Life,* March 17, 1961, 59. The Bond films boosted sales of Fleming's novels around the world. By late 1963, after the release of *Dr. No,* sales of Fleming's paperbacks climbed to almost ten million in the U.S. Lewis Nichols, "In and Out of Books," *New York Times Book Review,* December 15, 1963, 8; see also figures for paperback sales of Fleming's novels in Britain, 1955–1977 in Bennett and Woollacott, *Bond and Beyond,* 26–27.

14. "Charges Dismissed: Rioters Called 'Idiots,'" *Boston Globe,* May 7, 1967, 1, 4; "Disappointed Fans of James Bond Mob a Theater in Boston," *New York Times,* May 7, 1967, 58; "Boston Riot over Bond Film," *Times* of London, May 8, 1967, 4. Fifteen to twenty Bond fans were arrested on charges ranging from drunkenness to unlawful assembly, though for most their charges were dismissed as too vague— Municipal Court Justice Elijah Adlow called the detainees "idiots."

15. Cable No. A-195 from AmEmbassy Zanzibar to Department of State, March 31, 1964, RG 59, General Records of the Department of State, Central Foreign Policy files, 1964–6, Culture and Information, Box 420, National Archives.

16. "Move Over, Mr. Moto, for Agent 007," *New York Times,* January 24, 1966, 39; Ian Johnson, "007 + 4," *Films & Filming* 12, no. 1 (October 1965): 5; Lietta Tornabuoni, "A Popular Phenomenon," in del Buono and Eco, *The Bond Affair,* 19; Andrew Mulligan, "A France Fit for 007s to Live In," *Observer,* February 28, 1965 [BFI microfiche]; "The Bondanza," *Newsweek,* May 10, 1965, 94.

17. Hans Sturm, "Bond und Bonn," *Junge Welt,* July 16/17, 1966, 3. Although the majority of official 007 labels were to be found on men's clothing, women also had the opportunity to indulge their Bond fantasies. French women in 1965, for example, were encouraged to dress like Pussy Galore in their 007 negligees and Secret Agent Baby Doll nightgowns. "Golden Touch," *Daily Telegraph,* March 1, 1965 [BFI microfiche].

18. Although James Coburn's portrayal of Derek Flint on screen (*In Like Flint,* 1965, and *Our Man Flint,* 1967) made perhaps the most blatant attempt to emulate and even parody Bond, there are numerous other American examples from both film and television. Notable among them are film adaptations of Donald Hamilton's

Matt Helm books, starring Dean Martin as a nonchalant, alcoholic secret agent (four films, 1966–1968) and the tongue-in-cheek *The Man From U.N.C.L.E.* TV series (NBC, 1964–1968), which matched American agent Napoleon Solo (Robert Vaughn)—whose name was invented by Ian Fleming—with Russian agent Illya Kuryakin (David MacCallum). *Get Smart* (NBC, 1965–1969), *I Spy* (NBC, 1965–1968), and *Mission: Impossible* (CBS, 1966–1973) were also directly inspired by Bond. Bosley Crowther, "Screen; Inferior Burlesque of Bond," *New York Times,* January 26, 1966, 23; Ian Johnson, "007 + 4," *Films & Filming* 11, no. 1 (October 1965): 8–11; James Chapman, *Licence to Thrill: A Cultural History of the James Bond Films,* 285; Richard A. Schwartz, *Cold War Culture: Media and the Arts, 1945–1990.*

19. "New Italo Trend—Spy Epics: Bond-Type Pix Big Yen Today," *Variety,* February 24, 1965, 25, 28. Several of these Bond imitations were being made as Franco- or American-Italian co-productions.

20. For information on Tuovinen and Stolitksy, see http://www.kirjasto.sci.fi/artotuov.htm.

21. Cam Nguyet Nguyen, "Z.28 and the Appeal of Spy Fiction in Southern Vietnam, 1954–1975," unpublished master's thesis, University of California, Berkeley, 2002, 61, 62.

22. Fleming's novels were translated into Vietnamese by Hoang Hai Thuy (Nguyen 8).

23. See, for example, Christopher Booker, *The Neophiliacs: A Study of Revolution in English Life in the Fifties and Sixties,* 179–80. Bennett and Woollacott also take up this interpretation, seeing in Bond "mythic encapsulations of the then prominent ideological themes of classlessness and modernity" (34–35).

24. Julie d'Acci, "Nobody's Woman? Honey West and the New Sexuality," 73–93; and on "James Bond in skirts," see p. 81; Jeffrey Miller, *Something Completely Different,* 51–74. *The Girl From U.N.C.L.E.* (NBC, 1966–1967); *Get Smart* (NBC, 1965–1969); *The Avengers* (ABC, 1966–1969). James Chapman makes the insightful comment that although a number of British spy television shows, including *The Avengers,* predated the advent of the Bond films, they were influenced by 007 just the same (*Saints & Avengers* 12).

25. The article also noted that it was now possible for Yemeni girls to go unveiled before marriage. Eric Pace, "Action Movies from the West Are Socko in Yemen," *New York Times,* October 23, 1968, 2. By contrast, Egypt's *un*progressive stance was reflected in its ban on American films, including the popular Bond thrillers, to protest U.S. support for Israel in the 1967 war. "American Films Barred by U.A.R.," *New York Times,* September 17, 1967, 121.

26. "He is the embodiment, not of fantasy, but of sanity; he is *mens sana in corpore sano.*" Simon Raven, "The Natural Man," *Spectator,* October 28, 1966, 552, 554 (italics in original). Not everyone saw Bond's contemporary relevance as necessarily liberal-minded. The March 1965 issue of *The New Guard,* the publication of the right-wing Young Americans for Freedom, found parallels between Bond and, of all people, Barry Goldwater: "With his rather uncomplicated philosophy of life, his pronounced loyalty to his country, and his excessive interest in fine machinery, [Bond] coincides with the current conception of the conservative mystique." See *Newsweek,* May 10, 1965, 96.

27. Philippe Pilard, "003 Visages de James Bond," *Image et Son,* no. 184 (May 1965): 67.

28. See, for example, Thomas Wiseman, *Sunday Express,* October 9, 1962, n.p. [BFI microfiche]: "I find it disturbing that we should be offered as a hero . . . a man whose methods and morals are indistinguishable from those of the villain," and Paul

Mayersberg, "The Spies We Wish For," *New Society,* no. 136 (May 6, 1965): 24: "There is liaison between hero and villain which has its origin in the personality of James Bond, in his sado-masochistic fantasies, the way he sees himself as destroyer and saviour."

29. Eldridge Cleaver, *Soul on Ice,* 80. Interestingly, Ian Fleming's work was banned by South Africa's apartheid government in 1965; see "007 Is Banned in South Africa; Objection Is to 'Spy Who Loved,' " *New York Times,* June 20, 1965, 7.

30. "Bulldog Drummond Was a Gentleman: Moral Decline Illustrated by James Bond," *Times* of London, August 16, 1966, 8.

31. Lycurgus M. Starkey, Jr., *James Bond's World of Values,* 10–11, 18. Starkey held a Ph.D. from Columbia and was formerly a professor of Church History at St. Paul School of Theology Methodist, Kansas City.

32. Claudio Sorgi, "Il caso James Bond," *L'Observatore Romano,* no. 13 (May 17–18, 1965): 3.

33. These views came from both sides of the political spectrum—not only from conservative religious voices, but also from the left. See, for example, Nina Hibbin's comments in the *Daily Worker:* "The cult of James Bondism is a vicious one, a symptomatic sickness of our age . . . all this is one vast, gigantic confidence trick to blind the audience to what is going on underneath." "Goldfinger—Slickest: Bond's Latest Film Repeats the Dose," *Daily Worker,* September 16, 1964, n.p. [BFI microfiche].

34. Peter H. Schröder, "Film in der Nähe des Faschismus: James Bond oder Sex und Sadismus," *Zeit,* no. 12 (March 20, 1964): 16.

35. Andre Müller, "Bond und Bonn," *Junge Welt,* July 16/17, 1966, 3.

36. It was, for example, on the request of the Soviet embassy that *From Russia with Love* was banned from public viewing in Zanzibar in 1964, much to popular dismay.

37. Yurii Zhukov, "Morality of the Bourgeois World: The Advocate of the 'Right to Kill,' " *Pravda,* no. 272 (17224) (September 29, 1965): 6. Thanks to Adam S. Albion for his help with translation.

38. Zhukov, 6.

39. Grigor Chernev, "The Man with the Gun: Present All over the Screens of the West," *Narodna Kultura,* April 22, 1966, 7. Thanks to Mariana Lenkova for her help with translation.

40. Chernev, 7.

41. Zhukov, "Morality of the Bourgeois World: The Advocate of the 'Right to Kill,' " *Pravda,* September 29, 1965, 6. This same argument is made in "Bond und Bonn," *Junge Welt,* July 16/17, 1966, 3. Zhukov also mentions Western agents in the Congo, the Dominican Republic, Aden and Hong Kong, as well as making an analogy between Bond's credo and that of Hitler or Rudolph Hess: "what is the difference between the 'ideal' heroes of the bourgeoisie in the 1960s . . . and the ideal of Hitler?" Zhukov's theories might have had some credence; a *New York Times* article from 1967 reported the existence of "007" squads in northeastern Thailand—so dubbed by a district officer who trained them to guard their villages against incursions by communist guerrillas. Peter Braestrup, "The 'Little Vietnam' in Thailand: How the Guerillas Came to Koh Noi," *New York Times,* December 10, 1967, 297.

42. "Bond und Bonn," *Junge Welt,* July 16/17, 1966, 3.

43. A. Soskohvyi, *Komsomolskaya Pravda,* September 17, 1966, 3. Soskohvyi is in part here citing Bulgarian author Andrei Gulyashki's interpretation of Bond (see discussion of Gulyashki below).

44. "Bond und Bonn," *Junge Welt,* July 16/17, 1966, 1, 3. The article lays out

specific training tactics of the "Bonn Ultras" that mimic Bond's practices on the screen, to explain how the West Germans will launch first a covert war and then open war on the East. "And then, as is well known, the Bonn Ultras in the first hours of a war will want to use nuclear weapons, and atomic world war will have been inflamed!" (3).

45. "James Bond as Villain in Soviet Novel," *Daily Telegraph,* October 8, 1965, 25; "Bulgarian Hero Meets James Bond," *The Bookseller,* no. 3136 (January 29, 1966): 262; *New York Times,* January 27, 1966, 30.

46. *Komsomolskaya Pravda* serialized Andrei Gulyashki's "Avakum Zakhov vs. 07" when it first came out, September 17–October 2, 1966. Citations above are from Parts II and III. Copyright laws prohibited Gulyashki from using the character "007."

47. A. Soskohvyi in his introduction to the serialization of Gulyashki's story, *Komsomolskaya Pravda,* September 17, 1966, 3

48. Paula James, "Zakho [*sic*] the One-Girl Spy Will Beat Bond" *Daily Mirror,* January 26, 1966, 4.

49. Robert O. Keohane and Joseph S. Nye, "Introduction," in Nye and Donahue, *Governance in a Globalizing World,* 2. See also Neal M. Rosendorf's "Social and Cultural Globalization: Concepts, History, and America's Role," in the same volume (109–28), and Keohane and Nye, *Power and Interdependence: World Politics in Transition,* chapter 10.

50. See Keohane and Nye, "Introduction," 8, and Rosendorf, "Social and Cultural Globalization."

51. "Soviet Explorers Visit U.S. Antarctic Station," *New York Times,* March 9, 1967, 47. "How did the groups get along? Extremely well—there was said to have been much socializing, and a James Bond film."

52. Akira Iriye, "Culture and International History," in *Explaining the History of American Foreign Relations,* 222; Iriye, "Culture and Power: International Relations as Intercultural Relations," SHAFR presidential address December 29, 1978, in *Diplomatic History* 3, no. 2 (Spring 1979): 115–28.

53. This is clearly demonstrated by the worldwide publicity that accompanied the opening of the latest Bond film, *Die Another Day,* in December 2002. Moreover, Bond is now being experienced by a new generation of fans through computer games.

54. See, for example, Chapman, *Licence to Thrill;* Jeremy Black, *The Politics of James Bond: From Fleming's Novels to the Big Screen;* and Cork and Scivally, *Legacy.*

55. North Korea's Secretariat of the Committee for the Peaceful Reunification of the Fatherland denounced the United States (rightly identified as the financiers and distributors of the film) as "the root cause of all disasters and misfortune of the Korean nation and . . . an empire of evil," and called *Die Another Day* "a deliberate and premeditated act of mocking at and insulting the Korean nation." See "North Korean Denounces James Bond Film," *New York Times,* December 15, 2002, 25; Jenny Booth, "North Korea Declares War on James Bond," *Daily Telegraph,* December 15, 2002; "North Korea Takes Aim at Bond," *BBC News,* December 14, 2002, http://news .bbc.co.uk/1/hi/world/asia-pacific/2575889.stm. On the response from Seoul, see "Two Koreas Blast New James Bond Film," *The Associated Press,* January 3, 2003, http://cgi.wn.com/?t=print1.txt&action=display%article=17701270; Joohee Cho, "In Koreas, Latest Bond Movie Provokes Outcry, Calls for Boycott," *Washington Post,* December 26, 2002.

56. See, for example, Jack Garland, AP Press, "British Forces Use James Bond Code Names," *Seattle Post-Intelligencer,* March 31, 2003.

57. David C. Earnest and James N. Rosenau, "Department: The Spy Who Loved

Globalization," *Foreign Policy,* September/October 2000. "That [Fleming and the Bond film scriptwriters] . . . identified themes that resonate so well—across not only four decades of movies but also across cultures—should stir humility in every international affairs scholar."

58. The organization called SPECTRE, Bond's best-known adversary, stands for the Special Executive for Counterintelligence, Terrorism, Revenge and Extortion.

IV

Structures
of Feeling

13 Why Size Matters

CHRISTOPH LINDNER

It's the BIGGEST. It's the BEST. It's BOND. And B-E-Y-O-N-D.
—1977 film poster of *The Spy Who Loved Me*

Despite the connotations of my title, this chapter is not about James Bond's penis. This area of the Bond corpus, however, has recently come under close inspection, partly due to renewed critical and theoretical interest in the cultural representation of masculinity. Most notably, in his provocatively titled essay "James Bond's Penis," Toby Miller moves between analysis of the 007 novels and films to show how the superspy's relationship with his sexuality is not nearly so confident or comfortable as we might think. Revisiting classic screen moments such as the laser castration scene in *Goldfinger* (1964), Miller goes on to argue that the male body in the 007 series represents both a site and a source of cultural anxiety about power and control.

In many ways, Miller's essay reinforces a view that has dominated critical thinking about 007 since the 1960s—namely, the view that Bond is a highly unstable and often ambiguous cultural icon, what Tony Bennett and Janet Woollacott have called "a mobile signifier" (42). For Miller, one place where this mobility of signification registers is in the shifting configurations of Bond's penis as a site of discipline, mirroring, domination, and communication:

> The *disciplined* penis is trained to be obedient . . . to be under control in a satisfactorily self-policed body, as per . . . Bond's time spent at the health farm in *Never Say Never Again* and *Thunderball*. The *mirroring* penis is a desirable icon, used in the Bond saga to represent and produce excitement, anxiety, and failure, as per the bedroom triumph and

decline of *Goldfinger.* The *dominating* penis is a physical sign and technique for exerting force over others, especially women—Bond's instant
attraction to those he meets in the street or anywhere else in all the
films. And the *communicative* penis stands for a combination of the
aesthetic and the sublime, as in the complex relations of size, race,
sexual activity, and the Bondian organ's wry history—Bond sickened
by desire and terror in the *Dr. No* spider sequence. . . . James Bond's
penis comes in many sizes. (243–44)

Whether or not we agree with this line of thought, Miller's focus on "the
Bondian organ" and its changing symbolic valences does identify one of
the most obvious places where the 007 saga's obsession with size can be
observed. Pursuing a different line of inquiry, this chapter considers
some other, less obvious ways in which size matters in the sensational
world of James Bond.

To refocus on the issue of size from another perspective, I want to
start by looking at some recent comments about Bond from an unlikely
critical source—the Slovenian cultural theorist Slavoj Žižek. In *Welcome
to the Desert of the Real,* his extended essay on the events of September
11, 2001, Žižek notes the uncanny similarities between the real images of
mass destruction in New York and the fantastical disaster scenarios of
recent Hollywood blockbusters like *Independence Day* (1996) and *The
Matrix* (1999). He goes on from this rather obvious observation to argue
that "the unthinkable which happened was the object of fantasy, so that,
in a way, America got what it fantasized about, and this was the greatest
surprise" (16–17). Part of Žižek's point is that what we experienced on
September 11 was a violent eruption of the "Real"—in Jacques Lacan's
sense of the term—as the "impossible thing," experienced only as "rup-
ture, break, or interruption," that "turns our symbolic universe upside
down" (Zupancic 235). Another part of Žižek's point is that the mass-
mediated images of destruction also produced a flash of "hyperreality"—
in Jean Baudrillard's sense of the term—as the disorienting and illusory
state, endemic to the post-modern era of the Image, in which reality itself
is "always already reproduced" (146).

So how is this relevant to James Bond? Žižek goes on to cite the Bond
films both as an example of the uncanny fantasies that came to life on
September 11 and as an example of the blurring of boundaries between
reality and representation. Specifically, Žižek suggests that "Osama Bin
Laden, the suspected mastermind behind the bombings," can be understood as "a real-life counterpart of Ernst Stavro Blofeld, the master-

criminal in most of the James Bond films" whose "acts of global destruction" are defeated by Bond's "fireworks" (21). What I find particularly interesting is that, in looking to popular culture for a way into talking and thinking seriously about the events of September 11, Žižek turns to the James Bond films. It seems to me that one of the reasons is an implicit recognition of the importance of size in the world of Bond. Why does Žižek explicitly link bin Laden with Blofeld? Because Blofeld, the leader of the fictional terrorist network SPECTRE, is the only cinematic villain large enough to measure up to bin Laden, the leader of the real terrorist network al-Qaeda. In fact, I would suggest that the entire point of Blofeld is to be in every possible way larger than life and, in the process, to function in the Bond texts as an outrageously exaggerated threat of the eruption of the Lacanian "Real." Like the "specter" of bin Laden discussed by Stephen Watt in the next chapter, Blofeld is the threat of that phantasmal apparition—the unthinkable, unknowable, impossible "Thing" poised to turn our symbolic universe upside down.

Following these thoughts, I want to step back from the mass-mediated cultural spectacle that is the Bond phenomenon today and look at one of the early sources of the Bondian obsession with size: Ian Fleming's original spy novels. In an earlier essay, Brian Patton considers Fleming's writing in relation to the British cultural moment of "the angry young man," offering a reading of *Moonraker* (1955)—with its concerns over issues of gender, class, and nation—as a variation on the 1950s "condition of England" novel. Extending this line of critique in a related direction, this chapter considers Fleming's writing in relation to the British cultural moment of the postwar spy thriller. In particular, I want to suggest that one of the reasons size matters in the world of James Bond is because of the way Fleming conceives crime, conspiracy, and human agency in the 007 texts, and also because of how that conception moves on from earlier detective writing.

In the 1950s and 1960s, writers such as Len Deighton, John le Carré, and Ian Fleming in particular pioneered the formulaic British spy thriller to unprecedented commercial success. The mass publication of Fleming's Bond novels in Pan paperback beginning in 1956, for example, has been credited with triggering the American paperback revolution in Britain (Denning 92–93; Sutherland 176). In fact, more than half of the first eighteen million Pan paperback sales in Britain were 007 adventures. And in 1962, as the film adaptation of *Doctor No* grossed record sales at the box office, Bond profitably crossed over into the most popular of popular media. Popular demand in turn led to the subsequent serialization of the films (twenty and still counting), along with the continued serialization of the novels until Fleming's death in 1964. In effect, the appearance of a screen version of James Bond created a circular market. The books sold film tickets while the films sold books.

By the early 1960s, it seemed as if everyone was reading Fleming. *From Russia with Love* (1957) popped up on President Kennedy's list of top ten favorite books, and even Jean-Paul Sartre, to the dismay of the French intellectual elite, was reported to be an avid 007 fan. Perhaps the most telling event in terms of Bond's commercial and cultural significance, however, occurred in 1965 when the soundtrack from the *Goldfinger* film became the top-selling album in the United States, knocking the Beatles from the number one spot. The first Bond novel, *Casino Royale,* was published in 1953. Less than a decade later, the cultural spectacle we now call the James Bond phenomenon was in full swing.

Significantly, the secret agent story was by no means a new popular genre when *Casino Royale* first hit the bookstores, any more than it was when *Dr. No* first hit the screens. The film industry had been churning out spy thrillers for decades, and publishers had been printing them long before that. So why, then, did the 007 series, and the British spy thriller more generally, have such a heavy impact on popular culture in the postwar decades? It is, I want to argue, in large part because Fleming, among others, developed a variation on the popular genre of detective fiction that registered and responded to specifically postwar concerns about crime, conspiracy, and human agency.

As spy thrillers, the Bond novels adopt many of the formal and thematic characteristics of detective fiction. For example, as Umberto Eco's structuralist analysis of Fleming has shown, the Bond novels not only share the same basic narrative structures found in detective fiction, but also feature many of the same archetypal figures of adventure—including, among others, the villain/criminal and the hero/victor. Like detective fiction, moreover, the Bond novels are also concerned with questions of truth and reason, transgression and justice, and of course secrecy and surveillance. Yet, because Fleming locates these themes within the broader context of Britain's Cold War ideology and postwar geopolitics, the Bond novels also mark a departure from a trans-Atlantic tradition in detective writing. That is, the secret agent novel that Fleming constructs plays out at a global and ideological level what the detective novel typically plays out at a regional, social, and intimately private level—and here, in contrast to 007's jet-setting world of international travel and luxury tourism, I am thinking of the myopic world of Agatha

Christie's drawing-room dramas as well as the insular underworld of Raymond Chandler's hard-boiled Los Angeles.

So although both detective and secret agent narratives share a common preoccupation with crime and the people who pursue it, the specific character of that crime—and so that of its pursuers—sets the two apart. In Fleming's case, the Bond novels mark a shift in a cultural understanding of crime that, following the disillusioning experience of two world wars and the dawn of the atomic age, also came to include crimes against humanity. This legacy of Europe's massive political upheavals in the first half of the twentieth century finds expression in the size of what I want to call the Bond novels' "criminal vision."

In *You Only Live Twice* (1964), the final novel in the SPECTRE trilogy, Blofeld's latest criminal project, a Japanese "suicide garden," leaves this strong impression on Bond:

> And what a garden! A garden that would be like a deadly fly-trap for human beings, a killing bottle for those who wanted to die. . . . Blofeld must have gone off his head, but with a monstrous, calculating madness—the madness of the genius he undoubtedly was. And the whole demonic concept was on Blofeld's usual grand scale—the scale of a Caligula, of a Nero, of a Hitler, of any other great enemy of mankind. (127–28)

Aligning the head of SPECTRE with "monsters" of history like Caligula, Nero, and Hitler, these comments on the "calculating madness" of Blofeld's criminal vision perfectly capture the titanic scale on which crime is conceived in the 007 series as a whole. In Fleming's writing, crimes are no longer directed toward individuals, but rather toward entire nations, whole continents, and often humanity itself. *Moonraker, Thunderball* (1961), and *Doctor No* (1958) all contain potentially genocidal atomic conspiracies. *On Her Majesty's Secret Service* (1963) threatens biological warfare in an attempt to annihilate Britain's agricultural and livestock industries. In *Goldfinger* (1959), equally devious and devastating is Auric Goldfinger's scheme, backed by the Soviet machine, to plunder the gold reserves at Fort Knox and trigger the collapse of the global market economy. And though not all the Bond novels contain criminal plots of this destructive caliber, each offers at a very minimum some oblique though crippling stab at Western stability. In *From Russia with Love,* for example, Soviet intelligence chiefs reach a policy decision to undermine NATO intelligence and confidence. Their solution is to assassinate Bond in a compromising (sexual) position. Along similar lines, *Casino Royale* features Le Chiffre, a KGB paymaster who funds terrorist and subversive activities in France.

Taken together, the Bond novels contain a portfolio of monumental criminal conspiracies that played on British cultural anxieties of the 1950s and 1960s: atomic paranoia, currency crises, the threat of communist expansion, organized crime, freelance terrorism, and even resurgent Nazism. In its humbled postwar condition, compounded by the accelerating collapse of Empire, Britain could not afford another Hitler, another Hiroshima, another sterling crash, or another Suez-style embarrassment, and these are precisely the kinds of paralyzing threats to Britain and the larger Western world that Fleming's criminals conspire to deliver. As such, crime in Fleming is at once political and nihilistic, so that acts of political aggression or ideological heresy—in short, all that stands against Britain, capitalism, democracy, and cultural imperialism in general—double as trespasses against humanity.

Although the nature and scale of crime remain largely constant throughout the 007 series, the criminals themselves come in two waves: the Soviet-controlled operatives and the independent criminal masterminds. In the early Bond novels, Fleming typically casts his villains as agents who work either directly or indirectly for the Soviet government. Le Chiffre in *Casino Royale,* the aptly named Mr. Big in *Live and Let Die* (1954), Red Grant and Rosa Klebb in *From Russia with Love,* Dr. No, and Goldfinger all take orders or receive funds and training from SMERSH. As one of M's top-secret briefs in *Casino Royale* explains, SMERSH is the KGB's assassination squad:

> SMERSH is a conjunction of two Russian words: "Smyert Shpionam," meaning roughly: "Death to Spies." . . .
>
> Its task is the elimination of all forms of treachery and backsliding with the various branches of the Soviet Secret Service and Secret Police at home and abroad. It is the most powerful and feared organization in the USSR and is popularly believed never to have failed in a mission of vengeance. (14–15)

With Western hostility toward the Eastern bloc at an all-time high in the 1950s, the Soviet government, and its intelligence department in particular, made an easy typecast for villainy. As Lars Ole Sauerberg notes, at this time Fleming "could paint an unaffected and wholly negative picture of the Soviet Union confident that it would be positively received" (160). One notable exception to the early Bond villain, however, occurs in *Moonraker*'s Sir Hugo Drax, the megalomaniac German Nazi who masquerades as an English gentleman. But here again, Fleming exploits another British cultural antipathy of the 1950s. Germans, in the immediate wake of the Second World War, made another easy and obvious target for bad press.

The second wave of Bond villains begins with the 1961 publication of *Thunderball,* in which Fleming abandons the Soviet-backed operative for the freelance criminal Goliath. It begins, in other words, with the move from SMERSH to Blofeld's brainchild: the international crime syndicate SPECTRE (Special Executive for Counterintelligence, Terrorism, Revenge, and Extortion). In the early 1960s, as the Cold War began to emerge from a deep freeze (despite the setback and panic of the 1962 Cuban missile crisis) and edge slowly toward the atmosphere of détente that would see it through the 1970s, public attitudes toward the Communist bloc softened just enough in Britain to make the slandering of Soviets less politically fashionable than it had been in the mid to late 1950s. As a consequence, and in order to reflect the Cold War politics of the moment, Fleming decided to look beyond the Soviet Union for his criminals. In a reported comment made in 1961, Fleming explains the shift: "I could not see any point in going on digging at [the Soviets], especially when the co-existence thing seemed to be bearing some fruit. So I closed down SMERSH and thought up SPECTRE instead" (in Gant 148). But as many critics point out, the two organizations, like their members, are fundamentally the same.

SPECTRE, notes Umberto Eco, "has all the characteristics of SMERSH," including "the use of torture, the elimination of traitors, and the sworn enmity to all the powers of the Free World" (152). Sauerberg in turn suggests that the later Bond villain represents "a toning down of the adversary's political attachment and a strengthening of his criminal and/or morbid pursuits" (161). As an autonomous organization, SPECTRE possesses no direct political affiliation. Yet its criminal philosophy, expressed so exactly by the acronym itself, is in perfect tune with that of SMERSH. Similarly, SPECTRE's operations match in kind those envisioned by the earlier Bond villains. For example, Blofeld's plan in *Thunderball* to blackmail the West with stolen nuclear weapons boils down to the same scheme hatched in the earlier novel *Doctor No*—a recurring feature of the Bond world exploited to comic effect by the character of Dr. Evil in the 007 spoof *Austin Powers* (1997). And though SPECTRE lacks official government resources, its finances, technology, and task force rival those of any small nation. As such, the move to SPECTRE in the later Bond novels enables Fleming to dodge the exhausted topic of communist villainy without altering the Bond formula, downsizing the crimes, or even radically rethinking criminality. So, whether under the umbrella of SMERSH, SPECTRE, or some other sinister organization, each of Fleming's villains is hell-bent on crippling the West. More importantly, each commands the criminal apparatus with which to do it.

The point I want to make on the back of these observations is deceptively simple. In the 007 series as a whole, the size and sophistication of the various criminal organizations mirror the size and sophistication of their criminal conspiracies. Fleming provides various ways of gauging the size of these criminal visions, but one of the most obvious and accurate gauges in both the textual and cinematic worlds of Bond is the material structure of the secret base. In Fleming's writing, large-scale international crime requires an equally large-scale base of operations. It requires—in the world of Bond, at least—enough space to accommodate the ranks of sub-villains, thugs, saboteurs, and assassins; to house the string of torture chambers, holding cells, laboratories, and nerve centers; and to squeeze in the obligatory suite of gothic dining rooms, en-suite bedrooms, and futuristic cocktail lounges. Doctor No's Caribbean island, for example, houses "the most valuable technical intelligence centre in the world" (175), hidden appropriately under a mountain of guano. In *On Her Majesty's Secret Service,* Blofeld builds his clinic on the summit of his own personal Swiss Alp. And in the next novel, *You Only Live Twice,* he sets up shop in a fortified Japanese castle. Hugo Drax's private missile complex in *Moonraker,* complete with sunken concrete bunkers, watchdogs, and a perimeter patrol, flaunts all the bells and whistles of a high-tech military installation. Bond says it best when, in *Doctor No,* he describes these lavish hideaways as "private kingdoms— away from the beaten track, where there were no witnesses, where they could do what they liked" (172).

While Fleming's long, indulgent, and minutely detailed descriptions of these "private kingdoms" give a clear sense of what Bond is talking about here, the film adaptations of Fleming's work do it even better. From the beginning, but spiraling out of control in the Roger Moore years, the 007 films have taken Fleming's vision of the high-tech and large-scale secret base to conceptual extremes. In the 1967 screen adaptation of *You Only Live Twice,* for example, SPECTRE's base is relocated from the medieval castle featured in the novel to the hollowed-out crater of an inactive volcano. The volcano base contains, to name just a few of its most prominent features, an underground monorail, a helicopter pad, and launch facilities for nuclear missiles and space rockets. So sweeping and indulgently spectacular was the vision behind the volcano base that the actual set used in the film proved to be the most expensive ever built at the time of its production.

In the 1970s, these cinematic visions of the secret base became increasingly outlandish and, so far as it was possible, were conceived on increasingly larger scales by 007 production designer Ken Adam. In the 1977 film *The Spy Who Loved Me* (which takes only its title from the Fleming novel), the villain's base, strangely reminiscent of Nemo's *Nautilus* submarine in the film *20,000 Leagues under the Sea* (1954), goes underwater in the fantastic shape of a submersible marine laboratory evocatively named *Atlantis*. Two years later, in the 1979 screen version of *Moonraker*, Hugo Drax's missile complex literally takes to the skies in the even more fantastic shape of an orbiting space station that makes MIR look like a Lego toy. As James Chapman stresses in *Licence to Thrill*, these 007 set designs are where the "visual spectacle of the Bond films" reaches "its fullest expression," creating "an overwhelming sense of space and size" (61). Even in the current cycle of Pierce Brosnan films—some twenty years after *Moonraker* and the retirement of Ken Adam from the Bond production team—the same look of space and size continues to dominate and define the 007 set designs. In *Tomorrow Never Dies* (1997), for example, Elliot Carver prowls the South China Sea in a futuristic cross between an aquatic stealth bomber and the submersible *Atlantis* from *The Spy Who Loved Me*. Even more spectacular—yet far more preposterous—is the translucent "Ice Palace" that serves as operational headquarters for Gustav Graves' Icarus project in *Die Another Day* (2002).

When it comes to secret bases, Fleming may think big but the films think even bigger. The films blow up to almost absurd proportions what the novels already exaggerate beyond credibility. As measuring sticks for gauging criminality, these cinematic visions of the secret base make the point even more bluntly and unmistakably. Anyone with a private stockpile of nuclear weapons, a command center hidden away under a volcano or under the sea or even out in space, and with a billboard-sized, illuminated map of the world behind their desk, has to be up to something magnificently sinister—something Slavoj Žižek similarly notes in *Welcome to the Desert of the Real*, commenting that:

> The only place in Hollywood films where we see the production process in all its intensity is when James Bond penetrates the master-criminal's secret domain and locates there the site of intense labor

(distilling and packaging drugs, constructing a rocket that will destroy New York . . .). When the master-criminal, after capturing Bond, usually takes him on a tour of his illegal factory, is this not the closest Hollywood comes to the socialist-realist proud presentation of the production in a factory? And the function of Bond's intervention, of course, is to explode in fireworks this site of production. (21)

Here, Žižek's Marxist fascination with processes of labor and production leads to a reading of the "secret domain" that helps to explain one of the more contrived elements of the Bond film formula—namely, that clumsy cinematic moment when the overconfident villain offers the recently captured Bond a guided tour of his secret lair, usually accompanied by cocktails or champagne and a full revelation of his diabolical plan for world domination. One purpose of the tour, of course, is to enable the viewer/reader to experience gratuitously the sweep and spectacle of the secret base. Another, more abstract purpose is, as Žižek suggests, to establish the villain as an abuser of the "legitimate" capitalist system, and thus as an opponent of the West. Seen in this way, the secret base figures as a site of illegitimate labor and production backed by illegitimate capital, what he wonderfully describes as an "illegal factory" in need of shutting down by a lawful agent of the system. So, while the Bond films do feature a "proud presentation" of production that is uncharacteristic of Hollywood, that production is nonetheless criminalized—and deliberately so—by its explicit alignment with the figure of the villain.

More to the point, however, as a hugely elaborate and expensive construction, as well as a site of collective labor and mass production, the secret base functions as a material index that both registers and expresses the titanic scale on which crime is conceived in the Bond series. It testifies to the series' magnified scope of criminal vision, reconfirming the superlative, almost comic-strip proportions to which Fleming inflates the issues of crime and criminality. Here, we have super villains directing super crimes at superpowers. Enter the superspy.

In Fleming's writing, the threat of extreme disasters such as nuclear armageddon, biological warfare, and global economic meltdown means that the Western political establishment cannot afford for the novels' crimes to be made public or even for them to take place at all. The sheer magnitude of criminal vision accordingly shifts the Bond thriller's emphasis away from detecting crime to preventing it. Similarly, the political character of crime in the 007 series shifts the novels' emphasis away from the exposure of criminality toward its containment. Together, then, the political crime—what doubles as criminal politics—and the scope of criminal vision give rise to a corresponding ideology of prevention. That is, they generate new imperatives for the figure of the detective, imperatives that register the political status Fleming accords to crime and the criminals who commit it. For just as Fleming conceives crime and criminality in the context of Britain's Cold War ideology and postwar geopolitics, so too does he conceive the figure of the detective. The detective is now reconfigured as secret agent, licensed to kill.

James Bond as secret agent represents a new embodiment of the detective trained and dispatched to avert the crime against humanity and in the process defuse the political crisis. What this really means, however, is that Bond represents the transformation of the highly cerebral figure of the detective into a cold-blooded and unthinking professional who kills for a living. In other words, rather than being defined or driven by the activity of detection—as in the case of more conventional detectives like Sherlock Holmes, Hercule Poirot, Miss Marple, and Philip Marlowe—Bond is defined by the act of assassination, as his double-0 prefix specifically designates. Fleming makes this point disturbingly clear in the opening passage of *Goldfinger,* in which Bond ruminates about death while killing time in an airport lounge:

> It was part of his profession to kill people. He had never liked doing it and when he had to kill he did it as well as he knew how and forgot about it. As a secret agent who held the rare double-O prefix—the licence to kill in the Secret Service—it was his duty to be as cool about death as a surgeon. If it happened, it happened. Regret was unprofessional—worse, it was death-watch beetle in the soul. (3)

It is no accident, of course, that killing does happen on every job despite Bond's reluctant attitude toward it. The British government sanctions 007 to kill precisely because his assignments always require him to kill. In *The Man with the Golden Gun* (1965), M sums it up concisely in his reading of the Scaramanga case—a case involving a hit man/drug smuggler/all-around Soviet and Cuban crony:

> And James Bond, if aimed straight at a known target—M put in the language of battleships—was a supremely effective firing-piece. Well, the target was there and it desperately demanded destruction. Bond had accused M of using him as tool. Naturally. Every officer in the Service was a tool for one secret purpose or another. The problem on hand could only be solved by a killing. James Bond would not possess

the Double-O prefix if he had not high talents, frequently proved, as a gunman. (25)

Killing is how Bond averts the crime against humanity, how he defuses the political crisis, how he contains criminal politics. Killing is Fleming's final answer to the criminal who would topple the free world, his paradoxically humane solution to inhumanity played out on a global scale.

As Fleming makes a point of stressing in every novel from *Doctor No* to *The Man with the Golden Gun,* Bond's identity and success as a killer are inextricably linked to his gun and—more generally speaking—to his mastery over technology. In *Doctor No,* Fleming offers this particularly revealing insight into Bond's intimate relationship with his piece:

> [Bond] thought of his fifteen years' marriage to the ugly bit of metal. He remembered the times its single word had saved his life—and the times when its threat alone had been enough. He thought of the days when he had literally dressed to kill—when he had dismantled the gun and oiled it and packed the bullets carefully into the springloaded magazine and tried the action once or twice, pumping the cartridges out on to the bedspread in some hotel bedroom somewhere round the world. Then the last wipe of a dry rag and the gun into the little holster and a pause in front of the mirror to see that nothing showed. (20–21)

The eroticizing of the gun in this passage is hard to overlook, for Fleming not only explicitly describes Bond's relationship with his gun as a "marriage," but goes on to transform the "ugly bit of metal" into a phallic extension of Bond's body. In particular, the image of Bond playing with his weapon alone on a hotel bed is quite obviously masturbatory. At one level, the imagery of masturbation gestures toward Bond's loneliness, commenting perhaps on his inability to maintain long-term relationships with women. At another and more disturbing level, however, the same imagery also blurs the distinction between sex and violence. Far from exceptional, this conflation of sex and violence is repeated almost everywhere in the world of Bond, from the testicular torture scene of *Casino Royale* through the laser castration scene of *Goldfinger* to the loaded symbolism of 007's popular nickname "Mr. Kiss Kiss Bang Bang."

Important here is that, as a professional assassin, Bond kills for and in the name of Britain. Which is to say that Bond kills for and in the name of what Britain represents in Fleming's writing—namely, Western capitalist imperialism. In such terms, Bond acts as a political weapon and fulfills the ideological function within the 007 texts of protecting Britain's international footing and promoting its international interests. In *You Only Live Twice,* Blofeld restates the case even more bluntly in a sardonic speech given to the recently captured Bond:

> You are a common thug, a blunt instrument wielded by dolts in high places. Having done what you are told to do, out of some mistaken idea of duty or patriotism, you satisfy your brutish instincts with alcohol, nicotine and sex while waiting to be dispatched on the next misbegotten foray. Twice before, your Chief has sent you to do battle with me, Mister Bond, and, by a combination of luck and brute force, you were successful in destroying two projects of my genius. You and your government would categorize these projects as crimes against humanity, and various authorities still seek to bring me to book for them. (192)

Blofeld's observations in this passage are interesting for several reasons. Not only do the comments identify Bond as an unthinking agent of government, but in the process they allude perceptively to the ideology of nation underpinning 007's lethal actions. Also interesting is the way Blofeld implies that, at some psychological level, Bond seeks release from the stress of his job through material and physical self-gratification—effectively linking 007 to the emergent consumer society and swinging Britain of the late 1950s and early 1960s.

Panning back to the larger 007 picture, another aspect of the postwar context of the Bond novels also becomes relevant. In the following passage from *You Only Live Twice,* Fleming comments on Britain's international standing since 1945. Tiger Tanaka, head of the Japanese Secret Service, taunts Bond:

> Now it is a sad fact that I, and many of us in positions of authority in Japan, have formed an unsatisfactory opinion about the British people since the war. You have not only lost a great Empire, you have seemed almost anxious to throw it away with both hands . . . when you apparently sought to arrest this slide into impotence at Suez, you succeeded only in stage-managing one of the most pitiful bungles in the history of the world, if not the worst. (79–80)

As Fleming touches upon in this passage, the 1956 Suez fiasco marks a decisive moment in Britain's postwar history. In many ways, it publicly signaled the end of Britain's international clout—a death rattle of the British Empire. As Suez made clear, in the geopolitical reshuffle that followed the end of the Second World War, Britain lost out to its more influential wartime ally, the United States. And with its Empire contracting, Britain was rapidly losing its remaining spheres of influence to what was diplomatically termed "decolonization." By the 1950s, further frustrated by the U.S.'s reluctance to admit it fully into the "atomic club," Britain had no choice but to recognize what historian Kenneth Morgan aptly calls its "second-rate-power status" (158).

Within the James Bond texts, Fleming plays on—and even aggravates—Britain's postwar inferiority complex and Cold War insecurities. The crimes attempted in the novels not only endanger humanity but also, and more significantly, threaten to relegate Britain right down to a third-rate power. In terms of Fleming's contemporary British readership, they represent the threat of yet another blow to an already battered national pride. Yet, by introducing the character of James Bond, Fleming goes on to alleviate those anxieties, to re-inflate Britain's deflated confidence. In novel after novel, Bond safeguards not just humanity itself but also Britain's reputation in the process, thereby restoring at least the façade of the nation's superpower status. In effect, James Bond saves everything for a country and a world that cannot save themselves. And it is precisely in this way that the 007 series, nostalgic for Empire, achieves its ideological effect—namely, the effect, as Tony Bennett argues, of "putting England back on top" (20). Moreover, by inscribing the Bond texts with resurrected dreams of Empire and global influence reconstructed in the face of the Cold War, the arms race, and decolonization, Fleming articulates the very ideology that not only defines the character of James Bond, but also fixes his place politically in a postwar world order.

It is no accident, however, that the James Bond phenomenon—still with us today particularly in film—took off in the 1950s. With horrors such as trench warfare, the Holocaust, Stalin's purges, and the dropping of atomic bombs over Japan, the first half of the twentieth century witnessed war, destruction, and genocide on an unprecedented and previously inconceivable scale. This string of events, culminating in the U.S.'s decision to deploy the atomic bomb in 1945, is what made Fleming's particular conception of large-scale crime conceivable in the first place. It is also this same string of events, which, through its heavy impact on the popular imagination, created a contemporary audience in whose collective consciousness such large-scale crime would find deep resonance. By first magnifying the scope of criminal vision to include crimes against humanity and then locating those crimes politically in a postwar world order—however fictional and fantastic—Fleming effectively captured the popular cultural imagination with a fear that has been haunting it ever since.

Recently, in the wake of the September 11 terrorist attacks, this fear has been greatly accentuated. As a consequence, the original 007 novels have arguably become more relevant and resonant today than they have been for a long time—if for no other reason than because, as Stephen Watt argues in the next chapter, "Fleming uncannily anticipates the contemporary state of global terrorism both in strategy and representation" (246). And if we consider these big bangs alongside all the others that have also come to define the cult of James Bond—including the glamorous fantasies of gadgets, girls, and globetrotting—we begin to see why, for more than fifty years, Mr. Kiss Kiss Bang Bang has been leaving his public shaken and stirred.

NOTE

I would like to acknowledge and thank The British Academy for its generous financial support of the work carried out for this essay, which draws on material revised from chapter 4 of Lindner, *The James Bond Phenomenon.*

14 007 and 9/11, Specters and Structures of Feeling

Stephen Watt

> "I hate to say it," [Bond] said, "but [New York] must be the fattest atomic-bomb target on the whole face of the globe."
> "Nothing to touch it," agreed Halloran. "Keeps me awake nights thinking what would happen."
>
> —Ian Fleming, *Live and Let Die* (1954)

Given the reemergence of what might be characterized as Cold War paranoia and such largely forgotten phenomena as 1960s bomb shelters, now renovated with plastic sheeting and duct tape, one footnote to our 2003 military action in Iraq hardly seemed surprising. As reported by the Associated Press, British soldiers conducted operations named after characters from Ian Fleming's novels—"Operation James," most notably, in memory of "a No. 1 Brit and hero," as one military expert put it[1]—and concentrated their efforts on targets bearing such code names as Goldfinger and Blofeld, named after two infamous opponents of James Bond, 007. Although the motivation for such allusions and their effect on the morale of the coalition's troops are unclear, their appearance seemed scarcely exceptional. For just two months earlier, *U.S. News and World Report* published an issue with the title "Spy Stories" emblazoned on the cover that featured an essay on Fleming entitled "To Be a Spook." And while nothing in the *U.S. News* essay adduced connections between Fleming, the Cold War, and the conflict in the Middle East, this special issue concluded with an opinion piece by editor-in-chief Mortimer Zuckerman that announced "Midnight for Baghdad" and adverted pointedly to 9/11 in endorsing a preemptive strike against terrorism: "We have been kicked once," Zuckerman observed. "We will not be kicked again—and we will not let the Security Council whistle in the dark."[2] Why conclude a volume on espionage and "spook" stories, many of which concerned spy fiction written during the Cold War, with invective against Saddam Hussein and al-Qaeda? More particularly, how might we understand the resurfacing of Ian Fleming, James Bond, and 007's arch-enemy Ernst Stavro Blofeld in the withering deserts of Iraq?

Both questions might generate a host of predictable answers: our seeming need for a hero to save the day, for example, or the larger tendency evident in contemporary film (*Executive Action* or *True Lies*, to name but two) to narrativize contemporary tensions caused by terrorism as essentially melodramatic with good guys, inordinately bad guys, and heroines in distress. Indeed, one might argue that because coalition forces have been unable to find a large cache of Iraqi weapons of mass destruction, the putative reason for our military action, Jessica Lynch or even the Iraqi people collectively have become cast as heroines waiting to be saved.[3] If, as Zuckerman warns, some terrorist groups are eager to poison us with ricin and others are determined to annihilate us with nuclear weapons, then we need brave men and women with the where-withal to stop them. What sorts of men and women would these be? Further, assuming that the complexity of such matters exceeds the inher-ently reductive capacities of melodrama or tabloid reportage, how might we fairly represent the "terrorists" they oppose? Answers to this question, at times, have reached a kind of low-comic nadir, as when the *Weekly World News* (June 24, 2003) ran a front-page pictorial of Saddam Hus-sein and Osama bin Laden, flower in hand, reclining together on pillows and locked in an embrace under the headline "Saddam & Osama in Love!" and later in October published "Shocking Photos Obtained by the CIA" of the two lovers' "Gay Wedding." On a more serious note, it was precisely this matter—the representation of the 9/11 attackers as some-thing other than cowards or "perverted madmen," as the *Weekly World News* put it—that placed talk show host Bill Maher in the glare of an excoriating public spotlight just days after the attack.[4] Making comments similar to Maher's, Susan Sontag also found herself adrift in political hot water when she declared in *The New Yorker* that whatever else might be said about the attacks on the Twin Towers and the Pentagon, they were not "cowardly" strikes at " 'humanity' or 'the free world.' " "If the term 'cowardly' is to be used," she insisted in reference to the campaign of U.S. bombing of Iraq after the Gulf War, "it might be more aptly applied to those who kill from beyond the range of retaliation, high in the sky, than to those willing to die themselves" in furthering their cause.[5] *Representa-tion*, then, a highly debated issue in the wake of 9/11, remains crucial to recognizing parallels between the Cold War Fleming describes and the war on global terrorism today.

So, too, I believe, is *feeling*. For the first time in nearly half a century,

Osama bin Laden and Saddam Hussein in love. Photo courtesy *Weekly World News.*

since the Cold War era in which many of us built bomb shelters in our basements and garages, Americans were advised in the spring of 2003 to fortify their homes against potential attacks from our enemies. In the wake caused by legions of panicked shoppers storming hardware stores in search of duct tape and plastic sheeting, even the retraction of an embarrassed Secretary of Homeland Security could not dispel the anxiety caused by this feckless warning. How has the resultant anxiety produced by similar public scares affected what Raymond Williams famously described as our "structure of feeling"? Rather like the persistence of the death-instinct in Freud's thought, "structure of feeling" appears in Williams's writing from such earlier works as *Modern Tragedy* (1966) through *Marxism and Literature* (1977), defining a "particular quality of social experience and relationship," one "historically distinct from other particular qualities." Endeavoring to provide "a sense of a generation or of a period," the phrase denotes our shared sense of the present, not merely our personal responses or neuroses (*Marxism* 131). Here, Williams emphasizes social experiences that are both fluid enough to be describable as a *process* yet, because they also contain "specific internal relations, at once interlocking and in tension" (*Marxism* 132), fixed enough to possess an identifiable *structure*.

In what follows, I want to suggest that one representation in particular of the terrorist, not as some generic "spook" or ghost, but specifically as a "specter," finds resonance both in Fleming's fiction and in the present moment. Moreover, such a metaphor might help illuminate a structure of feeling composed both of present fears and of residues of the Cold War about which Ian Fleming was prescient in understanding. Central to my argument is Fleming's creation of SPECTRE and its founder Blofeld through three of his most accomplished novels: *Thunderball* (1961), *On Her Majesty's Secret Service* (1963), and *You Only Live Twice* (1964).[6] The film versions of these books are not pertinent to my discussion, save for several carefully composed shots of Blofeld from *From Russia with Love* (1963) and *Thunderball* (1965) and the extensive use of a disembodied voice from the very beginning of the Bond film series, *Dr. No* (1962), all of which might help us understand analogies between SPECTRE and the psychical effect of contemporary terrorist cells. Throughout, I want to underscore the importance of reading the novels in the order they were written, constituting both what James Chapman has suggestively termed the "Blofeld trilogy" and a complex revenge drama with several conventions intrinsic to the genre.[7] Such a reading, to echo the title of Christopher Hitchens's recent book on George Orwell, thus might not only underscore why Fleming the novelist still "matters" to a twenty-first-century readership, but might also enhance our understanding of a critical trope prominent these days in discussions of literary modernism: namely, ghosts and other figures of haunting. In *Ghostwriting Modernism* (2002), for instance, Helen Sword observes that in nearly every journal she has read and at every conference she has attended, scholars seem obsessed with such otherworldly figures. Yet too often, as she justly complains in reference to Jacques Derrida's *Specters of Marx,* ghosts and specters appear "in so many different permutations and contexts" that "they threaten to become verbal specters themselves, suggestive, thought-provoking, ethereal entities drained of all stable referential meaning" (163). Fleming, I believe, might help us stabilize distinctions between ghosts and specters, and, in an uncanny way, commentators on contemporary terrorism have deployed specters in ways compatible with Fleming's use of the term a half-century ago to capture what he believed to be

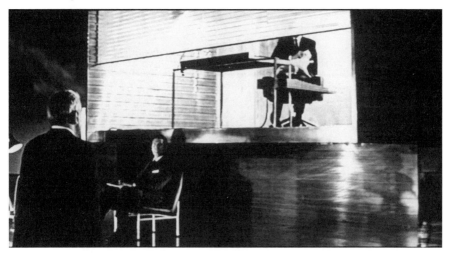

The hidden Blofeld at a SPECTRE meeting in *Thunderball* (1965).

the next threat to the West after Russia had devolved into little more than a nuisance—or relic.

Here is where the conventions of revenge tragedies like Shakespeare's *Hamlet* and the present battle against terrorism, as odd and ahistorical congeries as these may seem, bear directly on Fleming, and where Fleming can help unpack elements of a post-9/11 structure of feeling. Especially useful in this unpacking are Jacques Derrida's reading of the "visor effect" in *Hamlet,* the notion that vengeful spirits can survey us without our being able to see them, and Slavoj Žižek's conception of the Invisible Master, particularly the "emergence of a voice that is neither attached to an object (a person) . . . nor simply the voice of an external commentator, but a spectral voice, which floats freely in a mysterious intermediate domain and thereby acquires the horrifying dimension of omnipresence and omnipotence" ("'I Hear You'" 92). Director Terence Young intuitively understood and exploited Žižek's point, as I have implied earlier, shrouding Blofeld in mystery by not showing his face in the film adaptations of *From Russia with Love* and *Thunderball.* Instead, when ordering the execution of a traitor or threatening the West with nuclear destruction, Blofeld was represented by a frightening, authoritarian voice more terrifying than a cycloptic Emilio Largo or his henchmen could ever be. How different from that haunting voice in *Thunderball* are the audiotapes of Osama bin Laden with a voice asserting the prerogative, as it did in October of 2003, to "respond at the appropriate time and place against all the countries participating" in an "unjust war" against Islam and his "righteous jihad"?[8] How different are both the voice and the ominous message it delivers from those of ghosts in *Hamlet,* Thomas Kyd's *The Spanish Tragedy* (1587?), John Marston's *Antonio's Revenge* (1600–1601), and others? And, finally, what resemblances might be identified between the feelings these spectral voices and eyes produce—in both Elizabethan drama and twenty-first-century terror—and those created by Fleming in his "Blofeld trilogy"?

The Specter of SPECTRE, The Excesses of Revenge

[Blofeld is] altogether an expression of hypocrisy, tyranny, and cruelty on a Shakespearean level.

—Umberto Eco

Of Umberto Eco's many insights into Ian Fleming's fiction, this may not rank as the most significant. But that doesn't make the observation any less trenchant, as is another implication of Eco's reading that when Fleming "ceased to identify the wicked with Russia" (161), the creation of SPECTRE augured the birth of a far greater, more ruthless menace to the West. Borrowing Tiger Tanaka's phrase in *You Only Live Twice* that Blofeld is "a devil who has taken human form," Eco labels Bond's antagonist "a master of planning, an organizational genius" who is as "treacherous as needs be" (153). This is unfortunate for Bond at the beginning of *Thunderball*, where SPECTRE's history is introduced, because the simple fact is that he is scarcely imposing or even fit enough to prove a formidable opponent to Blofeld. Suffering from a hangover as the novel opens, he must also endure M's admonition: "All your troubles . . . the deep-seated toxaemia revealed by your Medical, are the result of a basically unnatural way of life" (4–5). More than a single night's excesses are at issue, however, as Bond smokes sixty or more cigarettes a day and imbibes a half-bottle of liquor. Such habits and the inherent stresses of his job have resulted in high blood pressure (160/90), chronic headaches, and other symptoms of a "toxic state which could finally have the effect of reducing his fitness as an officer" (3). In this crucial respect, the fictional Bond only partially resembles his filmic counterpart, especially the one played by Sean Connery and described by Rebecca Carpenter as "suave, sophisticated, powerful, sexually irresistible, brave, stoical, an essential member of an important and exclusive secret service" (187). At times in the Bond novels, he is indeed many of these things, but neither he nor the Secret Service Fleming depicts is quite so powerful or invulnerable as the films would have us believe. Quite to the contrary.

Equally diminished is 007's psyche—his "feelings," if you will—especially in the transition between Tracy's murder in the concluding chapter of *On Her Majesty's Secret Service* and the beginning of *You Only Live Twice*. In fact, M is so concerned about Bond's prolonged depression after Tracy's murder that he seeks the advice of a Nobel laureate psychologist, who prescribes a "desperately important but apparently impossible" mission, one that appeals to [Bond's] deep sense of patriotism, to jolt him from his state of shock (18). "Shock" and "neurosis," though, terms employed by Sir James Molony, are only proximate ones; in another era in which excesses of the bodily "humors" underpinned diagnoses, melancholy might also have been identified as the culprit. Obsessed with signs of death all around him early in the novel, Bond dawdles in Regent's Park, gazing at roses and contemplating the corpses of ants and bees that surround him. There must be thousands—or millions—of them, he reflects, but mercifully, "It was three-thirty. Only two more hours to go before his next drink!" (22), and an escape from death. Bond has contemplated this topic before, in the opening paragraphs of *Goldfinger* for instance, where while waiting to board an airplane he despairs momentarily about having killed a Mexican drug baron and imagines the production of death as an occupation at which we all labor in one way or another: "Was there any person in the world who wasn't somehow, perhaps only statistically, involved in killing his neighbour?" (9). He chastises himself for "glooming about" the murder of a Mexican *capungo* and for "being so damned morbid," resolving to pursue a change and enjoy a "slice of life" (9). And he does. The Bond in *You Only Live Twice* is not so fortunate. In the novel's prologue, set in Japan one month after the passage cited above, Bond drinks as much *sake* as a Sumo wrestler and is playfully admonished by Tanaka that this consumption will render him unfit later as a companion to his geisha girl. Bond is able to laugh the insinuation away, but the next chapter—and M's concern—makes it clear that his depression is no laughing matter.

A prominent double space, a kind of balancing caesura, divides the two expository sections of "Curtains for Bond?" the second chapter of *You Only Live Twice* in which the eminent psychologist recommends the therapeutic benefits of a desperate mission. The earlier section in which this prescription is formulated is counterbalanced by a brief second section in which a disaffected Bond is summoned to headquarters, and neither should be ignored, however inconsequential they might at first appear. The chapter begins on the eve of the annual closing of Blades, the fashionable club to which M belongs and the scene of Bond's fleecing of Hugo Drax in *Moonraker*. Its closing for a month requires those members unfortunate enough to be stranded socially in London to "pig it" at White's, Boodles, or other less desirable establishments. This month "in the wilderness" doesn't appear to bother M, who "couldn't care less"; he could go fishing for two weeks and take his lunch at his desk (12). To do otherwise, to seek another social habitus, would be to risk running into former shipmates who might inquire about his present occupation and, equally unpalatable, launch him into boring patter. Like Bond, who had been given a month's leave after Tracy's murder and returned only to occupy an emotional hell, a recurrent metaphor in Bond's meditation on the world around him, M is set adrift from life as he typically enjoys it. Of course, he has not arrived at the depression Bond suffers, nor has he descended to Hamlet's level of "ontological despair" and "affective withdrawal from the 'stale, flat, and unprofitable . . . uses of the world' (1.2.133–34),"[9] but his temporary liminality ought not be ignored. The world is a different place than it used to be for both men; something is out of joint.

In the chapter's second section, the "urgent thrill of the red telephone" on Mary Goodnight's desk augurs a meeting between M and Bond, setting her atwitter with eagerness to reach 007: "James! James! M wants you! M wants you! M wants you!" (*Live Twice* 17–18). Goodnight knows that Bond has recently neglected to carry his syncrophone and will be more difficult to reach than he should be, another sign of his alienation. What seems most significant about this summoning, however, is neither Bond's unreliability nor Goodnight's affection for him, but M's means of communication and her response to M's request: M, the disembodied voice on the telephone, a kind of friendly or paternal ghost displaced from his typical "haunt," announces that he "wants" Bond. That voice, importantly, also summons the avenger to take action, much as King Hamlet urges his son to action and the ghost of Andrugio calls upon Antonio to exact revenge in *Antonio's Revenge*, a Senecan revenge tragedy written very near the time Shakespeare composed *Hamlet*:

> Revenge my blood! Take spirit, gentle boy,
> Revenge my blood! (3.1.36–37)

Like Žižek's specter, who occupies a "mysterious intermediate domain," and M, who has been banished from Blades for a month, the ghost of Andrugio in Marston's play must wander before he can "touch / The banks of rest." King Hamlet and Kyd's ghost of Andrea are similarly made liminal, languishing uncertainly between life and eternal rest, the latter roving the underworld until brought to "serve for Chorus in this tragedy" by means "I wot not how—in twinkling of an eye" (1. Induction. 85). If the "domains" of these specters are mysterious, however, their commands to their charges are uncomplicated: take action in the name of justice against overwhelmingly powerful opponents.

In *You Only Live Twice,* a desperate mission that calls upon 007's patriotism—his duty, his debt—is thus analogous to that of most Elizabethan avengers inflected by a personal desire for revenge and instantiated by a spectral hailing or call to action. Such a hailing, I should add, amounts to less an Althusserian interpellation than a kind of Deleuzean confirmation of the merging of filiation and inscription, which then produces a recoding of Bond's desire. That is, expanding upon Eco's parallel between Fleming and Shakespeare, filial obligation—and I am hardly alone in suggesting this relationship between M and Bond[10]— almost always signals duty or indebtedness in both. Much the same might be said about the familial basis upon which most revenge plays are based. After his father's death, Hamlet, for example, is "Bound in filial obligation for some term / To do obsequious sorrow" (1.2.91–92), or so his uncle advises him; for the reformed Prince Hal in *2 Henry IV,* "filial tenderness" amounts to a "due" he will "pay" his ailing father "plenteously" (4.5.38–39). Like Hamlet, 007 is called upon to act, and the survival of the nation hangs in the balance. The "impossibility" of the mission—Deleuze and Guattari wonder, "Is that not the nature of desire, that one desires the impossible?" (*Anti-Oedipus* 162)—stokes Bond's "desiring machine," which lacks only appropriate direction (or recoding). To give both M and Sir James Molony their due, the project of avenging himself upon Blofeld proves more successful in curing Bond than regaining "his manhood" by "having a woman" (19). The two possibilities are braided together throughout: virility and death, Eros and Thanatos. For one temporary effect Bond suffers after avenging himself upon Blofeld in *You Only Live Twice* is impotence that, thanks to Kissy Suzuki's ministrations, is eventually cured. But Bond's potency can only be restored after revenge is exacted, and the desire for revenge has to be rechanneled as well into a larger, more nationalist project.

Equally important, in this trilogy Bond *is* Britain, and throughout the novels Britain is as diminished as he is. Jeremy Black regards the "shift from SMERSH to SPECTRE" as evidence of a "surrender to fantasy occasioned, in part, by the decline of the British Empire" (50), and the later Bond novels bear this out. "England is a sick nation by any standards" (194), Blofeld snarls to Bond in *You Only Live Twice,* a more direct characterization than M's when earlier explaining the mission to Japan: America is "worried about our security. Can't blame them" (26). This concern over security, occasioned in part by the defection of British intelligence officers in the early 1950s, some of them notoriously homosexual, merges with a sense that post–World War II Britain had declined precipitously, one reason for the empaneling of the Wolfenden Committee in 1954 to study British law insofar as homosexuality and prostitution were concerned. *The Wolfenden Report,* published in 1957 and the catalyst for acrimonious debate because of its largely liberal recommendations, was opposed by conservative Parliamentarians who lobbied against relaxation of the laws restricting homosexual intimacy, viewing the report as a threat to the family, "moral fibre," and "physique of the nation."[11] While Bond's sexual dalliances scarcely uphold a monogamous procreative ideal—one reason why conservatives attacked Fleming and Bond as immoral—his heterosexual potency nonetheless remained central to the novels from the beginning and was often projected upon a detumescent nation of diminished vitality. For if it wasn't weakened or "sick," England was like Bond immediately after his revenge of Tracy's murder or after Le Chiffre's torture in *Casino Royale:* impotent, powerless. Doctor No extends this very point to political power at the dinner table to 007 and Honeychile Rider, hinting at the potency of terrorism: "You talk of kings and presidents. How much power do they possess? . . . Who in the world has the power of life and death over his people?" Then, he arrogantly answers his own question. He wields such power through "privacy. Through the fact that nobody knows. Through the fact that I have to account to no one" (131).

Given the terms developed in *You Only Live Twice* and witnessed today in the tactics of contemporary terrorism, Doctor No seems only half correct in this assertion. To be sure, stealth or "privacy" is important, but so too are a quite particular definition of honor and its demand for self-sacrifice in Eastern culture. Speaking to Bond about Americans living in Japan, Tanaka observes that they "enjoy the remaining strict patterns of our life," patterns that both provide them with an "underlying hint of deep meaning" in Japanese culture and starkly oppose the "chaos that reigns in America" (60). Honor, self-sacrifice, and death constitute expressions of this deeper meaning, for "[t]here is no apology more sincere than the offering up of your own life. It is literally all you have to give" (73). Bond rejoins this thesis with the contention that suicide is "dishonourable," even "cowardly—a refusal to stand up to reverses, to life" (73). More than this, he argues, suicide is merely a "form of hysteria" and a sign that the Japanese "hold" life—their own and others'—"cheaply" (73). Tanaka disagrees. As he explains to Bond, although suicide is vulgarly understood by the West as *hara-kiri* or "belly-cutting," it might more properly be regarded as *seppuku,* an honorable expiation of guilt or negligence memorialized by the reverence of pilgrims. Blofeld understands this, as his Garden of Death is visited—and used by Japanese travelers—as if it were a shrine. Bond, in this scene standing in for British and Western culture more generally, is incapable of recognizing this sign of "deep" cultural meaning, as these religious connotations of suicide are utterly foreign to him. "To be or not to be," in short, remains a question in this dispute: "Whether 'tis nobler in the mind to suffer / The slings and arrows of outrageous fortune," or to risk violation of God's "canon 'gainst self-slaughter" (*Hamlet* 3.1.57–58; 1.2.132) remains a crucial question in the novel. Can self-sacrifice in the name of the deeper meaning to which Tanaka alludes be transposed slightly into the contemporary register of suicide bombings and their redress of the wrongs Hamlet lists: "Th' oppressor's wrong, the proud man's contumely / The pangs of despis'd love, the law's delay" (3.1.71–72) and so on?

All of this returns me to the title of this essay, my epigraph from Eco, and comparisons between the "Blofeld trilogy," al-Qaeda and Osama bin Laden, and the conventions of such revenge tragedies as *Hamlet.* Restated, my claims are that Fleming uncannily anticipates the contemporary state of global terrorism in both strategy and representation; and that Shakespeare's *Hamlet,* a play he consciously invokes in *You Only Live Twice,* constitutes both an apt figure of his design for the trilogy *and* a metaphor for his characterization of a postwar West. Again, perhaps most important, besides braiding together such issues as sexual and national power in the "Blofeld trilogy," Fleming introduces the spectral as a definitive trope in the representation of international terrorism. The trope as conceived by Derrida and his valorization of the specter's vision are anticipated in *Doctor No* by No's privileging both of sight and "privacy." In this way, Fleming's Cold War West and the forces bent upon destroying it find counterparts in our own times and resemble our own structure of feeling in telling ways.

Let's take these claims one at a time, beginning with Fleming's his-

Donald Pleasence as Blofeld in *You Only Live Twice* (1967).

tory of Blofeld and SPECTRE, a multinational organization composed of six cells of three, every man of whom, an expert in conspiracy and "secret communication," possessed a "solid cover," a resolute "cleanliness after a lifetime in big crime" (*Thunderball* 49–50). Cleanliness, a motif in the chapter in *Thunderball* entitled "SPECTRE," might be redacted to connote "purity" or austerity, as reflected in the deportment of its leader. For unlike Bond and Emilio Largo, Blofeld refrains from drinking, smoking, and sexual intimacy and, while not demanding such abstemiousness from others, does enforce a strict, if perverse, code of behavior. When one of his confederates takes sexual liberties with a girl SPECTRE had kidnapped and held for ransom, Blofeld returns half of the money to her parents with a note of apology, delivers a homily on self-discipline, and electrocutes the offender. Blofeld is also a model of industry who inspires reverence from his colleagues. Born in Gdynia of a Polish father and Greek mother, he studied engineering and radionics in Warsaw, where he grew convinced that "fast and accurate communication lay, in a contracting world, at the very heart of power" (44). Before founding SPECTRE, he created networks specializing in espionage, communications, and surveillance, winning decorations during World War II for what amounted to having "plumped for the Allies" by "selling his wares" (47). In the process, he excised information about his birth from the Gdynia registry, obtained a phony passport, and traveled under an assumed name.

By the time of the second installation of the trilogy, *On Her Majesty's Secret Service*, Blofeld pursues the ruse that he was descended from an aristocratic family, employing the British College of Arms to verify his claim. His shrewd investments have afforded him sufficient capital to

buy a pedigree, and his plan to destroy the British economy by conveying bacterial agents into agricultural areas promises to enhance his
wealth. Of particular interest to my thesis, not surprisingly, is the chapter
"Something Called 'BW,' " in which the effects of biological and chemical
agents including anthrax, smallpox, and botulism are outlined. An official from the Ministry of Agriculture explains a reality of which we are
all, by now, acutely aware (and one Bond confronts in such post-Fleming
"continuation" novels as Raymond Benson's *The Facts of Death* [1998]).
While marchers protest the development of nuclear weapons, the official
observes, biological agents pose an even greater danger. Why? Because
they are "very adaptable for covert or undercover operations. . . . The fact
that these agents are so concentrated, cannot be detected by physical
senses, and have a delayed casualty effect, would enable an operator
quietly to introduce effective amounts into building ventilation systems,
food and water supplies, and other places where they would be spread
rapidly through contact with a heavily concentrated population" (207).
Such a prediction, juxtaposed to the panic over anthrax after 9/11
and terrorist threats to the ventilation systems of high-rise apartment
buildings, resonates more ominously now than it might have just a few
years ago.

All of this suggests the applicability of two comments Sven Lindquist
makes in *A History of Bombing* (2000): first, that the "conventional, large-
scale war is on its deathbed," a diagnosis not to be celebrated, as this
passing will only produce "new forms of warfare"; and, second, referring
to the Gulf War of 1990–91, that while "selling weapons for years to Iraq
for its rearmament," Britain and America knew "perfectly well that Iraq
considered Kuwait an Iraqi province," that it was ruled by "a harsh
dictatorship that waged war on its own citizens," and that it posed "a
threat to Israel" (173–74). Twelve years later, a smaller coalition would
return to Iraq to destroy some of the very weapons with which they had
armed it, and then languish in the quagmire that has been the inevitable
result. To take up the former point, one of the "new forms" warfare has
taken is often described as "low intensity warfare," the definition of
which for Noam Chomsky eerily resembles that of terrorism: "the use of
coercive means aimed at civilian populations in an effort to achieve
political, religious, or other aims" (57). Blofeld's plan to ruin the British
economy in *On Her Majesty's Secret Service* illustrates this point, as what
could more clearly epitomize an assault on a civilian population than the
ruination of its food supply, starting with the contamination of turkeys
at Christmastime? In this regard, Slavoj Žižek's purchase on the tactics of

contemporary terror seems more potentially horrifying: namely, that the attacks on the WTC constituted "the last spectacular cry" of a twentieth-century warfare that was irreducibly materialist. Worse times lie ahead:

> What awaits us is something much more uncanny: the spectre of an "immaterial" war where the attack is invisible—viruses, poisons, which can be anywhere and nowhere. On the level of visible reality, nothing happens, no big explosions; yet the known universe starts to collapse, life disintegrates.[12]

Like Derrida, Žižek is no more able to avoid the metaphor of a specter than Fleming is in describing such threats not merely to Western hegemony, but to the quotidian realities of American, Brits, Israelis, Palestinians, and others. Given Blofeld's schemes in *On Her Majesty's Secret Service*, these threats extend even to the menus of holiday dinners.

Žižek's characterization of a spectral terrorism capable of launching attacks "anywhere and nowhere" at the same time coincides with Derrida's specter and Elizabethan figures of revenge: both are simultaneously present and not-present, always hovering nearby, watching and poised to act—or not. Here terror *itself* collapses into the terrorist *himself*, or more recently *herself*, method becoming entity or essence as the material becomes the immaterial. Chomsky, however unwittingly, makes a similar point in his reluctance even to employ the name al-Qaeda, opting instead for the phrase "bin Laden network," a powerful terrorist force "so lacking in hierarchical structure and so dispersed throughout much of the world as to have become largely impenetrable" (36). However compelling the observation, an oxymoronic quality obtains in Chomsky's phraseology: on the one hand, a "network" replaces responsible parties with an anonymous circuitry of power, much as boards of directors in late capitalism replace individual industrialists; on the other hand, this potentially anonymous and dispersed force is nonetheless identified with a single man, Osama bin Laden. One might object that such a reduction does not exist in Fleming's fiction, as Blofeld's SPECTRE is irreducibly hierarchical, hence vulnerable, while in this formulation Osama's network is not. Perhaps, although one might recall that the rotating number system SPECTRE employs, one that allows its operatives to switch positions regularly, renders this hierarchy more fluid, more difficult to detect. Moreover, Fleming's narrators often work hard to project Blofeld directly toward the invisibility of the Žižekian specter. In *On Her Majesty's Secret Service*, for example, Bond is frustrated by his inability to uncover anything about Blofeld, blaming his ignorance largely on the uncooperative nature of Swiss intelligence. But more than bureaucratic inefficiency or obstinance may be at issue:

> Their "friends" in Zürich were continuing to prove obtuse, or more probably, obstinate. There was no trace of any man ... called Blofeld in the whole of Switzerland. Nor was there any evidence of the existence of a reborn SPECTRE on Swiss soil. (52)

Hierarchically organized or not, SPECTRE often proves as dispersed and impenetrable—as spectral—as today's terrorist "networks."

This point might be converted to illuminate further resemblances between Fleming's SPECTRE and terrorists in our own times. To begin, Blofeld's ruthlessness extends to the murder of his own people to further his cause, perhaps one reason why he and Osama bin Laden are often allegorized as Satanic, incarnations of an "ultimate evil" (Chomsky's phrase). Numerous biographical parallels also exist between Blofeld and Osama. For example, like Blofeld—indeed, like Bond himself—Osama is the product of a mixed marriage: his father was a Yemeni immigrant to Saudi Arabia, an engineer and architect; his mother a Syrian. Osama, as Simon Reeve stresses, was not always a "raging Islamic fundamentalist" (159); in the early 1970s, while living in Beirut, he could be found drinking and "serial" womanizing before joining the Muslim Brotherhood at College. Reeve even suggests that Osama's conversion to fundamentalism was a refutation not only of his own decadent past, but of the jet-setting "playboy lifestyle" of his older brother Salim. Salim bin Laden —tall, muscular, fond of well-tailored Western suits, and the obvious successor to the billion-dollar family construction business—cast a shadow too large for Osama to overcome. Much like Blofeld's self-imposed abstemiousness, Osama's self-fashioning repudiates the Bond/*Playboy* lifestyle vilified in Christian attacks on Fleming like the Reverend Lycurgus Starkey's book *James Bond's World of Values* (1966). (As James Chapman reminds us in his essay, *Casino Royale,* the first Bond novel, was published in the same year that the first issue of *Playboy* appeared. Quite obviously, the connection between 007 and *Playboy* manifests itself in various ways in the Bond corpus, as Patrick O'Donnell outlines earlier in this volume.)

But the self-imposed austerity and mixed heritage of both terrorists mark just the beginning of more serious economic and political parallels between this pair. Like Blofeld, the recipient of several "decorations and citations from the British, Americans, and French" after World War II (*Thunderball* 47), Osama was once considered an ally of the West, which during Ronald Reagan's administration armed him with Stinger missiles and other basic weapons to battle the Soviets in Afghanistan. And, most obviously, like Blofeld, Osama bin Laden has used his "genius"—not to mention a large inheritance—to amass a private fortune sufficient to carry out his projects. Blofeld's pre-SPECTRE activities allowed him to "widen his market" for communications services before establishing his "private enterprise for private profit" (50), and the biological war he threatens in *On Her Majesty's Secret Service* is accurately characterized by Bond as an "economic weapon" which will cause British currency to drop "through the floor—and the country with it" (210). Bin Laden similarly understands the utility of agricultural products as economic weapons. By cornering the market in the production of Sudanese gum arabic, which prevents ingredients from settling at the bottoms of cans and bottles, he might profit "every time someone buys an American soft drink" (Reeve 179). Reeve also speculates that the exportation of sesame seeds affords bin Laden both substantial profit and a legitimate cover for trafficking in arms.

Such gross materialism—Žižek in one version of *Welcome to the Desert of the Real* (2002) regards Blofeld as representing capitalism's inherent excess—is complicated by the mythic and religious self-fashioning of both Fleming's villain and America's arch-enemy. That is to say, both proclaim their heritage with ancient, in some ways venerated, warriors: Blofeld regards himself as a "latter-day *samurai*" (*Live Twice* 191), Bin Laden and his associates as holy warriors or soldiers of Allah—mujaheddin. But more than martial prowess or religious arrogations are at work here. I want to return to Doctor No's explanation of the source of his power and to one other boast he makes while tapping his contact lenses with his steel claws: "These," said Doctor No, "see everything" (158). Similarly, Blofeld's eyes, "deep black pools surrounded—totally surrounded as Mussolini's were—by very clear whites" exert extraordinary power. Constantly roving in acute analysis, they "stripped the guilty of the false and made him feel transparent" (*Thunderball* 47). Blofeld's gaze, Fleming's narrator confides, is "microscopic" and always turned on—in secret—watching with "a focus that had been sharpened by thirty years of danger" (48). In this way SPECTRE and Blofeld most resemble the force Derrida describes in *Specters of Marx*. For Derrida, speaking of the ghost of Hamlet's father, this "spectral *someone other looks at us* [his emphasis], we feel ourselves being looked at by it" (7); at the same time, paradoxically, "one does not [always] know if it is living or if it is dead": "*It is* something that one does not know, precisely, and one does not know if precisely it *is,* if it exists" (6). In this respect, Derrida's ghost corresponds exactly with Žižek's specter, whose voice is "neither dead or alive; its primordial phenomenological status is rather that of the living dead" ("'I Hear You'" 103). The spectral is a thing "that looks at us," he reiterates, and because of the "the visor effect"—the effect of the helmet King Hamlet wears that covers his face—"we do not see who looks at us." The spectral is secret and anterior to our gaze: it sees us first, but we are not precisely sure who it is and where it is. This "thing," as Derrida describes it, simply "is": watching, hovering nearby. Similarly, to invoke the title and cover of Bill Maher's sharply ironic political tract *When You Ride ALONE You Ride with bin Laden* (2002), the West's current enemy is always nearby, in this specific instance in the passenger's seat right next to you, although you cannot see him. It is the specter of a SPECTRE, in other words, the threat posed by eyes constantly assessing the vulnerability of America's airports, power plants, bridges, waterways, and tunnels, that now defines our structure of feeling and marks yet another parallel between international tensions today and Fleming's "Blofeld trilogy."

The analogy between *Hamlet* and Fleming's fiction is obviously an imperfect one, but it consists of more than a comparison of apparitions—or "spooks." To succumb momentarily to the intentional fallacy and recall Eco's invocation of Shakespearean evil, Fleming clearly had *Hamlet* in mind in staging the confrontation between Bond and Blofeld in *You Only Live Twice.* Borrowing the thesis of Christoph Lindner's essay, "size" does indeed matter in this final showdown, as Fleming not only compares Blofeld to Hitler, as he had in *Thunderball,* but adds grandeur to the scene by comparing the eventual encounter between Blofeld and Bond to those in the Elizabethan revenge play, Wagnerian opera, and *Kabuki* theater. The most overt parallel between *You Only Live Twice* and *Hamlet* is Blofeld's boast that he provides a solution to the problem of "whether to be or not to be" (217). But there is more. Earlier, in Bond's first view of Blofeld in the Garden of Death, the latter appears much as King Hamlet does by being attired in full armor. In Act One of Shakespeare's play, Horatio reports seeing "A figure like your father, / Armèd at point exactly, cap-a-pe" (1.2.199–200), and in this instance King Hamlet's "beaver" or visor was up, allowing Horatio to see his face. By contrast, Blofeld's face is initially concealed by his visor, much as King Hamlet's is later in Act One when summoning his son to action. The specter "beckons" or waves to Hamlet three times, urging him to follow, and finally identifies himself as "thy father's spirit," an identification Horatio did not require earlier:

> Hamlet: Then saw you not his face?
> Horatio: O, yes, my lord. He wore his beaver up. (1.2.229–30)

Like M calling for Bond on the telephone earlier in *You Only Live Twice*, King Hamlet beckons his son as a disembodied voice. In Fleming's novel, however, the armored, initially faceless Blofeld is here not summoning him to an act of revenge, but rather serving as Bond's "prey," the object of his revenge. Yet, as Bond, in his "ghostly" black ninja uniform, awaits his confrontation with Blofeld, another parallel with Hamlet emerges. Bond is preoccupied, cursing his "fate"—an echo of "O cursèd spite / That ever I was born to set it right!" (1.5.188–89)—when a "small voice" whispers in his ear to take action immediately: "But don't you want to kill Blofeld? Don't you want to avenge Tracy?" (163). Admittedly, this self-recrimination and the delay that motivates it scarcely reach the scale of Hamlet's, but they are present nonetheless within a castle and a hellish Garden that provide a "true banquet of death" for its victims.

Consider also the parallels in plot structure between *Hamlet* and *You Only Live Twice*: a youngish man, out of shape and in deep mourning, is asked by a metonymical figure of the state—one diminished in power, perhaps even sinful or "rotten"—to perform a desperate mission that evolves into or serves as a cover for an act of revenge. The avenger—much as Linda Charnes reads *Hamlet*—is at the same time entrapped between "two fathers": one noble and one fallen into sin. The godlike King Hamlet compared to Claudius is akin to "Hyperion" juxtaposed to a "satyr"; yet, however noble, this godlike figure has also been "Cut off even in the blossoms of [his] sin" and sent to his reckoning "With all [his] imperfections on [his] head" (1.5; 76,79). M, in so many ways the paternal "good father" figure to Bond, sends him to his death in *You Only Live Twice*, where Blofeld is eager to complete the job, as is Claudius in Shakespeare's play. M, confined to his desk and a monotonous social life until Blades reopens, is at least not in such dire straits as King Hamlet, who is "Doomed for a certain time to walk the night / And for the day confined in fast fires" until his sins are purged (1.5.10–11). In this regard, he resembles his best-known precursor on the Elizabethan stage, the ghost of Don Andrea in Kyd's *The Spanish Tragedy*, who in the underworld was denied admission onto Charon's boat until his "funeral and obsequies were done" (1. Induction. 260); and they could not be deemed as "done" until Don Balthazar, the "author" of his death, is violently "deprived of life." Nor will Tracy's obsequies be completed until Blofeld is dead.

There isn't sufficient space here to do justice either to Charnes's deft reading of *Hamlet* and *film noir*—the avenger as detective—or to the psychoanalytic substrate of her argument. Still, a number of her observations about revenge tragedy and detective fiction, a cousin of Fleming's spy fiction, seem relevant. The emergence of the "obscene father," for example, who supplants the father living up to his "symbolic function" (Charnes 5), might be said to occur later in *You Only Live Twice* as Blofeld rises to the father who "knows." Threatening Blofeld with discovery after extricating himself at precisely the right moment from the seatless chair perched over a geyser that would have incinerated him, Bond warns him that "many people in London and Tokyo know" of his presence there. Blofeld is unmoved; he claims to "know the ways of officialdom," and if Blofeld's own presence were "known" to the authorities, police would have already been swarming his enclave (189). Further, Blofeld "happens to know" all about Tiger Tanaka and is confident he will make no extraordinary effort to save Bond; he has secured "certain information" and other facts that assure him of this (190). The obscene father who knows, like Claudius, will also kill the son—or try to. The obvious differences between *You Only Live Twice* and *Hamlet* include Kissy Suzuki's successful ministrations to her fallen "husband" in the novel's final chapter, and the fact that the son does not die *literally* in the act of avenging the wrong done to his family, although Bond doesn't know his own name at the end of the novel. And Blofeld, albeit bloodied and eventually suffocated, does not die in such spectacular a fashion as, say, Claudius, the evil brothers in John Webster's *The Duchess of Malfi*, or Tamora and her sons in Shakespeare's earlier revenge play *Titus Andronicus*. Nor does Bond, who ascends the balustrade and escapes from Blofeld's castle to the sea below.

Perhaps as much as British spy fiction or gangster novels, then, revenge tragedies like *Hamlet* inform *You Only Live Twice*. Before this novel, Fleming had introduced the motive of revenge in his fiction in M's desire to avenge the murders of an old friend and his wife, for example, in the short story "For Your Eyes Only" (1960). There, Bond found rationalization of the act of revenge fairly easy: it wouldn't be advisable for anyone to think England had grown "soft" and further, "[t]his is a case for rough justice—an eye for an eye" (47). Later in the story, Bond rationalizes his mission in terms more resonant after September 11:

> Bond argued to himself, these men were as much enemies of his coun-
> try as were the agents of SMERSH or of other enemy Secret Services.
> They had declared war and waged war against British people on British
> soil and they were currently planning another attack. (69)

The revenge tradition typically projects the avenger's desire onto larger
issues as well, offering religious or supernatural justifications or, as
Charnes suggests, national or political ones as well. And one wonders, to
extend the analogy between yesterday's fiction and today's headlines,
how the grisly conventions of revenge tragedy might be revisited in our
present war on terrorism: How much blood will be spilled? How many
more beheadings? And worse, if we can imagine such things?

Ghosts and Specters: For Your Eyes—and Ears—Only

> [Bond] had the impression that there was a crowd behind him at each elbow, and
> that faces were peering over his shoulder. . . . He somehow felt that the ghosts
> were friendly, that they approved of the rough justice that was about to be done.
> —Bond, poised to beat Hugo Drax in *Moonraker*

> Have you ever heard the Japanese expression *kirisute gomen*? . . . It dates from
> the time of the *samurai*. It means literally "killing and going away."
> —Blofeld, preparing to kill Bond in *You Only Live Twice*

The ghosts in *Hamlet* and *The Spanish Tragedy* share another
characteristic as well with Blofeld and Osama bin Laden: from their
mysterious places, on audiotapes or with chilling voices, they not only
order the murder of others and countenance the possibility of mass
murder, they also induce people to commit suicide for what they believe
are just causes against an essentially corrupt state. Like Blofeld, bin
Laden is even arrogant about the ease with which the battle might be
won. He is quoted as saying that after defeating the Soviets in Afghanistan, toppling America should prove much simpler. Yet, unlike the
kirisute gomen Blofeld defines in *You Only Live Twice* as a practice that
means "killing and going away" (213), Osama and specters kill and do
not go away. They feel themselves justified in lopping off the head of any
person who, in their estimation, fails to exhibit "proper respect" for
them. Ghosts, by stark contrast, are often "friendly" and usually stay
where they are supposed to, and when they don't, they may return in an
amicable fashion to view a few hands of bridge and lend their support to
the chastisement of a cheater like Hugo Drax. Specters and SPECTRE
never do. They are, by definition, ruthless and at some level unknowable.

Equally or even more dangerously, they may also understand or believe fervently in some version of Tiger Tanaka's lecture on honor, self-sacrifice, and the deep cultural meaning that inheres in both. They may beckon their sons and daughters to help restore their honor—or exact their revenge. And they may be dead. Or they may be watching with Doctor No's analytical gaze, probing and then striking. We just don't know.

These are some of the qualities inherent in the present moment and the structure of feeling I have been laboring to define. Out there somewhere, dead or alive, are invisible masterminds, geniuses like Blofeld, watching. We feel ourselves surveyed by them and by an administration prone to respond to surveillance with even more surveillance. On occasion, they call out in that frightening, disembodied voice Doctor No uses when ordering Dent to pick up a caged tarantula in the film version of the novel. Dent really doesn't want to pick up the spider, but he has no choice. He is terrified, knowing that he is being watched and, at the same time, is assailed by a voice coming from somewhere else. Unlike Osama, that voice doesn't overtly threaten Dent. Still, he knows. He feels the danger, and so do we. Every month or so, covers of *Time* and *Newsweek* exacerbate the feeling of dread, with masked terrorists peering directly at us; and our director of homeland security orders yet another state of heightened security. Every new audiotape, properly authenticated, of course, reminds us of what we would like to forget, yet cannot. That's what Fleming might tell us about a post-9/11 world—about its specters and structures of feeling.

NOTES

1. This information comes from Jack Garland, AP Press, "British Forces Use James Bond Code Names," *Seattle Post-Intelligencer*, March 31, 2003.

2. Mortimer Zuckerman, "Midnight for Baghdad," *U.S. News and World Report,* January 27–February 3, 2003, 76.

3. I am indebted to Dennis Allen for suggesting this reading of Iraq as melodramatic heroine.

4. In fact, Maher's comments were heard in the September 17, 2001, episode of his now-defunct ABC series *Politically Incorrect.* Comparing the 9/11 terrorists to those who lob cruise missiles "from 2,000 miles away," Maher observed, "Staying in the airplane when it hits the building, say what you want about it, it's not cowardly." Interviewing Maher for *Salon,* Jake Tapper dubs this the "quote that got him fired

from ABC" ("The Salon Interview: Bill Maher," www.salon. com/people/interview/
2002/12/11/maher/print).

5. Susan Sontag, "The Talk of the Town," *The New Yorker,* September 24, 2001, 32.

6. Almost all topics relating to *Thunderball,* the novel in which SPECTRE first
appears, are vexed ones, as is well-known by students of Fleming's works. The notion that Fleming "created" SPECTRE follows the historical argument Andrew Lycett makes in his biography that, regardless of Kevin McClory's insistence that he
first "suggested" that an international terrorist group ought to replace Russia and
SMERSH as Bond's adversaries, Fleming appears to have conceived of the idea two
months earlier. See Lycett, *Ian Fleming* 352–54.

7. See James Chapman, *Licence to Thrill: A Cultural History of the James Bond
Films,* p. 121. Chapman makes the salient point that "the different order" in which
these three novels were adapted for film "had significant implications for the continuity of the films." One might add that this disordering almost completely erases
the motive of revenge and Bond's near depression at the beginning of *You Only Live
Twice.*

8. This quotation comes from Johanna McGeary, "When No One Is Truly Safe,"
Time, December 1, 2003, 56.

9. I have borrowed this formulation from Linda Charnes, "Dismember Me:
Shakespeare, Paranoia, and the Logic of Mass Culture," *Shakespeare Quarterly* 48
(Spring 1997): 5.

10. At times in the later novels M's fatherly and repressive demeanor is signaled
in more comic ways than his lecture on lifestyle in the early pages of *Thunderball.* In
On Her Majesty's Secret Service, for example, M fusses with Bond about "qualities of
the Swiss," who at least "keep their trains clean and cope with the beatnik problem
[two very rampant bees in M's bonnet!]" (85). The narrator's aside about bees and
bonnets intimates the distance not only between son and father, but also between an
amused narrator and a kind of old-fashioned fuddy-duddy. More seriously—and
more Hamlet-like—Fleming in creating Bond may have been projecting onto his
hero the image of his father, which "he spent his life measuring up to and not quite
emulating" (Lycett 223).

11. See Frank Mort, "The Legal Regulation of Sexuality in the 1950's and '60's:
The Case of the Wolfenden Report." A typescript of this paper, presented at a conference on "Deviance and Social Control" at the University of Essex, December 1978,
may be found in the library of the Kinsey Institute on Sexuality and Reproduction.
This quotation is from p. 4.

12. See Slavoj Žižek, *Welcome to the Desert of the Real* (New York: Verso, 2002),
p. 37. I want to thank Christoph Lindner and Skip Willman for calling to my
attention an alternative version of this book that includes a short paragraph on
Blofeld as capitalist-industrialist. Žižek's point is well taken that few heroes are so
routinely given a tour of a factory before facing the machinations of an adversary; my
interests, however, more concern the very metaphors of immateriality he uses in
making this case.

ACKNOWLEDGMENTS

The conference from which these essays are taken was made possible through the generous support of the Arts and Humanities Institute of the College of Arts and Sciences, Indiana University, Kumble R. Subbaswamy, Dean, and Andrea Ciccarelli, Director of the Institute. Additional support was provided by the Ian Fleming Foundation, which also furnished vehicles for display during the meeting; Moya Andrews, Dean of the Faculties; and George Walker, Dean of Research at the University Graduate School at Indiana University. We thank in particular Doug Redenius, Michael van Blaricum, Raymond Benson, David Reinhardt, and Brad Frank from the Ian Fleming Foundation for their hard work on the symposium; and also Robert Laycock, Zoe Watkins, and Kate Grimond from Ian Fleming Publications for their enthusiasm for the event. We also owe special debts of gratitude to Andrew Lycett for his generous participation, and to Lee Pfeiffer of SPYGUISE productions for his sharing of materials for the film series connected to the conference, particularly in regard to the 1954 CBS television production of *Casino Royale*. We appreciate the cooperation of Danielle McClelland, director of the beautifully restored Buskirk-Chumley Theatre in downtown Bloomington, for hosting this film series.

Additional thanks go to Breon Mitchell and Joel Silver of the Lilly Library, which organized a magnificent exhibition of items from its Ian Fleming Collection; to Mary Morgan of IU Conferences, who made certain (as always!) that everything ran smoothly; to Matthew Scott Johnson, who designed a beautiful website; and to the many faculty and graduate students at Indiana who participated in what became an engaging three days of conversation. We also want to acknowledge the work of Caitlin Watt, who helped with the manuscript, and the enthusiastic support of Bob Sloan and Jane Quinet from Indiana University Press, who encouraged us from the start, long before the conference began.

Our greatest debt, of course, is owed to the conferees themselves, many of whom traveled long distances to attend: from Britain, Canada, and from across the United States. In addition to the authors whose work is included here, we also want to thank in particular Jeremy Black, Dan

Mills, Charles Helfenstein, Ian Borton, Cynthia Walker, Mark Best, James South, Ishay Landa, Brian Doan, De Witt Kilgore, David Halloran, David Higgins, Jill Hochman, Justus Nieland, and Katie McNamara. Thanks so much for making this a truly memorable event.

WORKS CITED

This bibliography includes, for the most part, references only to monographs, an-thologies, and scholarly essays and journal articles. For citations from most news-papers and popular periodicals—and from films—see the notes to individual essays.

Addison, Paul. "British Historians and the Debate over the 'Postwar Consensus.'" In *More Adventures with Britannia: Personalities, Politics, and Culture in Britain*, ed. William Roger Louis, 255–64. Austin: University of Texas Press, 1998.

Adorno, Theodor W. "Freudian Theory and the Pattern of Fascist Propaganda." In *The Essential Frankfurt School Reader*, ed. Andrew Arato and Eike Gebhardt, 118–37. New York: Urizen Books, 1978.

Amis, Kingsley. *The James Bond Dossier*. New York: New American Library, 1965.

Anderson, Benedict. *Imagined Communities: Reflections on the Origin and Spread of Nationalism*. London: Verso, 1983.

Appadurai, Arjun. *Modernity at Large: Cultural Dimensions of Globalization*. Public Worlds Series 1. Minneapolis: University of Minnesota Press, 1996.

Awkward, Michael. *Negotiating Difference: Race, Gender, and the Politics of Positionality*. Chicago: University of Chicago Press, 1995.

Barnes, Alan, and Marcus Hearn. *Kiss Kiss Bang! Bang! The Unofficial James Bond Film Companion*. London: BT Batsford, 1997.

Baron, Cynthia. "*Doctor No*: Bonding Britishness to Racial Sovereignty." *Spectator: The University of Southern California Journal of Film and Television Criticism* 14, no. 2 (1994): 68–81.

Baudrillard, Jean. *Simulations*. Translated by Paul Foss, Paul Patton, and Philip Beitchman. New York: Semiotext(e), 1983.

Benítez-Rojo, Antonio. *The Repeating Island: The Caribbean and the Postmodern Perspective*. Translated by James E. Maraniss. 2nd ed. Durham, N.C.: Duke University Press, 1996.

Benjamin, Walter. *Illuminations*. Translated by Harry Zohn. Edited by Hannah Arendt. New York: Schocken Books, 1968.

Bennett, Tony. *U203 Popular Culture: Unit 21*. Milton Keynes: Open University Press, 1982.

Bennett, Tony, and Janet Woollacott. *Bond and Beyond: The Political Career of a Popular Hero*. London: Macmillan, 1987.

Bergonzi, Bernard. "The Case of Mr Fleming." *The Twentieth Century*, March 1958, 220–28.

Black, Jeremy. *The Politics of James Bond: From Fleming's Novels to the Big Screen*. Westport, Conn., and London: Praeger, 2001.

Bond, Mary Wickham. *How 007 Got His Name*. London: Collins, 1966.

Booker, Christopher. *The Neophiliacs: A Study of Revolution in English Life in the Fifties and Sixties*. London: Collins, 1969.

Boyd, Ann S. *The Devil with James Bond!* Richmond, Va.: John Knox Press, 1967.

Braine, John. *Room at the Top*. London: Arrow, 1989.

Bright, Susie. *Sexual Reality: A Virtual Sex World Reader*. Pittsburgh: Cleis, 1992.

Butler, Judith. "Imitation and Gender Insubordination." In *The Lesbian and Gay*

Studies Reader, ed. Henry Abelove, Michele Barale, and David Halperin, 307–20. New York: Routledge, 1993.

Byers, Thomas. "Terminating the Postmodern: Masculinity and Phobia." *Modern Fiction Studies* 41, no. 1 (1995): 5–34.

Cannadine, David. "James Bond and the Decline of England." *Encounter* 53, no. 3 (1979): 46–55.

Carpenter, Rebecca. "Male Failure and Male Fantasy: British Masculine Mythologies of the 1950s, or Jimmy, Jim, and Bond. James Bond." *the minnesota review* 55–57 (2002): 187–201.

Carpentier, Alejo. "On the Marvelous Real in America." In *Magical Realism: Theory, History, Community,* ed. Lois Parkinson Zamora, 75–88. Durham, N.C.: Duke University Press, 1995.

Cawelti, John G. *Adventure, Mystery, and Romance: Formula Stories as Art and Popular Culture.* Chicago: University of Chicago Press, 1976.

Chapman, James. *Licence to Thrill: A Cultural History of the James Bond Films.* New York: Columbia University Press, 2000.

———. *Saints & Avengers: British Adventure Series of the 1960s.* London and New York: I. B. Tauris, 2002.

Charnes, Linda. "Dismember Me: Shakespeare, Paranoia, and the Logic of Mass Culture." *Shakespeare Quarterly* 48, no. 1 (1997): 1–16.

Chomsky, Noam. *9-11.* New York: Seven Stories Press, 2002.

Cleaver, Eldridge. *Soul on Ice.* New York: Delta Book, 1968.

Colby, William, and Peter Forbath. *Honorable Men: My Life in the CIA.* New York: Simon and Schuster, 1978.

Colley, Linda. *Britons: Forging the Nation 1707–1837.* London: Pimlico, 1994.

Colls, Robert. *Identity of England.* Oxford: Oxford University Press, 2002.

Cooper, Rence, and Chris Morris, eds. *Mr. Boston: Official Bartender's and Party Guide.* 64th ed. New York: Warner Books, 1994.

Cork, John, and Bruce Scivally. *James Bond: The Legacy.* New York: Harry N. Abrams, 2002.

D'Acci, Julie. "Nobody's Woman? Honey West and the New Sexuality." In *The Revolution Wasn't Televised: Sixties Television and Social Conflict,* ed. Lynn Spiegel and Michael Curtin, 73–93. New York: Routledge, 1997.

Dallek, Robert. *An Unfinished Life: John F. Kennedy, 1917–1963.* New York: Little, Brown, 2003.

Del Buono, Oreste, and Umberto Eco, eds. *The Bond Affair.* Translated by R. A. Downie. London: MacDonald, 1966.

Deleuze, Gilles. *Coldness and Cruelty.* In *Masochism,* by Leopold von Sacher-Masoch and Gilles Deleuze, 9–138. New York: Zone Books, 1991.

Deleuze, Gilles, and Félix Guattari. *Anti-Oedipus: Capitalism and Schizophrenia.* Translated by Robert Hurley, Mark Seem, and Helen R. Lane. Minneapolis: University of Minnesota Press, 1983.

———. *A Thousand Plateaus: Capitalism and Schizophrenia.* Translated by Brian Massumi. Minneapolis: University of Minnesota Press, 1987.

DeLillo, Don. *Libra.* New York: Penguin, 1988.

Denning, Michael. *Cover Stories: Narrative and Ideology in the British Spy Thriller.* London: Routledge & Kegan Paul, 1987.

———. "Licensed to Look: James Bond and the Heroism of Consumption." In *Contemporary Marxist Literary Criticism,* ed. Francis Mulhern, 211–29. London: Longmans, 1992.

Derrida, Jacques. *Specters of Marx: The State of Debt, the Work of Mourning, & the New International.* Translated by Peggy Kamuf. New York: Routledge, 1994.

Disch, Thomas M. *The Dreams Our Stuff Is Made Of.* New York: Touchstone, 1988.

Drummond, Lee. *American Dreamtime: A Cultural Analysis of Popular Movies and Their Implications for a Science of Humanity.* Lanham, Md.: Littlefield Adams, 1996.

Dulles, Allen W. Letter to Ian Fleming, April 24, 1963. Lilly Library, Bloomington, Indiana.

Durgnat, Raymond. *A Mirror for England: British Movies from Austerity to Affluence.* London: Faber and Faber, 1970.

Eagleton, Terry. *After Theory.* New York: Basic Books, 2003.

Early, Gerald. "Jungle Fever: Ian Fleming's James Bond Novels, the Cold War, and Jamaica." *New Letters* 66, no. 1 (1999): 139–63.

Eco, Umberto. *The Role of the Reader: Explorations in the Semiotics of Texts.* Bloomington: Indiana University Press, 1979.

Edelman. Lee. *Homographesis: Essays in Gay Literary and Cultural Theory.* New York: Routledge, 1994.

Eliot, T. S. "Tradition and the Individual Talent." In *Selected Prose of T. S. Eliot,* ed. Frank Kermode, 37–44. San Diego, Calif.: Harcourt Brace and Company, 1975.

Ewen, Stuart. *PR! A Social History of Spin.* New York: Basic Books, 1996.

Faderman, Lillian. *Odd Girls and Twilight Lovers: A History of Lesbian Life in Twentieth-Century America.* New York: Columbia University Press, 1991.

Fleming, Ian. *Casino Royale.* 1953. New York: Penguin, 2003.

———. *Diamonds Are Forever.* 1956. New York: Penguin, 2003.

———. *Doctor No.* 1958. New York: Penguin, 2002.

———. *For Your Eyes Only: Five Secret Exploits of James Bond.* 1960. New York: Penguin, 2003.

———. *From Russia with Love.* 1957. New York: Penguin, 2003.

———. *Goldfinger.* 1959. New York: Penguin, 2002.

———. "How to Write a Thriller." *Books and Bookmen,* May 1963, 14.

———. "If I Were Prime Minister." *The Spectator,* October 9, 1959, 466–67.

———. "Introducing Jamaica." In *Ian Fleming Introduces Jamaica,* ed. Morris Cargill, 11–21. New York: Hawthorn Books, 1965.

———. Letter to Robert Kennedy. June 20, 1962. L. Russell MSS. Lilly Library, Bloomington, Indiana.

———. *Live and Let Die.* 1954. New York: Penguin, 2003.

———. *The Man with the Golden Gun.* 1965. New York: Penguin, 2004.

———. *Moonraker.* 1955. New York: Penguin, 2003.

———. *On Her Majesty's Secret Service.* 1963. New York: Penguin, 2003.

———. *Thunderball.* 1961. New York: Penguin, 2003.

———. *Thrilling Cities.* 1959. New York: New American Library, 1964.

———. *You Only Live Twice.* 1964. New York: Penguin, 2003.

Freedman, Lawrence. *Kennedy's Wars: Berlin, Cuba, Laos, and Vietnam.* Oxford: Oxford University Press, 2000.

Freud, Sigmund. "Character and Anal Erotism." In *The Freud Reader,* ed. Peter Gay, 293–97. New York: W.W. Norton, 1989.

———. *The Ego and the Id.* Translated by Joan Riviere. Edited by James Strachey. New York: W.W. Norton, 1960.

———. *Group Psychology and the Analysis of the Ego.* Translated by James Strachey. New York: W.W. Norton, 1959.

———. "On Narcissism: An Introduction." In *The Freud Reader,* 545–61.

———. *Three Case Histories.* New York: Touchstone, 1996.

———. "Three Essays on the Theory of Sexuality." In *The Freud Reader,* 239–92.

———. *Totem and Taboo.* New York: W.W. Norton, 1950.

———. *The "Wolfman" and Other Case Studies.* Translated by Louise Adey Huish. New York: Penguin, 2002.

Gant, Richard. *Ian Fleming: The Man with the Golden Pen.* London: Mayflower-Dell, 1966.

Giroud, Mark. *The Return to Camelot: Chivalry and the English Gentleman.* New Haven, Conn.: Yale University Press, 1981.

Gubar, Susan. *Racechanges: White Skin, Black Face in American Culture.* New York: Oxford University Press, 1997.

Halberstam, Judith. "O Behave! Austin Powers and the Drag Kings." *GLQ* 7, no. 3 (2001): 425–52.

Hamer, Emily. *Britannia's Glory: A History of Twentieth-Century Lesbians.* London: Cassell, 1996.

Haraway, Donna. *Simians, Cyborgs, and Women: The Reinvention of Nature.* New York: Routledge, 1991.

Hebdige, Dick. *Subculture: The Meaning of Style.* London: Routledge, 1991.

Heffer, Simon. *Nor Shall My Sword: The Reinvention of England.* London: Wiedenfeld and Nicolson, 1999.

Heinlein, Robert. *The Puppet Masters.* New York: Signet, 1951.

Hellman, John. *The Kennedy Obsession: The American Myth of JFK.* New York: Columbia University Press, 1997.

Hersh, Burton. *The Old Boys: The American Elite and the Origins of the CIA.* New York: Scribner's, 1992.

Hersh, Seymour M. *The Dark Side of Camelot.* New York: Little, Brown, 1997.

Hewison, Robert. *In Anger: Culture and the Cold War 1945–60.* London: Wiedenfeld and Nicolson, 1981.

Hilferding, Rudolf. *Finance Capital: A Study of the Latest Phase of Capitalist Development.* Edited by Tom Bottomore. London: Routledge & Kegan Paul, 1981.

Hoggart, Richard. *The Uses of Literacy.* London: Penguin, 1958.

Horkheimer, Max, and Theodor W. Adorno. *Dialectic of Enlightenment.* New York: Continuum, 1996.

Hyde, H. Montgomery. *Room 3603: The Incredible True Story of Secret Intelligence Operations during World War II.* 1962. New York: Lyons Press, 2001.

Investigation of the Assassination of President John F. Kennedy: Hearings before the President's Commission on the Assassination of President Kennedy, Exhibits 1054 to 1512, Volume XXII. Washington: US GPO, 1964.

Iriye, Akira. "Culture and International History." In *Explaining the History of American Foreign Relations,* ed. Michael J. Hogan and Thomas G. Paterson. Cambridge: Cambridge University Press, 1991.

———. "Culture and Power: International Relations as Intercultural Relations." *Diplomatic History* 3 (Spring 1979): 115–28.

Jacobs, H. P. "Dialect, Magic and Religion." In *Ian Fleming Introduces Jamaica,* ed. Morris Cargill, 79–102. New York: Hawthorn Books, 1965.

Jaffe, Aaron. *Modernism and the Culture of Celebrity.* Cambridge: Cambridge University Press, 2005.

Jakes, Ian. *Theoretical Approaches to Obsessive-Compulsive Disorder.* Cambridge: Cambridge University Press, 1996.

Katz, Jonathan Ned. *The Invention of Heterosexuality.* New York: Plume, 1996.

Kennedy, John F. *Profiles in Courage.* 1956. New York: Perennial Classics, 2000.

Kennedy, Robert. Letter to Ian Fleming. June 1, 1962. L. Russell MSS. Lilly Library, Bloomington, Indiana.

Keohane, Robert O., and Joseph S. Nye. "Introduction." In *Governance in a Globalizing World,* ed. Joseph S. Nye and John D. Donahue, 1–12. Washington, D.C.: Brookings Institution Press, 2000.

——. *Power and Interdependence: World Politics in Transition.* Boston: Addison-Wesley, 2000.

Kyriazi, Paul. *How to Live the James Bond Lifestyle.* Ronin Audio Books, 1999.

Lacan, Jacques. *Écrits.* Translated by Alan Sheridan. New York: Norton, 1977.

——. *The Four Fundamental Concepts of Psychoanalysis.* Translated by Alan Sheridan. New York: Norton, 1981.

Lane, Sheldon, ed. *For Bond Lovers Only.* London: Panther, 1996.

Ledenson, Elizabeth. "Lovely Lesbians; or, Pussy Galore." *GLQ* 7, no. 3 (2001): 417–23.

Lewis, Wyndham. "Mr. Wyndham Lewis: Personal Appearance Artist." In *Men Without Art,* ed. Seamus Cooney, 95–105. Santa Rosa: Black Sparrow Press, 1987.

Lindner, Christoph. *The James Bond Phenomenon: A Critical Reader.* Manchester: Manchester University Press, 2003.

Lindquist, Sven. *A History of Bombing.* Translated by Linda Haverty Rugg. New York: The New Press, 2000.

Lycett, Andrew. *Ian Fleming: The Man behind James Bond.* Atlanta: Turner Publishing, 1995.

——. "Lesbians and 007: A License to Deconstruct." *The Times,* June 8, 2003, sec. 3.8, 8.

Marwick, Arthur. *British Society since 1945.* 3rd ed. Harmondsworth: Penguin, 1996.

McCallum, E. L. *Object Lessons: How to Do Things with Fetishism.* Albany: State University of New York Press, 1999.

McLachlan, Donald. *Room 39: A Study in Naval Intelligence.* New York: Atheneum, 1968.

McLuhan, Marshall. *Understanding the Media.* New York: Signet, 1964.

Miller, Jeffrey S. *Something Completely Different: British Television and American Culture.* Minneapolis: University of Minnesota Press, 2000.

Miller, Toby. "James Bond's Penis." In *The James Bond Phenomenon: A Critical Reader,* ed. Christoph Lindner, 232–47. Manchester: Manchester University Press, 2003.

Moniot, Drew. "James Bond and America in the Sixties: An Investigation of the Formula Film in Popular Culture." *Journal of the University Film Association* 28, no. 3 (1976): 25–33.

Morgan, Kenneth. *The People's Peace: British History 1945–1990.* Oxford: Oxford University Press, 1990.

Morrison, Blake. *The Movement: English Poetry and Fiction of the 1950s.* Oxford: Oxford University Press, 1980.

Nadel, Alan. *Containment Culture: American Narratives, Postmodernism, and the Atomic Age.* Durham, N.C.: Duke University Press, 1995.

Nestle, Joan. *A Restricted Country.* Ithaca, N.Y.: Firebrand Books, 1987.

Nguyen, Cam Nguyet. "Z.28 and the Appeal of Spy Fiction in Southern Vietnam, 1954–1975." M.A. thesis, University of California-Berkeley, 2013.

Nichols, Lewis. "In and Out of Books." *New York Times Book Review,* April 1, 1962, 8.

——. "In and Out of Books." *New York Times Book Review,* December 15, 1963, 8.

O'Connor, William Van. "Two Types of 'Heroes' in Post-War British Fiction." *PMLA* 77, no. 1 (1962): 168–74.

O'Donnell, Patrick. *Latent Destinies: Cultural Paranoia in Contemporary U.S. Fiction.* Durham, N.C.: Duke University Press, 2000.

Palmer, Jerry. *Thriller: Genesis and Structure of a Popular Genre.* London: Edward Arnold, 1978.

Paxman, Jeremy. *The English: A Portrait of a People.* London: Michael Joseph, 1998.

Pearson, John. *The Life of Ian Fleming.* New York: McGraw-Hill, 1966.

Perkin, Harold. *The Rise of Professional Society: England since 1880.* New York: Routledge, 1989.

Price, James. "Our Man in the Torture Chamber: The Novels of Ian Fleming." *The London Magazine,* July 1962, 67–70.

Pritchett, V. S. "These Writers Couldn't Care Less." *The New York Times Review of Books,* April 28, 1957, 1.

Proledge, Fred. "Clues to Oswald Traced in Books: He Borrowed Library Texts on Kennedy, Communists, and Huey Long Slaying." *New York Times,* November 28, 1963, 1, 23.

Puzo, Mario. *The Godfather.* New York: Putnam, 1969.

Reeve, Simon. *The New Jackals: Ramzi Yousef, Osama bin Laden and the Future of Terrorism.* Boston: Northeastern University Press, 1999.

Richards, Jeffrey. *Films and the British National Identity: From Dickens to Dad's Army.* Manchester: Manchester University Press, 1997.

Riebling, Mark. *Wedge: From Pearl Harbor to 9/11: How the Secret War between the FBI and CIA Has Endangered National Security.* New York: Touchstone, 2002.

Rock, Paul, and Stanley Cohen. "The Teddy Boy." In *The Age of Affluence 1951–1964,* ed. Vernon Bogdanor and Robert Skidelsky, 288–320. London: Macmillan, 1970.

Roof, Judith. *A Lure of Knowledge: Lesbian Sexuality and Theory.* New York: Columbia University Press, 1991.

Rosendorf, Neal M. "Social and Cultural Globalization: Concepts, History, and America's Role." In *Governance in a Globalizing World,* ed. Joseph S. Nye and John D. Donahue, 109–34. Washington, D.C.: Brookings Institution Press, 2000.

The Rough Guide to James Bond. New York: Penguin, 2002.

Rubin, Gayle. "Thinking Sex: Notes for a Radical Theory of the Politics of Sexuality." In *Pleasure and Danger: Exploring Female Sexuality,* ed. Carol S. Vance, 267–319. Boston: Routledge and Kegan Paul, 1984.

Russo, Vito. *The Celluloid Closet: Homosexuality in the Movies.* New York: Harper and Row, 1987.

Sauerberg, Lars Ole. *Secret Agents in Fiction: Ian Fleming, John le Carré, and Len Deighton.* London: Macmillan, 1984.

Schwartz, Richard A. *Cold War Culture: Media and the Arts, 1945–1990.* New York: Facts on File, 1998.

Sidey, Hugh. "The President's Voracious Reading Habits." *Life,* March 17, 1961, 55–56, 59–60.

Starkey, Jr., Lycurgus M. *James Bond's World of Values.* Nashville: Abingdon Press, 1966.

Stevenson, William. *A Man Called Intrepid.* New York: HBJ, 1976.

Street, Sarah. *British National Cinema.* London: Routledge, 1997.

———. *Transatlantic Crossings: British Feature Films in the USA.* London: Continuum, 2002.

Sutherland, John. *Fiction and the Fiction Industry.* London: Athlone, 1978.

Sword, Helen. *Ghostwriting Modernism.* Ithaca: Cornell University Press, 2002.

Thomas, Evan. *Robert Kennedy: His Life.* New York: Touchstone, 2000.

———. *The Very Best Men: The Early Years of the CIA.* New York: Simon and Schuster, 1995.

Usborne, Richard. *Clubland Heroes: A Nostalgic Study of Some Recurrent Characters in the Romantic Fiction of Dornford Yates, John Buchan and Sapper.* London: Barrie and Jenkins, 1953.

Venturi, Robert, Denise Scott Brown, and Steven Izenour. *Learning from Las Vegas: The Forgotten Symbolism of Architectural Form.* Cambridge, Mass.: MIT Press, 1977.

Walton, John K., ed. *Relocating Britishness.* Manchester: Manchester University Press, 2003.

Watson, Colin. *Snobbery with Violence: English Crime Stories and their Audience.* London: Methuen, 1973.

Weight, Richard. *Patriots: National Identity in Britain 1940–2000.* London: Macmillan, 2002.

White, Mark J., ed. *The Kennedys and Cuba: The Declassified Documentary History.* Chicago: Ivan R. Dee, 1999.

Williams, Raymond. *Marxism and Literature.* New York: Oxford University Press, 1977.

———. *The Year 2000.* New York: Pantheon, 1984.

Wills, Gary. *The Kennedy Imprisonment: A Meditation on Power.* 1981. Boston: Houghton Mifflin, 2002.

Wolfe, Tom. *The Right Stuff.* New York: Bantam, 1979.

Žižek, Slavoj. " 'I Hear You with My Eyes'; or, The Invisible Master." In *Gaze and Voice as Love Objects,* ed. Reneta Salecl and Slavoj Žižek, 90–126. Durham, N.C.: Duke University Press, 1996.

———. *The Sublime Object of Ideology.* New York: Verso, 1989.

———. *Welcome to the Desert of the Real.* New York: The Wooster Press, 2001, and New York: Verso, 2002.

Zupancic, Alenka. *Ethics of the Real: Kant, Lacan.* London: Verso, 2000.

CONTRIBUTORS

ALEXIS ALBION is a Ph.D. candidate in International History at Harvard University and is completing a dissertation entitled "The Spy in All of Us: The Public Image of Intelligence in the 1960s," an Anglo-American study of the interaction between public perception and intelligence work in the sixties. She has presented her work at the Society for Historians of American Foreign Relations, the Institute for Contemporary British History (London), the Center for Cold War Studies at the University of California at Santa Barbara, and the Weatherhead Center for International Affairs at Harvard. She recently left the International Spy Museum in Washington, where she served as the museum's historian, and is a professional staff member on the National Commission on Terrorist Attacks Upon the United States (the 9-11 Commission).

DENNIS W. ALLEN teaches literary theory and Gay and Lesbian Studies at West Virginia University. He is the author of *Sexuality in Victorian Fiction* (1993) and articles on topics ranging from queer pedagogy to aesthetic activism in such journals as *Genders, Narrative,* and *Modern Fiction Studies.* He is currently working on a book on the impact of postindustrial capitalism on contemporary gay culture. His favorite Bond is Sean Connery.

JAMES CHAPMAN is Senior Lecturer in Film and Television History at the Open University. He has wide-ranging research interests in British cultural history, especially cinema and popular television genres. His books include *The British at War: Cinema, State and Propaganda, 1939–1945* (1998), *Licence to Thrill: A Cultural History of the James Bond Films* (1999), and *Saints and Avengers: British Adventure Series of the 1960s* (2002). His next book, *Past and Present: National Identity and the British Historical Film,* is forthcoming in 2005. He saw his first Bond film, *The Spy Who Loved Me,* at the Odeon cinema, St. Peter Port, Guernsey, on a family holiday in 1977 and began reading Bond novels on another holiday in 1979 at the age of ten. His favorite Bond novel and film is *On Her Majesty's Secret Service.*

EDWARD P. COMENTALE is Assistant Professor of English and teaches modernism, the avant-garde, and critical theory at Indiana University in Bloomington. He is also the founder and leader of an interdisciplinary study group called The Modernist Exchange. He has published several articles on issues relating to modernism in journals such as *Modernism/Modernity* and *The International Review of Modernism,* and his work on D. H. Lawrence and Wyndham Lewis appeared in the inaugural issue of *Modernist Cultures.* He is the author of *Modernism, Cultural Production, and the British Avant-Garde* (2004) and co-editor of a forthcoming collection *T.E. Hulme and the Question of Modernism* (2005).

VIVIAN HALLORAN is Assistant Professor of Comparative Literature at Indiana University in Bloomington. Her primary research interest is Caribbean literature written in Spanish, English, and French. At present, she is completing a manuscript on the continuing popularity of historical novels about slavery in contemporary Caribbean and African literature. Her other interests include diaspora studies, postmodern literature, popular culture, and ethnic memoirs and autobiographies. She has published work and presented scholarly papers on the persistence of memory in the face of historical amnesia in Caribbean, African American, and Latino/a texts.

JAIME HOVEY is Assistant Professor of English and Gender and Women's Studies at the University of Illinois-Chicago. She is the author of essays on sexuality, gender, and modernism; her forthcoming book is concerned with sexuality and style in modernist literary portraiture.

AARON JAFFE is Assistant Professor of English at the University of Louisville. His book *Modernism and the Culture of Celebrity,* a study of the poetics and cultural politics of modernist reputation, was published in 2004. His work has appeared in such journals as *The Yale Journal of Criticism* and *Restoration,* and he is planning a book on modernism, cosmopolitanism, and obsolescence.

CHRISTOPH LINDNER is Lecturer in English at the University of Wales, Aberystwyth. His research and teaching interests include modern and contemporary literature, popular culture, and critical theory. He has published essays on a wide range of topics, including Conrad and urban decay, Henry James and Cubism, and postmodernism in the age of the TV talk show. His recent books include *Fictions of Commodity Culture: From the Victorian to the Postmodern* (2003) and *The James Bond Phenomenon: A Critical Reader* (2003). He is currently researching an interdisciplinary study of urban modernity.

ANDREW LYCETT is the biographer of Ian Fleming. He has also written lives of Colonel Qaddafi, Rudyard Kipling, and—most recently—Dylan Thomas.

PATRICK O'DONNELL is Professor and Chair of English at Michigan State University. A major contributor to discussions of contemporary fiction and narrative theory more generally, his books include *Latent Destinies: Cultural Paranoia and Contemporary U.S. Narrative* (2000), *Echo Chambers: Figuring Voice in Modern Narrative* (1992), and *Passionate Doubts: Designs of Interpretation in Contemporary American Fiction* (1986).

CRAIG N. OWENS is Assistant Professor of English at Drake University, where he teaches courses in modern and contemporary literature, especially Irish literature and modern drama, and literary theory. He has published essays in such journals as *The Harold Pinter Review* and *M/MLA: The Journal of the Midwest Modern Language Association,* and he is currently finishing a book manuscript on post-Brechtian British political drama.

BRIAN PATTON is Associate Professor of English Literature at King's College in London, Ontario, where he teaches courses in twentieth-century British literature, popular culture, and renaissance literature. His major research interests include British literature and culture of the postwar period and the multicultural nature of postimperial Britain. His recent publications include articles on Irvine Welsh, Hanif Kureishi, Salman Rushdie, Daniel Clowes, Vikram Seth, and Katherine Mansfield.

JUDITH ROOF is Professor of English and the author of five books, including *All About Thelma and Eve: Sidekicks and Third Wheels* (2002) and *Reproductions of Reproduction: Imaging Symbolic Change* (1996). Much of her work examines how systems of order manifest their changes culturally in such discourses as film, literature, law, popular culture, and science.

STEPHEN WATT is Professor and Chair of English at Indiana University in Bloomington. He is the author of *Joyce, O'Casey, and the Irish Popular Theater* (1991), *Postmodern/Drama: Reading the Contemporary Stage* (1998), and—with Cary Nelson—*Academic Keywords: A Devil's Dictionary for Higher Education* (1999) and *Office Hours: Activism and Change in the Academy* (2004). His most recent book from Indiana University Press was *A Century of Irish Drama* (2000), co-edited with Eileen Morgan and Shakir Mustafa.

SKIP WILLMAN is Assistant Professor of English at the University of South Dakota, where he teaches critical theory and twentieth-century American literature. His work has appeared in *Contemporary Literature, Modern Fiction Studies,* and the volume *Conspiracy Nation: The Politics of Paranoia in Postwar America.* He is currently completing a book on conspiracy theory in contemporary American culture.

INDEX

"077 from France Without Love," 205
"007½ Mission Goldsinger," 205
20,000 Leagues under the Sea, 231

d'Acci, Julie, 217n.24
Adam, Ken, 231
Addison, Paul, 22n.3
Adorno, Theodor W., 22n.4, 22n.7, 23n.12
Agar, Herbert, 201n.2
al-Qaeda, xiii, 225, 238, 248, 251
Albion, Adam S., 218n.37
Albion, Alexis, xxii
Allen, Dennis W., xv, xix, 19, 259n.3
Althusser, Louis, 33, 246
Ambler, Eric, 215n.8
Amis, Kingsley, 11, 20, 32, 41n.12, 95, 105n.16, 143n.6, 143n.12, 145–46, 155–56, 203, 215n.4
Anderson, Benedict, 129, 142n.1
Andress, Ursula, 125n.1
Antonio's Revenge, 243, 245–46
Appadurai, Arjun, 159
Arbenz, Jacobo, 192
Arvad, Inga Marie, 188, 190
Asimov, Isaac, 59
Atkinson, Rowan, 141
Austin Powers: International Man of Mystery, 44, 229
"Avakum Zakhov vs. 07," 211–12, 219n.46
Avengers, The, 207, 217n.24
Awkward, Michael, 165

Baker, Bobby, 189–90
Bannon, Ann, 49
Barnes, Alan, 215n.3
Barnes, Tracy, 197
Baron, Cynthia, 143n.7
Batman, 24
Baudrillard, Jean, 224
Beardsley, Marion, 187
Beatles, The, 226
Bemis, Samuel Flagg, 201n.2
Benítez-Rojo, Antonio, 159–60

Benjamin, Walter, 23n.10
Bennett, Tony, xii, 11, 40n.2, 40n.4, 41n.12, 86n.6, 106n.33, 121, 136, 142n.2, 215n.11, 216n.13, 217n.23, 223, 236
Benson, Raymond, xii, 250
Bergonzi, Bernard, 133, 215n.7
Berle, Milton, 40n.5
Berry, Halle, 101
Bianchi, Daniela, 114, 117
bin Laden, Osama, 224–25, 239–40, 242, 248, 251, 252–53, 257–58
bin Ladin, Salim, 252
Bissell, Richard, 180, 191–94, 196, 197, 199
Black, Jeremy, xv, 40n.1, 40n.5, 102, 130, 142n.2, 147, 161, 219n.54, 246
Bogart, Humphrey, 138
Bond, Mary Wickham, 105n.15
Booker, Christopher, 134–35, 217n.23
Boyd, Ann S., 142n.2, 215n.12
Boys in the Band, The, 40n.7
Bradlee, Ben, 187
Braestrup, Peter, 218n.41
Braine, John, 145, 152–53, 155–56
Brandon, Henry, 176
Bright, Susie, 48
Broccoli, Albert R. ("Cubby"), 86n.4, 87
Brosnan, Pierce, 44, 73, 79, 101, 139–40, 143n.13, 213, 231
Bross, John, 179
Brown, Denise Scott, 106n.29
Bruce, David, 190
Buchan, John, 130, 133, 142n.3, 178, 191, 215n.8
Buffy the Vampire Slayer, xviii
Bui Anh Tuan, 206, 212
Bundy, McGeorge, 193
Burdick, Eugene, 195
Butler, Judith, 40n.5, 46, 47, 54n.1
Byers, Thomas, 68n.5

Caligula, 227
Cam Nguyet Nguyen, 217n.21, 217n.22
Canby, Vincent, 215n.5

Cannadine, David, 142n.2
Carpenter, Rebecca, 243
Carpenter, Richard C., 216n.12
Carpentier, Alejo, 175
le Carré, John, 60, 215n.8, 225
Case, Sue-Ellen, 47
Casino Royale (film), 73, 205
Castro, Fidel, xxii, 178–80, 191, 194–98, 200
Catch Me If You Can, 88
Cawelti, John G., 215n.8
Cecil, David, 186, 201n.2
Chamoiseau, Patrick, 175
Chandler, Raymond, 215n.8, 227
Chang, Suzy, 189
Chapman, James, xiv, xv–xvi, xxi, xxiii, 40n.3, 40n.5, 41n.12, 41n.13, 86n.5, 142n.2, 217n.18, 219n.54, 231, 241, 252, 259n.7
Charnes, Linda, 255–56, 259n.9
Chernev, Grigor, 210, 218n.39, 218n.40
Chomsky, Noam, 250, 251, 252
Chow Yun-Fat, 102
Christie, Agatha, 226–27
Chu, Jeff, 105n.17
Church Committee, 180
Churchill, Winston, 147, 162, 182–83, 201n.2
Clarke, Arthur C., 59
Cleaver, Eldridge, 161–64, 165, 176n.1, 208, 218n.29
Coburn, James, 216n.18
Cohen, Stanley, 157n.2
Coit, Margaret L., 201n.2
Colby, William, 196–97
Colley, Linda, 142n.1
Colls, Robert, 142n.1
Colman, Ronald, 140
Comentale, Edward P., xix, 30
Connery, Sean, 26, 40n.4, 43, 44, 59, 63, 64, 65, 78, 79, 110, 114, 117, 125n.1, 138, 141, 142n.4, 143n.10, 144, 162, 207, 208, 243
Cooper, Gary, 138
Cork, John, 215n.1, 215n.3, 219n.54
Crowther, Bosley, 202, 203, 215n.1, 217n.18
Cuba: Bay of Pigs invasion, xxii, 180, 191–93, 196–97, 198–99; Cuban missile crisis, 55, 58, 180, 198; Operation Mongoose, 180, 194–98

Dali, Salvador, 19
Dallek, Robert, 201n.2
Dalton, Timothy, 44, 139
de Foucauld, Charles, 74, 76
Deighton, Len, 215n.8, 225
Del Buono, Oreste, 142n.2
Deleuze, Gilles, xx, 22n.4, 67n.1, 115, 159, 246
DeLillo, Don, 199–200
Dench, Judi, xvii
Denning, Michael, 21n.1, 94, 98, 142n.3, 215n.8
Derrida, Jacques, 60, 61, 65, 241, 242, 248, 251, 253–54
Desert of the Heart, 49
Devil with James Bond!, The, 216n.12
Diagnostic and Statistical Manual of Mental Disorders, 35–36, 41n.15
Diamonds Are Forever (film), 24–39, 39n.1, 40n.5, 41n.9, 41n.11, 41n.16, 49, 51, 52, 80, 82, 86, 139
DiCaprio, Leonardo, 88
Die Another Day (film), 44, 96–97, 140, 213–14, 219n.53, 219n.55, 231
Diesel, Vin, 79, 101
Disch, Thomas M., 105n.13, 106n.34
Donahue, John D., 219n.48
Donat, Robert, 138
Donovan, William P. "Wild Bill," 183–84
Dr. No (film), xii, 45, 46, 52, 80, 86n.3, 96, 125n.1, 136, 137, 138–39, 142n.4, 143n.8, 143n.10, 215n.13, 224, 225, 226, 241
Dreams Our Stuff Is Made Of, The, 105n.13
Drummond, Lee, 129, 140–41
Dulles, Allen, 179, 180, 191–94, 197, 199
Durgnat, Raymond, 129, 136
Duchess of Malfi, The, 256

Eagleton, Terry, xviii
Early, Gerald, 161, 162, 168
Earnest, David C., 219n.57
Eastwood, Clint, 79
Eco, Umberto, 90, 142.n.2, 157n.5, 226, 229, 243, 246, 248, 254
Edelman, Lee, 28–29, 30, 40n.8
Eisenhower, Dwight D., 186, 191–92
Eliot, T. S., 19, 20, 23n.13
Emergence of Green, 49

Enemy Within, The, 190
L'Esclave vieil homme et le molosse, 175
Ewen, Stuart, 104n.7
Executive Action, 239

Facts of Death, The, 250
Faderman, Lillian, 46, 47, 48
Field Guide to Birds of the West Indies, 95
FitzGerald, Demond, 180, 198, 199
Flaubert, Gustave, 104n.6
Fleming, Ann, 190
Fleming, Ian, biography, xi, 5, 9–10, 19–
    20, 105n.9, 178–80, 181–84, 186, 190,
    195, 197, 226. Works: *Casino Royale,*
    xi, 7–8, 11, 13, 86n.3, 90, 106n.26,
    114, 122–23, 131, 134, 143n.8, 147,
    164, 171, 175, 176n.2, 226, 227–28,
    234, 247, 252; *Diamonds Are Forever,*
    xii, 24, 25, 72, 134, 143n.8, 161, 165,
    176n.2, 190, 194; *Doctor No,* 12, 72,
    102, 113–16, 118, 122, 131–32, 134,
    168–70, 171, 173, 176n.2, 176n.3,
    177n.6, 227, 230, 234, 248; "For Your
    Eyes Only," 131–32, 171, 173–75,
    177n.4, 256–57; *For Your Eyes Only,*
    99–100, 109, 115, 166; *From Russia
    with Love,* xii, xxii, 43, 96, 102, 106,
    113, 114, 117, 119, 161, 165–66,
    176n.2, 176n.3, 186, 188–89, 190,
    197, 199–200, 201n.2, 204, 218n.36,
    226, 227, 228; "From a View to a Kill,"
    171; *Goldfinger,* xii, 11, 12, 40n.6, 43,
    50, 51–52, 90, 132, 133–34, 135, 137,
    143n.8, 160, 161, 176n.2, 199, 227,
    233, 234, 241; "Hildebrand Rarity,
    The," 109; "How to Write," 145; "If I
    Were Prime Minister," 5, 22n.5; *Live
    and Let Die,* 86n.3, 100, 109, 113, 160,
    161, 164, 168–70, 171, 175–76,
    176n.2, 176n.3, 177n.8, 228, 238; *Man
    with the Golden Gun, The,* 95, 102,
    142n.4, 167, 171, 173–74, 176n.2,
    177n.4, 233, 234; *Moonraker,* 6, 8–9,
    10, 11–12, 97, 106n.27, 120–21, 133,
    134, 138, 144, 146–57, 164, 176n.2,
    199, 225, 227, 228–29, 245, 257; *On
    Her Majesty's Secret Service,* xiii, 6–7,
    13, 57, 112, 125n.1, 134, 167, 197, 227,
    230, 241, 244, 249–53, 259n.10;
    "Property of a Lady, The," 144;
    "Quantum of Solace," 166, 171;
    "Risico," 99; *Thrilling Cities,* 100–01,

175; *Thunderball,* xiii, 10–11, 16–17,
    105n.14, 106n.26, 109, 111, 125, 132,
    137, 157n.3, 159, 162, 171, 172, 174,
    176n.2, 176n.3, 177n.4, 199, 227, 229,
    241, 243, 249, 253, 254, 259n.6,
    259n.10; *You Only Live Twice,* 6, 11,
    99, 102–03, 123–24, 125n.1, 132, 137,
    142n.4, 163, 167, 168, 173, 176n.2,
    227, 230, 235, 241, 243, 244–48, 253,
    254–56, 257, 259n.7
For Your Eyes Only (film), 141
Forrest, Katherine V., 49
Foucauld, Charles de, 74, 76
Freedman, Lawrence, 195
French, Phil, 140
Freud, Sigmund, 17, 23n.9, 32, 33, 41,
    111, 114, 124, 180. Works: "Charac-
    ter and Anal Eroticism," 14, 22n.8;
    *Notes upon a Case of Obsessional Neu-
    rosis,* 30–31; "On Narcissism: An In-
    troduction," 22–23n.9; *Three Case
    Histories,* 41n.10; "Three Essays on
    the Theory of Sexuality," 13–14;
    Totem and Taboo, 15–16, 18–19, 20;
    The Wolfman and Other Cases, 15
Friday, Nancy, 48
From Russia with Love (film), 57, 58, 62,
    64, 80, 86n.3, 114, 117, 122, 124, 137,
    138–39, 141, 143n.8, 204, 241, 242
Furst, Alan, 215n.8

Gable, Clark, 138
Gagarin, Yuri, 55
Gardner, John, xii
Garland, Jack, 219n.56, 259n.1
Garner, Jennifer 104n.4
Get Smart, 207, 217n.18, 217n.24
Ghostwriting Modernism, 241
Gilbert, Lewis, 86n.4
Girl from U.N.C.L.E., The, 207, 217n.24
Giroud, Mark, 142n.1
Glass, Marvin, 215n.5
Glen, John, 86n.4
Glover, Bruce, 28
Godfather, The, 81
Godfrey, John, 181, 182, 183
GoldenEye (film), xvii, 139, 141
Goldfinger (film), 43, 45, 50, 51, 62, 64,
    82, 89, 115, 137, 138–39, 202, 205,
    210, 223, 224, 226
Goldwater, Barry, 217n.26
Greene, Graham, 195, 215n.8

Guattari, Félix, 22n.4, 66n.1, 159, 246
Gubar, Susan, 165
Gulyashki, Andrei, 211, 218n.46, 219n.47

Halberstam, Judith, 42, 44
Hall, Radclyffe, 49
Hall, Stuart, 161
Halloran, Vivian, xxi
Hamer, Emily, 46
Hamilton, Donald, 216n.18
Hamilton, Guy, 39n.1, 86n.4
Hammett, Dashiell, 215n.8
Hanks, Tom, 88, 104n.2
Haraway, Donna, 57, 58, 68n.5
Harvey, William, 196–98
Hebdige, Dick, 45
Heffer, Simon, 142n.1
Hefner, Hugh, 57–60, 64–65, 68n.5
Heinlein, Robert, 93, 105n.13
Hellman, John, 184–85
Helms, Richard, 196
Hemingway, Ernest, 185–86
Hersh, Burton, 192, 196
Hersh, Seymour, 178, 186, 187–88, 189
Hess, Rudolph, 218n.41
Hewison, Robert, 157n.1
Hibbin, Nina, 218n.33
Highsmith, Patricia, 49
Hilferding, Rudolf, 22n.2, 22n.6, 23n.11
History of Bombing, A, 250
Hitchcock, Alfred, 45
Hitchens, Christopher, 241
Hitler, Adolf, 183, 188, 192, 218n.41, 227, 228
Hoang Hai Thuy, 217n.22
Hoffa, Jimmy, 190
Hoggart, Richard, 157
Honey West, 207
Honorable Men: My Life in the CIA, 196–97
Hoover, J. Edgar, 188, 201n.1
Horkheimer, Max, 22n.4
Hovey, Jaime, xv, xix
How 007 Got His Name, 105n.15
How to Live the James Bond Lifestyle, 71
Hurry On Down, 145
Hussein, Saddam, 238, 239–40
Hyde, H. Montgomery, 201n.1

I Spy, 217n.18
Ian Fleming Foundation, xiv

Ian Fleming Introduces Jamaica, 169
Ian Fleming Publications Ltd., xiv
In Like Flint, 216n.18
Independence Day, 224
Iriye, Akira, 213, 219n.52
Izenour, Steven, 106n.29

Jacobs, H. P., 169
Jaffe, Aaron, xx
Jakes, Ian, 41n.14
James, Paula, 219n.48
James Bond: The Legacy, 215n.1, 215n.3, 219n.54
James Bond Dossier, The, 143n.6, 215n.4
James Bond's World of Values, 218n.31, 252
Jefferson, Thomas, 162
Johnson, Ian, 216n.16
Johnson, Lyndon B., 191
Johnson, Paul, 131, 203, 215n.7
Joyce, James, 20
Jung, Carl, 204, 216n.12

Katz, Jonathan Ned, 54n.1
Keeler, Christine, 189
Kennedy, John F., xii, xxii, 55, 59, 178–81, 184–90, 191–99, 200, 201n.2, 201n.3, 201n.4, 204, 226
Kennedy, Joseph P., 183, 185, 188, 189, 201n.4
Kennedy, Robert, 178, 180, 188–90, 191, 194–99, 201n.4
Kennedy Obsession, The: The American Myth of JFK, 184
Keohane, Robert O., 219n.49, 219n.50
Kerouac, Jack, 164
Kim Jong Il, 213–14
Kingdom of This World, The, 175
"Kiss Agent 088 on Sight," 205
Kiss Kiss Bang! Bang!: The Unofficial James Bond Film Companion, 215n.3
Korda, Alexander, 143n.9
Krassilnikov, Rem, 92–94, 105n.10
Khrushchev, Nikita, 62
Kyd, Thomas, 243, 246, 255
Kyriazi, Paul, 71, 78

Lacan, Jacques, 83, 86n.2, 109, 179, 180–81, 184, 192, 224
Lane, Sheldon, 141
Lansdale, Edward, 180, 195–96, 198, 199

Latour, Bruno, xvi–xvii
Laughton, Charles, 143n.9
Lawrence, D. H., 20
Learning from Las Vegas: The Forgotten Symbolism of Architectural Form, 100, 106n.29
le Carré, John, 60, 215n.8, 225
Lederer, William, 195
Leiter, Marion "Oatsie," 176
Lenin, Vladimir, 92, 105n.11, 105n.12
Lenkova, Mariana, 218n.39
Lewis, Wyndham, 20, 23n.13
Libra, 198
Licence to Kill, 139
Lindner, Christoph, xxii–xxiii, 40n.4, 158, 254, 259n.12
Lindquist, Sven, 250
Live and Let Die (film), 139
Living Daylights, The (film), 139
Look Back in Anger, 138, 145
Lord, Jack, 138
Lucky Jim, 145–46, 153
Luhrmann, Baz, 40n.5
Lumumba, Patrice, 191
Lycett, Andrew, 20, 22n.5, 102, 106n.31, 178, 181, 182, 183, 196, 259n.6, 259n.10
Lynch, Jessica, 239

M.A.D., 88
MacCallum, David, 2187n.18
Macmillan, Harold, 135, 189
Magee, John Gillespie, 68n.2
Maher, Bill, 239, 259n.4
Mailer, Norman, 186
Man from U.N.C.L.E., The, 217n.18
Man with the Golden Gun, The (film), 139
Mansfield, Jayne, 57
Mao Zedong, 62
Marnie, 45
Marshall Plan, 192
Marston, John, 243, 245
Martin, Dean, 217n.18
Marx, Karl, 22n.2, 22n.6, 124
Marxism and Literature, 240, 241
Matrix, The, 68n.6, 224
Maugham, W. Somerset, 76, 82, 146, 147
Mauriac, Claude, 202, 204, 215n.2, 216n.12
McCallum, E. L., 114

McCarthy, Joseph, 93
McClellan Committee, 190
McClory, Kevin, 259n.6
McGeary, Johanna, 259n.8
McLachlan, Donald, 182–83
McLuhan, Marshall, 104n.8
McNeile, Herman C. "Sapper," 130, 133, 142n.3, 215n.8
McQueen, Steve, 79
Miller, Jeffrey S., 216n.11, 217n.24
Miller, Toby, 40n.4, 223–24
Mission: Impossible, 217n.18
Moniot, Drew, 140
Moonraker (film), 139, 231
Moore, Roger, 44, 65, 73, 79, 139, 143n.13, 230
Morgan, J. P., 183
Morgan, Kenneth, 236
Morrison, Blake, 157n.1
Mort, Frank, 259n.11
Müller, Andre, 209, 218n.35
Mulligan, Andrew, 215n.2, 216n.6
Murdoch, Iris, 145
Mussolini, Benito, 253
My Secret Garden, 48

Nadel, Alan, 187–88
Narodna Kultura, 218n.39
NASA (National Aeronautics and Space Administration), 55
Nero, 227
Nestle, Joan, 47
Never Say Never Again (film), 73, 141, 223
Nevins, Allan, 201n.2
Nguoi Thu Tam, 206
Nguyen, Cam Nguyet, 217n.21, 217n.22
Nichols, Lewis, 216n.13
Niven, David, 138, 142n.4
Nixon, Richard, 192
Nye, Joseph S., 219n.49, 219n.50

Ocean's Eleven, 82
Odd Girl Out, 49
O'Donnell, Patrick, xix–xx, 34, 91, 252
On Her Majesty's Secret Service (film), 125n.1, 137
On the Road, 164
Operation Success, 192
Oppenheim, E. Phillips, 215n.8
Orwell, George, 95, 241
Oswald, Lee Harvey, 199–200

Our Man Flint, 216n.18
Owens, Craig N., xx, 91

Pace, Eric, 217n.24
Palmer, Jerry, 215n.8
Paris Is Burning, 40n.5
Patton, Brian, xxi, 225
Paxman, Jeremy, 142n.1
Pearson, John, 178
Perkin, Harold, 3, 4, 9, 18, 22n.6, 133
Persuaders!, The, 139, 143n.13
Philby, Kim, 196
Pilard, Philippe, 208, 217n.27
Playboy (magazine), 57–59, 68n.4, 88,
   135, 252
Playboy Club, 26
Pleasence, Donald, 249
Poe, Edgar Allan, 109
Politically Incorrect, 259n.4
Politics of James Bond, The, 147, 219n.54
Portrait of a President, 199
Pratt, Mary Louise, 160
Price, James, 133, 135
Price of Salt, The, 49
Pritchett, V. S., 145–46, 150
Private Life of Henry VIII, The, 143n.9
Profiles in Courage, 184–85, 199
Promise Keepers, 84
Promises, Promises, 57
Puppet Masters, 93

Queer Theory, 40n.5
Quennell, Peter, 201n.2
le Queux, William, 215n.8
Quiet American, The, 195

Racechanges, 165
Rat Pack, 79, 81–82
Raven, Simon, 131, 203, 207, 215n.6,
   217n.26
Reagan, Ronald, 68n.2
Red and the Black, The, 201n.2
Reeve, Simon, 252–53
Reid, Scott, 105n.18, 105n.19
Remington Steele, 140, 143n.13
Repeating Island, The, 159
Richards, Jeffrey, 137, 142n.1
Right Stuff, The, 56
Risen, James, 105n.10
Robert Kennedy, 179, 189–90, 194–97
Rock, Paul, 147n.2
Rogers, Edward, 208

Rometsch, Ellen, 189–90
Roof, Judith, xv–xvi, xx, 47, 54n.1
Room at the Top, The, 138, 145, 152–53
Roosevelt, Eleanor, 183
Roosevelt, Franklin Delano, 182–83
Rosenau, James N., 219n.57
Rosendorf, Neil M., 219n.48, 219n.50
Rubin, Gayle, 53
Rule, Jane, 49
Russo, Vito, 40n.7, 42

Saint, The, 139, 143.n.13
Sarris, Andrew, 41n.13
Sartre, Jean-Paul, 226
Saturday Night and Sunday Morning,
   138
Sauerberg, Lars Ole, 228, 229
Schirra, Wally, 55
Schlesinger, Arthur, Jr., 191, 193
Schröder, Peter, 208–09, 218n.34
Schwartz, Richard A., 217n.18
Schwarzenegger, Arnold, 139
Scivally, Bruce, 215n.1, 215n.3, 219n.54
September 11, 2001 (9/11), xiii, xxii,
   xxiii, 37–38, 41n.18, 231
Shakespeare, William, 242, 246, 254,
   256. Works: *Hamlet,* 112, 242–43,
   245–46, 248, 253–56, 257; *The Sec-
   ond Part of King Henry the Fourth,*
   246; *Titus Andronicus,* 256
Sidey, Hugh, 187, 201n.2
Sinatra, Frank, 71, 81–82, 83
Smith, Putter, 28
Sontag, Susan, 239, 259n.5
Sorgi, Claudio, 208, 215n.5, 218n.32
Soskohvyi, A., 218n.43, 219n.47
Soul on Ice, 161–63, 218n.29
Spanish Tragedy, The, 243, 255–56,
   257
Specters of Marx, 241, 253
Spielberg, Steven, 88–89, 104n.2
Spillane, Mickey, 215n.8
Spy Who Loved Me, The (film), 130,
   137, 223, 231
St. Laurent, Octavia, 40n.5
Stalin, Joseph, 92–93, 105n.10, 105n.11,
   236
Stallone, Sylvester, 139
Star Wars, 139
Starkey, Lycurgus, 208, 212, 218n.31,
   252
de Stendahl, M., 201n.2

Stephenson, William "Little Bill," 182–83, 201n.1
Stowe, Harriet Beecher, 162
Street, Sarah, 137, 139
Sturm, Hans, 216n.17
Sword, Helen, 241

Tam, Nguoi Thu, 206
Tapper, Jake, 258–59n.4
Taylor, Maxwell, 193
Thomas, Evan, 178–79, 189–90, 191, 193–98
Thunderball (film), 53, 61, 80, 81, 82, 139, 143n.9, 202, 209, 215n.1, 215n.2, 223, 241, 242
Thuy, Hoang Hai, 217n.22
Tomorrow Never Dies (film), 139, 231
Tornabuoni, Lietta, 216n.16
Transatlantic Crossings, 137
True Lies, 239
Trujillo, Rafael, 191
Tuan, Bui Anh, 206, 212
Tuovinen, Arto, 205, 217n.20

Ugly American, The, 195
Ulbricht, Walter, 189
Uncle Tom's Cabin, 162
Under the Net, 145
Usborne, Richard, 142n.3
Uses of Literacy, The, 157

Van O'Connor, William
Vaughn, Robert, 217n.18
Venturi, Robert, 100, 106n.29
Very Best Men, 179, 191, 193, 196–98
View to a Kill, A (film), 137, 138
Von Sacher-Masoch, Leopold, 118

Wagner, Richard, 254
Wain, John, 145
Warren Commission Report, The, 198

Washington, George, 162
Watson, Colin 142n.3
Watt, Stephen, xxiii, 225, 237
Webster, John, 256
Weight, Richard, 142n.1
Well of Loneliness, The, 49
White, Mark J., 195, 198
Williams, Raymond, 101, 106n.20, 240
Willis, Bruce, 139
Willman, Skip, xxii, 259n.12
Wills, Gary, 186–88, 201n.4
Winchell, Walter, 188
Wiseman, Thomas, 217n.28
Wolfe, Tom, 56
Wolfenden Report, The, 247
Woolf, Virginia, 20
Woollacott, Janet, xii, 11, 40n.2, 40n.4, 41n.12, 86n.6, 105n.33, 121, 136, 142n.2, 215n.11, 216n.13, 217n.23, 223
World Is Not Enough, The (film), 139–40
Wright, Richard, 163

Yeats, William Butler, 19
You Only Live Twice (film), 50, 61, 85, 137, 143n.9, 230, 249
Young Melbourne, The, 186–87
Young, Terence, 59, 82, 86n.4, 138, 242

Zhukov, Yurii, 209–10, 218n.37, 218n.38, 218n.41
Žižek, Slavoj, xii, xvii, 92–93, 179–80, 181, 184–85, 188, 245, 250–51. Works: "'I Hear You with My Eyes'; or, The Invisible Master," 242; *The Sublime Object of Ideology,* 92–93, 180, 184, 185; *Welcome to the Desert of the Real,* 224–25, 231–32, 253–54, 259n.12
Zuckerman, Mortimer, 238, 239, 259n.2

EDWARD P. COMENTALE is Assistant Professor of English at Indiana University, author of *Modernism, Cultural Production, and the British Avant-Garde, 1909–1915*, and co-editor of a forthcoming volume on Modernism and Classicism.

STEPHEN WATT is Professor and Chair of English at Indiana University and the author of *Postmodern/Drama: Reading the Contemporary Stage; Joyce, O'Casey, and the Irish Popular Theater*; and (with Cary Nelson) *Academic Keywords: A Devil's Dictionary for Higher Education* and *Office Hours: Activism and Change in the Academy.* He is co-editor (with Eileen Morgan and Shakir Mustafa) of *A Century of Irish Drama* (IU Press, 2000).

SKIP WILLMAN is Assistant Professor of English at the University of South Dakota, where he teaches courses in postmodern literature and cultural theory.